尾田栄一郎

Here's a little story for you. Long, long ago, a really long time ago, rabbits were able to fly. The fact that we count rabbits in Japanese (*ichiwa, niwa*) the same way we count birds is a holdover from that time. Rabbits, flapping their big ears across the vast, clear skies of ancient times...sounds like a horror story.

-Eiichiro Oda, 1999

Eiichiro Oda began his manga career at the age of 17, when his one-shot cowboy manga **Wanted!** won second place in the coveted Tezuka manga awards. Oda went on to work as an assistant to some of the biggest manga artists in the industry, including Nobuhiro Watsuki, before winning the Hop Step Award for new artists. His pirate adventure **One Piece**, which debuted in **Weekly Shonen Jump** in 1997, quickly became one of the most popular manga in Japan.

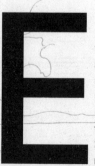

ONE PIECE VOL. 8
EAST BLUE PART 8

SHONEN JUMP Manga Edition

This volume contains material that was originally
published in English in **SHONEN JUMP** #29–32.

STORY AND ART BY EIICHIRO ODA

English Adaptation/Lance Caselman
Translation/Naoko Amemiya
Touch-up Art & Lettering/Mark McMurray
Additional Touch-up/Josh Simpson, Walden Wong
Design/Sean Lee
Editors/Megan Bates, Yuki Takagaki

Published by VIZ Media, LLC
P.O. Box 77010
San Francisco, CA 94107

10 9
First printing, September 2005
Ninth printing, April 2013

www.viz.com

THE WORLD'S
MOST POPULAR MANGA
www.shonenjump.com

SHONEN JUMP MANGA

Vol. 8

I WON'T DIE

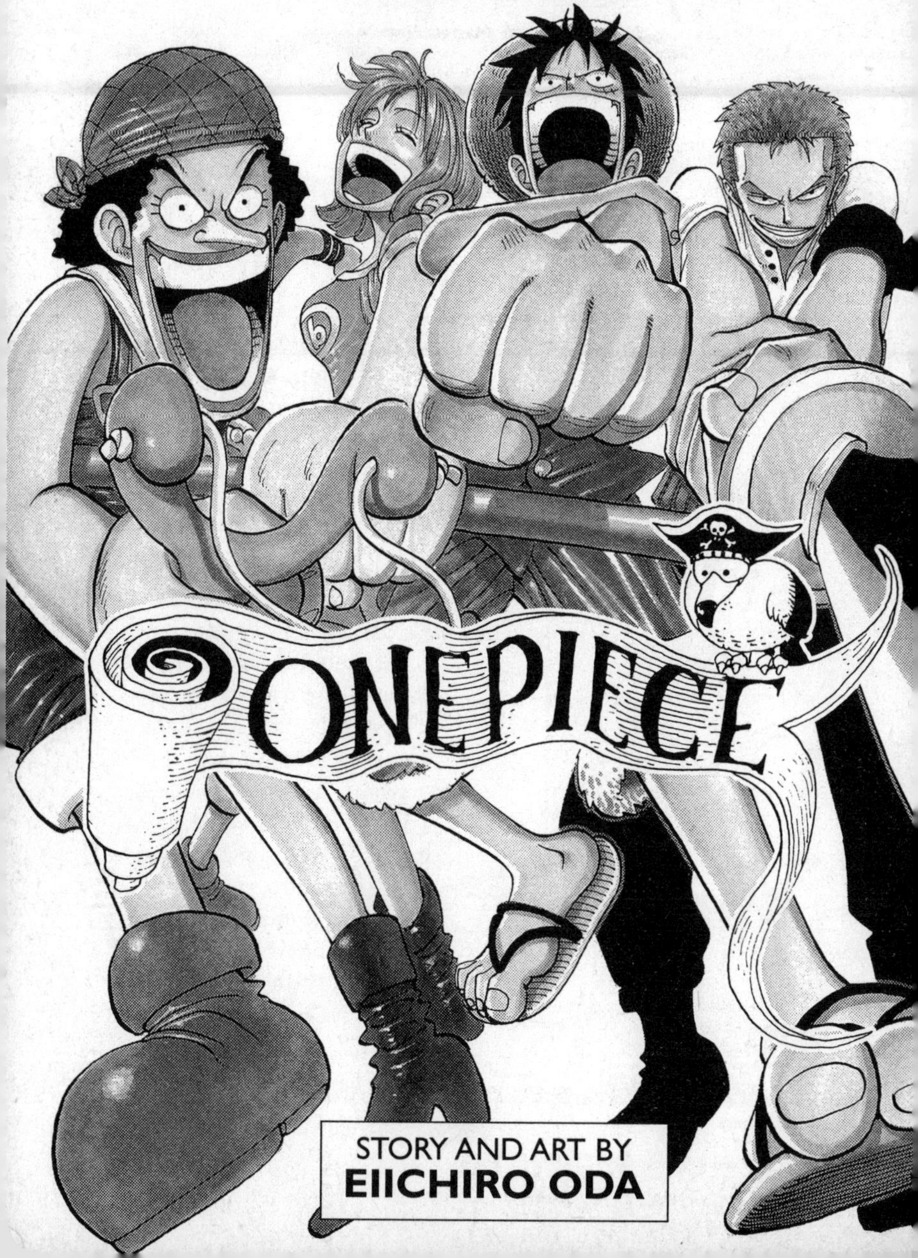
ONE PIECE

STORY AND ART BY
EIICHIRO ODA

THE STORY OF ONE PIECE

Volume 8

Monkey D. Luffy started out as just a kid with a dream – and that dream was to become the greatest pirate in history! Stirred by the tales of pirate "Red-Haired" Shanks, Luffy vowed to become a pirate himself. That was before the enchanted Devil Fruit gave Luffy the power to stretch like rubber, at the cost of being unable to swim – a serious handicap for an aspiring sea dog. Undeterred, Luffy set out to sea and recruited some crewmates: lying sharpshooter Usopp, master swordsman Zolo and treasure-hunting thief Nami.

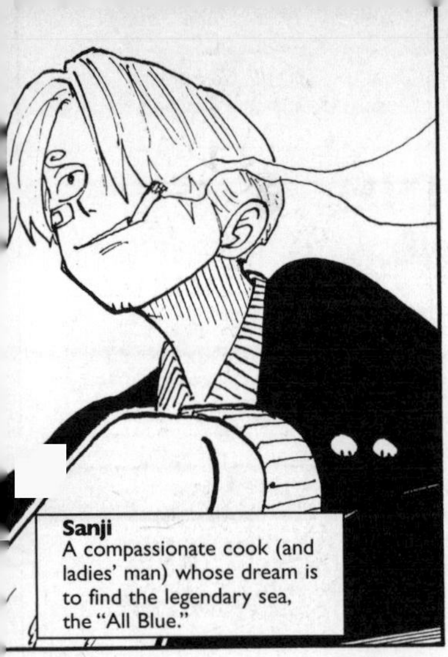
Sanji
A compassionate cook (and ladies' man) whose dream is to find the legendary sea, the "All Blue."

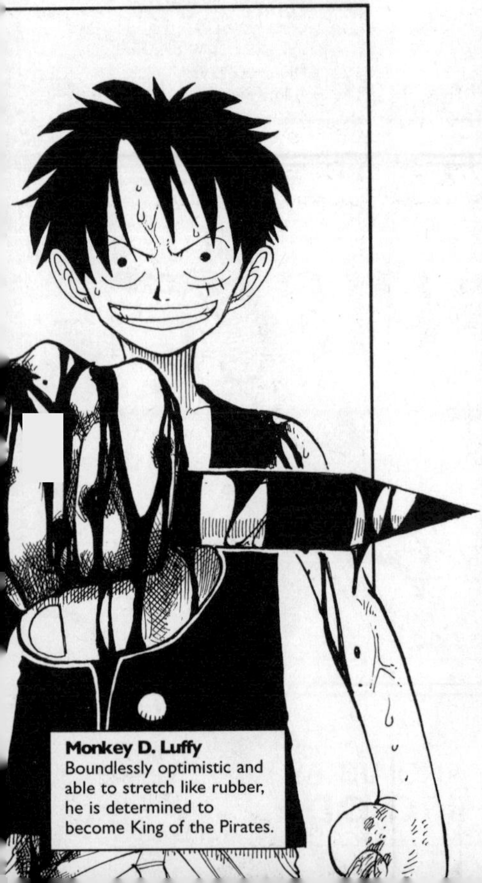
Monkey D. Luffy
Boundlessly optimistic and able to stretch like rubber, he is determined to become King of the Pirates.

Luffy and his crew visit the oceangoing restaurant Baratie, where they meet and befriend Sanji, the sous-chef. But the powerful and ruthless Don Krieg arrives with his pirates and declares that he wants Baratie for himself! So begins a battle royal for the restaurant ship. Sanji vows to defend the ship with his life, but when Chef Zeff is taken hostage, the situation turns desperate! Everyone wonders why Sanji is so determined to defend the ship, until he reveals a secret from the past: when Sanji was a young apprentice cook, he and Zeff (then known as "Red Shoes" Zeff, the pirate) were swept overboard by a sudden storm and cast upon a rock in the ocean! Because Sanji shared Zeff's dream, the pirate gave the boy all the food he had and ate his own leg to survive.

Nami
A thief who specializes in robbing pirates. Nami hates pirates, but Luffy convinced her to join his crew as navigator.

Roronoa Zolo
A former bounty hunter and master of the "three-sword" fighting style (one in each hand and one in his mouth!).

Don Krieg
Commander of the Pirate Armada.

Gin

Usopp
The newest addition to Luffy's crew, Usopp's known for his tall tales, but he has a way with a slingshot and a heart of gold.

"Red-Haired" Shanks
A pirate captain who saved the young Luffy's life and inspired him to be a pirate.

Chef Zeff

EAST BLUE
ONE PIECE

Vol. 8
I WON'T DIE

CONTENTS

Chapter 63:
I WON'T DIE

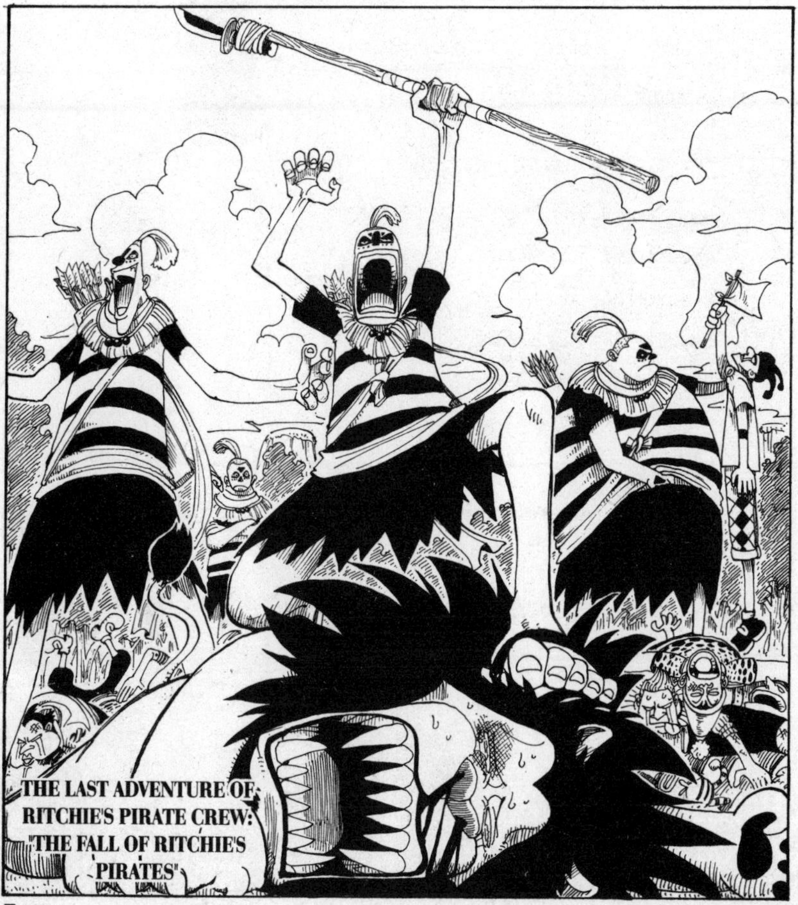
THE LAST ADVENTURE OF RITCHIE'S PIRATE CREW: "THE FALL OF RITCHIE'S PIRATES"

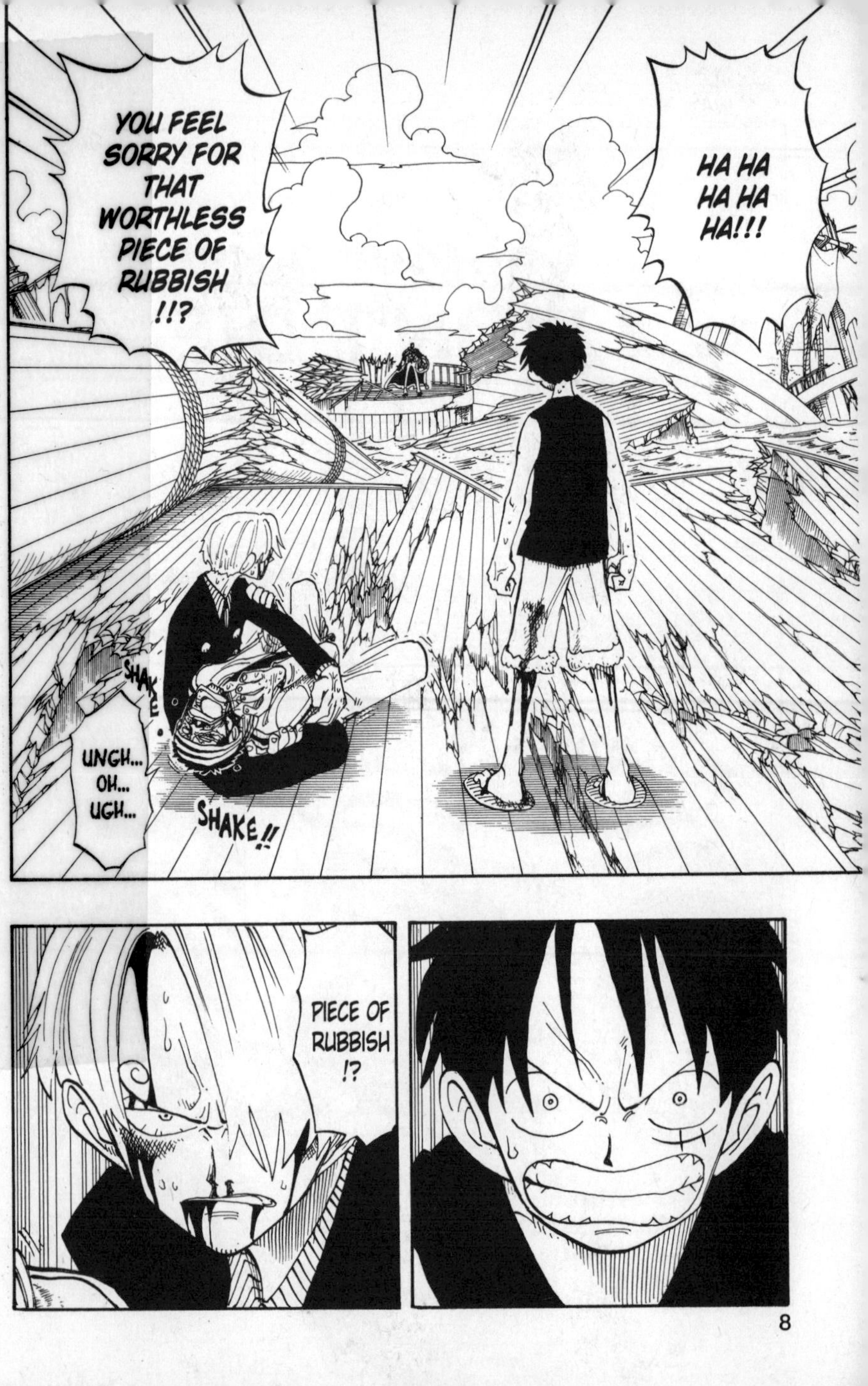
HA HA HA HA HA!!!
YOU FEEL SORRY FOR THAT WORTHLESS PIECE OF RUBBISH !!?
SHAKE
UNGH... OH... UGH...
SHAKE!!
PIECE OF RUBBISH !?

READ THIS WAY

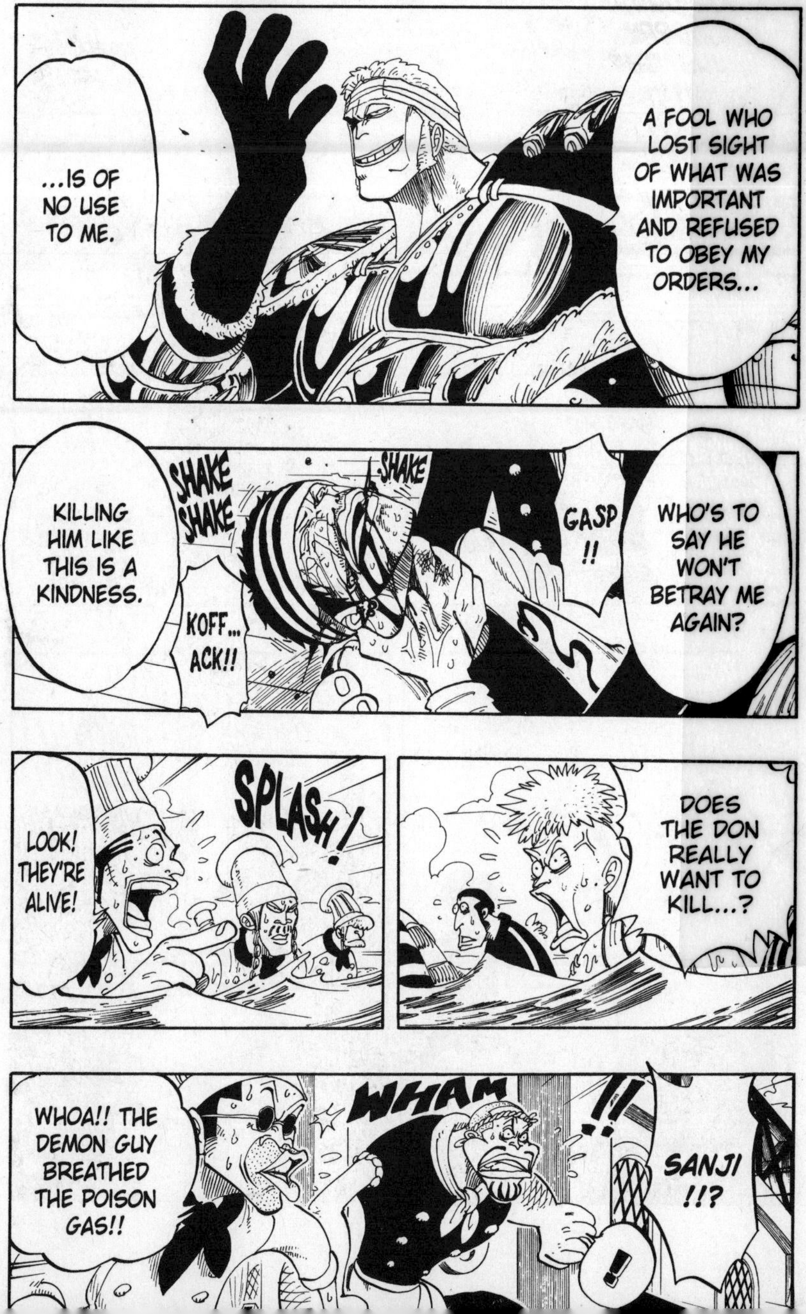
A FOOL WHO LOST SIGHT OF WHAT WAS IMPORTANT AND REFUSED TO OBEY MY ORDERS...
...IS OF NO USE TO ME.
WHO'S TO SAY HE WON'T BETRAY ME AGAIN?
GASP !!
SHAKE
SHAKE SHAKE
KOFF... ACK!!
KILLING HIM LIKE THIS IS A KINDNESS.
DOES THE DON REALLY WANT TO KILL...?
SPLASH!
LOOK! THEY'RE ALIVE!
!!
SANJI !!?
WHAM
WHOA!! THE DEMON GUY BREATHED THE POISON GAS!!
!

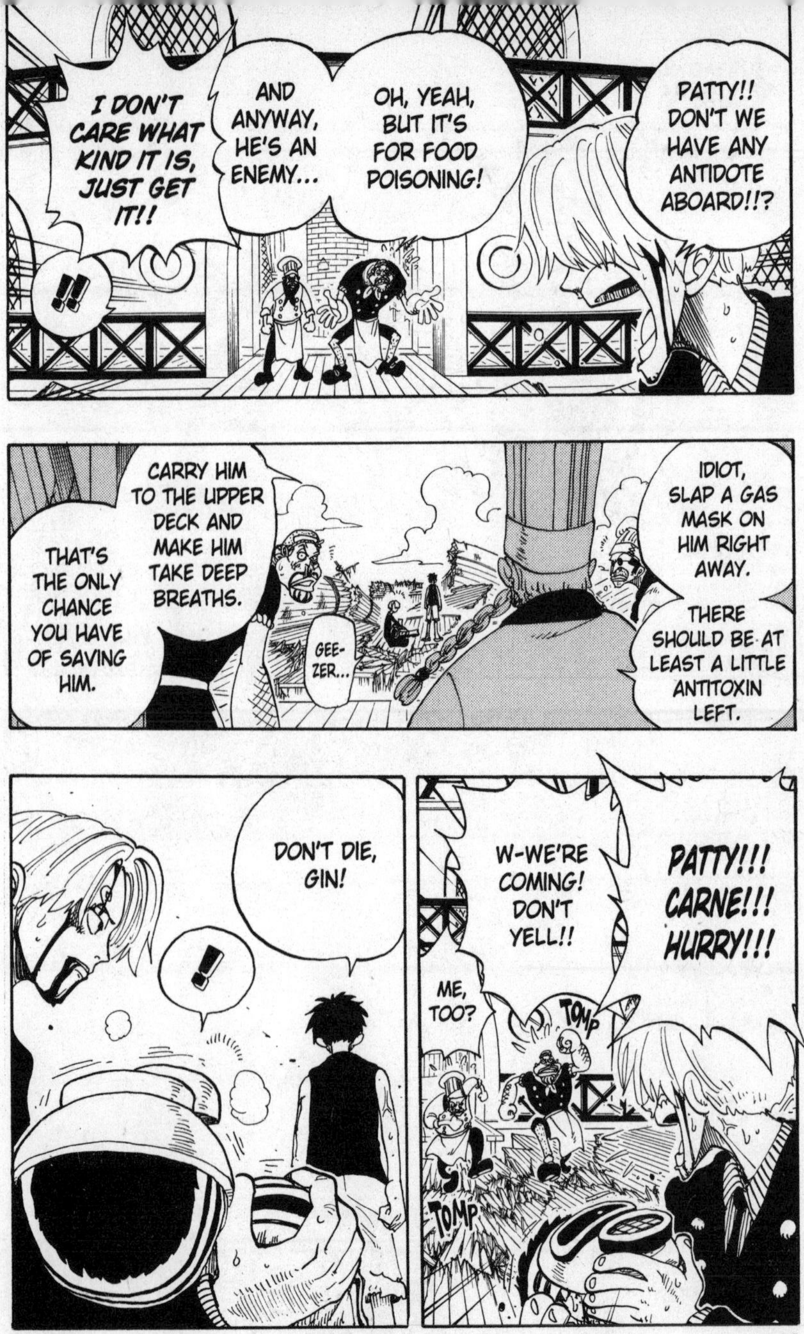
PATTY!! DON'T WE HAVE ANY ANTIDOTE ABOARD!!?
OH, YEAH, BUT IT'S FOR FOOD POISONING!
AND ANYWAY, HE'S AN ENEMY...
I DON'T CARE WHAT KIND IT IS, JUST GET IT!!
!!
IDIOT, SLAP A GAS MASK ON HIM RIGHT AWAY.
THERE SHOULD BE AT LEAST A LITTLE ANTITOXIN LEFT.
GEE-ZER...
CARRY HIM TO THE UPPER DECK AND MAKE HIM TAKE DEEP BREATHS.
THAT'S THE ONLY CHANCE YOU HAVE OF SAVING HIM.
PATTY!!! CARNE!!! HURRY!!!
W-WE'RE COMING! DON'T YELL!!
ME, TOO?
TOMP
TOMP
DON'T DIE, GIN!
!

READ THIS WAY

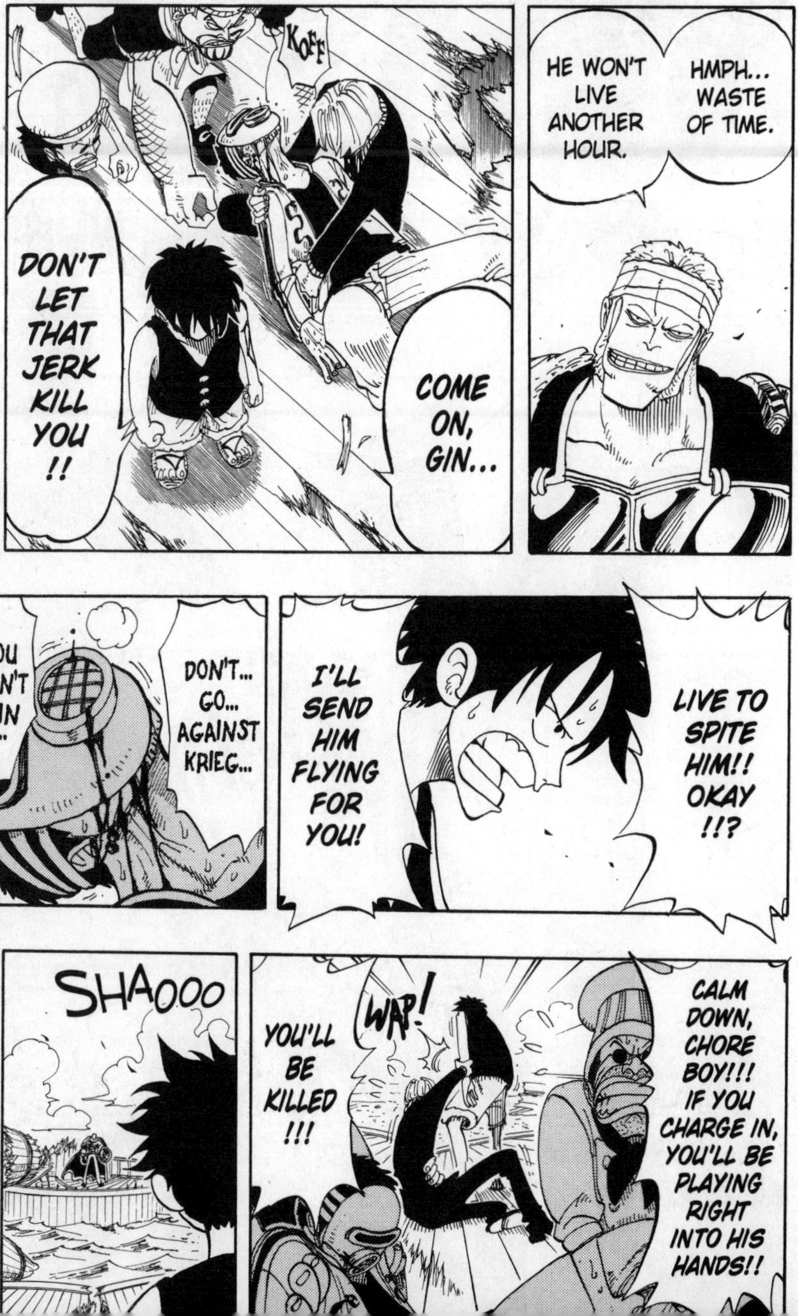

HMPH... WASTE OF TIME.
HE WON'T LIVE ANOTHER HOUR.
KOFF
COME ON, GIN...
DON'T LET THAT JERK KILL YOU!!
LIVE TO SPITE HIM!! OKAY!!?
I'LL SEND HIM FLYING FOR YOU!
DON'T... GO... AGAINST KRIEG...
YOU CAN'T WIN...
SHAKE
CALM DOWN, CHORE BOY!!! IF YOU CHARGE IN, YOU'LL BE PLAYING RIGHT INTO HIS HANDS!!
WAP!
YOU'LL BE KILLED!!!
SHAOOO

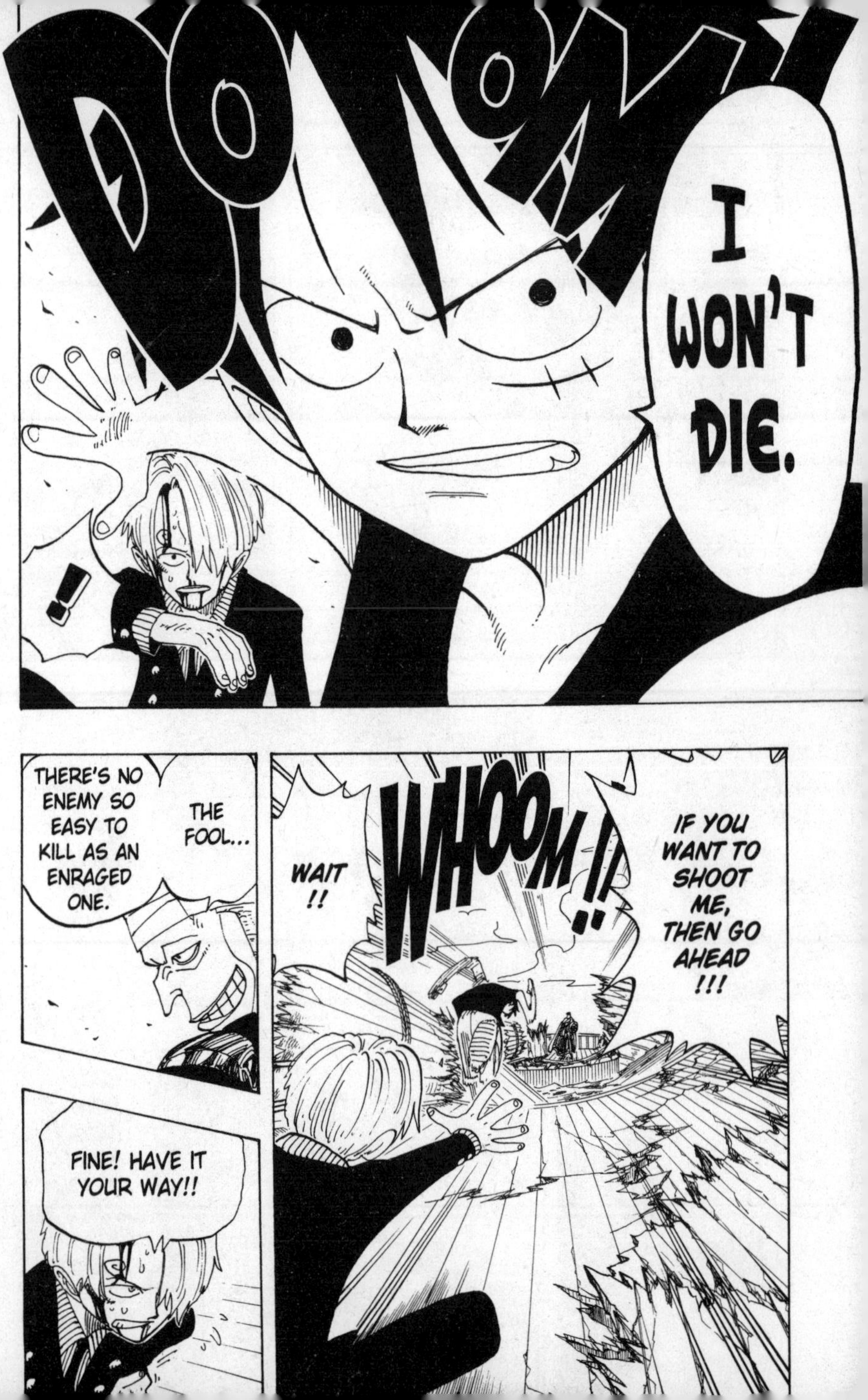
I WON'T DIE.
!
IF YOU WANT TO SHOOT ME, THEN GO AHEAD!!!
WHOOM!!
WAIT!!
THE FOOL...
THERE'S NO ENEMY SO EASY TO KILL AS AN ENRAGED ONE.
FINE! HAVE IT YOUR WAY!!

READ THIS WAY

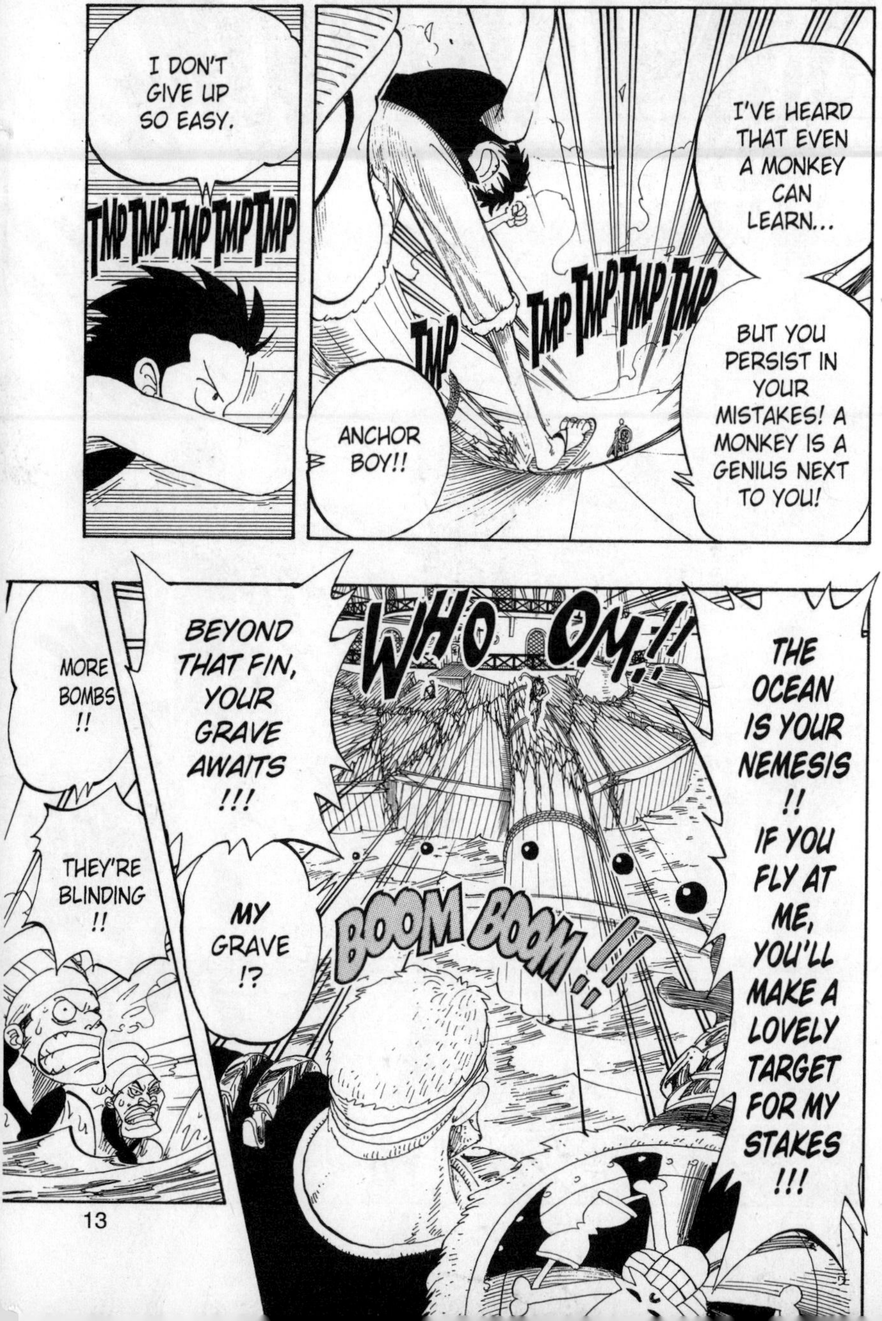
I'VE HEARD THAT EVEN A MONKEY CAN LEARN...
BUT YOU PERSIST IN YOUR MISTAKES! A MONKEY IS A GENIUS NEXT TO YOU!
TMP TMP TMP TMP
TMP
ANCHOR BOY!!
I DON'T GIVE UP SO EASY.
TMP TMP TMP TMP TMP
THE OCEAN IS YOUR NEMESIS!! IF YOU FLY AT ME, YOU'LL MAKE A LOVELY TARGET FOR MY STAKES!!!
WHOOM!!
BEYOND THAT FIN, YOUR GRAVE AWAITS!!!
BOOM BOOM!!
MY GRAVE!?
MORE BOMBS!!
THEY'RE BLINDING!!

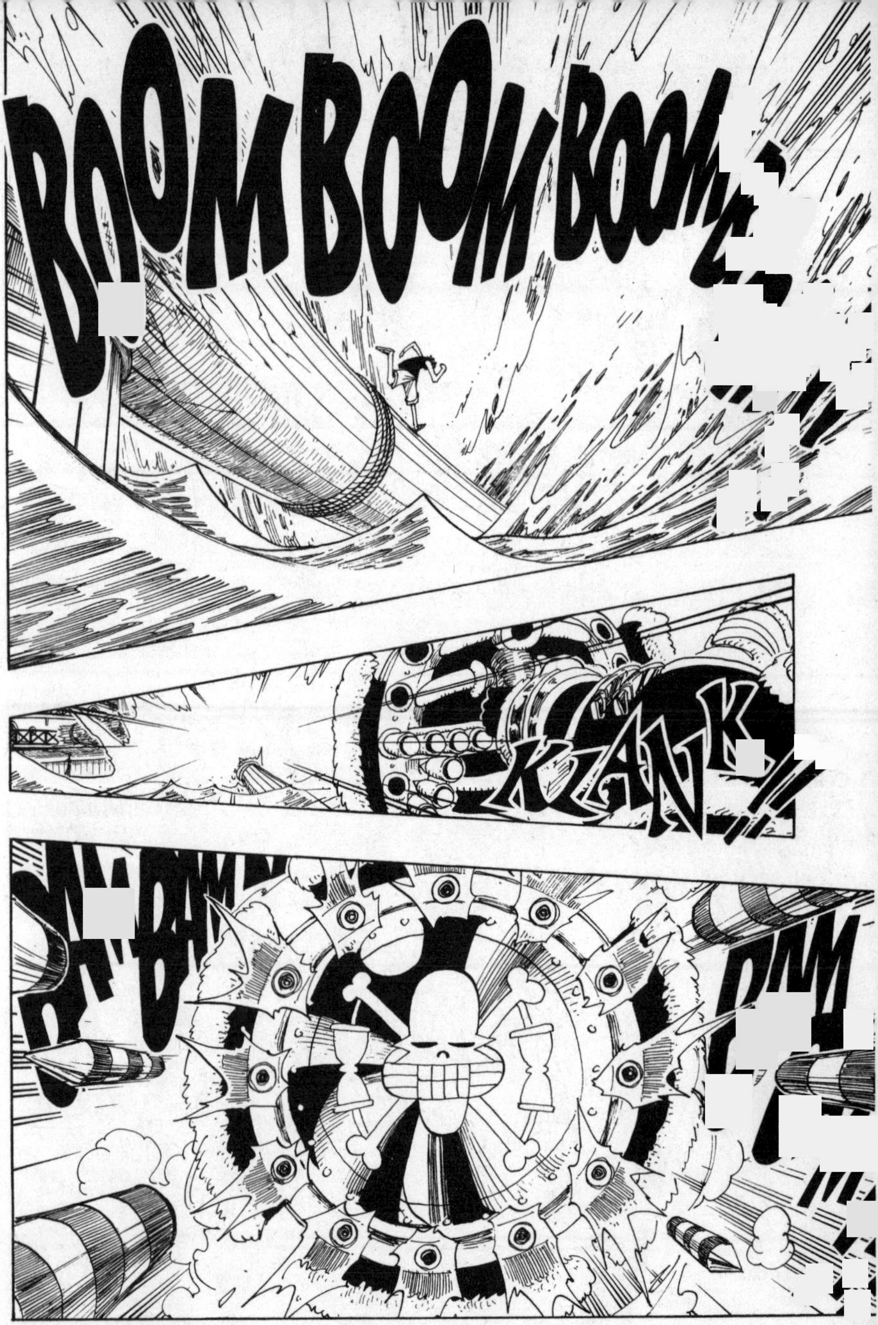
BOOM BOOM BOOM
KLANK!!
BAM BAM

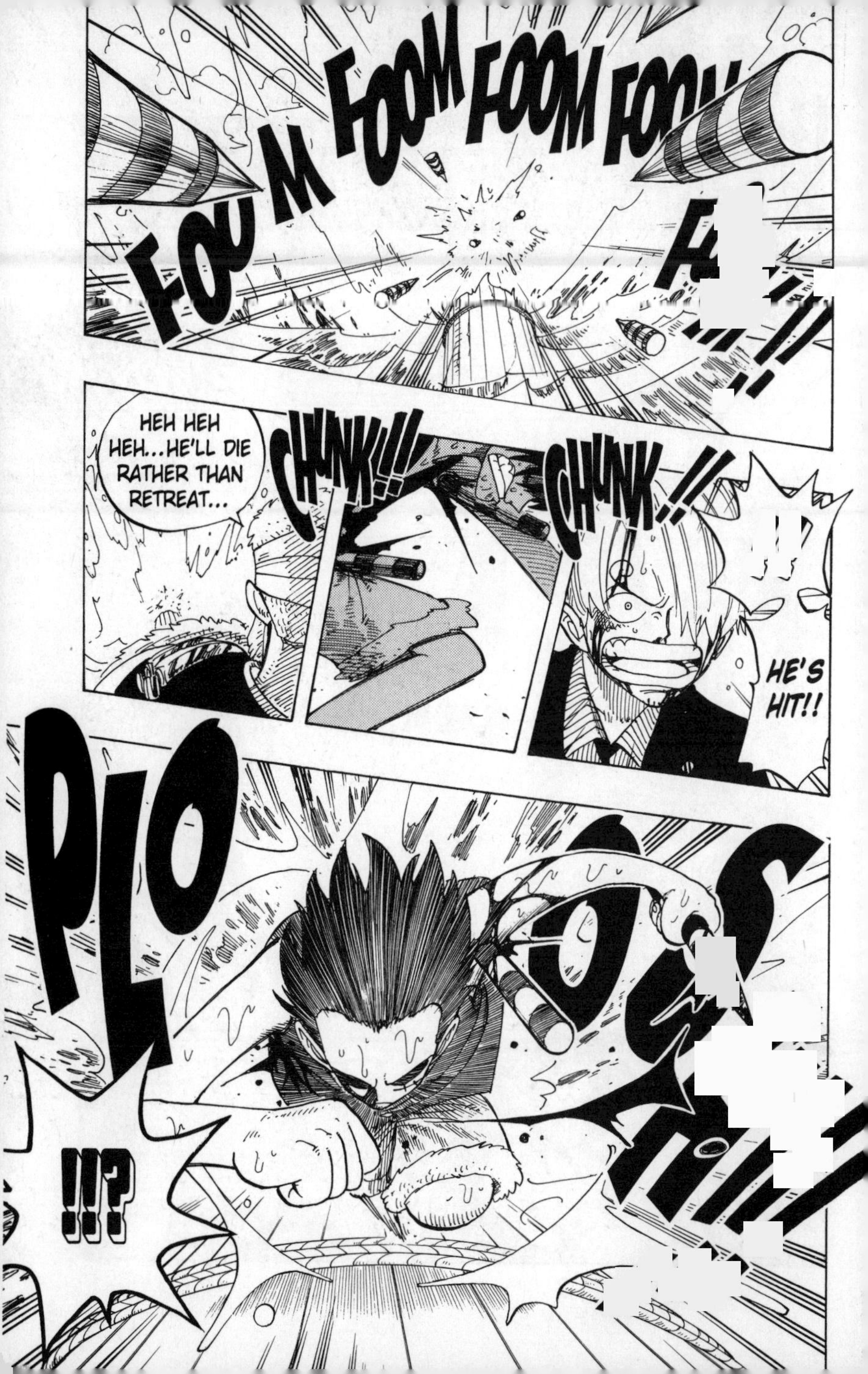

FOU M FOOM FOOM
CHUNK!!
HE'S HIT!!
CHUNK!!!
HEH HEH HEH...HE'LL DIE RATHER THAN RETREAT...
PLO
!!?

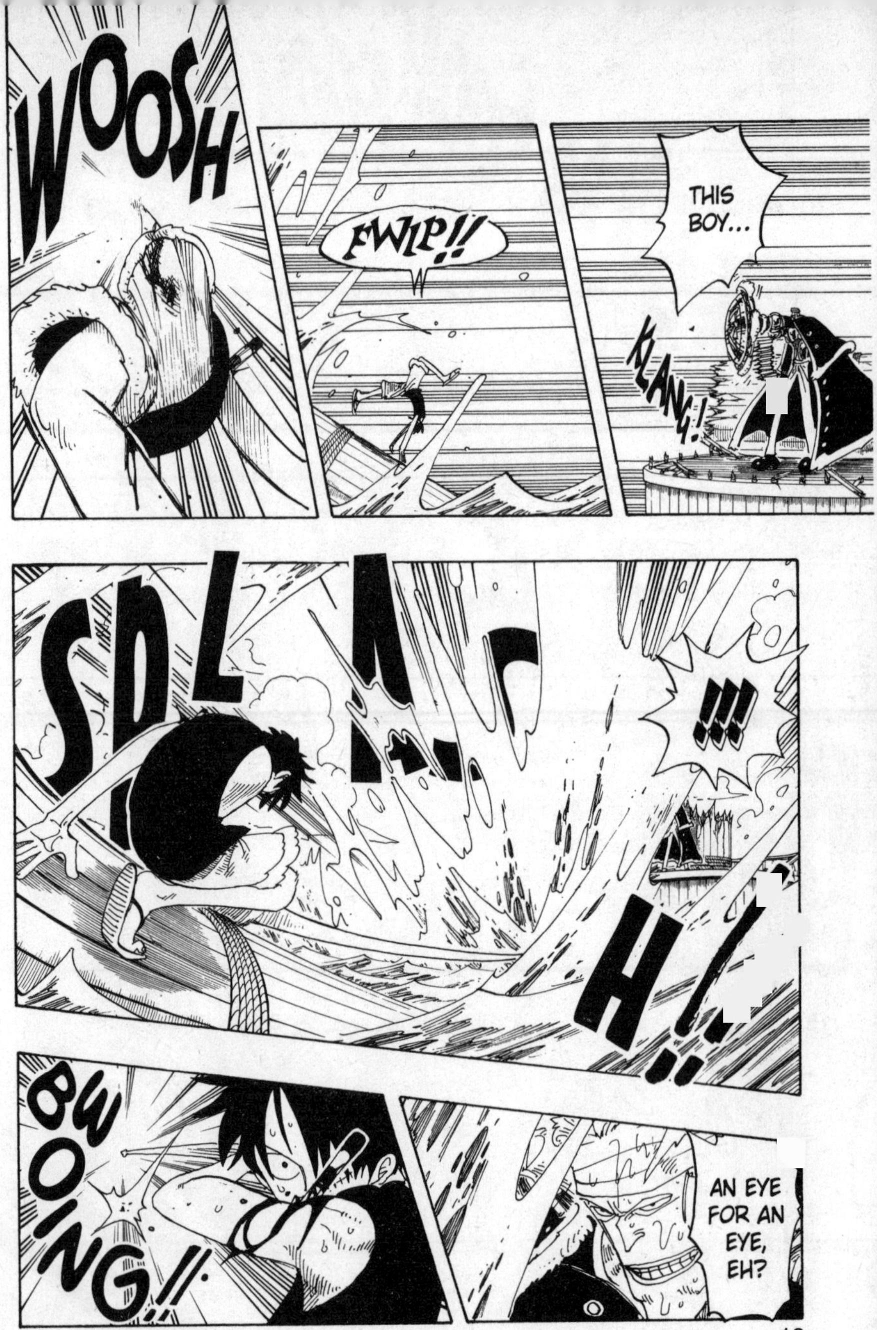
THIS BOY...
KLANG!
FWIP!!
WOOSH
!!!
SPLASH!!
AN EYE FOR AN EYE, EH?
BWOING!!

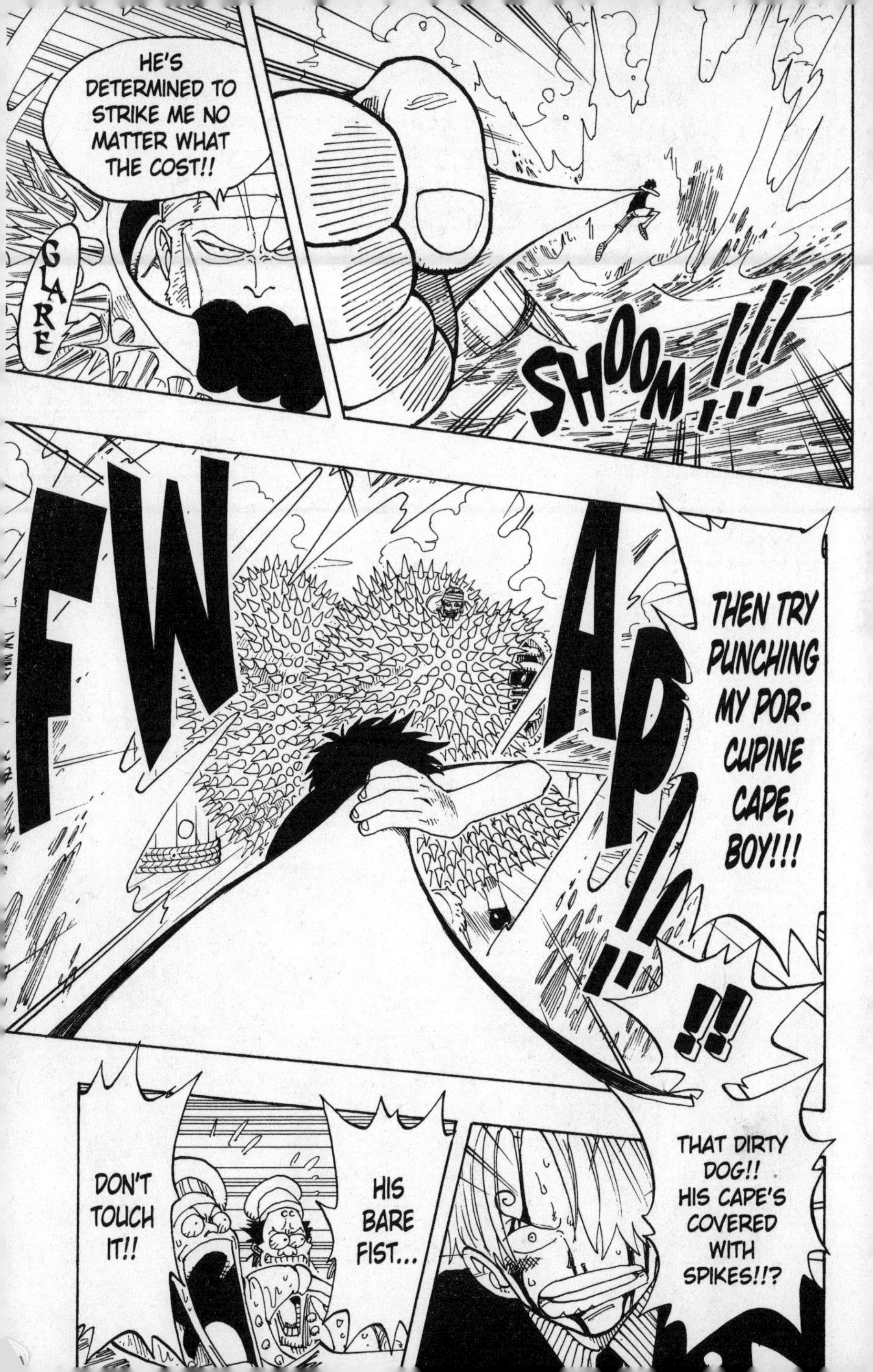

HE'S DETERMINED TO STRIKE ME NO MATTER WHAT THE COST!!
GLARE
SHOOM!!!
THEN TRY PUNCHING MY POR-CUPINE CAPE, BOY!!!
FWAP!!!!
THAT DIRTY DOG!! HIS CAPE'S COVERED WITH SPIKES!!?
HIS BARE FIST...
DON'T TOUCH IT!!

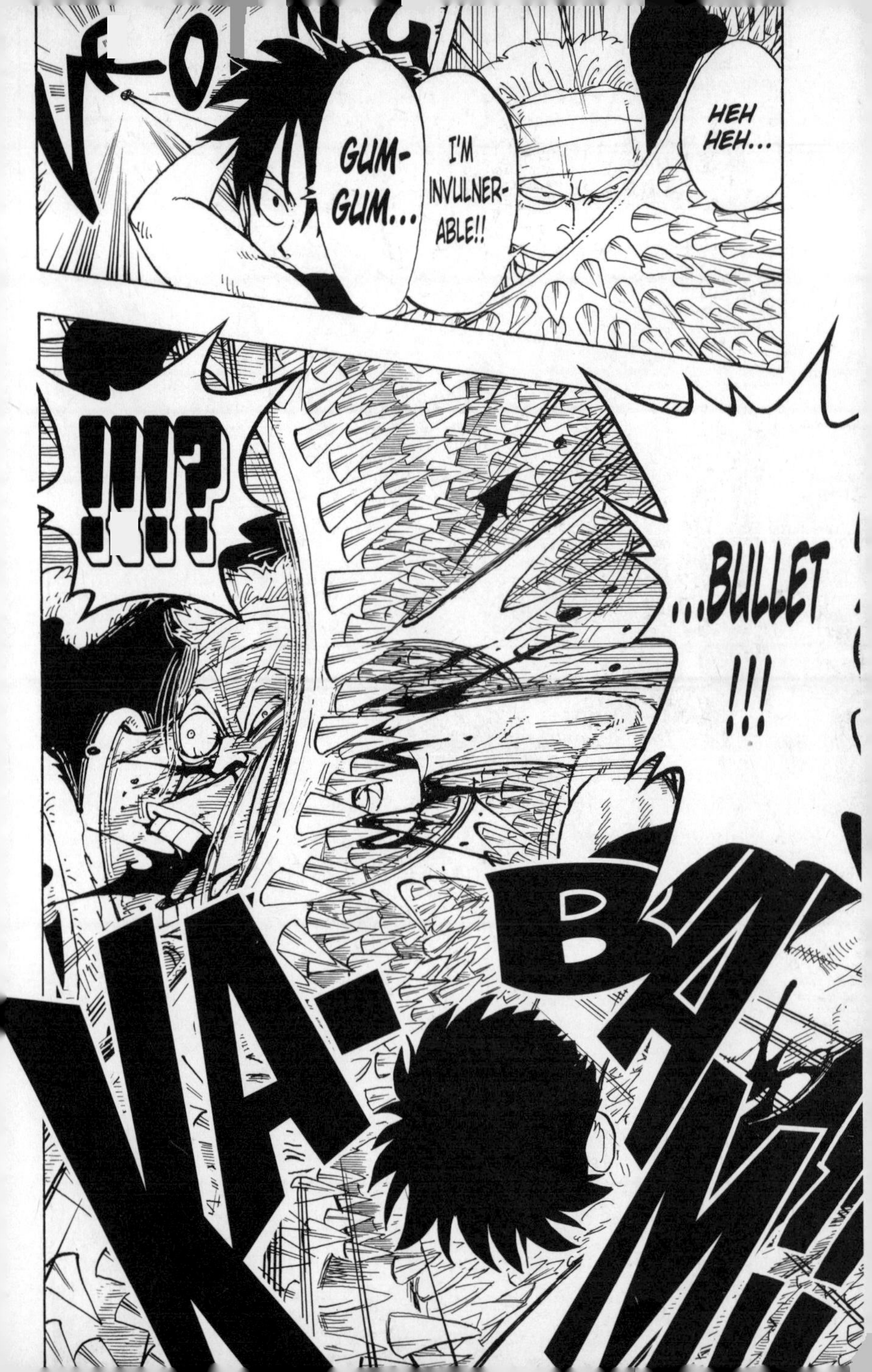
HEH HEH...
I'M INVULNER-ABLE!!
GUM-GUM...
...BULLET !!!
!!?

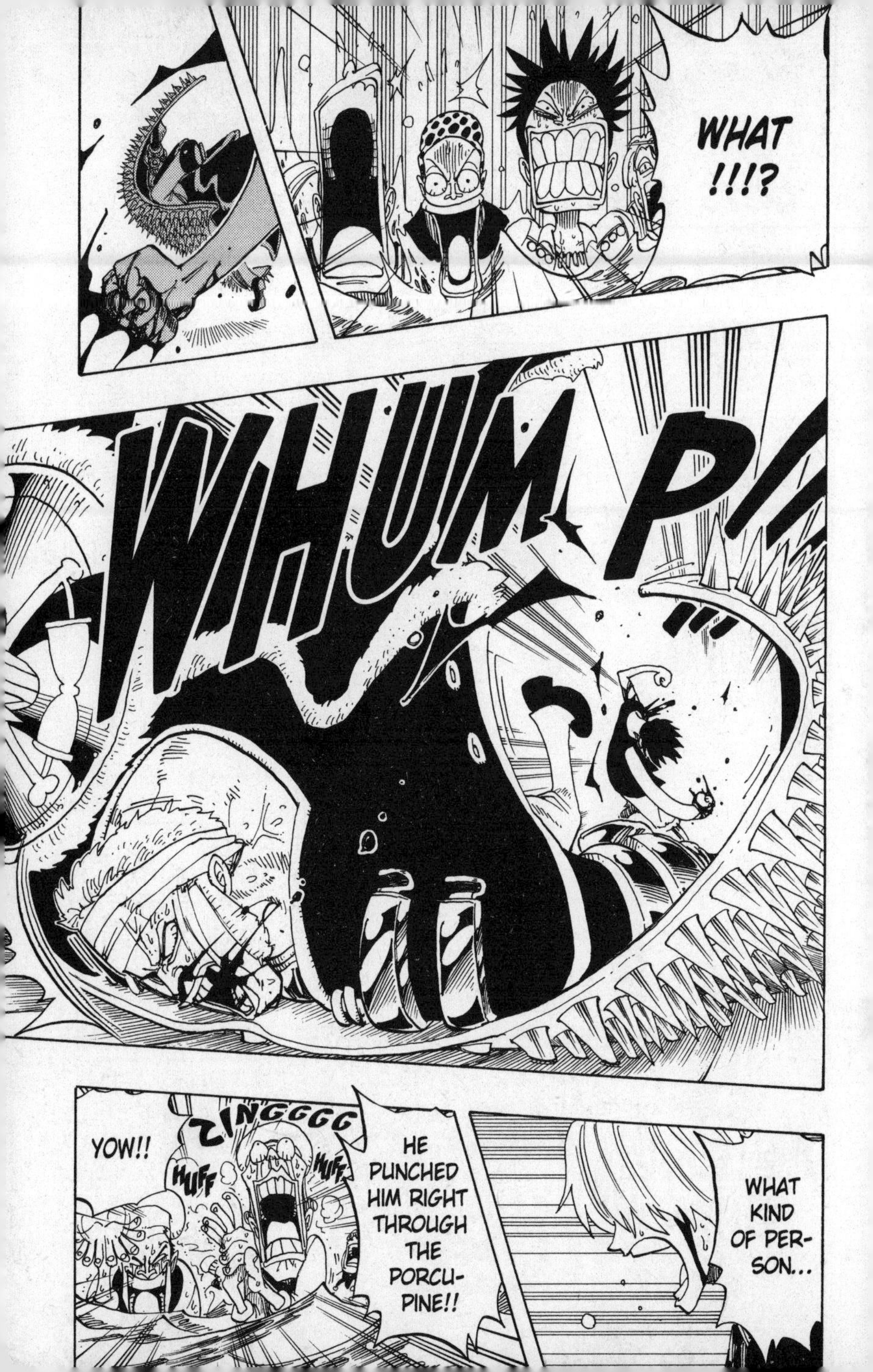
WHAT !!!?
WHUMP!!!
WHAT KIND OF PERSON...
ZINGGGG
HE PUNCHED HIM RIGHT THROUGH THE PORCUPINE!!
HUFF
HUFF
YOW!!

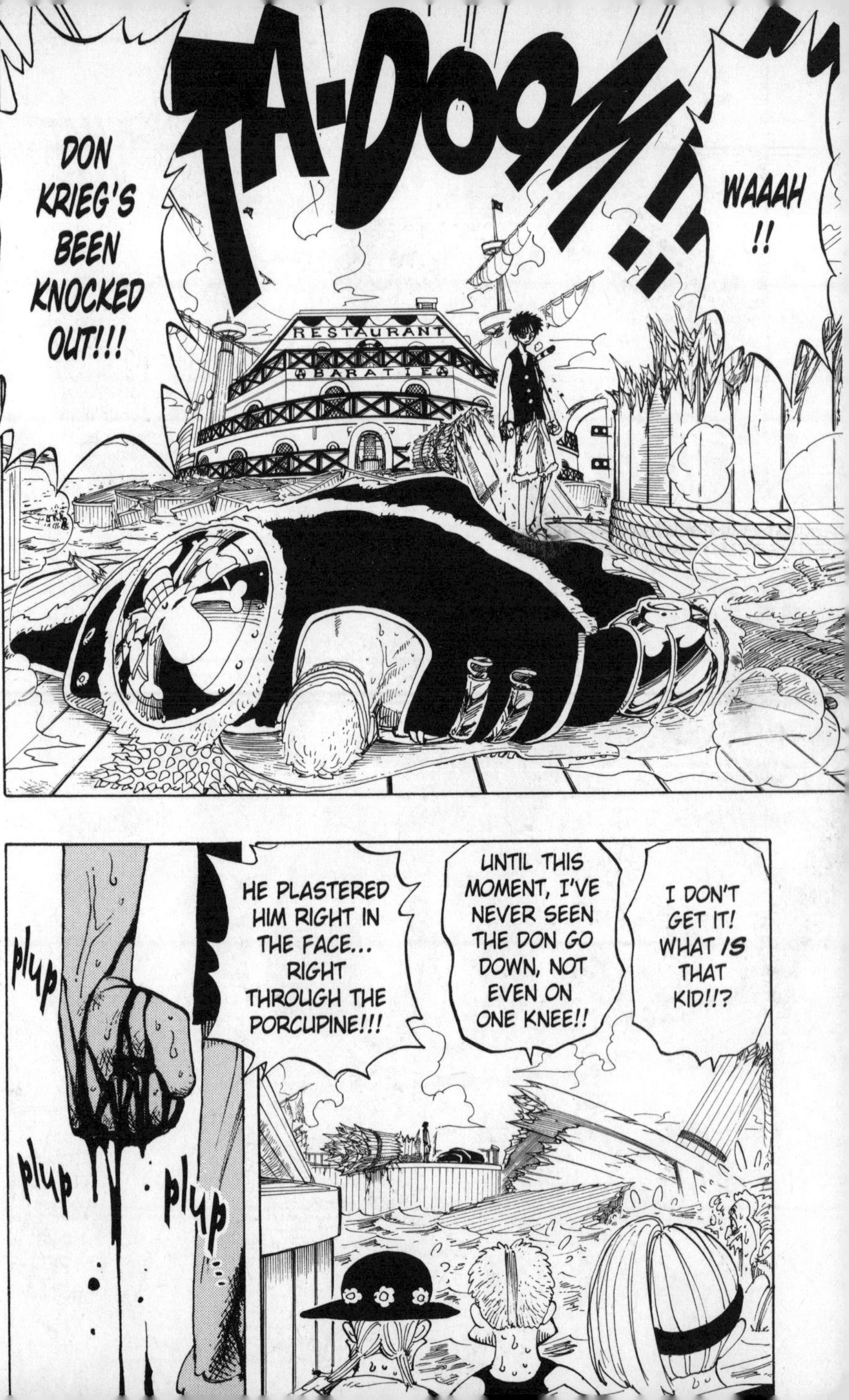
WAAAH!!
TA-DOOM!!
DON KRIEG'S BEEN KNOCKED OUT!!!
I DON'T GET IT! WHAT *IS* THAT KID!!?
UNTIL THIS MOMENT, I'VE NEVER SEEN THE DON GO DOWN, NOT EVEN ON ONE KNEE!!
HE PLASTERED HIM RIGHT IN THE FACE... RIGHT THROUGH THE PORCUPINE!!!
plup
plup
plup

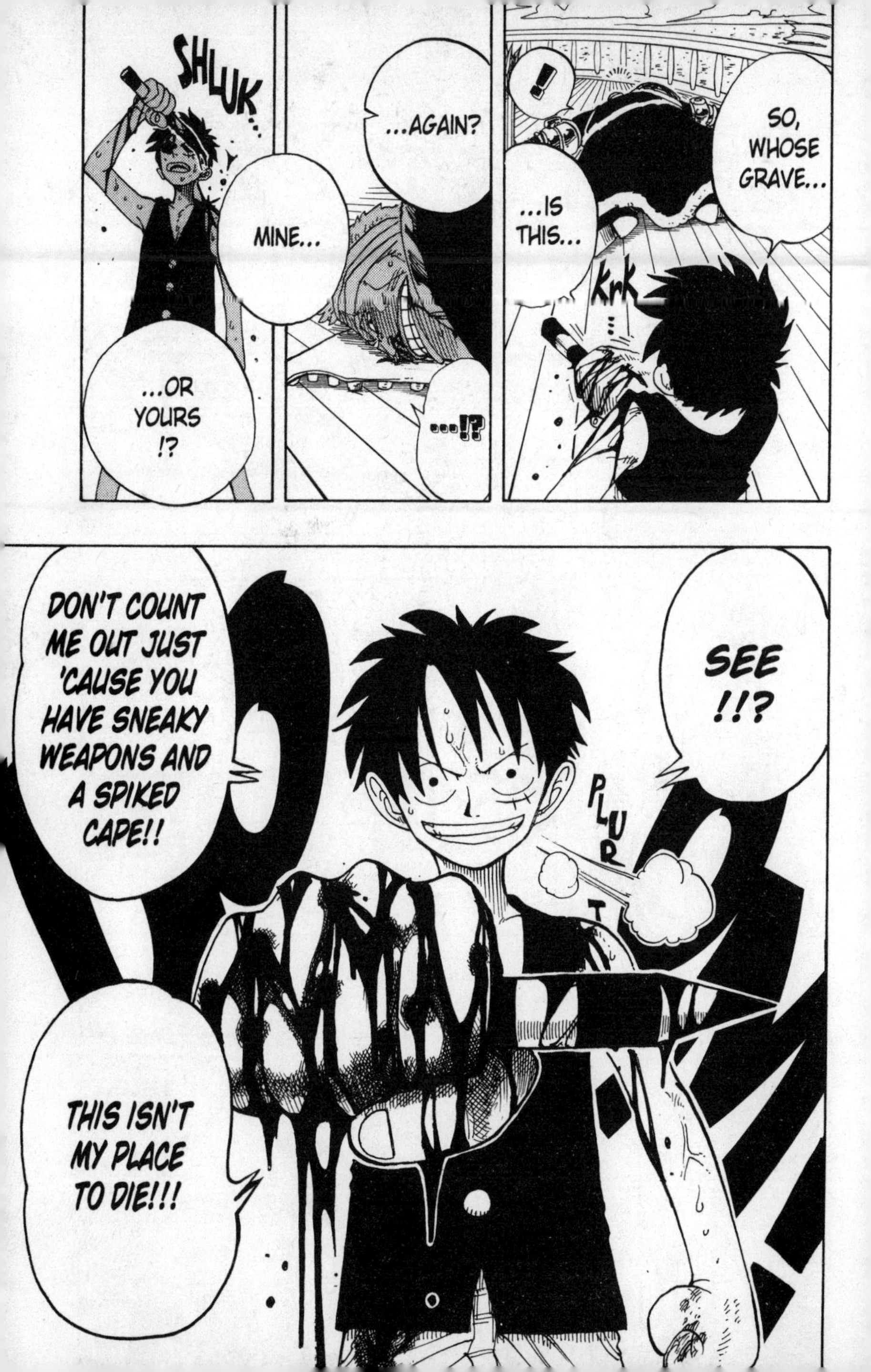
!
SO, WHOSE GRAVE...
...IS THIS...
KRK
...AGAIN?
...!?
SHLUK
MINE...
...OR YOURS !?
SEE !!?
PLURT
DON'T COUNT ME OUT JUST 'CAUSE YOU HAVE SNEAKY WEAPONS AND A SPIKED CAPE!!
THIS ISN'T MY PLACE TO DIE!!!

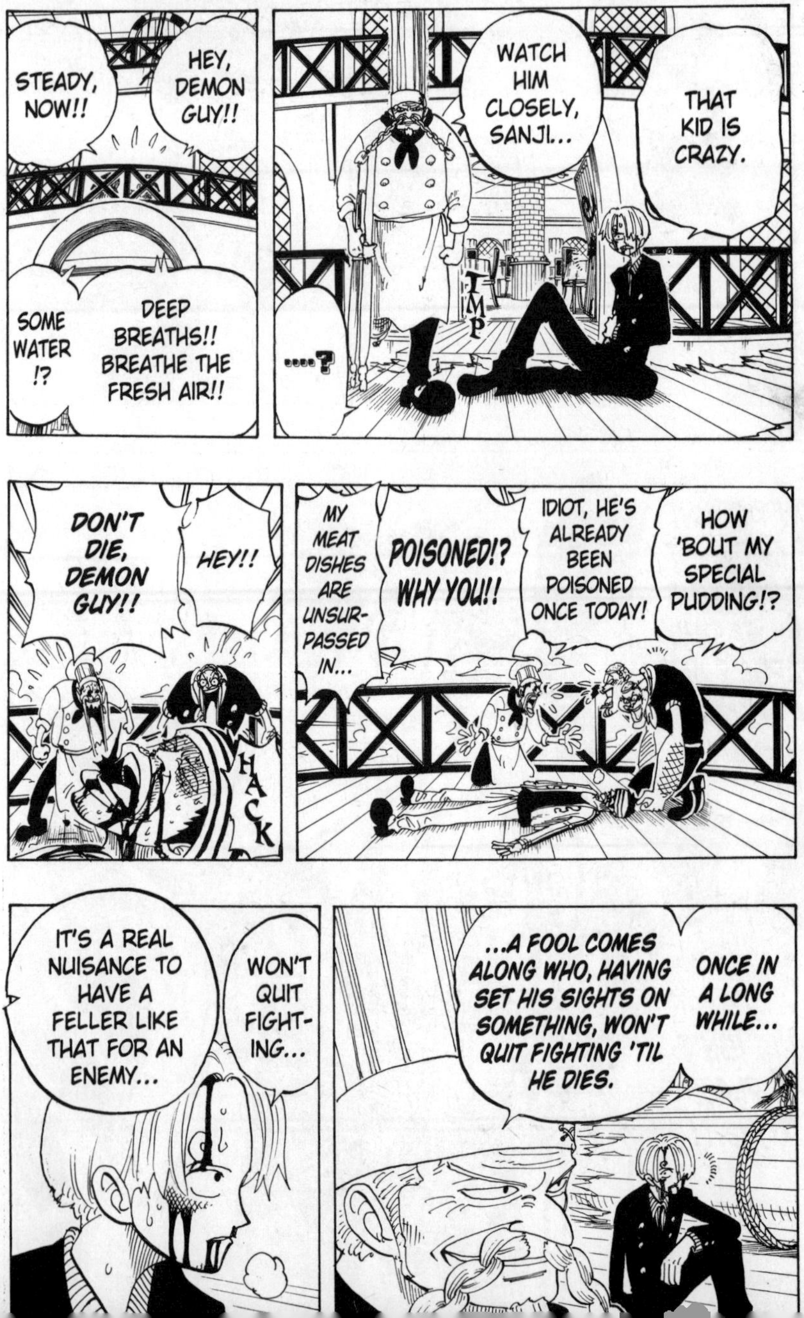
THAT KID IS CRAZY.
WATCH HIM CLOSELY, SANJI...
TMP
....?
HEY, DEMON GUY!!
STEADY, NOW!!
DEEP BREATHS!! BREATHE THE FRESH AIR!!
SOME WATER !?
HOW 'BOUT MY SPECIAL PUDDING!?
IDIOT, HE'S ALREADY BEEN POISONED ONCE TODAY!
POISONED!? WHY YOU!!
MY MEAT DISHES ARE UNSURPASSED IN...
HEY!!
DON'T DIE, DEMON GUY!!
HACK
ONCE IN A LONG WHILE...
...A FOOL COMES ALONG WHO, HAVING SET HIS SIGHTS ON SOMETHING, WON'T QUIT FIGHTING 'TIL HE DIES.
WON'T QUIT FIGHTING...
IT'S A REAL NUISANCE TO HAVE A FELLER LIKE THAT FOR AN ENEMY...

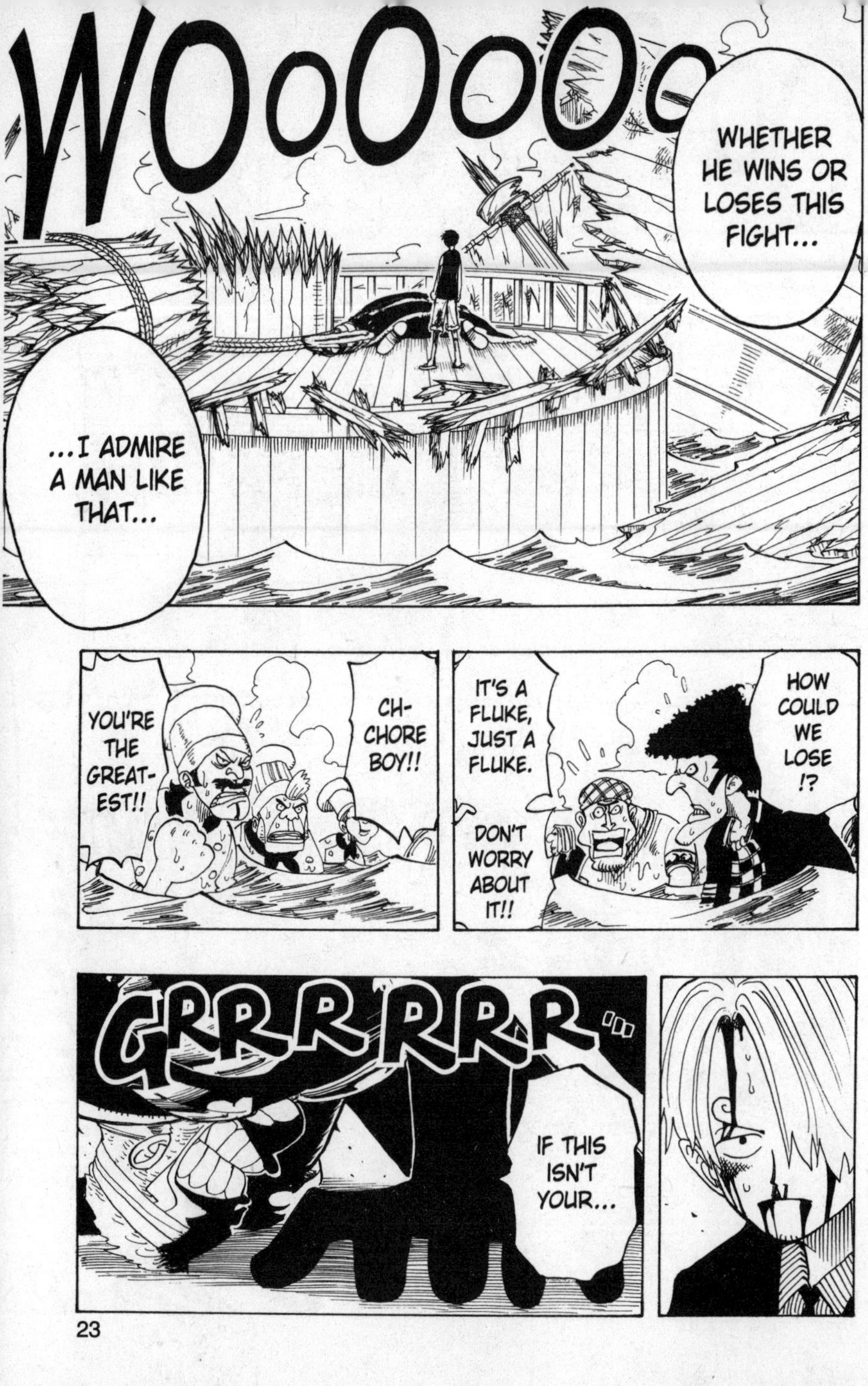
WOOOOOO
WHETHER HE WINS OR LOSES THIS FIGHT...
...I ADMIRE A MAN LIKE THAT...
HOW COULD WE LOSE !?
IT'S A FLUKE, JUST A FLUKE.
DON'T WORRY ABOUT IT!!
CH- CHORE BOY!!
YOU'RE THE GREAT- EST!!
GRRRRRR
IF THIS ISN'T YOUR...

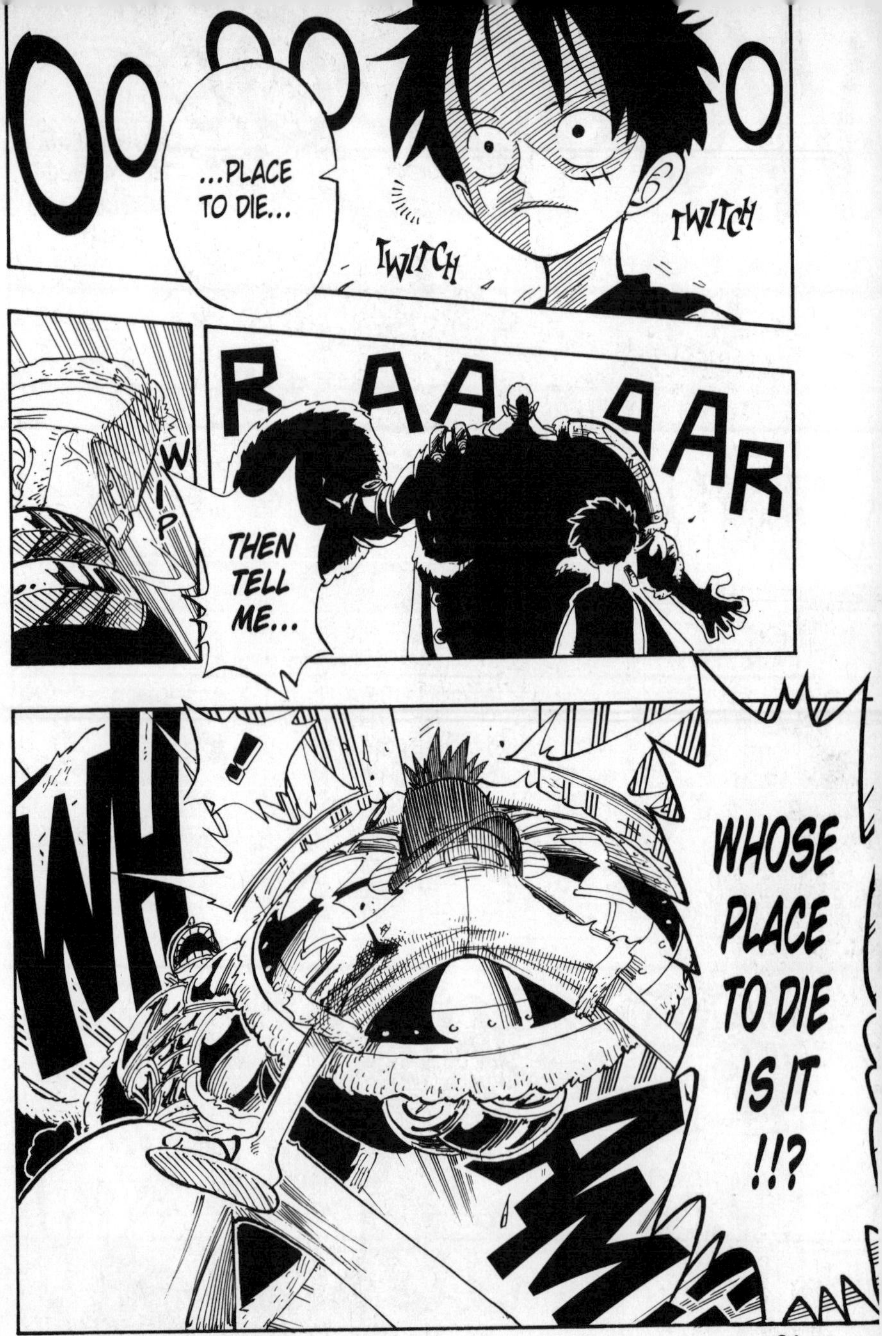
OOOOO
...PLACE TO DIE...
TWITCH
TWITCH
RAAAAR
THEN TELL ME...
WIP
WHOSE PLACE TO DIE IS IT !!?
!
WH

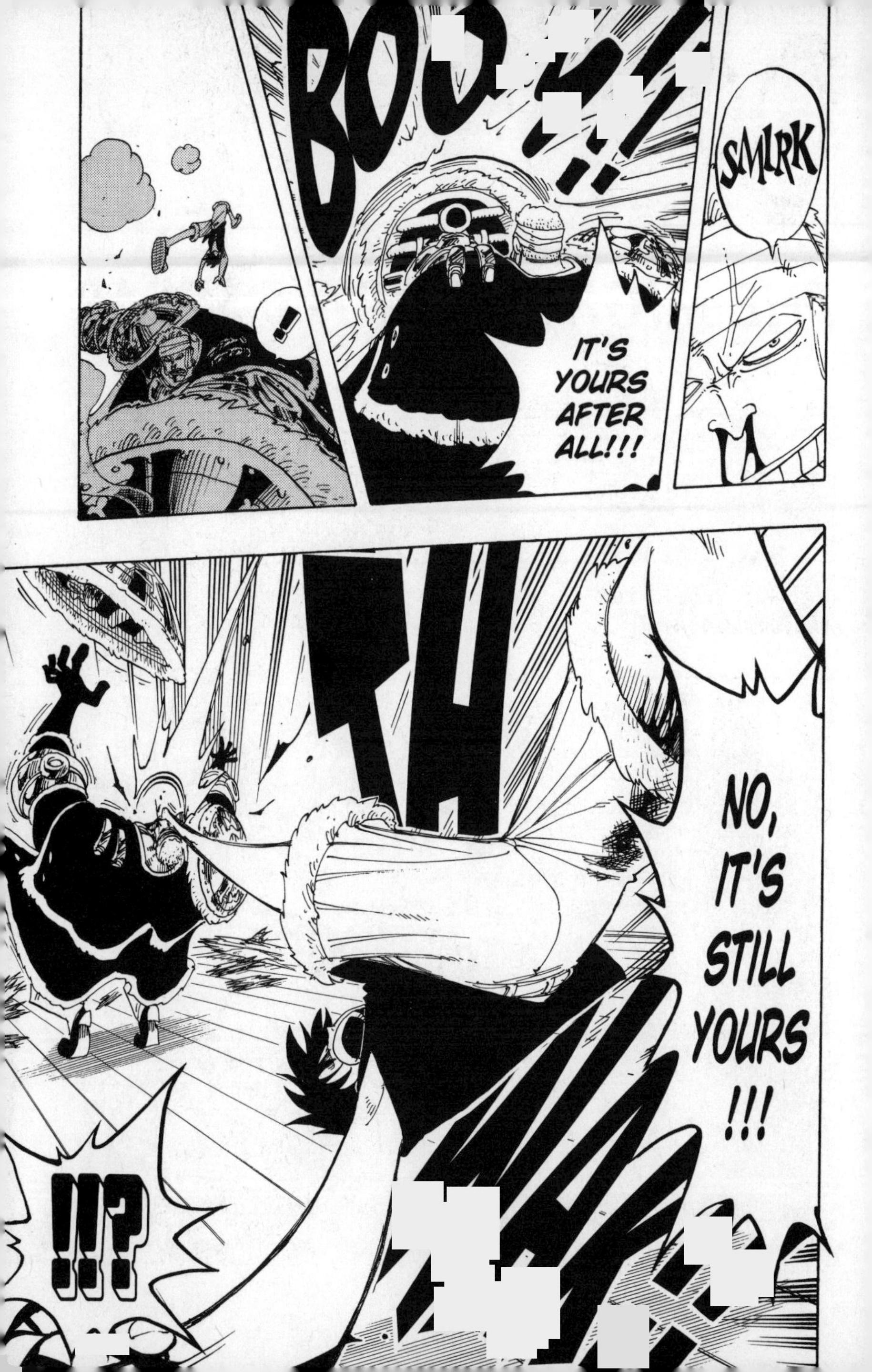
SMIRK
IT'S YOURS AFTER ALL!!!
!
NO, IT'S STILL YOURS!!!
!!?

Chapter 64:

THE MIGHTY BATTLE SPEAR

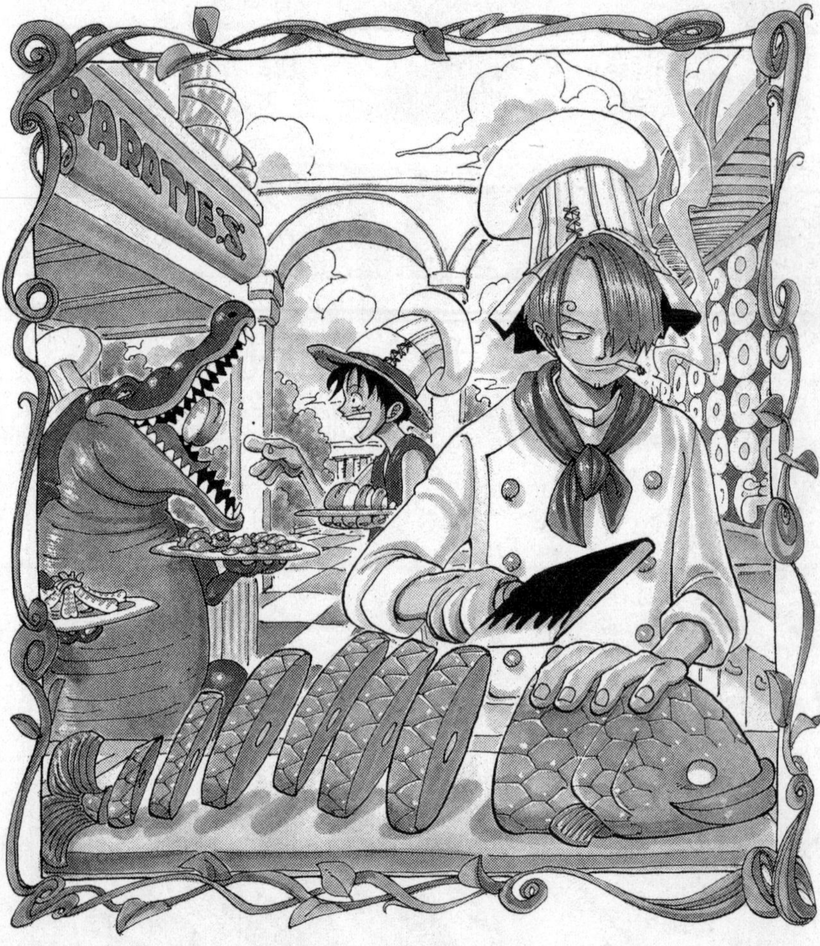
BARATIE'S

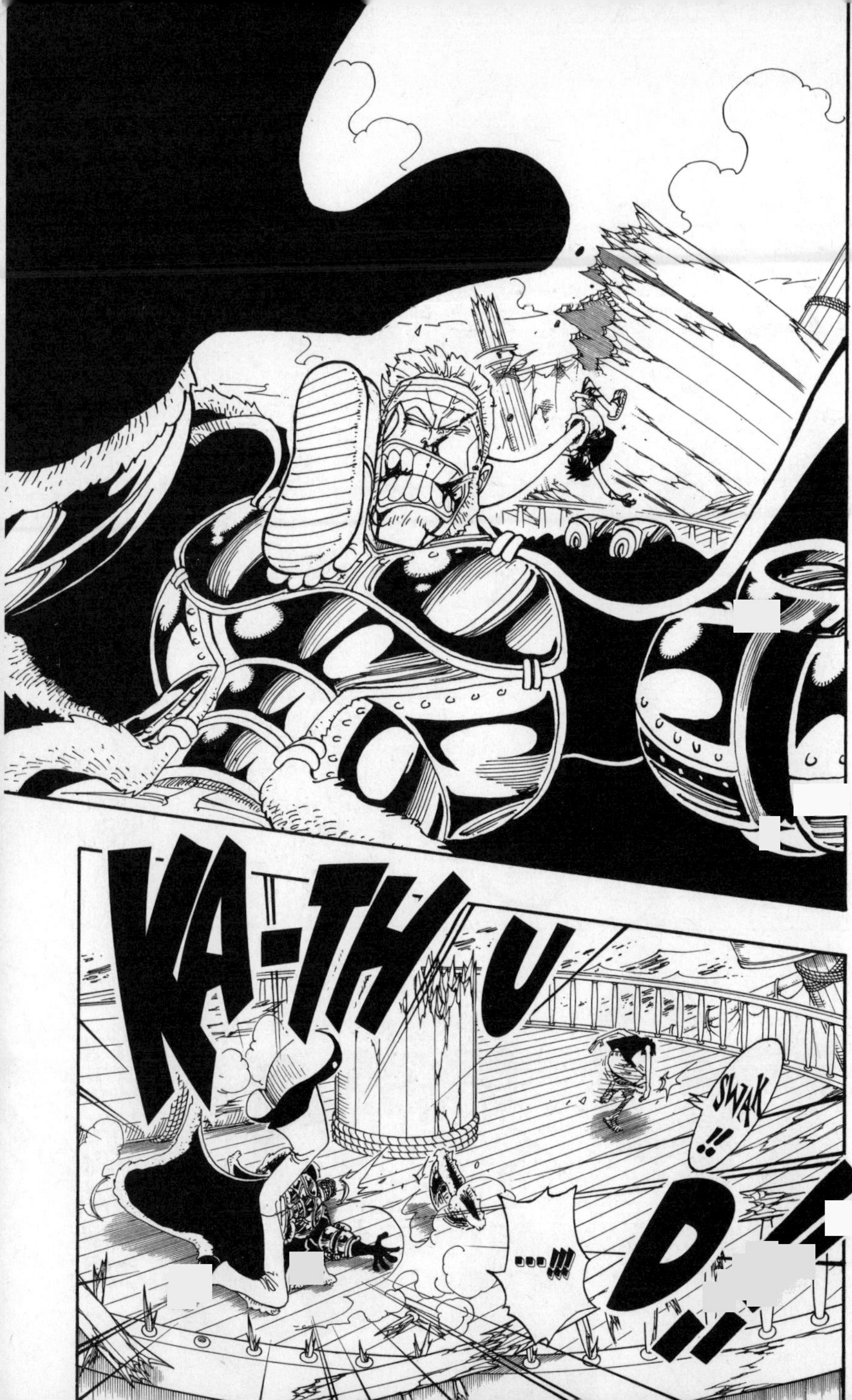
SWAK!!
KA-THU
D!!
...!!!

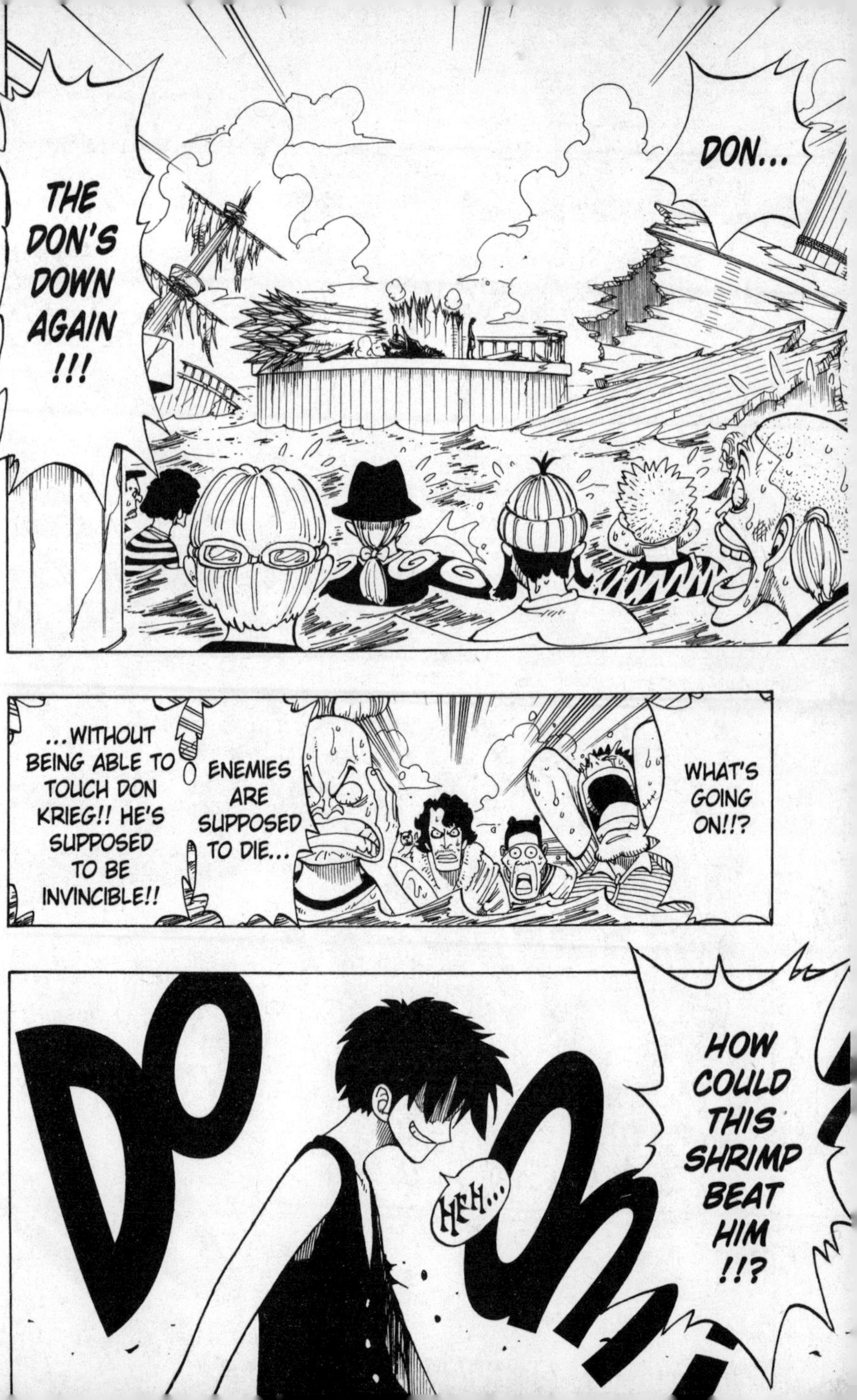
DON...
THE DON'S DOWN AGAIN!!!
WHAT'S GOING ON!!?
ENEMIES ARE SUPPOSED TO DIE...
...WITHOUT BEING ABLE TO TOUCH DON KRIEG!! HE'S SUPPOSED TO BE INVINCIBLE!!
HOW COULD THIS SHRIMP BEAT HIM!!?
HEH...
DOOM

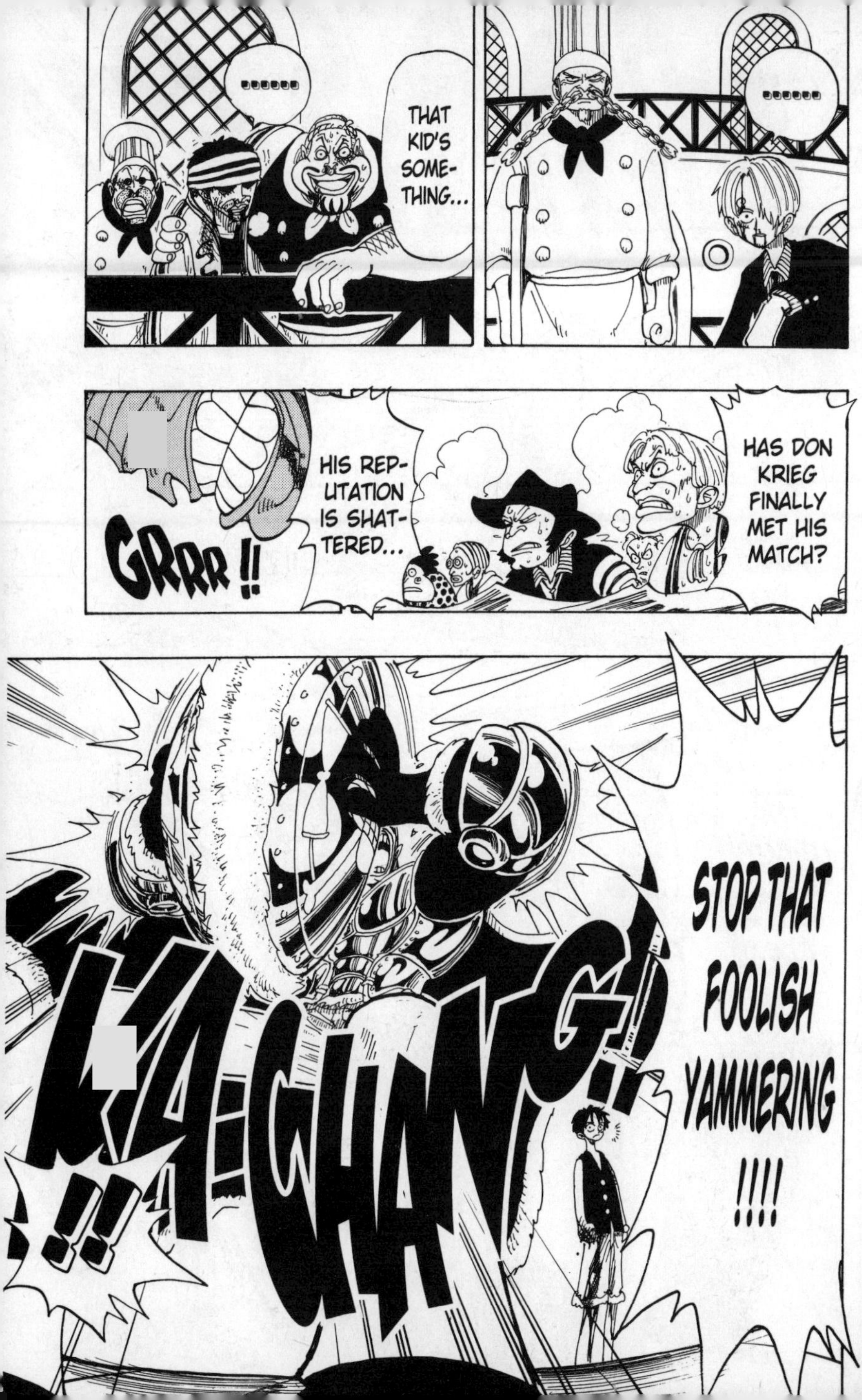
......
THAT KID'S SOME-THING...
......
HAS DON KRIEG FINALLY MET HIS MATCH?
HIS REP-UTATION IS SHAT-TERED...
GRRR!!
STOP THAT FOOLISH YAMMERING!!!!
A-CHANG!!

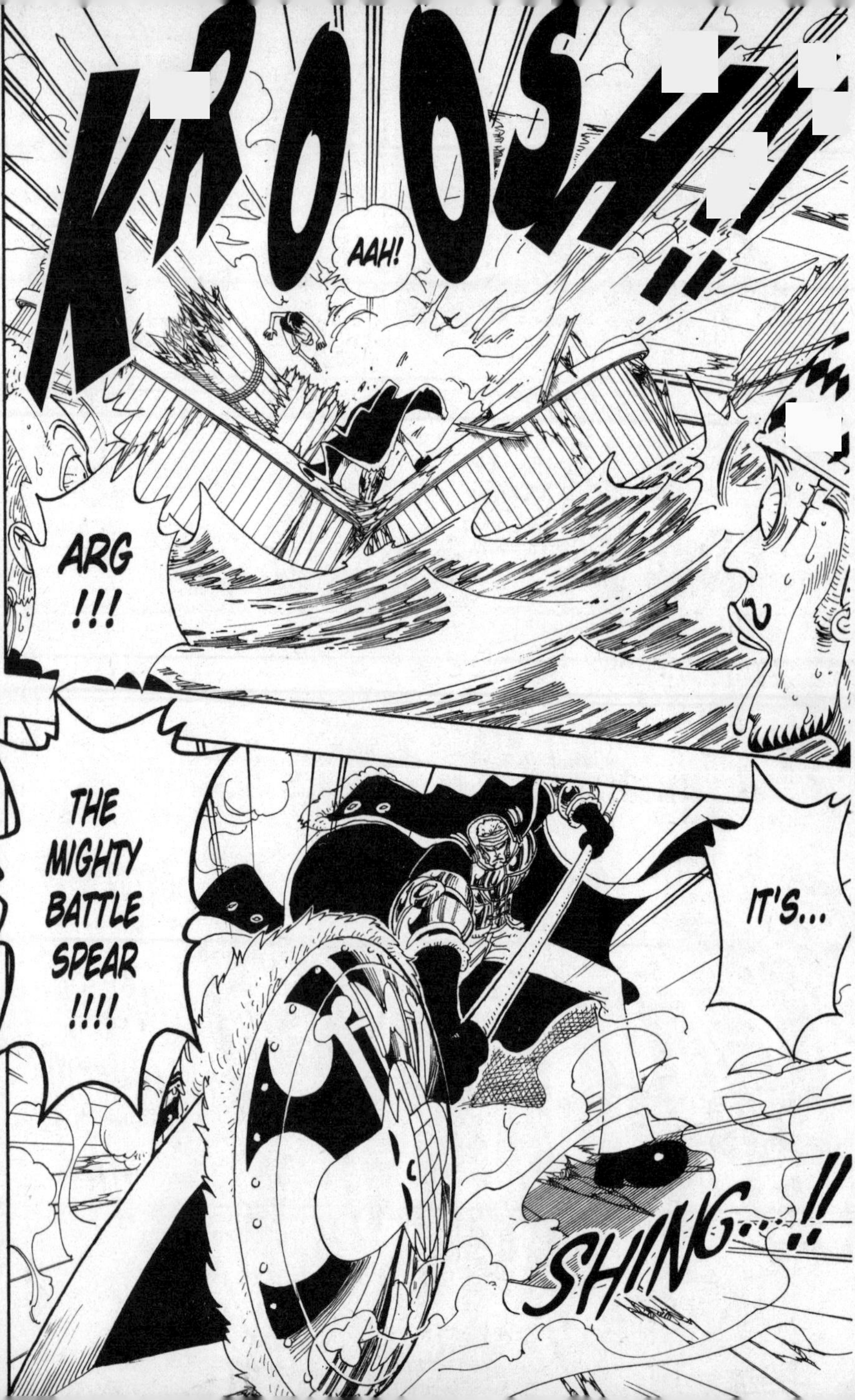
KROOSH!!
AAH!
ARG!!!
IT'S...
THE MIGHTY BATTLE SPEAR!!!!
SHING...!!

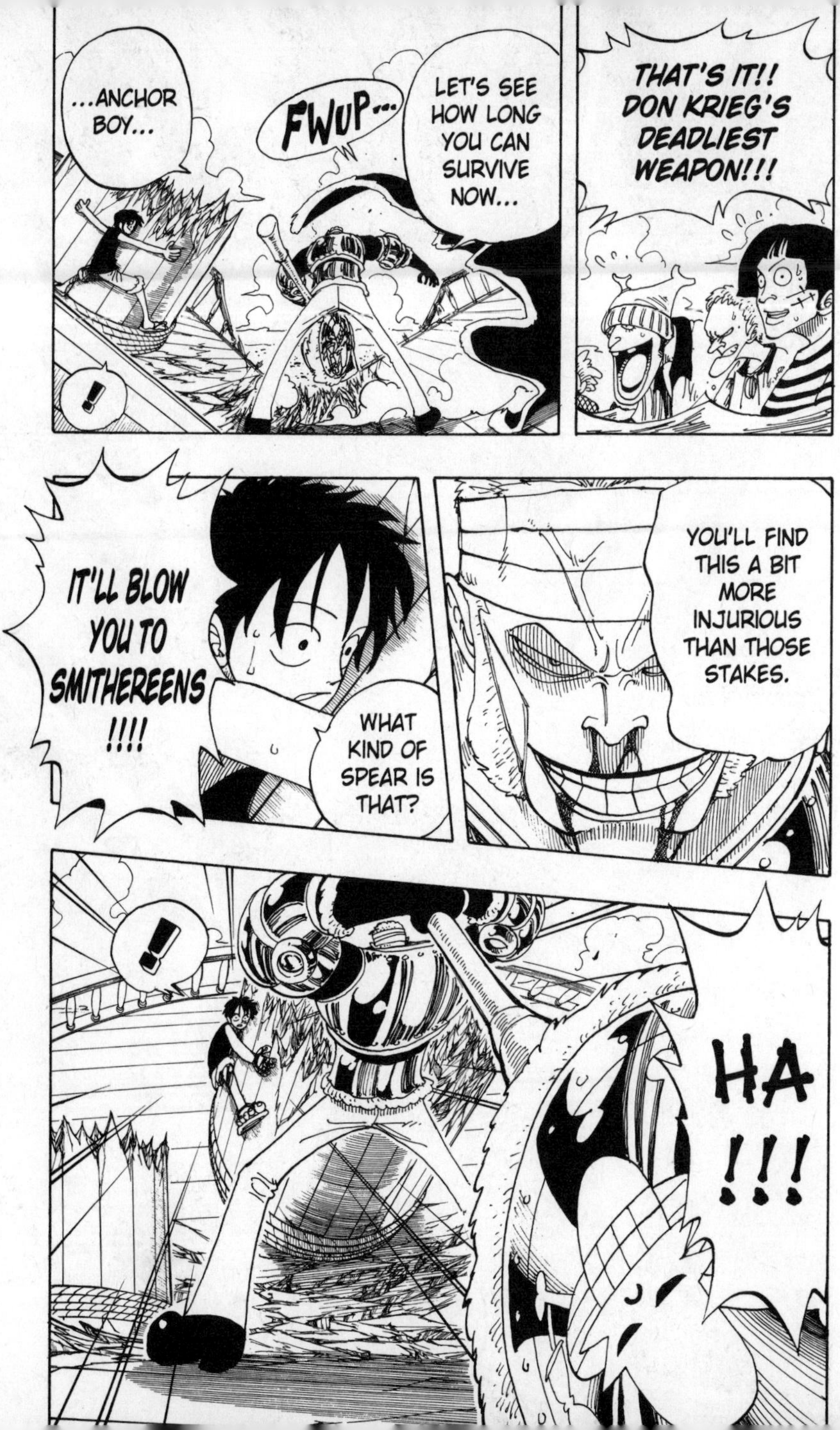
THAT'S IT!! DON KRIEG'S DEADLIEST WEAPON!!!
LET'S SEE HOW LONG YOU CAN SURVIVE NOW...
FWUP...
...ANCHOR BOY...
!
YOU'LL FIND THIS A BIT MORE INJURIOUS THAN THOSE STAKES.
WHAT KIND OF SPEAR IS THAT?
IT'LL BLOW YOU TO SMITHEREENS!!!!
HA!!!
!

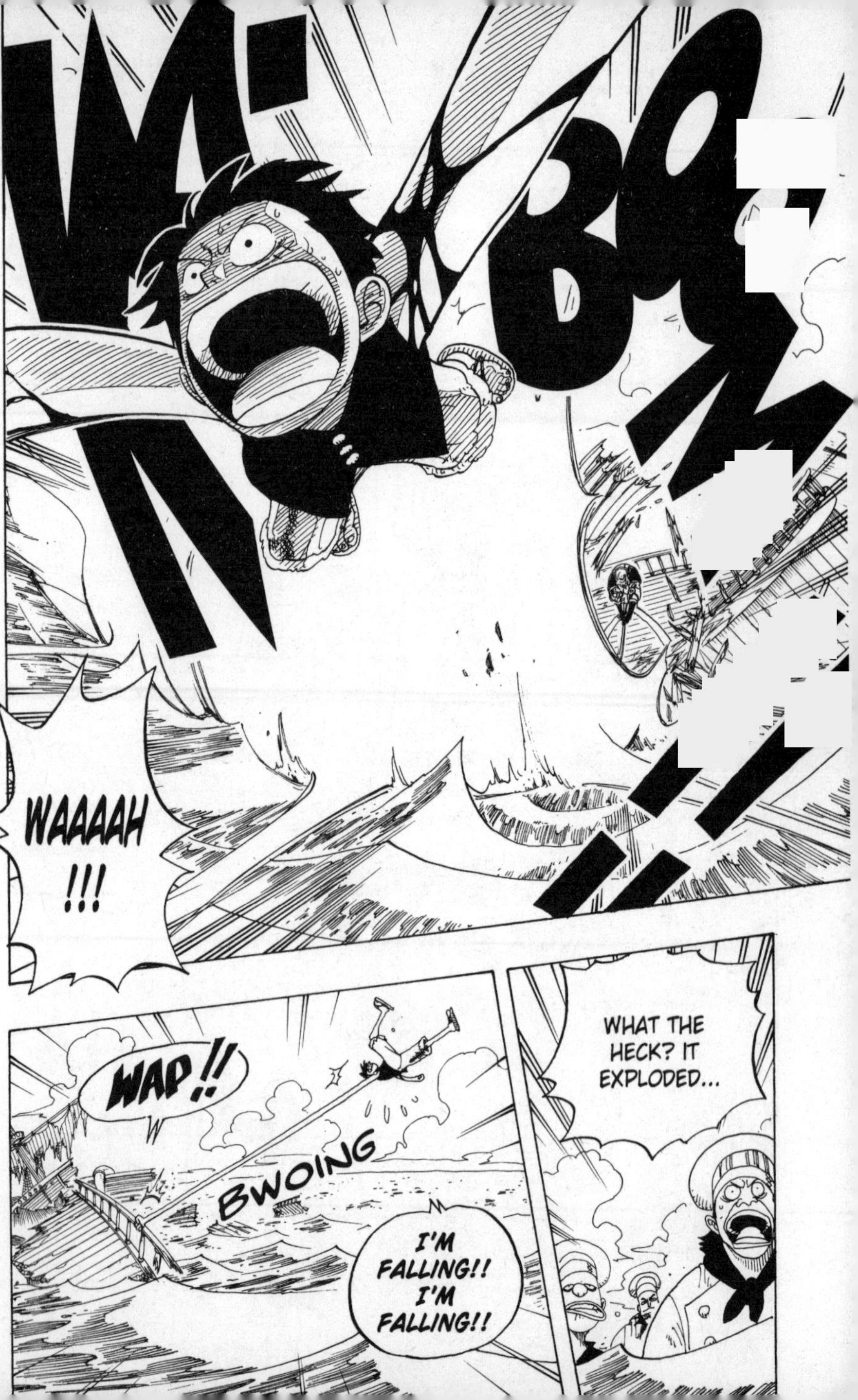
WAAAAH !!!
WHAT THE HECK? IT EXPLODED...
WAP!!
BWOING
I'M FALLING!! I'M FALLING!!

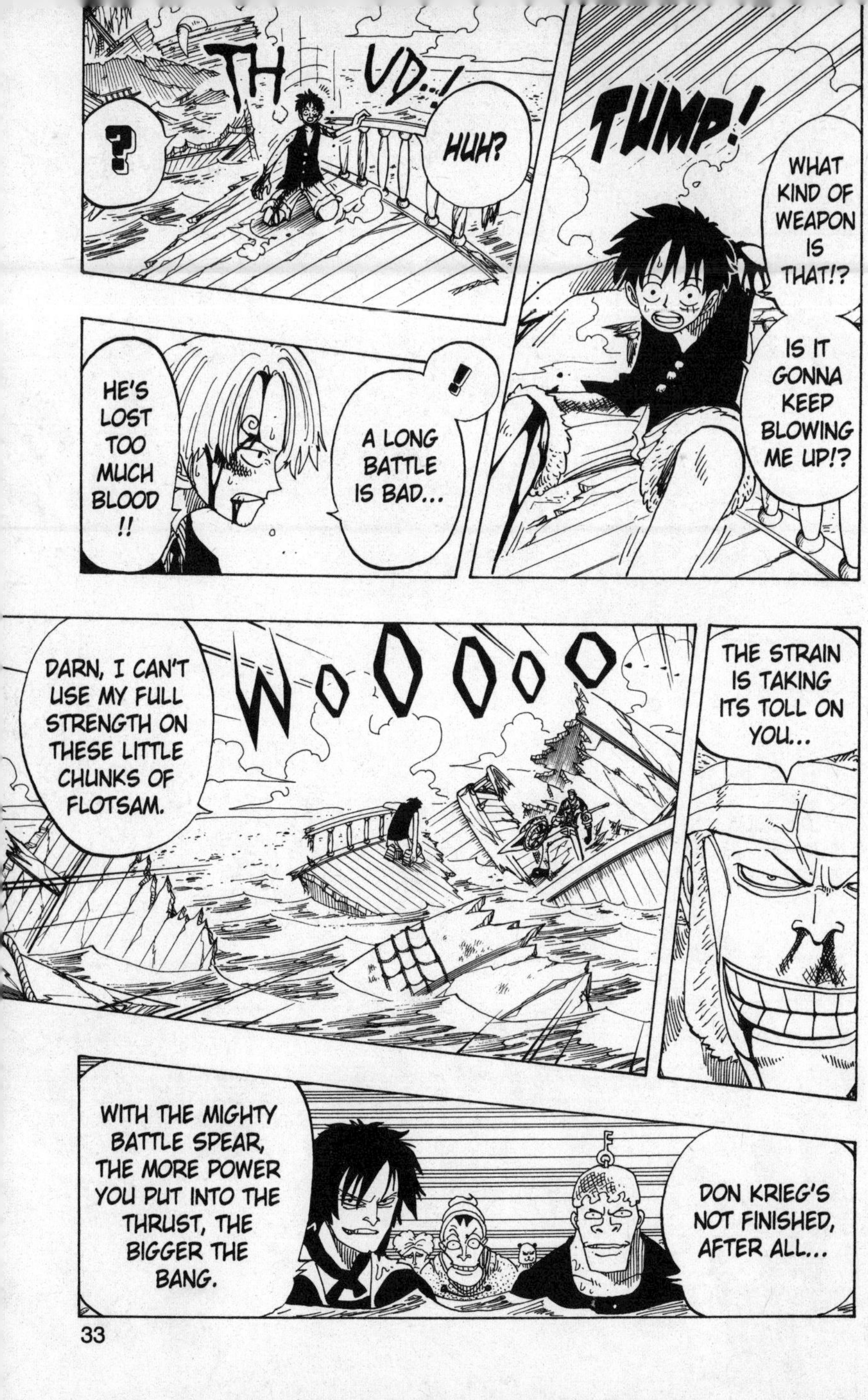
TUMP!
WHAT KIND OF WEAPON IS THAT!?
IS IT GONNA KEEP BLOWING ME UP!?
THUD..!
HUH?
?
!
A LONG BATTLE IS BAD...
HE'S LOST TOO MUCH BLOOD!!
THE STRAIN IS TAKING ITS TOLL ON YOU...
WOOOOO
DARN, I CAN'T USE MY FULL STRENGTH ON THESE LITTLE CHUNKS OF FLOTSAM.
DON KRIEG'S NOT FINISHED, AFTER ALL...
WITH THE MIGHTY BATTLE SPEAR, THE MORE POWER YOU PUT INTO THE THRUST, THE BIGGER THE BANG.

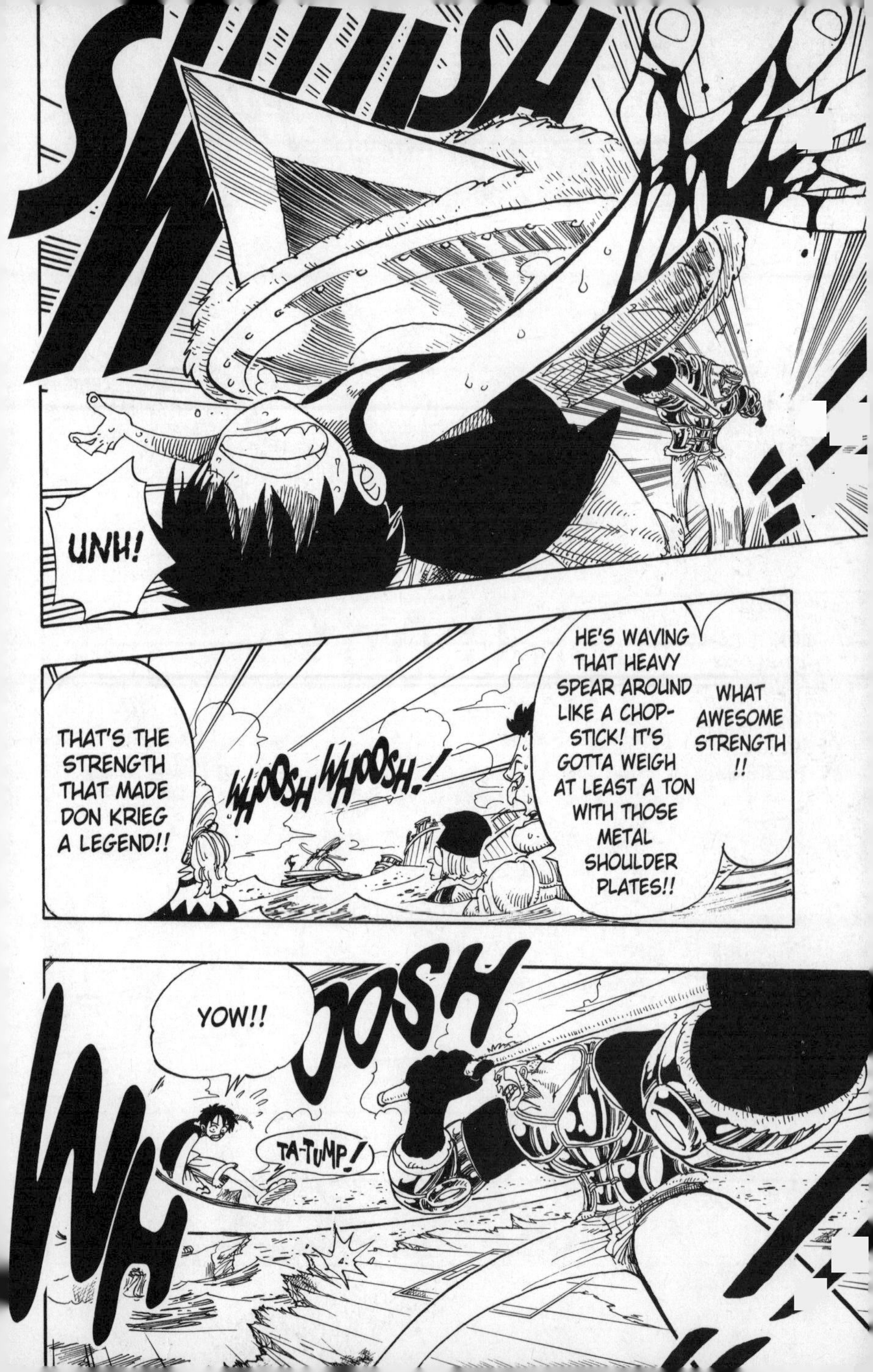
UNH!
WHAT AWESOME STRENGTH!!
HE'S WAVING THAT HEAVY SPEAR AROUND LIKE A CHOP-STICK! IT'S GOTTA WEIGH AT LEAST A TON WITH THOSE METAL SHOULDER PLATES!!
WHOOSH WHOOSH!
THAT'S THE STRENGTH THAT MADE DON KRIEG A LEGEND!!
WHOOSH
YOW!!
TA-TUMP!

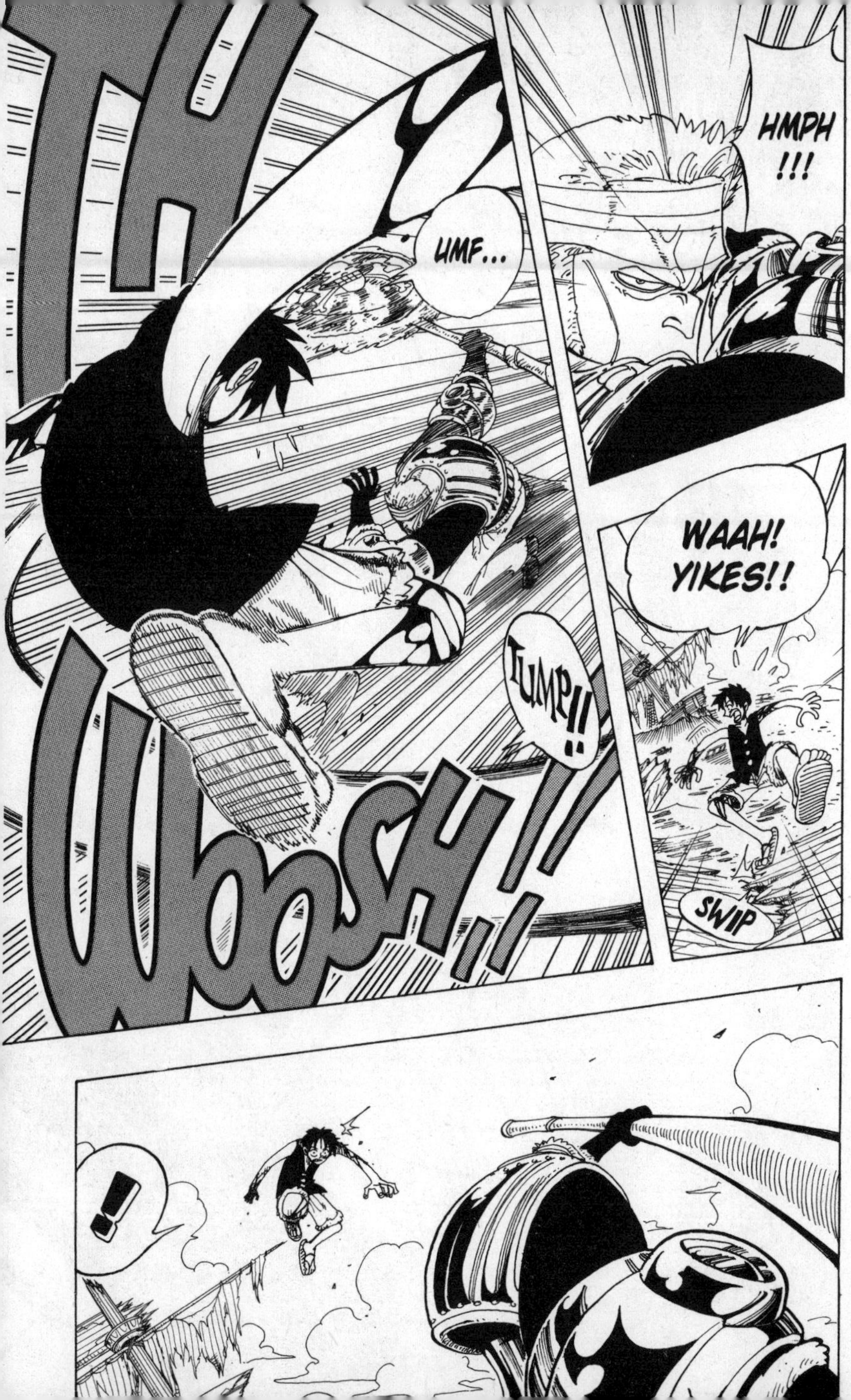
HMPH!!!
WAAH! YIKES!!
SWIP
UMF...
TUMP!!
WOOSH!!
!

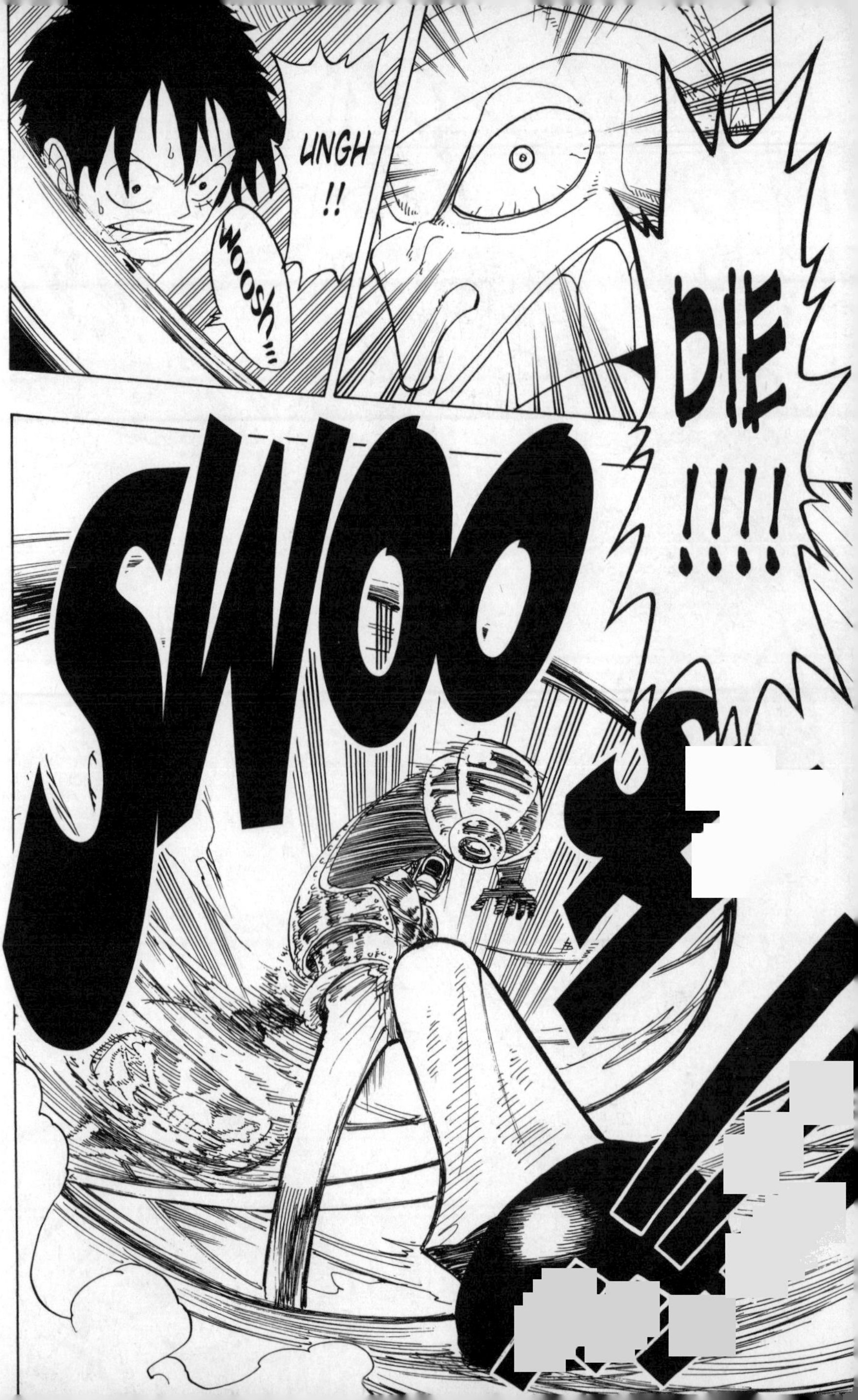
UNGH!!
DIE!!!!
WOOSH!!!
SWOO

READ THIS WAY

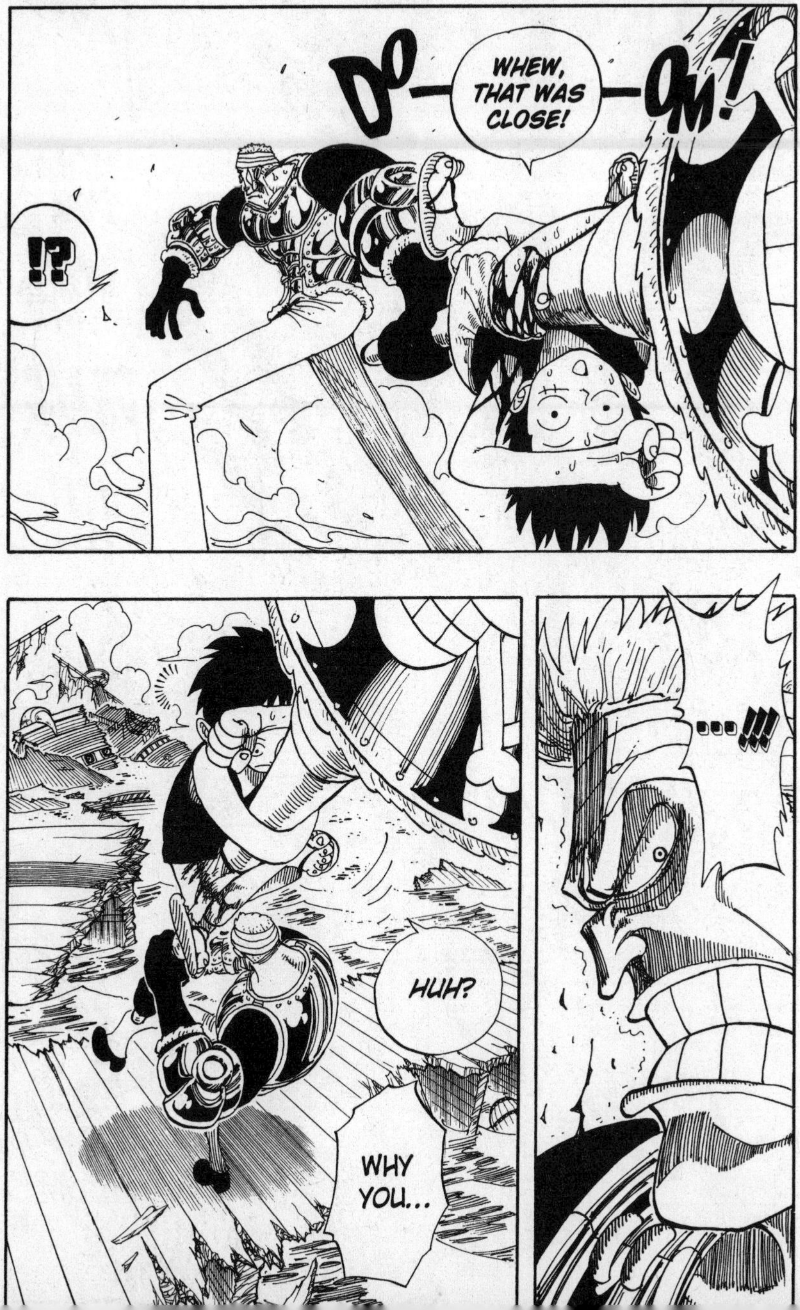
DO—OM!
WHEW, THAT WAS CLOSE!
!?
...!!!
HUH?
WHY YOU...

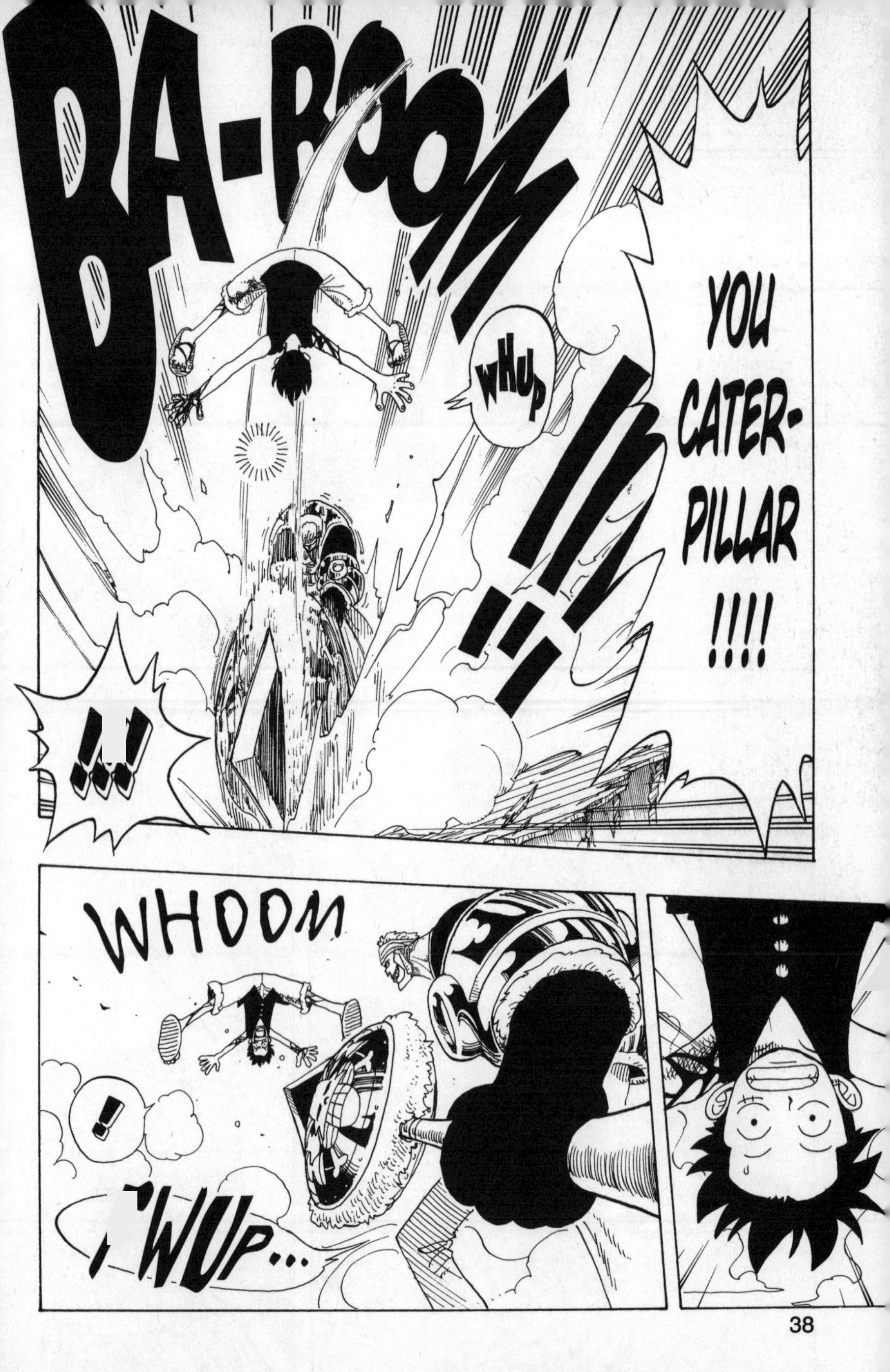
BA-BOOM
WHUP
YOU CATER-PILLAR !!!!
!!
WHOOM
!
WUP...

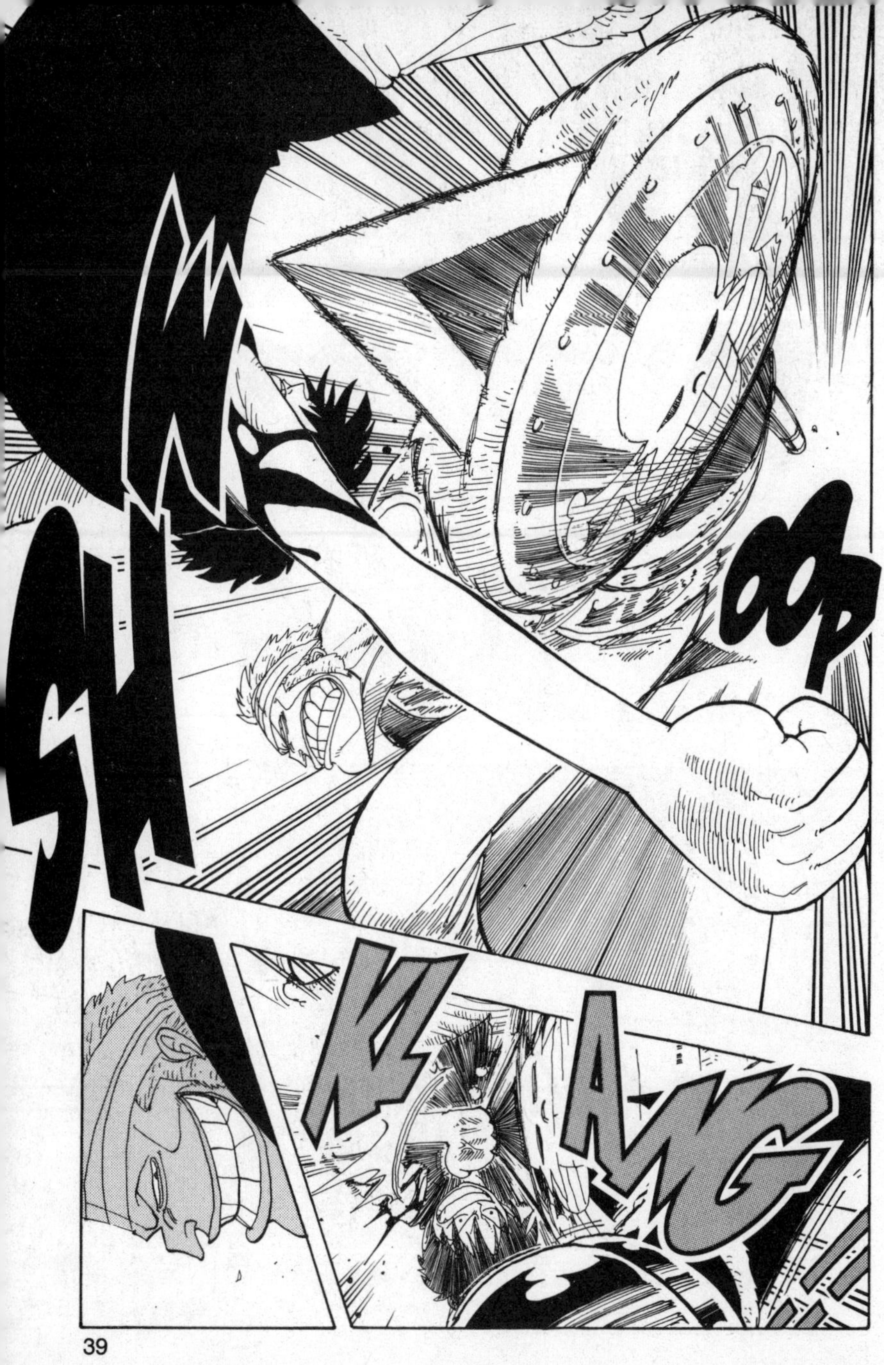
SHOOP
KA-ANG!!

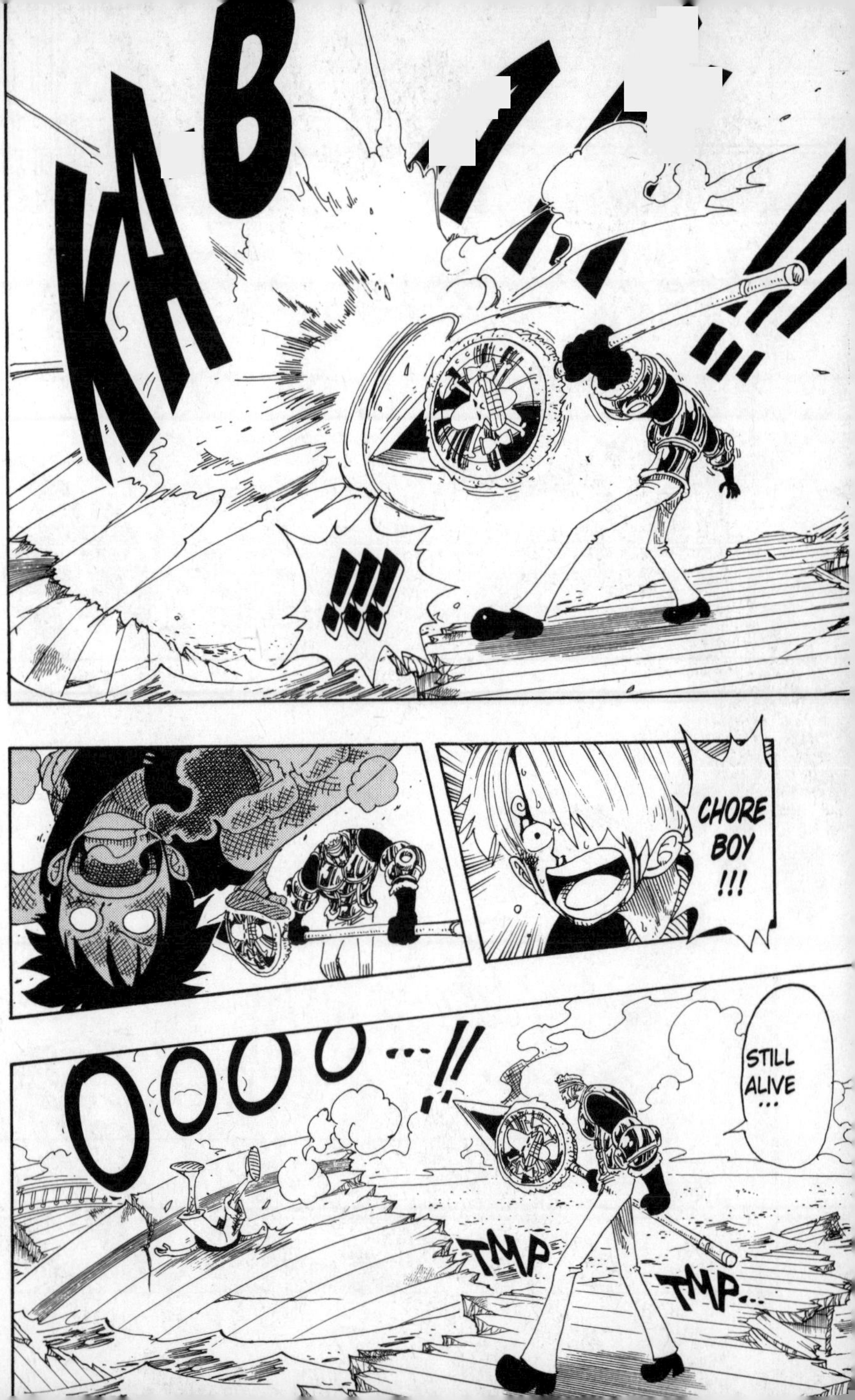
KA-B
!!!!
CHORE BOY !!!
STILL ALIVE ...
TMP...
TMP
OOOO...!!

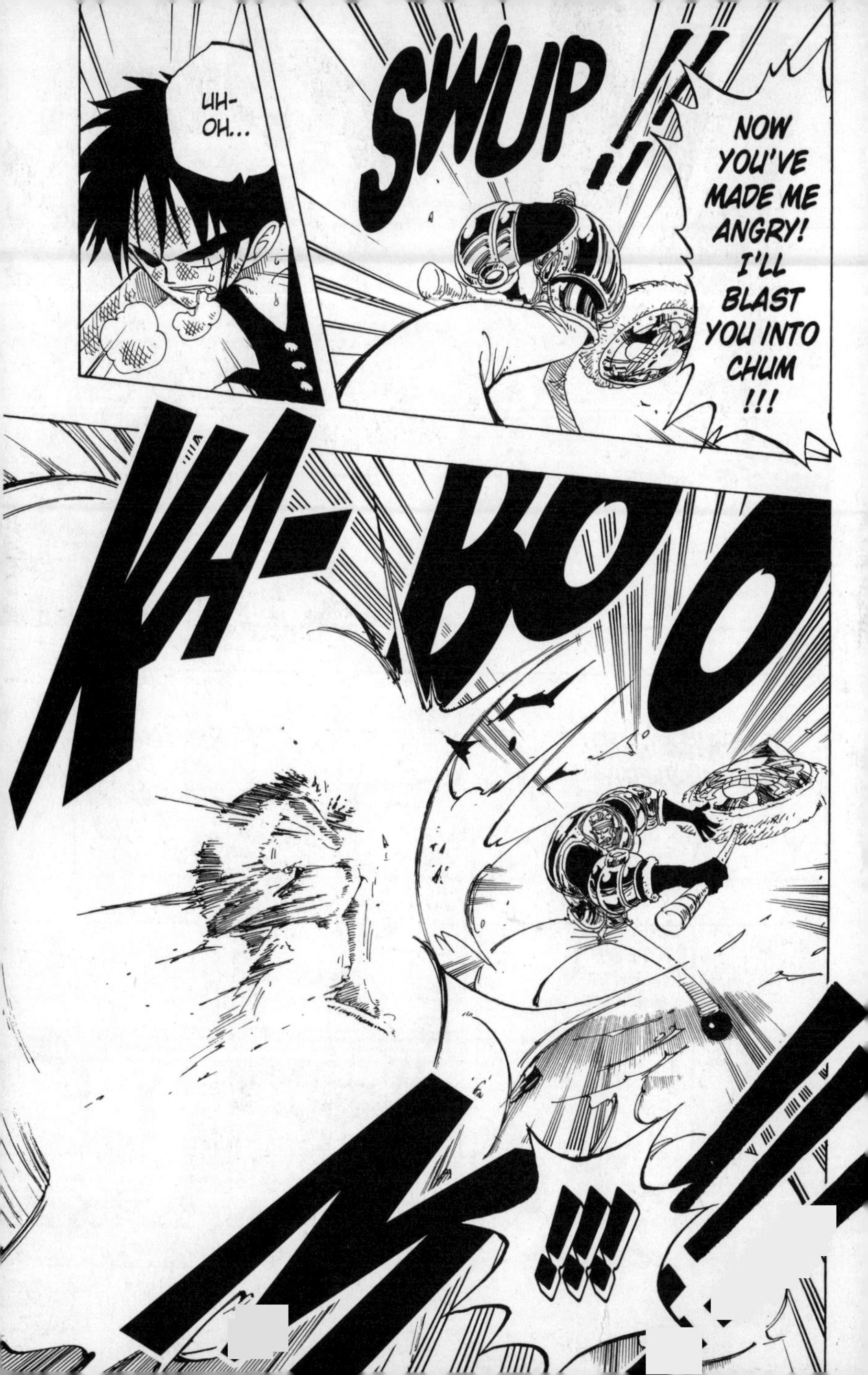
SWUP!!
NOW YOU'VE MADE ME ANGRY! I'LL BLAST YOU INTO CHUM!!!
UH-OH...
KA-BOOM!!!

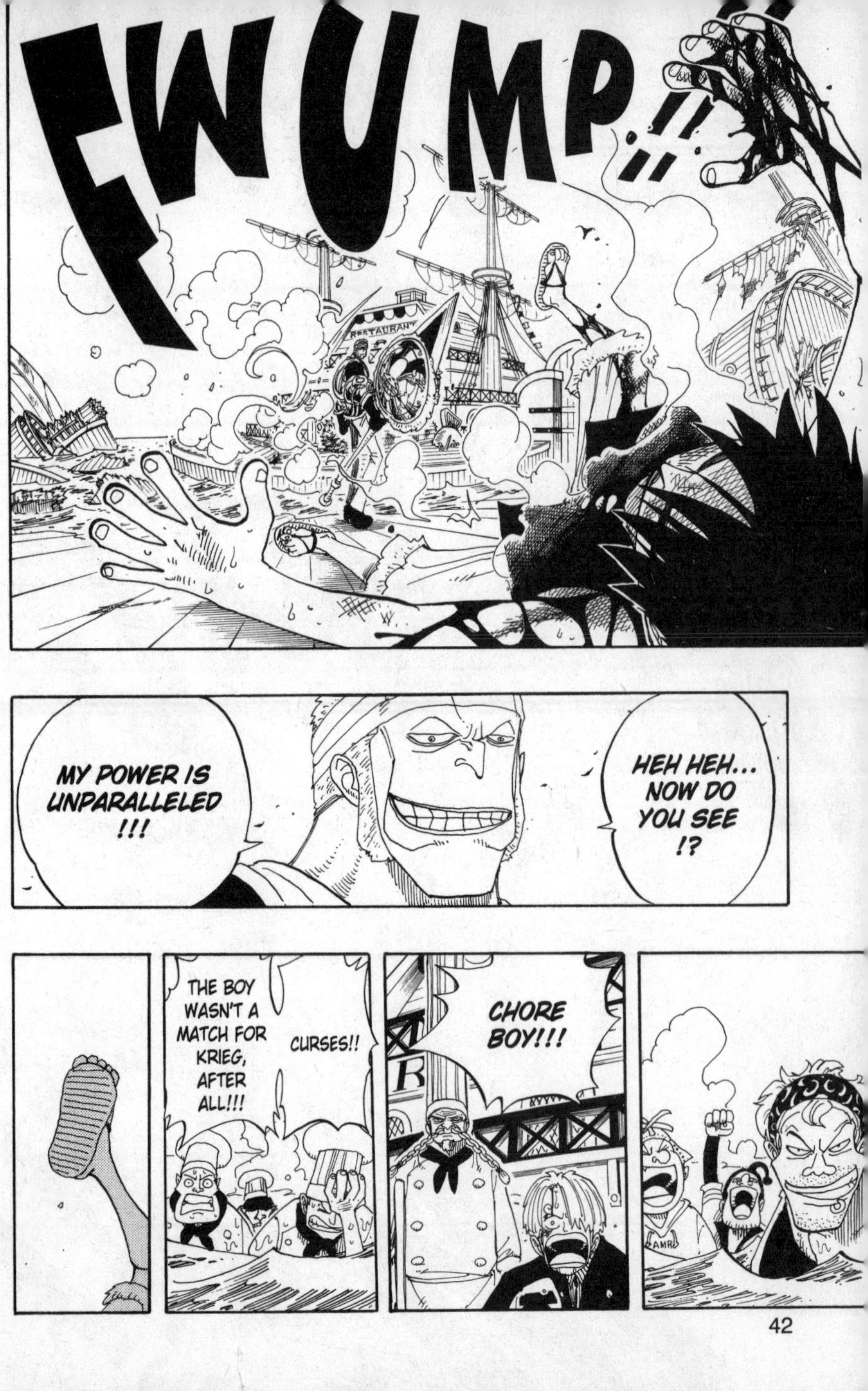
FWUMP!!
HEH HEH... NOW DO YOU SEE !?
MY POWER IS UNPARALLELED !!!
CHORE BOY!!!
CURSES!!
THE BOY WASN'T A MATCH FOR KRIEG, AFTER ALL!!!

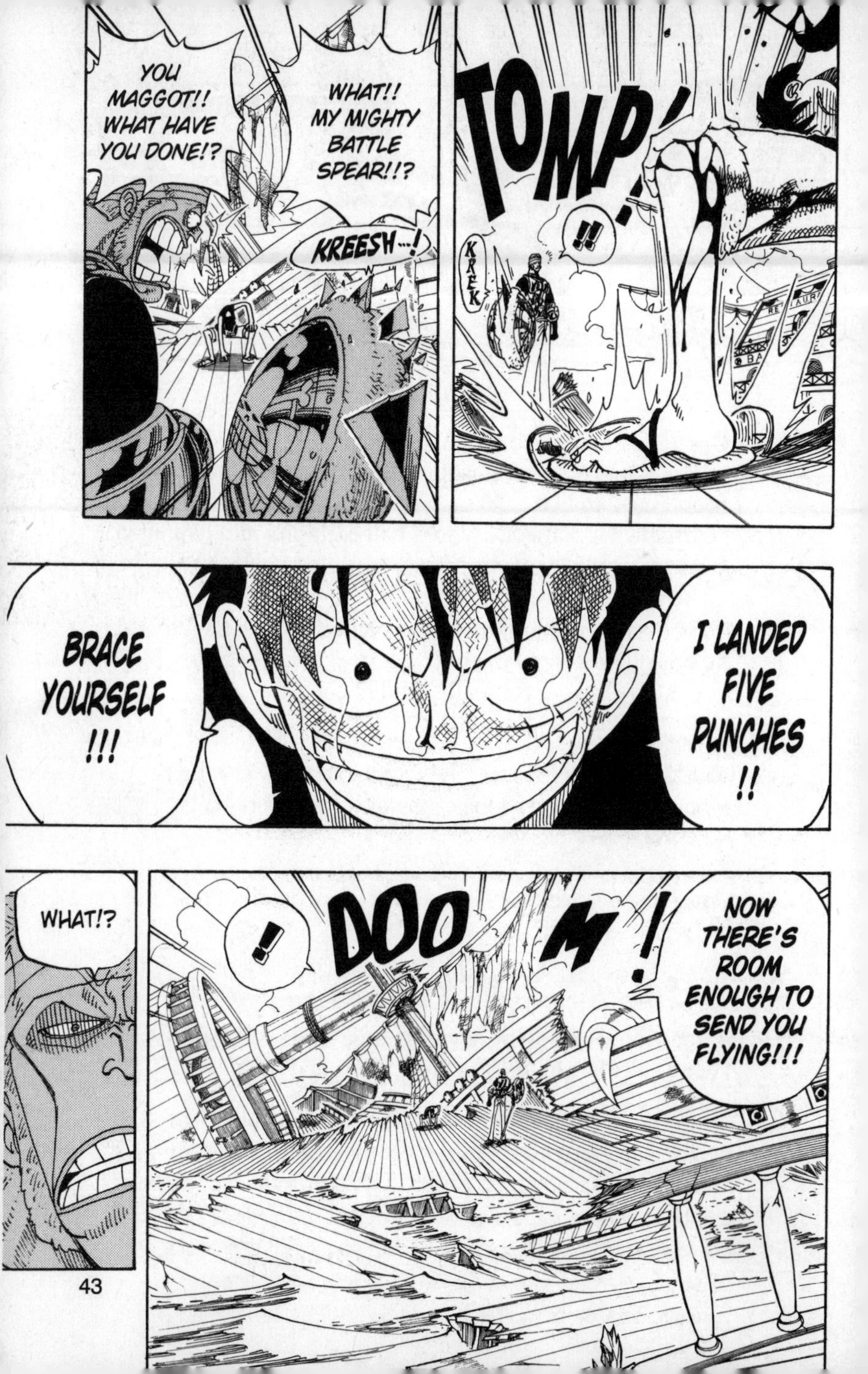
TOMP!
!!
KREK
WHAT!! MY MIGHTY BATTLE SPEAR!!?
YOU MAGGOT!! WHAT HAVE YOU DONE!?
KREESH...!
I LANDED FIVE PUNCHES!!
BRACE YOURSELF!!!
NOW THERE'S ROOM ENOUGH TO SEND YOU FLYING!!!
DOOM!
!
WHAT!?

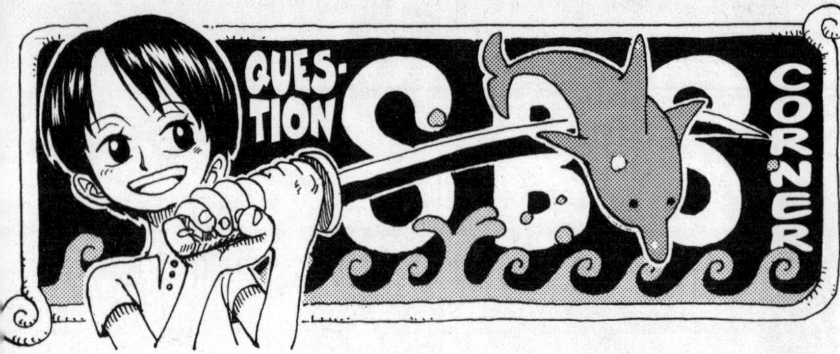
QUESTION
SBS
CORNER

Reader: Greetings. I am the earthalien living in the house where Usopp's father Yasopp's friend's brother's girl-friend used to live.
*Earthalien is someone who is half earthling and half alien.

Oda: Really? Question Corner is starting!! (Doom)

Q: On both sides of the skull on Don Krieg's pirate flag, there are hourglasses symbolizing the threat to his enemies, but were hourglasses ever really used like that?

A: There really were Jolly Roger flags with hourglasses on them. They symbolized the prey's appointment with death, basically: "Your time is running out!"

Q: Oda Sensei, since Luffy is a rubber man, do **all** of his body parts stretch?

A: Yes, everything stretches.

Q: A question. How many g/cm^3 is Sanji's kick strength? Please calculate to two decimal points and let me know.

A: To be frank, measurement is not possible. You know that game at the arcades where you can measure your kick strength? If, for example, Sanji did that, the whole machine would go flying out of the building. But if I had to put it into units, I'd say 21 bats--the energy required to break 21 wooden bats with one kick.

Chapter 65: PREPARED

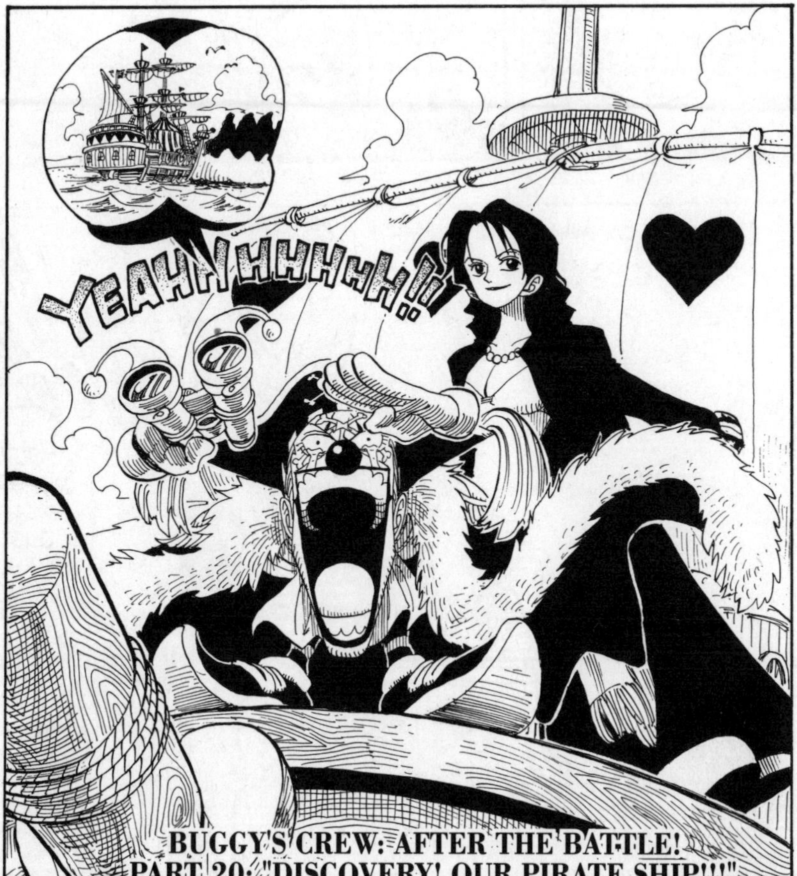
YEAHHHHHHH!!!
BUGGY'S CREW: AFTER THE BATTLE!
PART 20: "DISCOVERY! OUR PIRATE SHIP!!!"

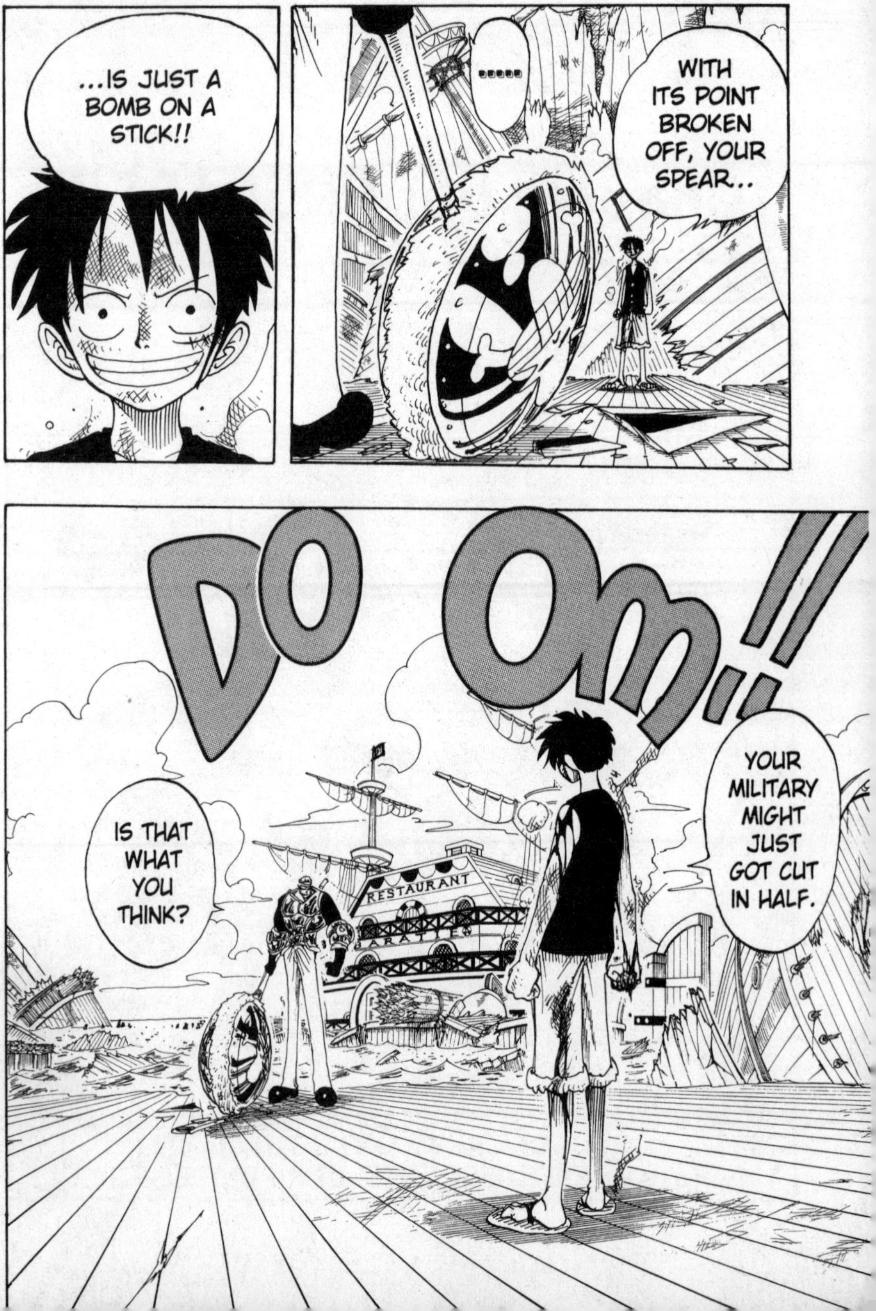
WITH ITS POINT BROKEN OFF, YOUR SPEAR...
......
...IS JUST A BOMB ON A STICK!!
DOOM!!
YOUR MILITARY MIGHT JUST GOT CUT IN HALF.
RESTAURANT
BARATIE
IS THAT WHAT YOU THINK?

READ THIS WAY

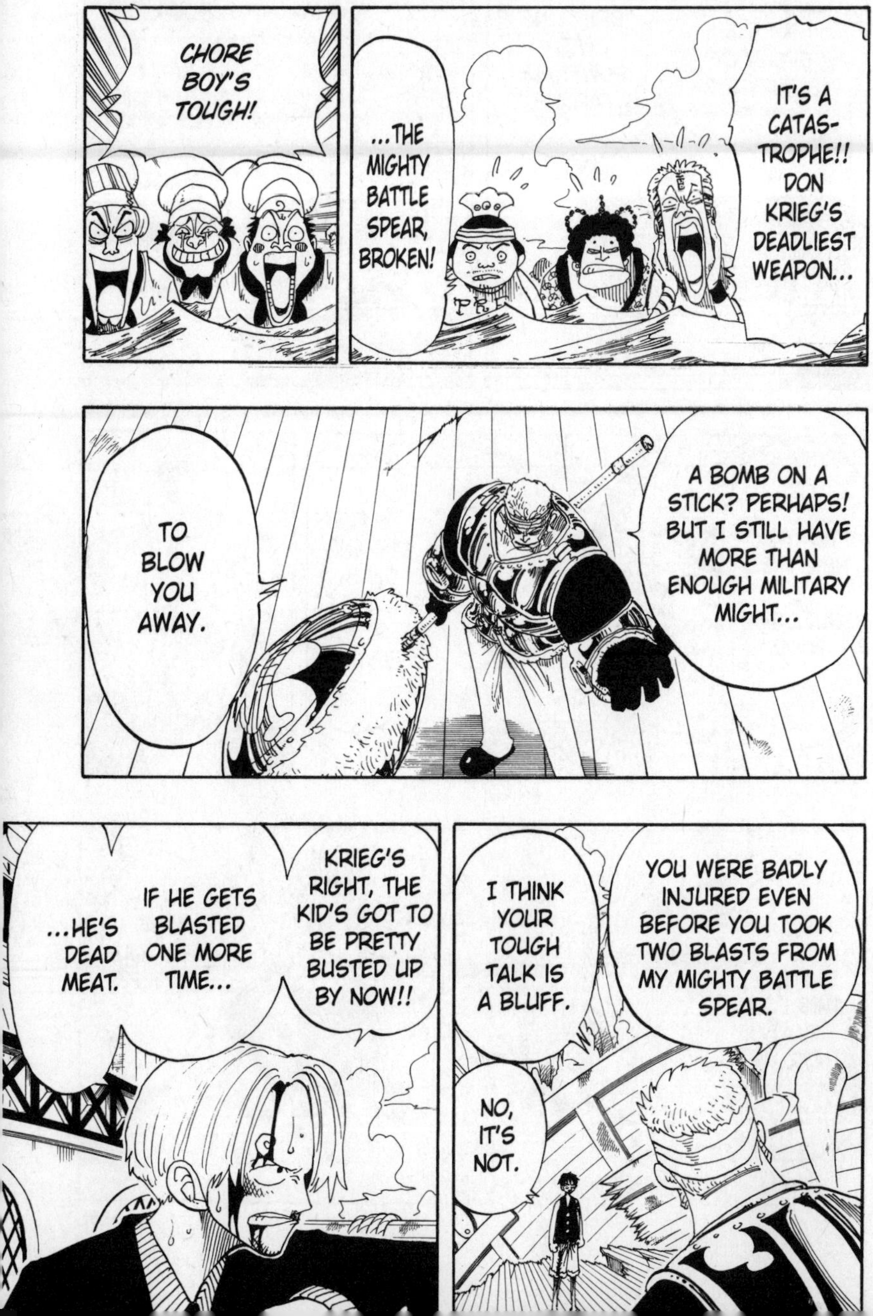
IT'S A CATASTROPHE!! DON KRIEG'S DEADLIEST WEAPON...
...THE MIGHTY BATTLE SPEAR, BROKEN!
CHORE BOY'S TOUGH!
A BOMB ON A STICK? PERHAPS! BUT I STILL HAVE MORE THAN ENOUGH MILITARY MIGHT...
TO BLOW YOU AWAY.
YOU WERE BADLY INJURED EVEN BEFORE YOU TOOK TWO BLASTS FROM MY MIGHTY BATTLE SPEAR.
I THINK YOUR TOUGH TALK IS A BLUFF.
NO, IT'S NOT.
KRIEG'S RIGHT, THE KID'S GOT TO BE PRETTY BUSTED UP BY NOW!!
IF HE GETS BLASTED ONE MORE TIME...
...HE'S DEAD MEAT.

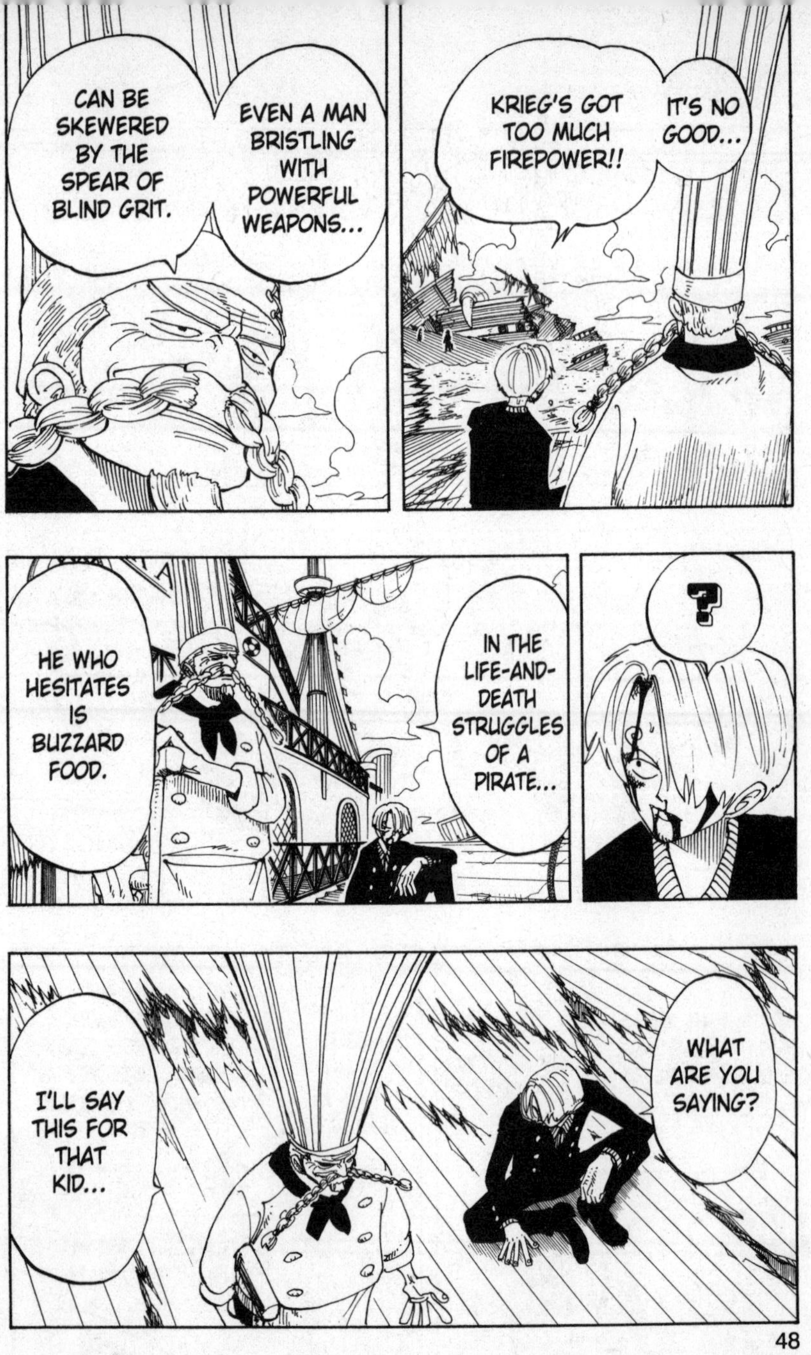
IT'S NO GOOD...
KRIEG'S GOT TOO MUCH FIREPOWER!!
EVEN A MAN BRISTLING WITH POWERFUL WEAPONS...
CAN BE SKEWERED BY THE SPEAR OF BLIND GRIT.
?
IN THE LIFE-AND-DEATH STRUGGLES OF A PIRATE...
HE WHO HESITATES IS BUZZARD FOOD.
WHAT ARE YOU SAYING?
I'LL SAY THIS FOR THAT KID...

READ THIS WAY

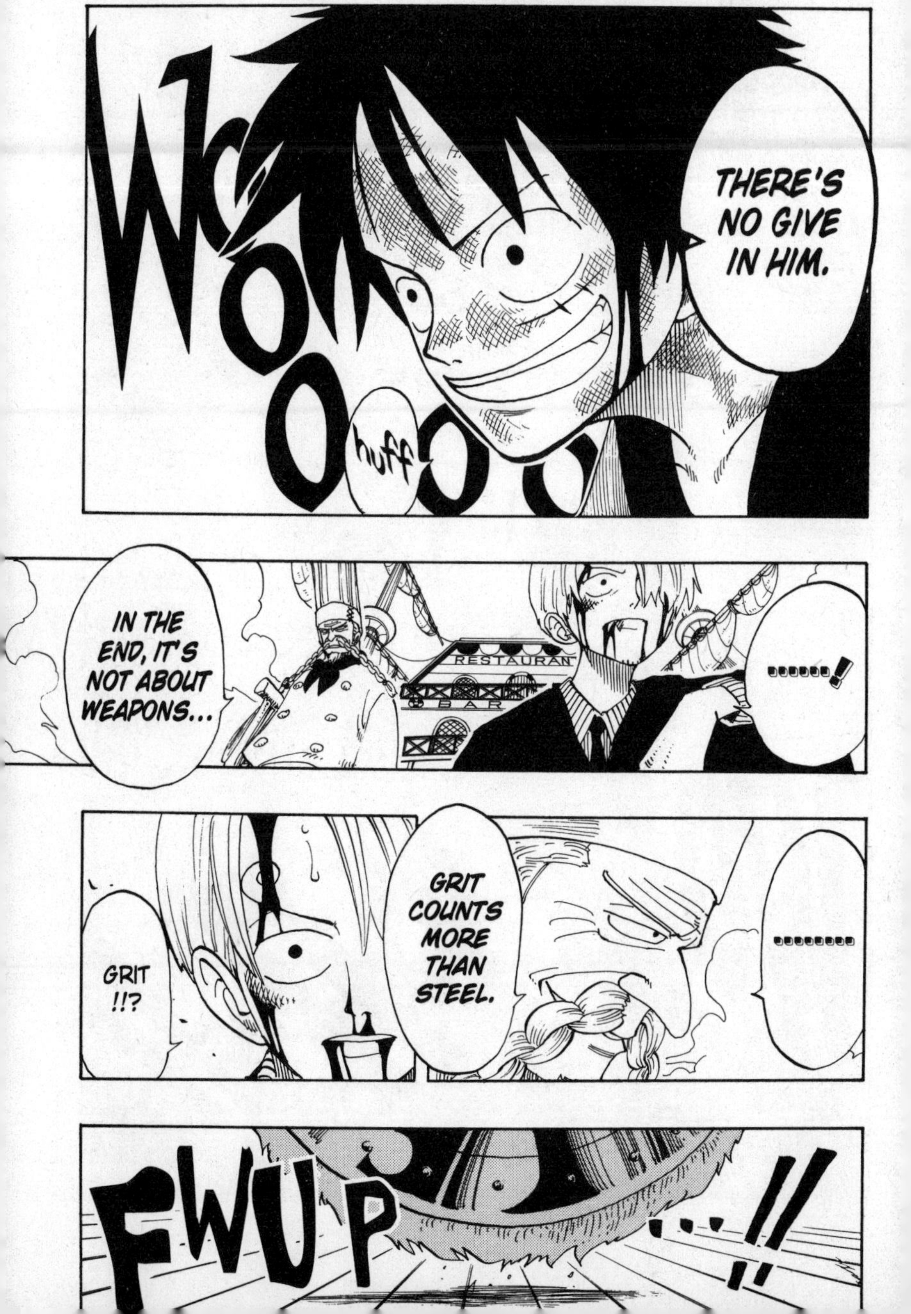
THERE'S NO GIVE IN HIM.
huff
WOOOOO
......!
RESTAURAN
BAR
IN THE END, IT'S NOT ABOUT WEAPONS...
....
GRIT COUNTS MORE THAN STEEL.
GRIT!!?
FWUP...!!

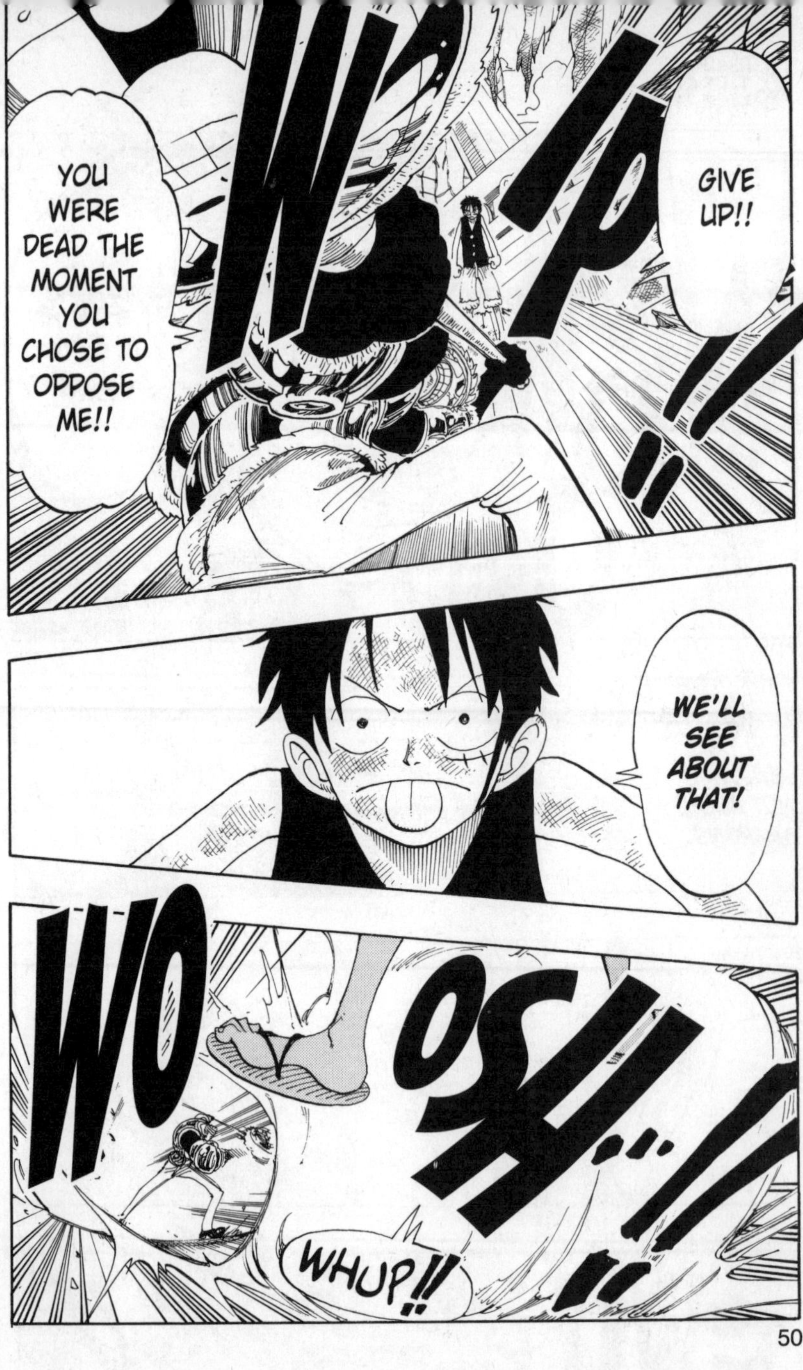
GIVE UP!!
YOU WERE DEAD THE MOMENT YOU CHOSE TO OPPOSE ME!!
WE'LL SEE ABOUT THAT!
WOOSH!!
WHUP!!

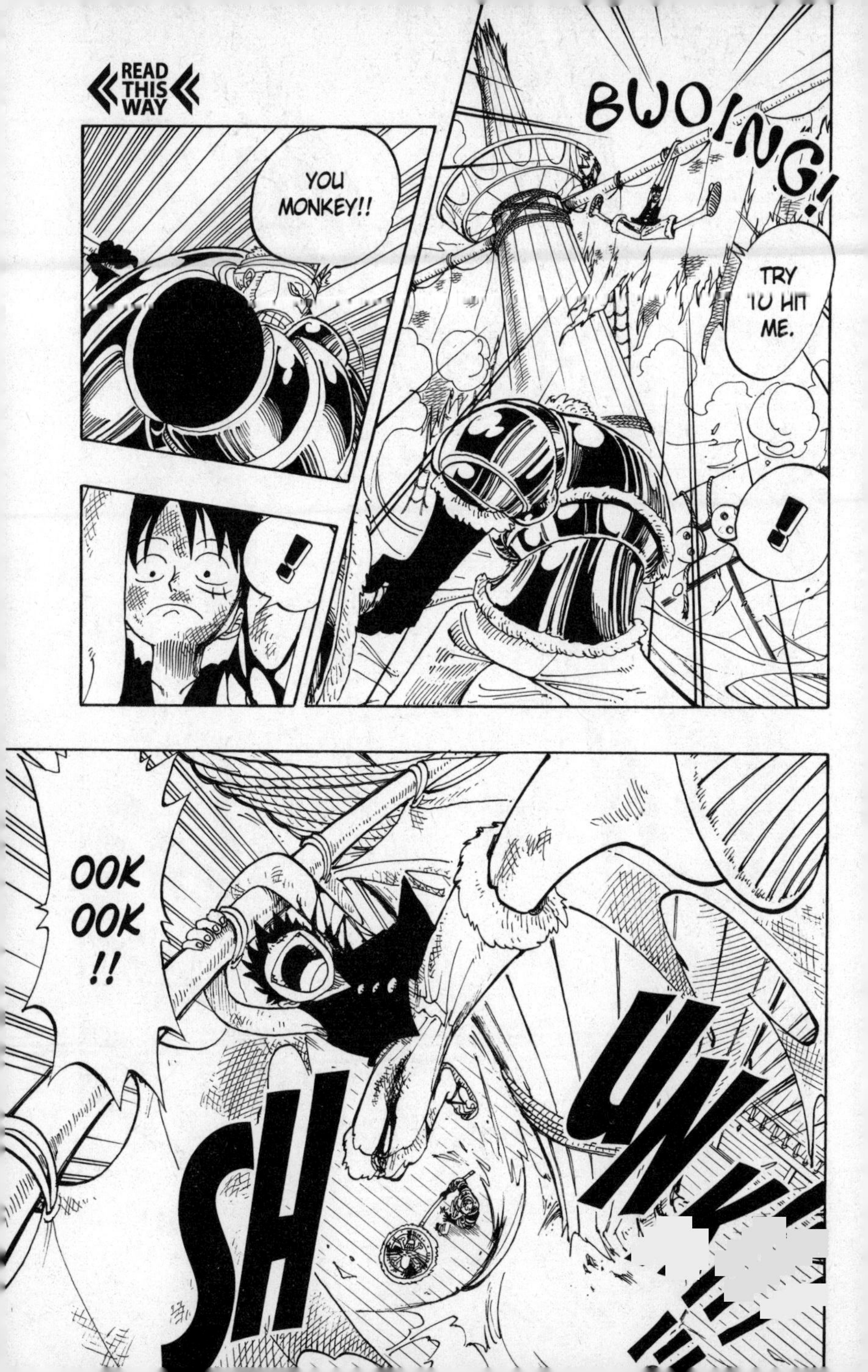
READ THIS WAY
BWOING!
TRY TO HIT ME.
!
YOU MONKEY!!
!
OOK OOK !!
SH
UNK

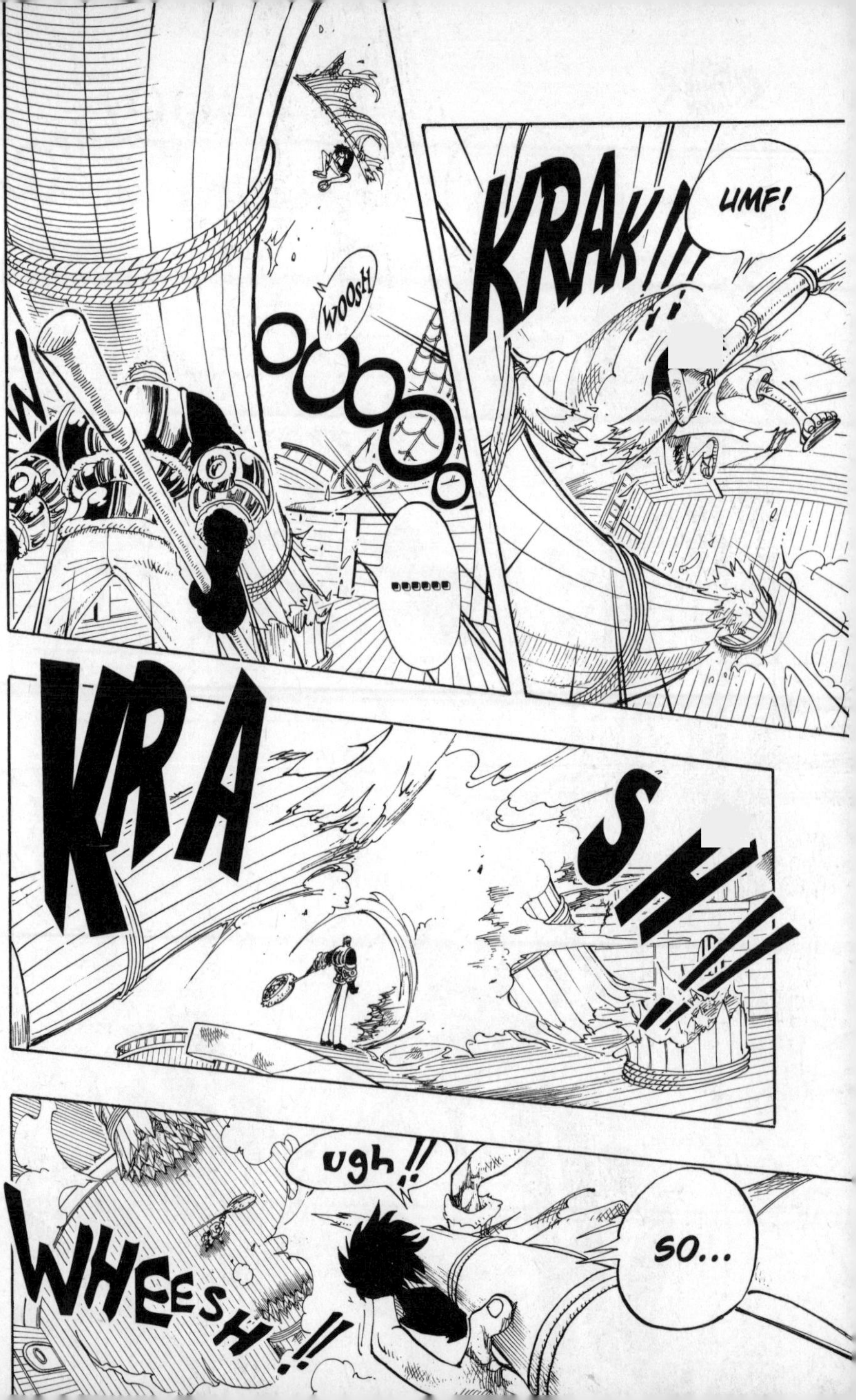
KRAK!!!
UMF!
WOOSH
OOOOOO
......
W
KRASH!!
SO...
ugh!!
WHEESH!!

READ THIS WAY

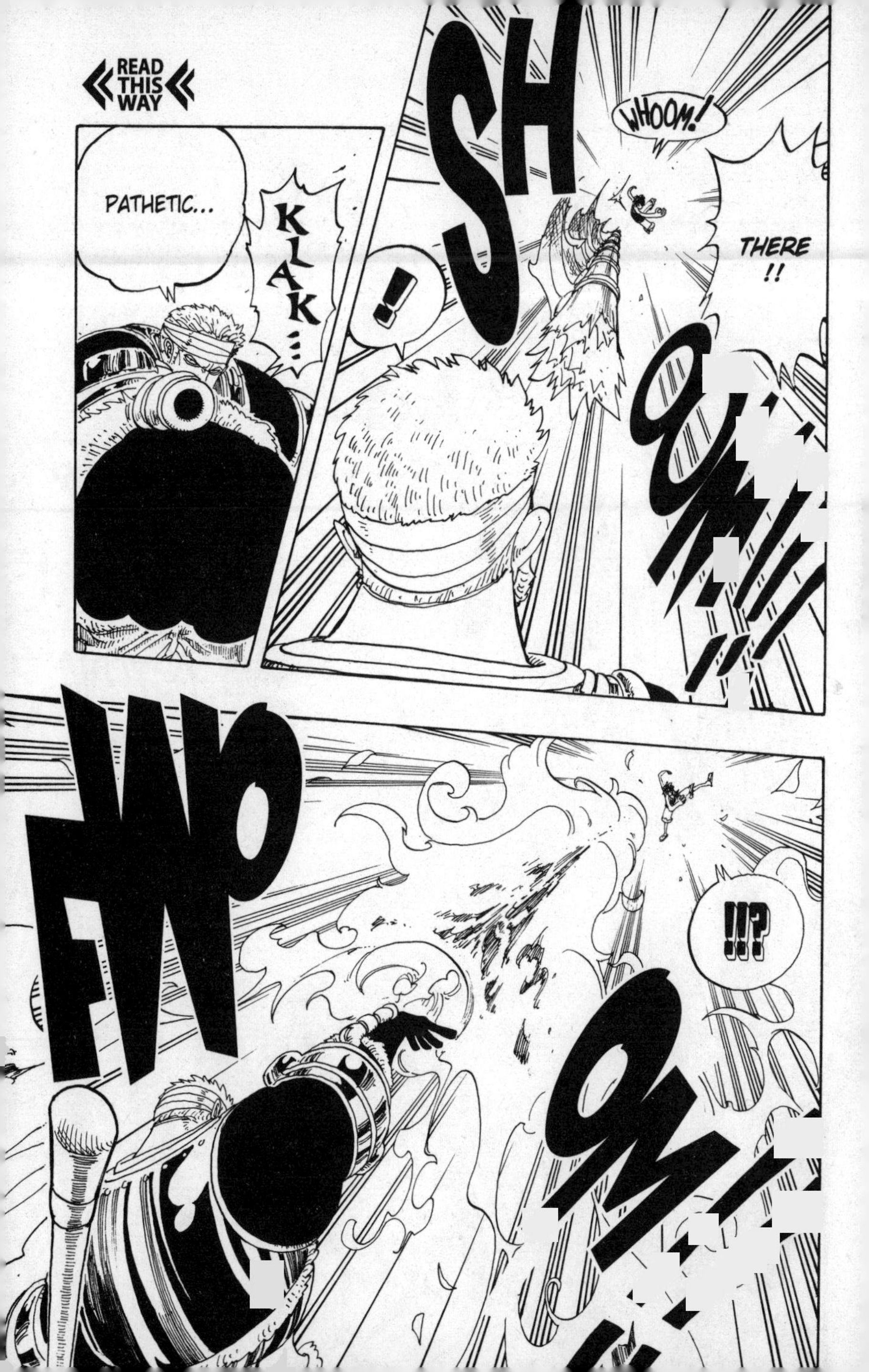
SH
WHOOM!
THERE !!
OOM!!
!
KLAK!!
PATHETIC...
FWO
!!?
OOM!!

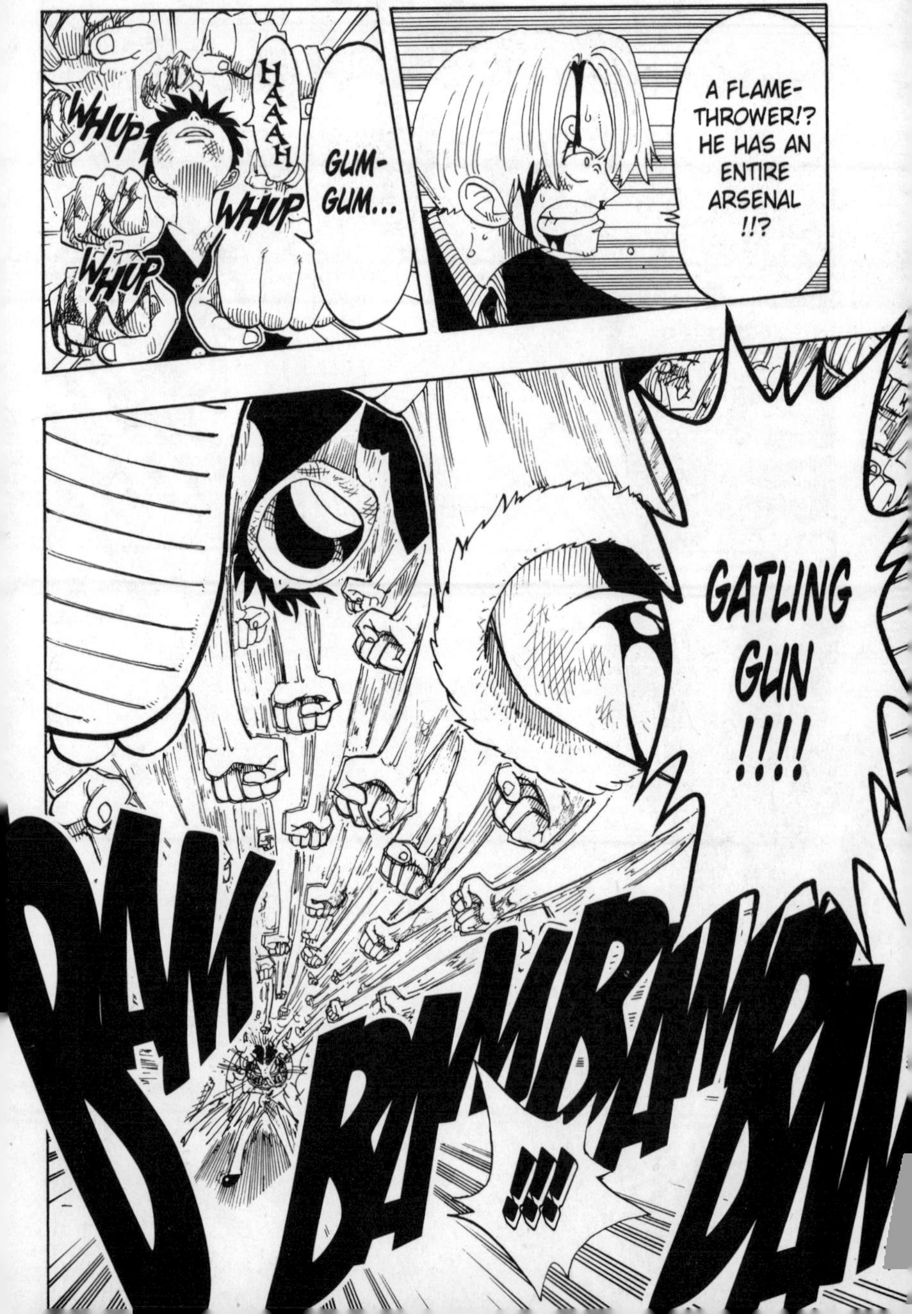
A FLAME-THROWER!? HE HAS AN ENTIRE ARSENAL !!?
GUM-GUM...
HAAAH
WHUP
WHUP
WHUP
GATLING GUN !!!!

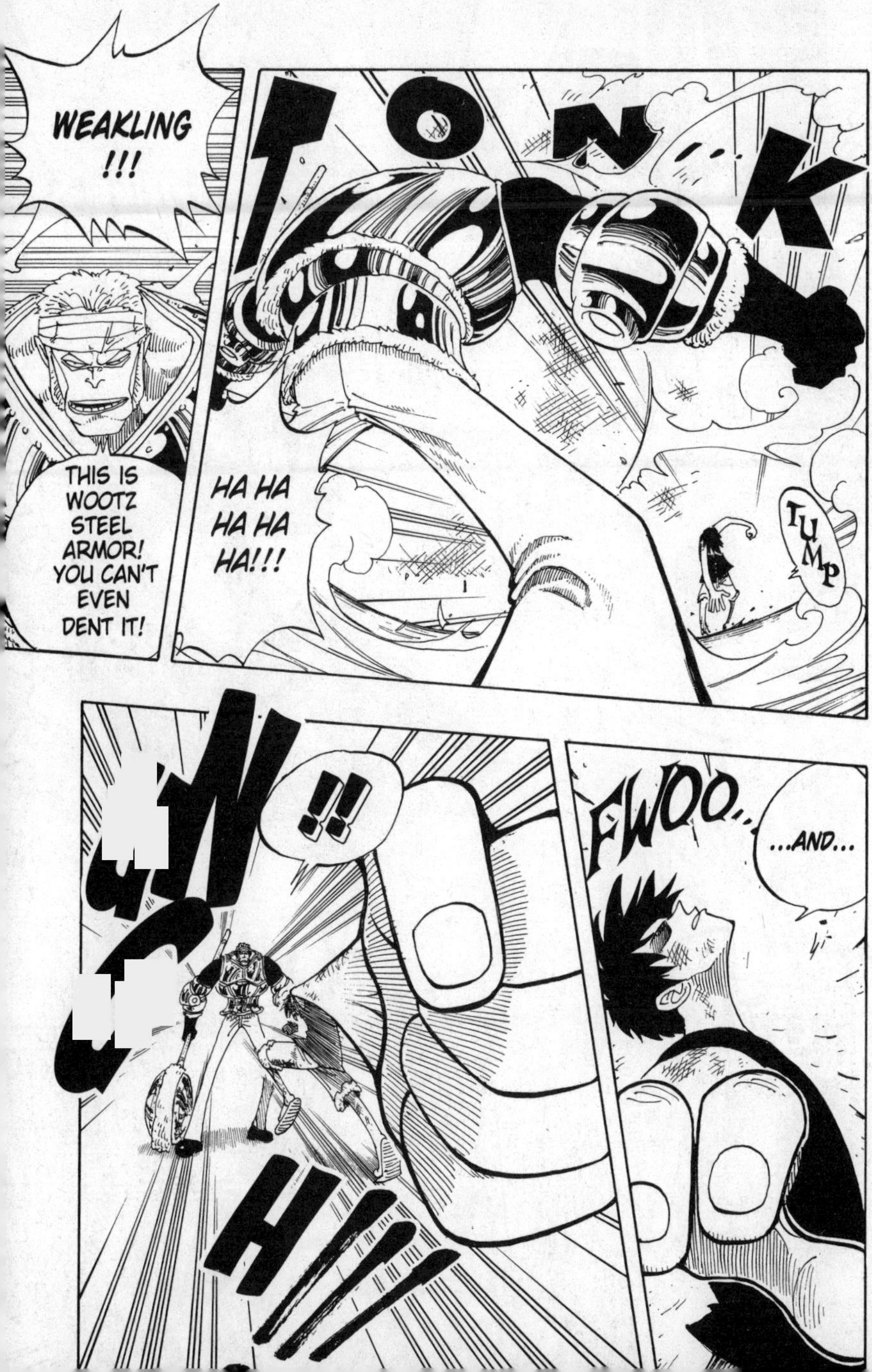
TONK
TUMP
HA HA HA HA HA!!!
WEAKLING !!!
THIS IS WOOTZ STEEL ARMOR! YOU CAN'T EVEN DENT IT!
FWOO...
...AND...
!!

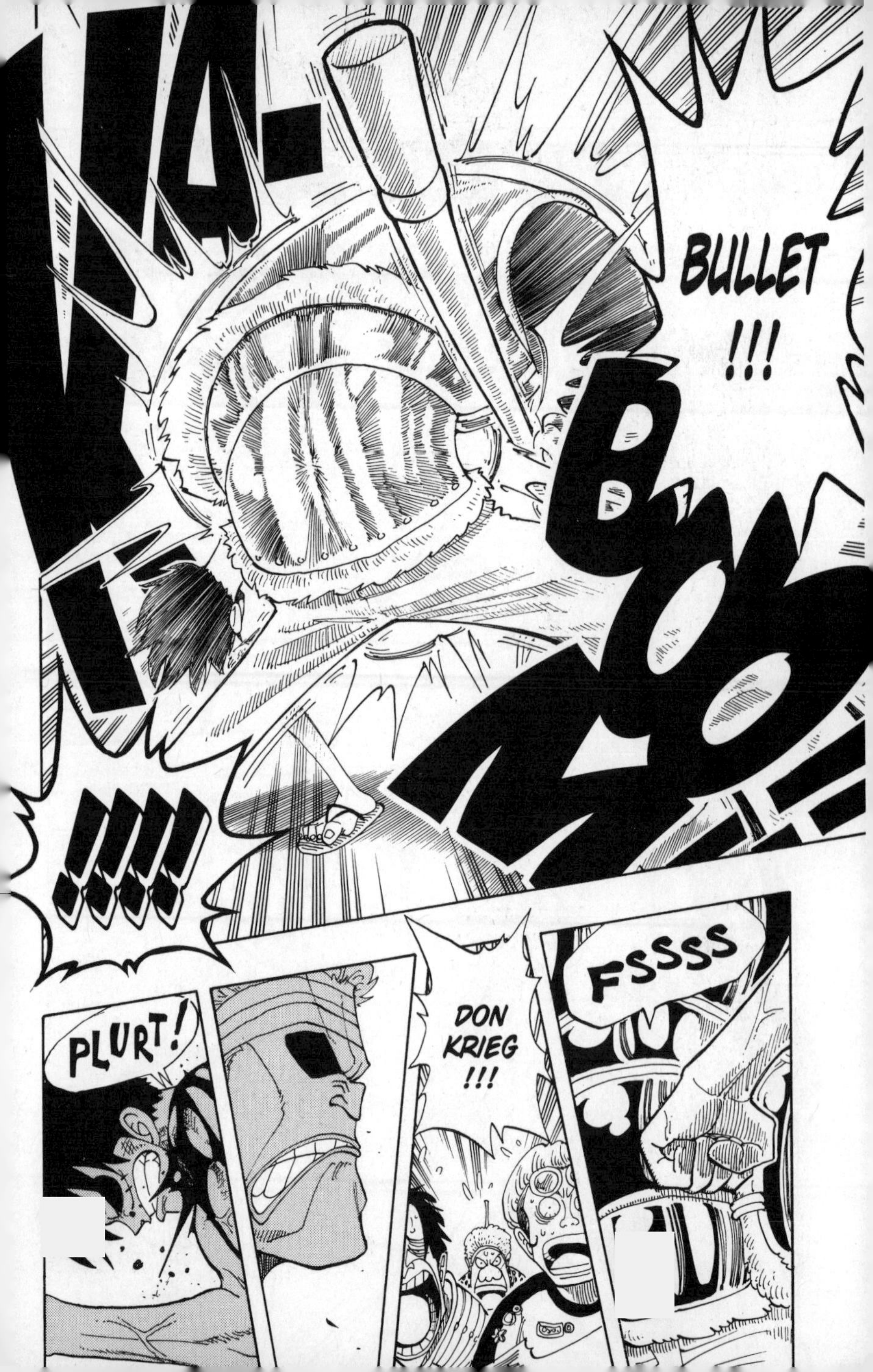
BULLET
!!!
HA-
!!!!
FSSSS
DON KRIEG !!!
PLURT!

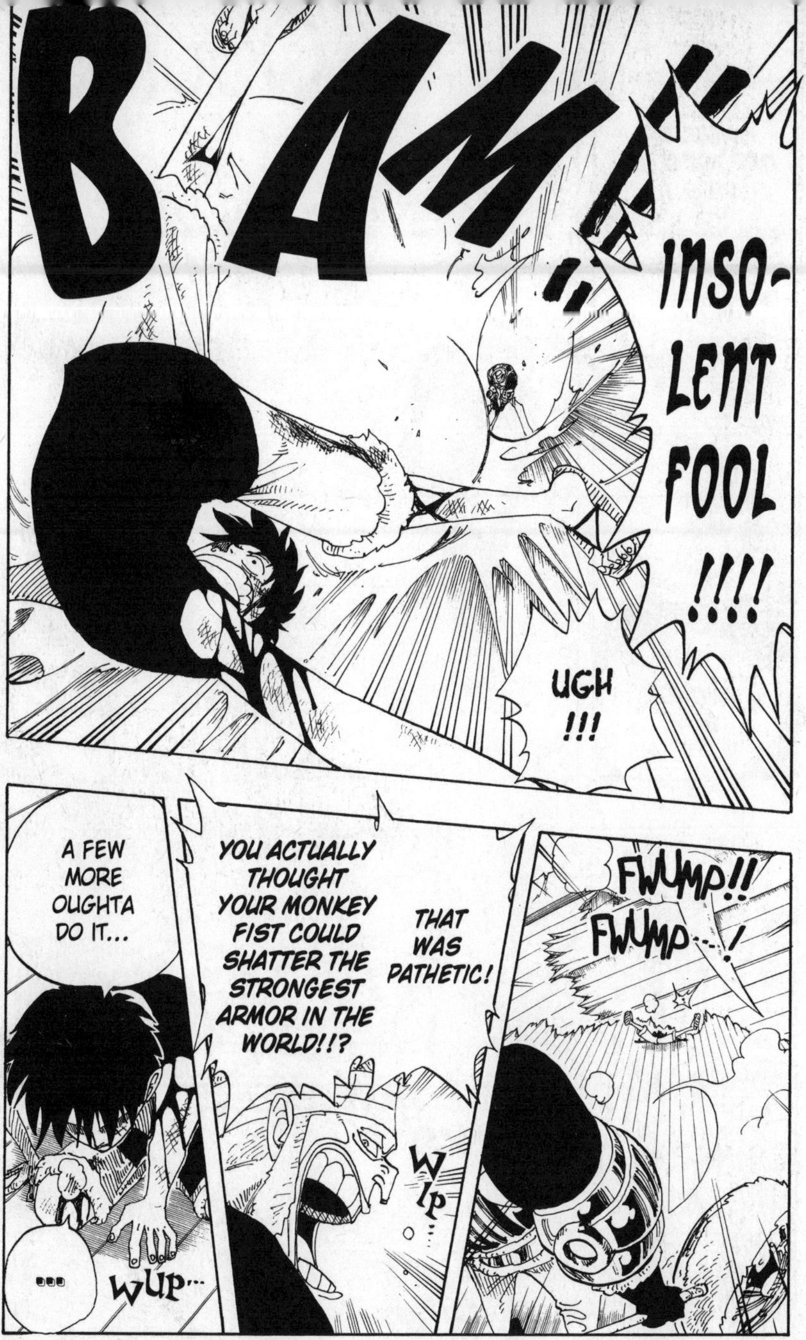
BAM!!
INSO-LENT FOOL!!!!
UGH!!!
FWUMP!!
FWUMP...!
THAT WAS PATHETIC!
YOU ACTUALLY THOUGHT YOUR MONKEY FIST COULD SHATTER THE STRONGEST ARMOR IN THE WORLD!!?
WIP...
A FEW MORE OUGHTA DO IT...
...
WUP...

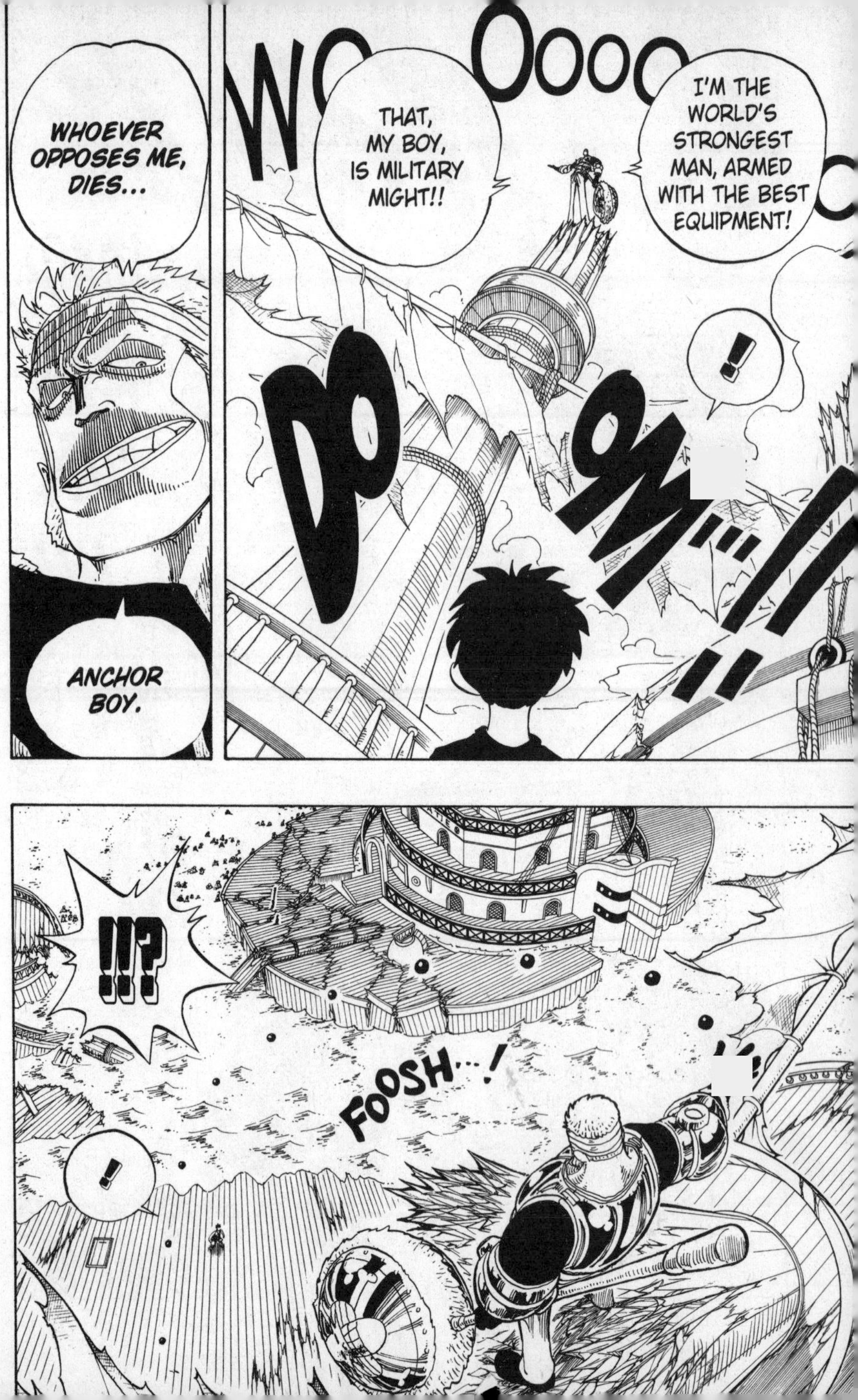
I'M THE WORLD'S STRONGEST MAN, ARMED WITH THE BEST EQUIPMENT!
THAT, MY BOY, IS MILITARY MIGHT!!
!
DOOM!!
WHOEVER OPPOSES ME, DIES...
ANCHOR BOY.
!!?
FOOSH...!
!

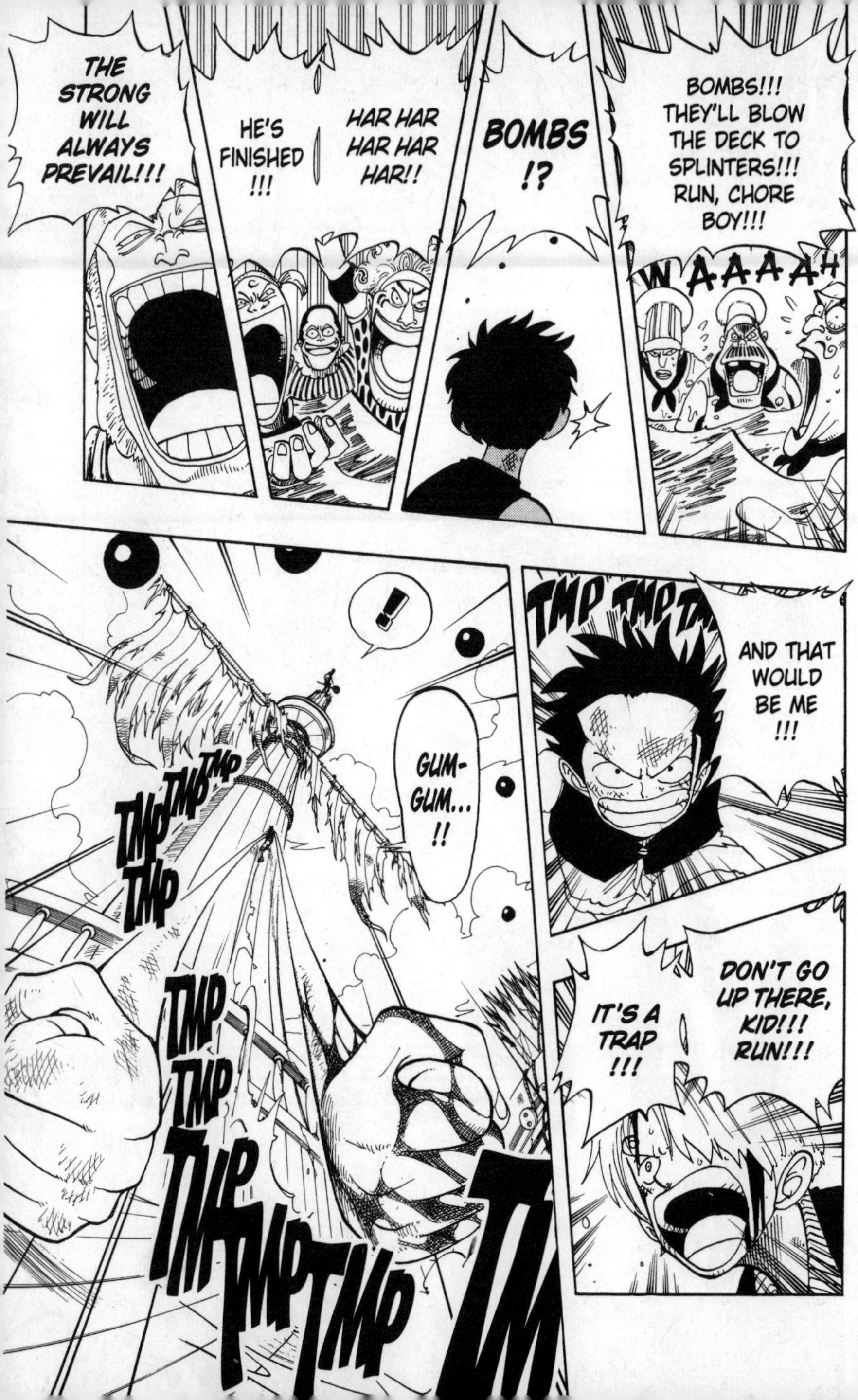
BOMBS!!! THEY'LL BLOW THE DECK TO SPLINTERS!!! RUN, CHORE BOY!!!
WAAAAAH
BOMBS !?
HAR HAR HAR HAR!!
HE'S FINISHED !!!
THE STRONG WILL ALWAYS PREVAIL!!!
TMP TMP TMP
AND THAT WOULD BE ME !!!
DON'T GO UP THERE, KID!!! RUN!!!
IT'S A TRAP !!!
!
GUM-GUM... !!
TMP TMP TMP TMP
TMP TMP TMP TMP TMP TMP
TM

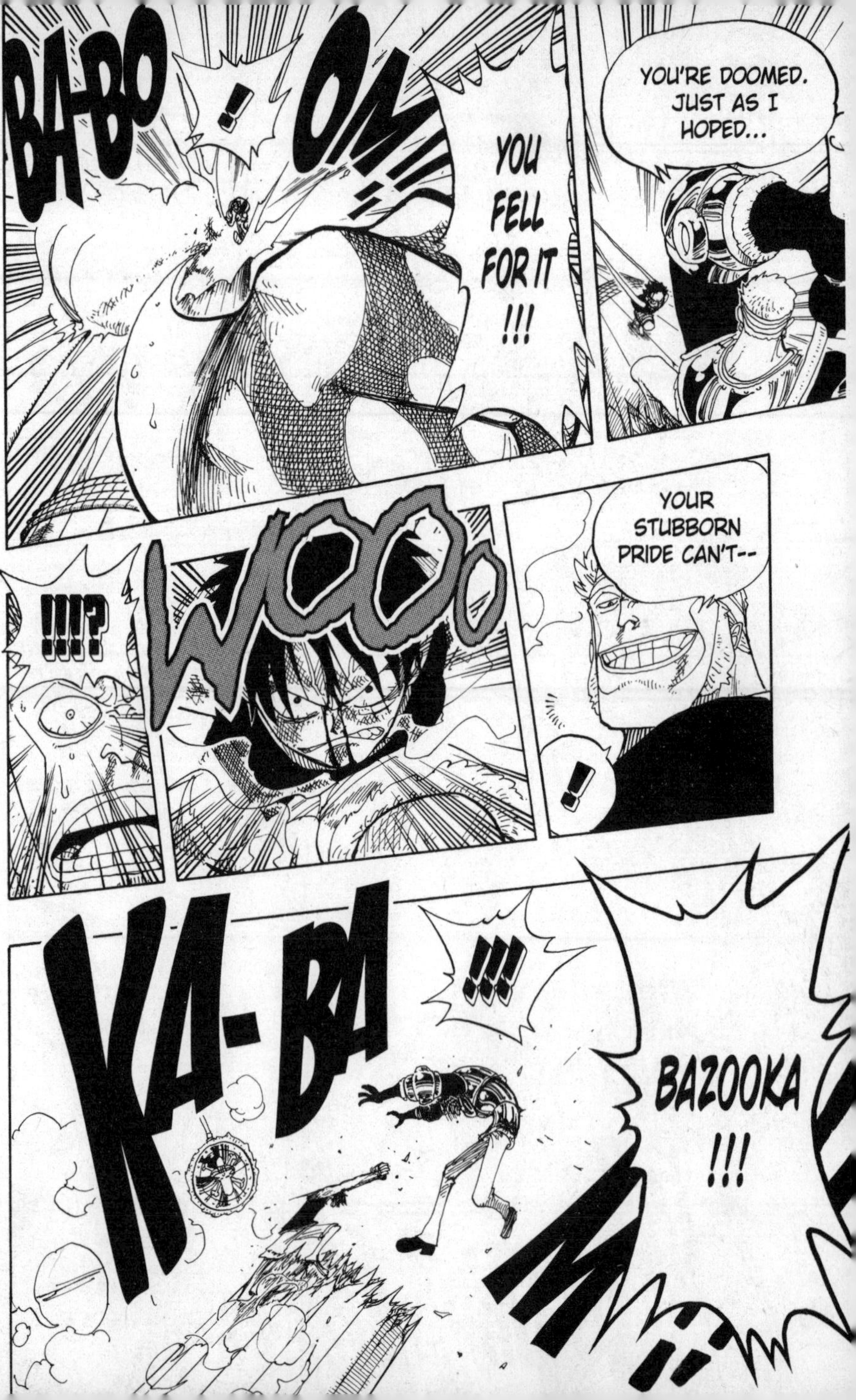
YOU'RE DOOMED. JUST AS I HOPED...
YOU FELL FOR IT !!!
!
BA-BO OM!!
YOUR STUBBORN PRIDE CAN'T--
!
WOOO
!!!?
BAZOOKA !!!
!!!
KA-BA M!!

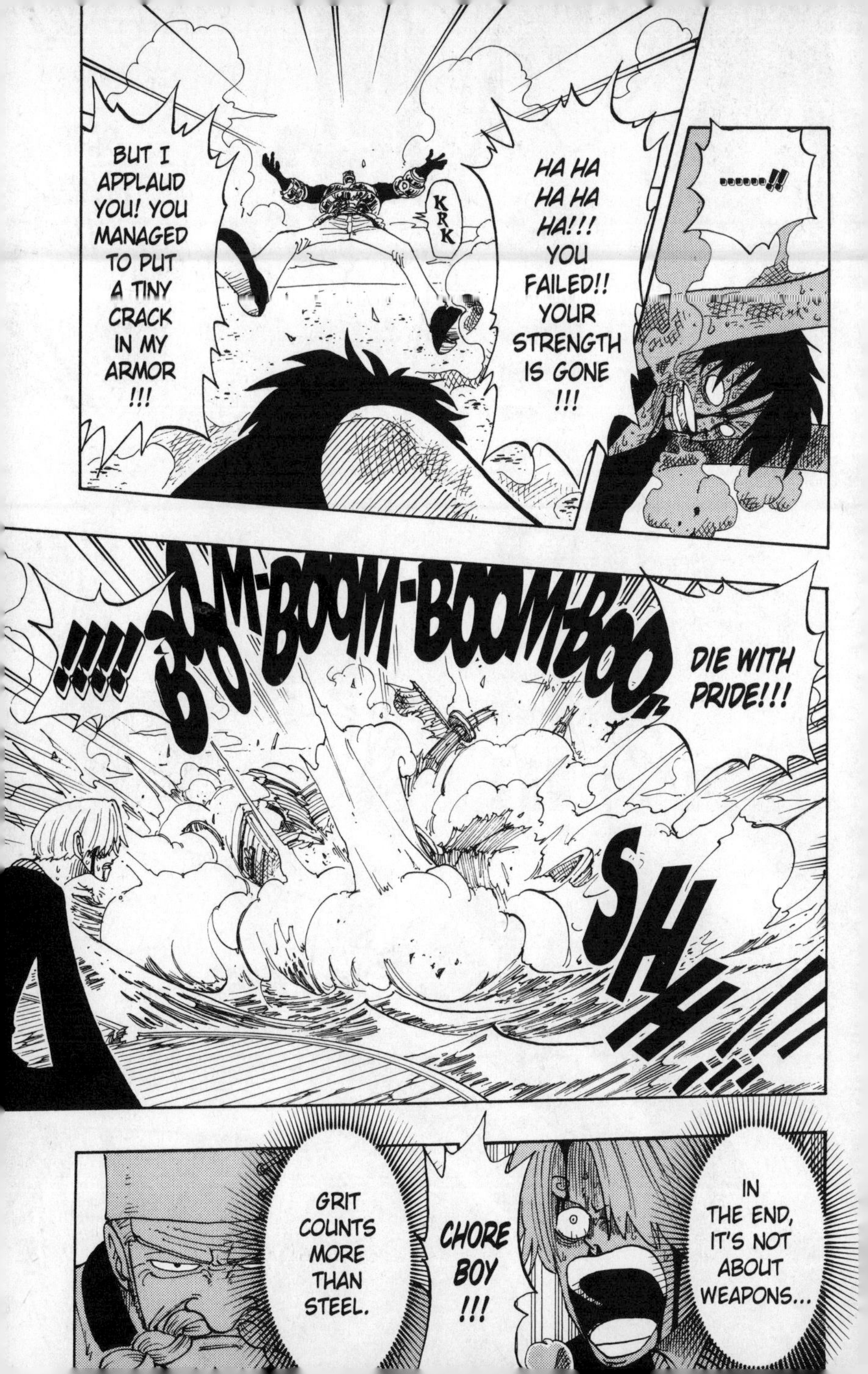
......!!
HA HA HA HA HA!!! YOU FAILED!! YOUR STRENGTH IS GONE!!!
KRK
BUT I APPLAUD YOU! YOU MANAGED TO PUT A TINY CRACK IN MY ARMOR!!!
DIE WITH PRIDE!!!
BOOM-BOOM-BOOMBOO
!!!!
SH!!!
IN THE END, IT'S NOT ABOUT WEAPONS...
CHORE BOY!!!
GRIT COUNTS MORE THAN STEEL.

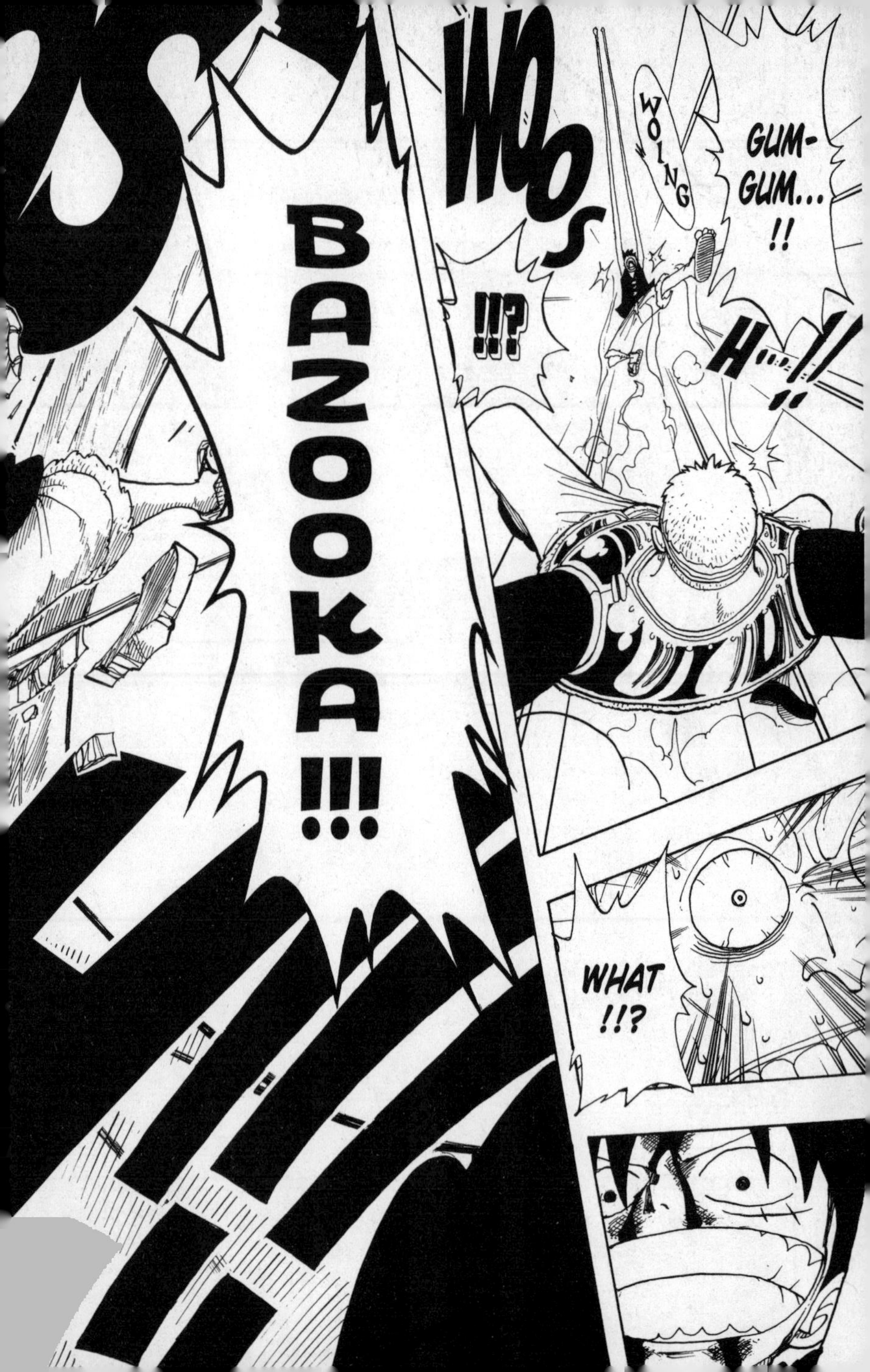
GUM-GUM...!!
WOING
H...!!
WOOOS
!!?
WHAT!!?
BAZOOKA!!!

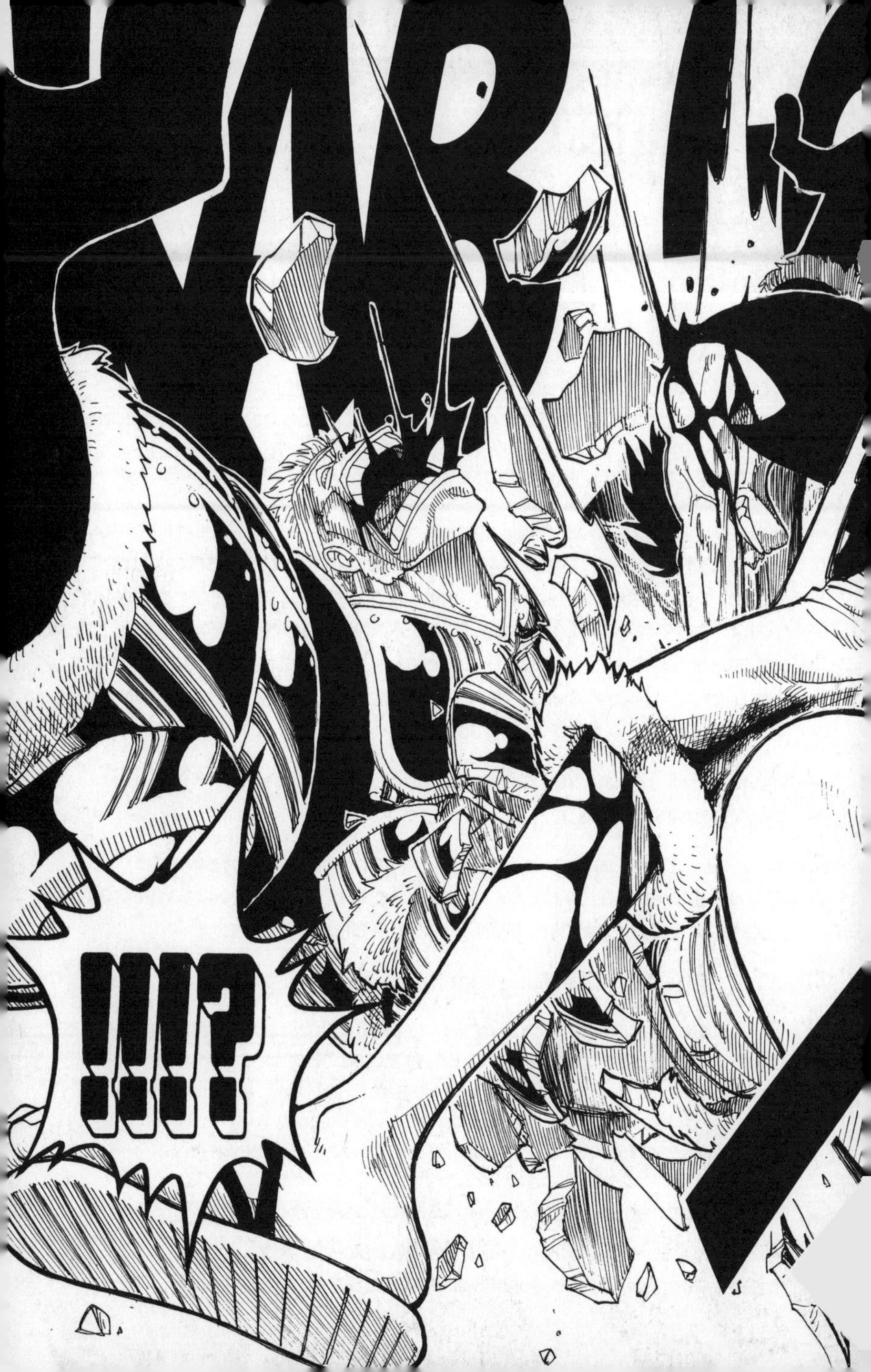
!!!?

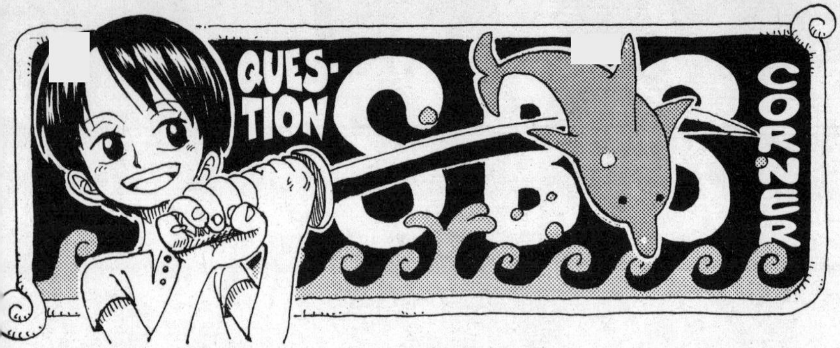
QUESTION
SBS
CORNER

Q: Hey, Ei-chan!! Have you been working on *One Piece* like you're supposed to? Draw your best!! All right, here's a question for you: which *One Piece* characters have the highest and lowest IQs?!! Okay, that's it for today.

A: I'll tell you, but this only applies to the characters that have appeared so far. The highest IQ belongs to Shanks' first mate, Benn Beckman--his unrivaled intelligence and brawn make him an excellent aid for Shanks. Next highest is probably Captain Kuro, then Nami. As for the characters with the lowest IQs, I can't decide who is number one--there are just too many idiots.

Q: Oda Sensei, is your house really made of cardboard? (My friend said it is.)

A: Yes. Yet through rain and wind and snow I persevere, drawing manga. But it's okay. The ink I use is waterproof!! (Note: Good children should not believe me!)

Q: What is the cape-like thing that Butchie of the Meowban Brothers wears? Is it a futon?

A: It's a **kotatsu-buton*, to be precise. He is a cat, after all.
*A kotatsu is a low, heated table that has a skirt-like quilt (futon or buton) that keeps people's legs warm when they sit at it. cats love to sleep under them on cold days.

Q: Is Luffy's pose on the cover of volume 3 Ken Shimura's* "Aiiin"?

A: Hey, you're right!! It's "Aiiin"!! You nailed it!!
*Ken Shimura is a famous Japanese comedian.

Chapter 66:
THE CHEWED-UP SPEAR

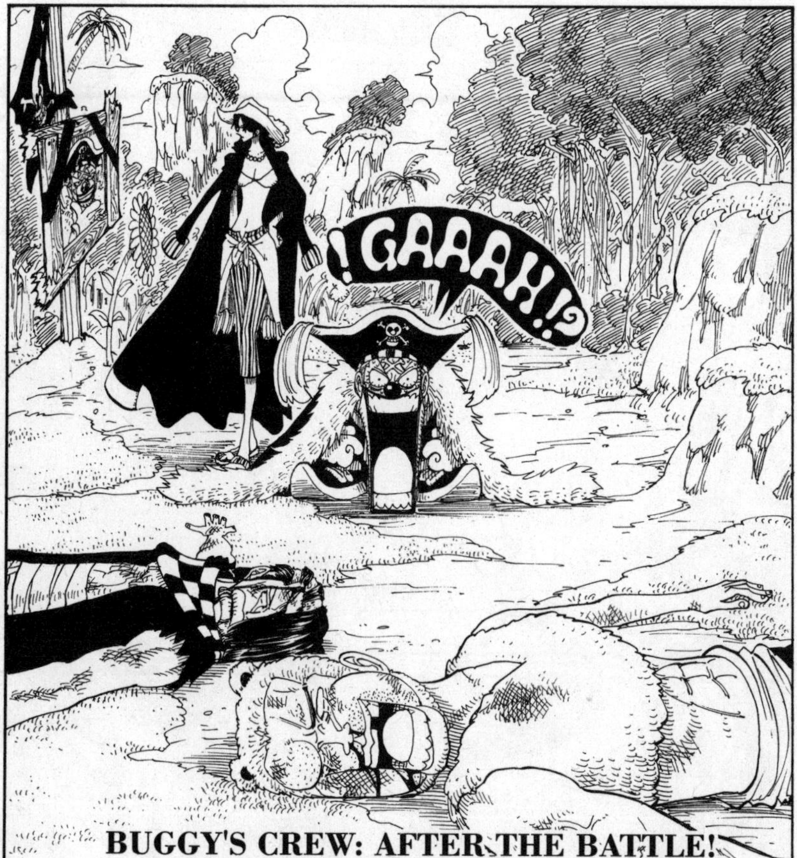
GAAAH!?

BUGGY'S CREW: AFTER THE BATTLE!
PART 21: "AN UNHAPPY REUNION"

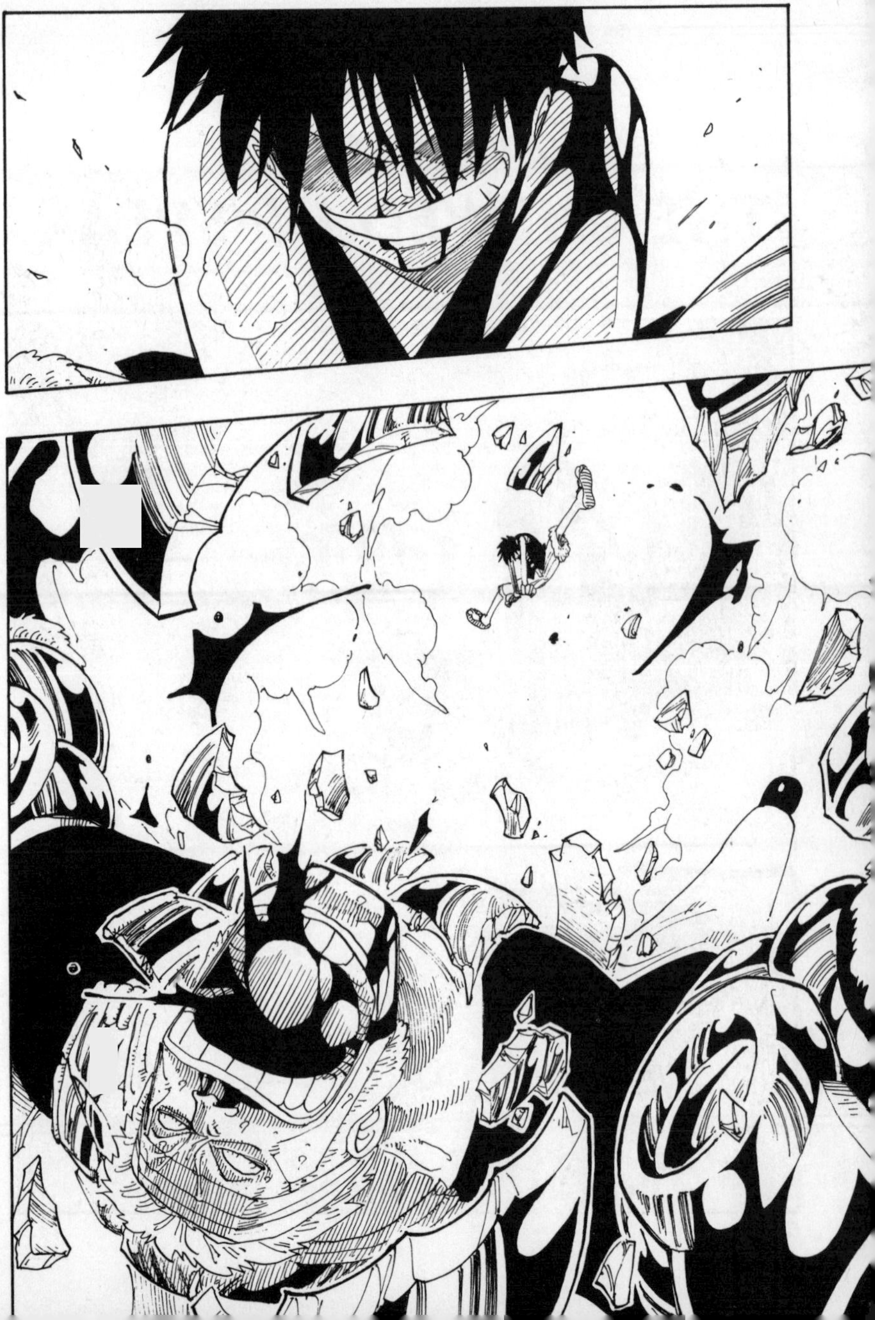

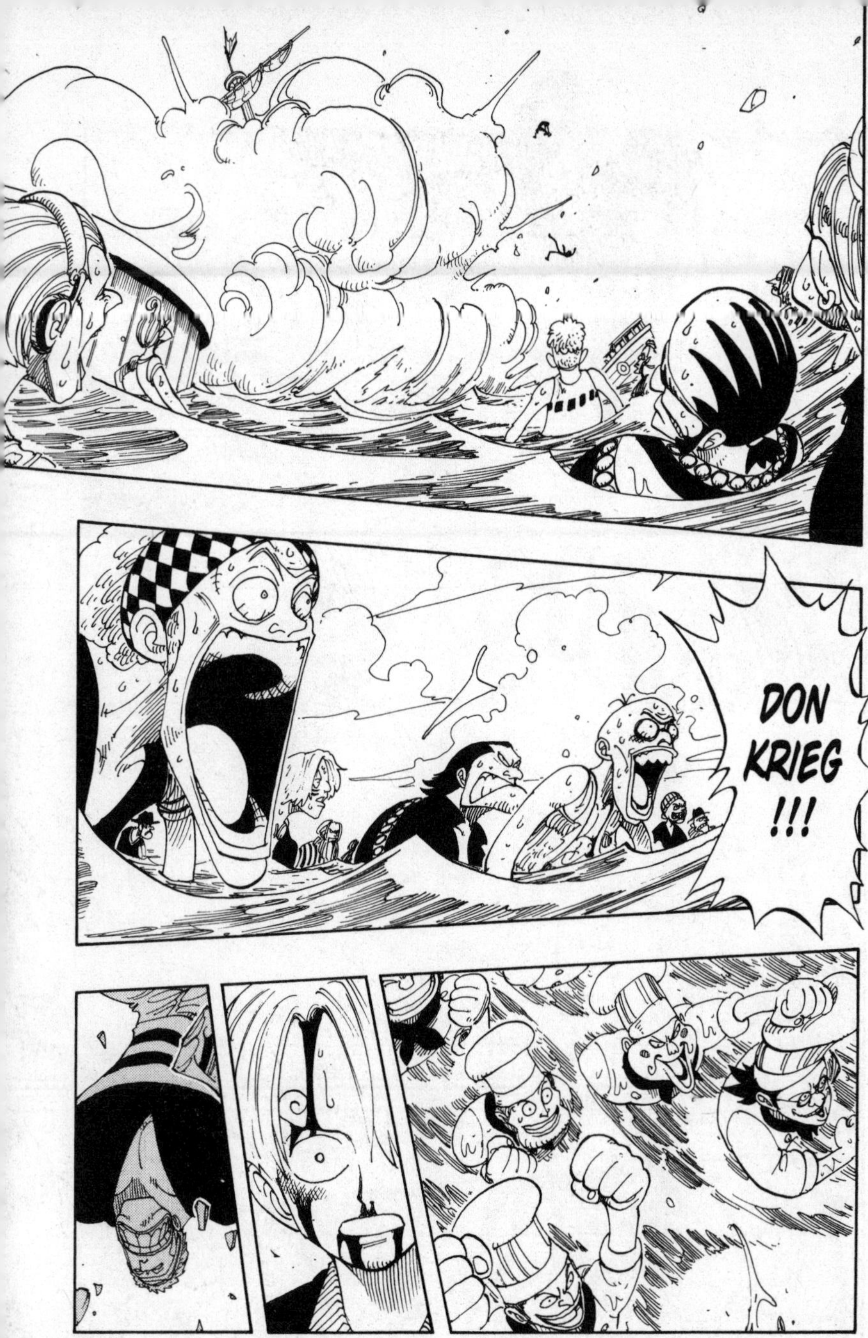
DON KRIEG !!!

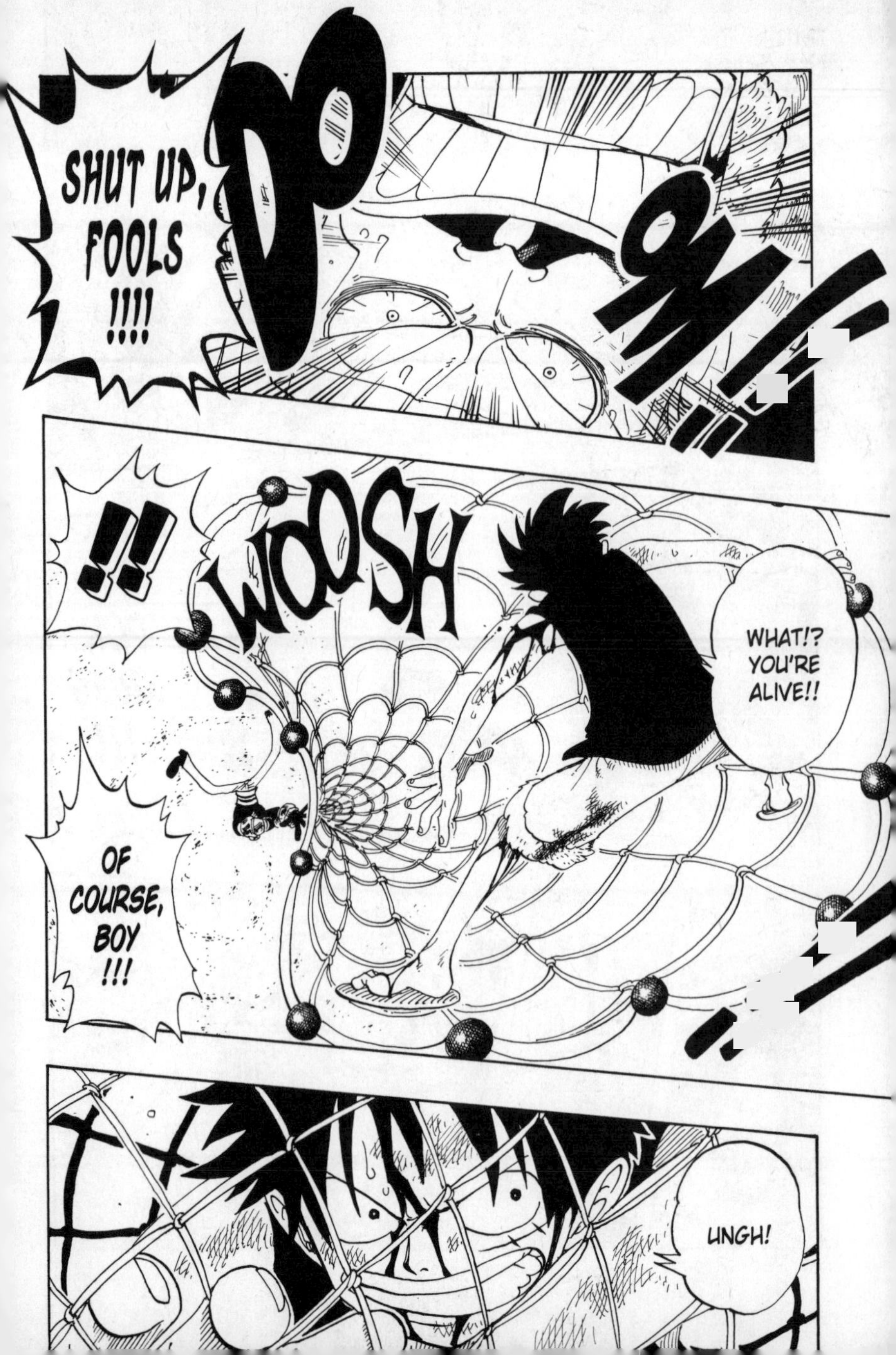
DOOM!!
SHUT UP, FOOLS!!!!
WHAT!? YOU'RE ALIVE!!
WOOSH
!!
OF COURSE, BOY!!!
UNGH!

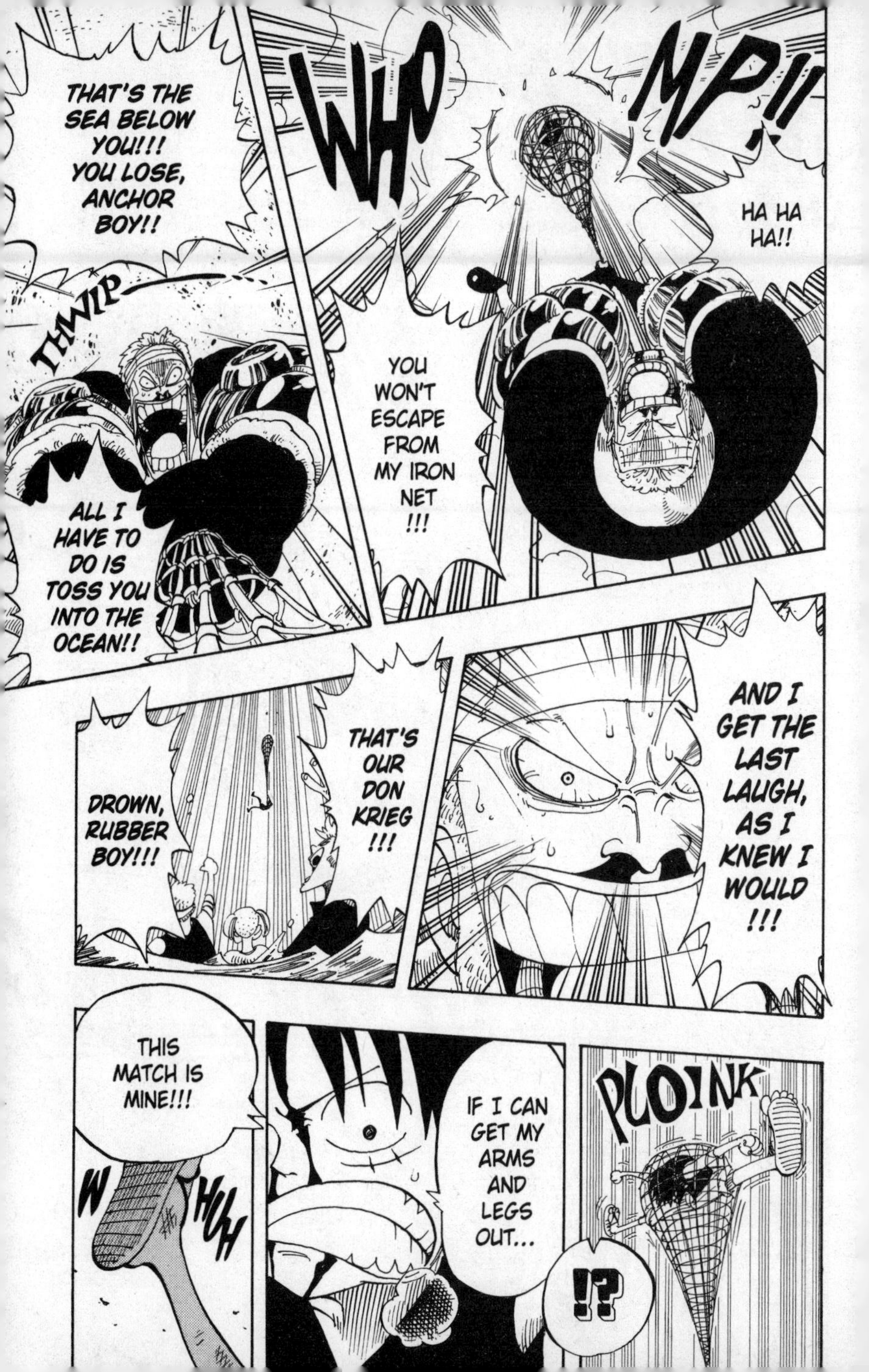
WHOMP!!
HA HA HA!!
YOU WON'T ESCAPE FROM MY IRON NET!!!
THAT'S THE SEA BELOW YOU!!! YOU LOSE, ANCHOR BOY!!
THWIP
ALL I HAVE TO DO IS TOSS YOU INTO THE OCEAN!!
AND I GET THE LAST LAUGH, AS I KNEW I WOULD!!!
THAT'S OUR DON KRIEG!!!
DROWN, RUBBER BOY!!!
PLOINK
!?
IF I CAN GET MY ARMS AND LEGS OUT...
THIS MATCH IS MINE!!!
WHUH

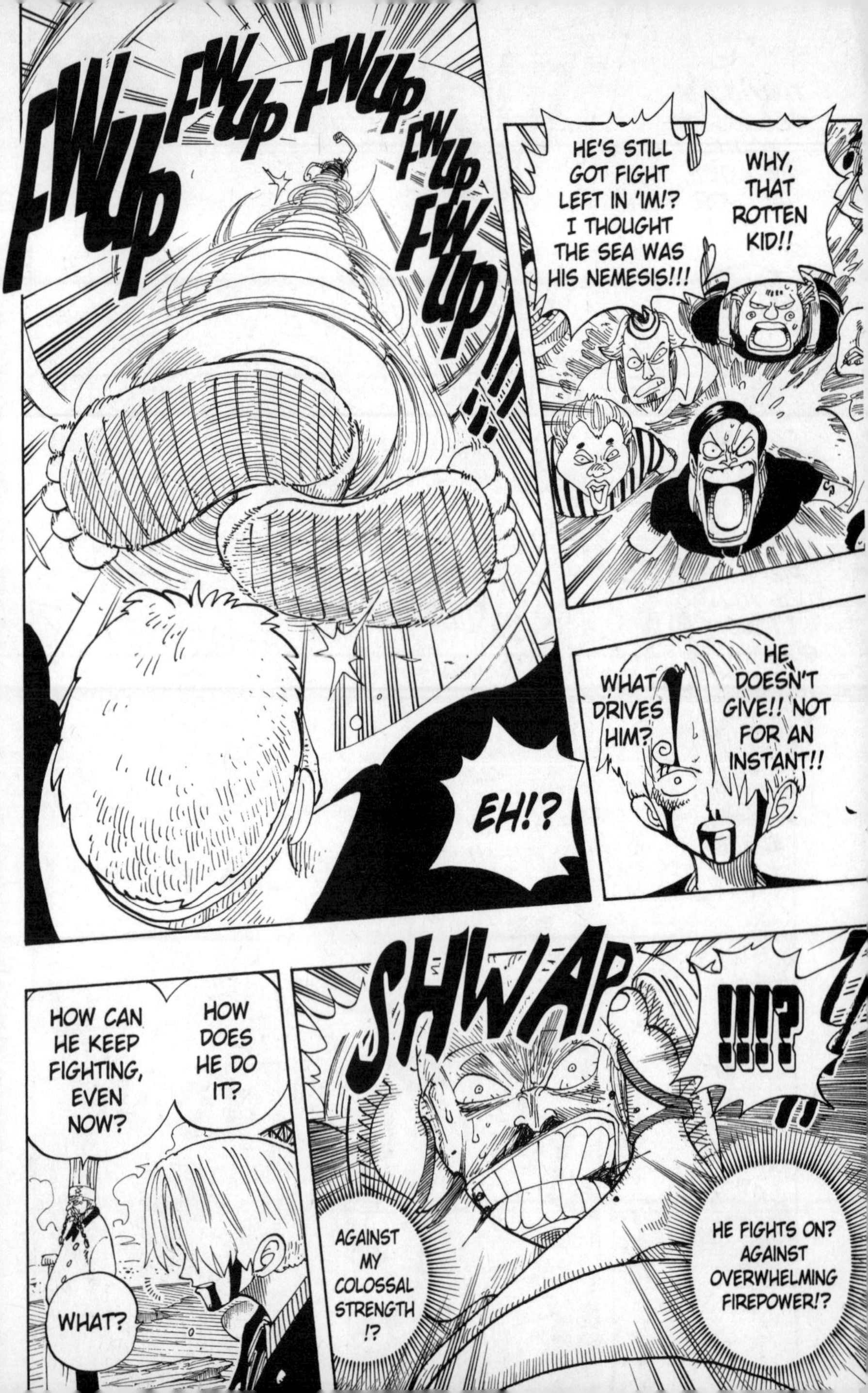
WHY, THAT ROTTEN KID!!
HE'S STILL GOT FIGHT LEFT IN 'IM!? I THOUGHT THE SEA WAS HIS NEMESIS!!!
HE DOESN'T GIVE!! NOT FOR AN INSTANT!!
WHAT DRIVES HIM?
FWUP FWUP FWUP FWUP FWUP!!!
EH!?
!!!?
SHWAP
HE FIGHTS ON? AGAINST OVERWHELMING FIREPOWER!?
AGAINST MY COLOSSAL STRENGTH !?
HOW DOES HE DO IT?
HOW CAN HE KEEP FIGHTING, EVEN NOW?
WHAT?

READ THIS WAY

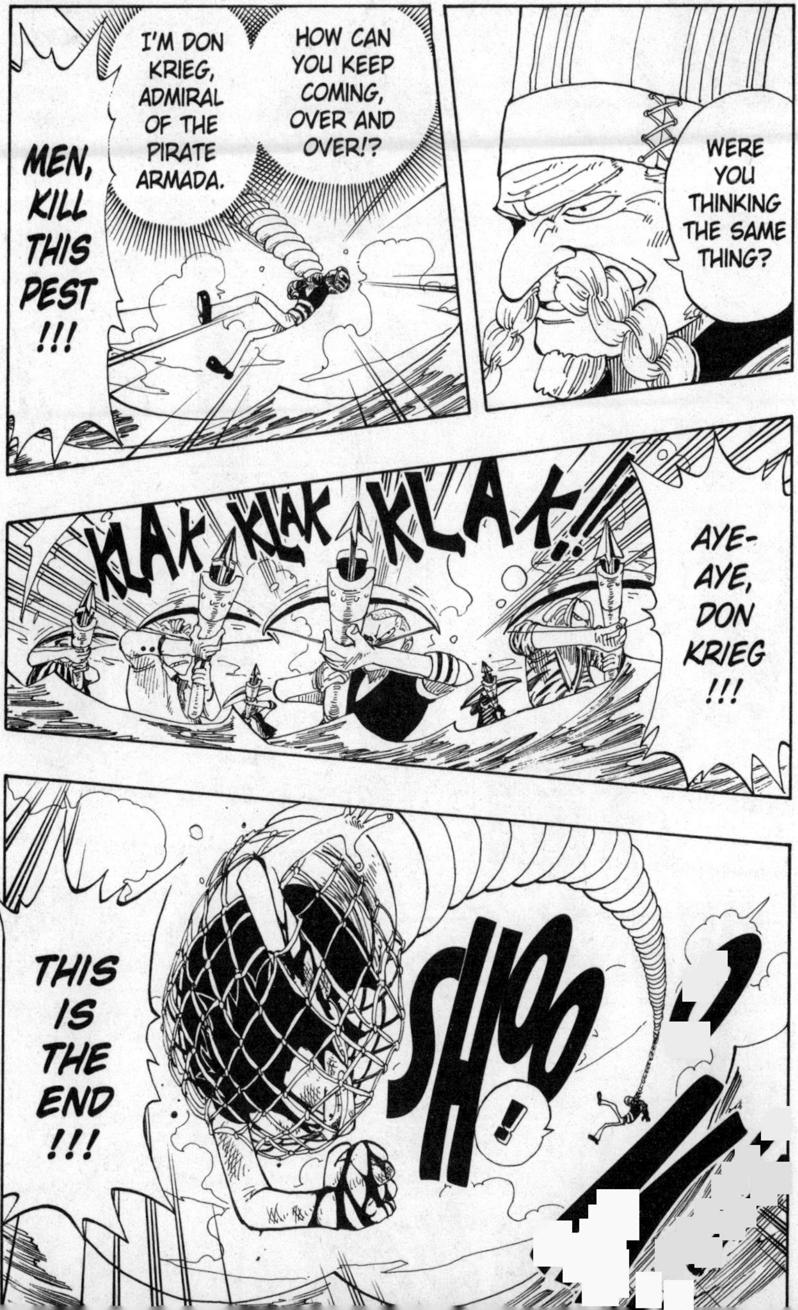
WERE YOU THINKING THE SAME THING?
HOW CAN YOU KEEP COMING, OVER AND OVER!?
I'M DON KRIEG, ADMIRAL OF THE PIRATE ARMADA.
MEN, KILL THIS PEST!!!
AYE-AYE, DON KRIEG!!!
KLAK KLAK KLAK!!
SHOO
THIS IS THE END!!!

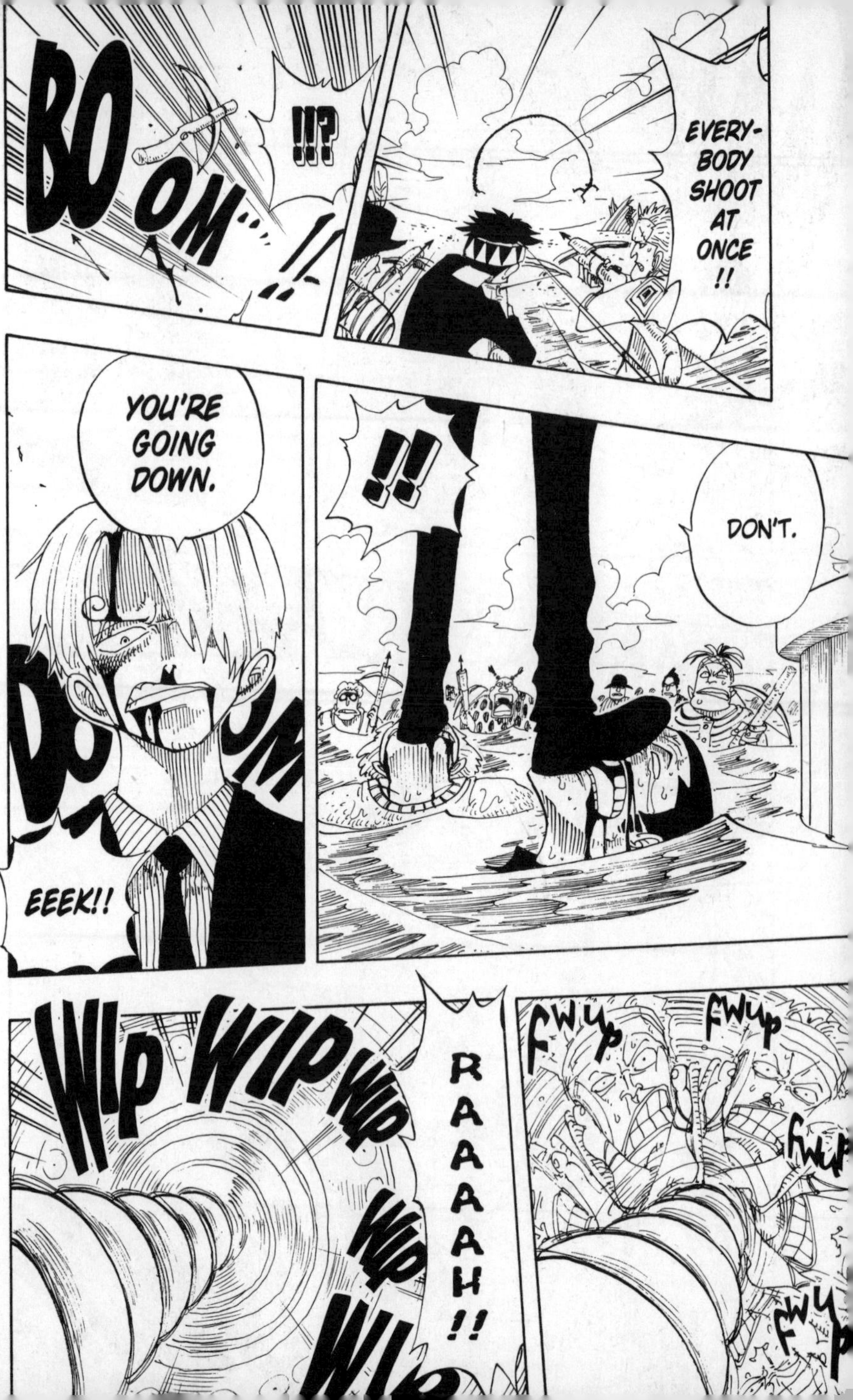
EVERY-BODY SHOOT AT ONCE !!
!!?
BOOM..!!
DON'T.
!!
YOU'RE GOING DOWN.
BOOM
EEEK!!
FWUP
FWUP
FWUP
FWUP
RAAAAAH!!
WIP WIPWIP
WIP
WIP

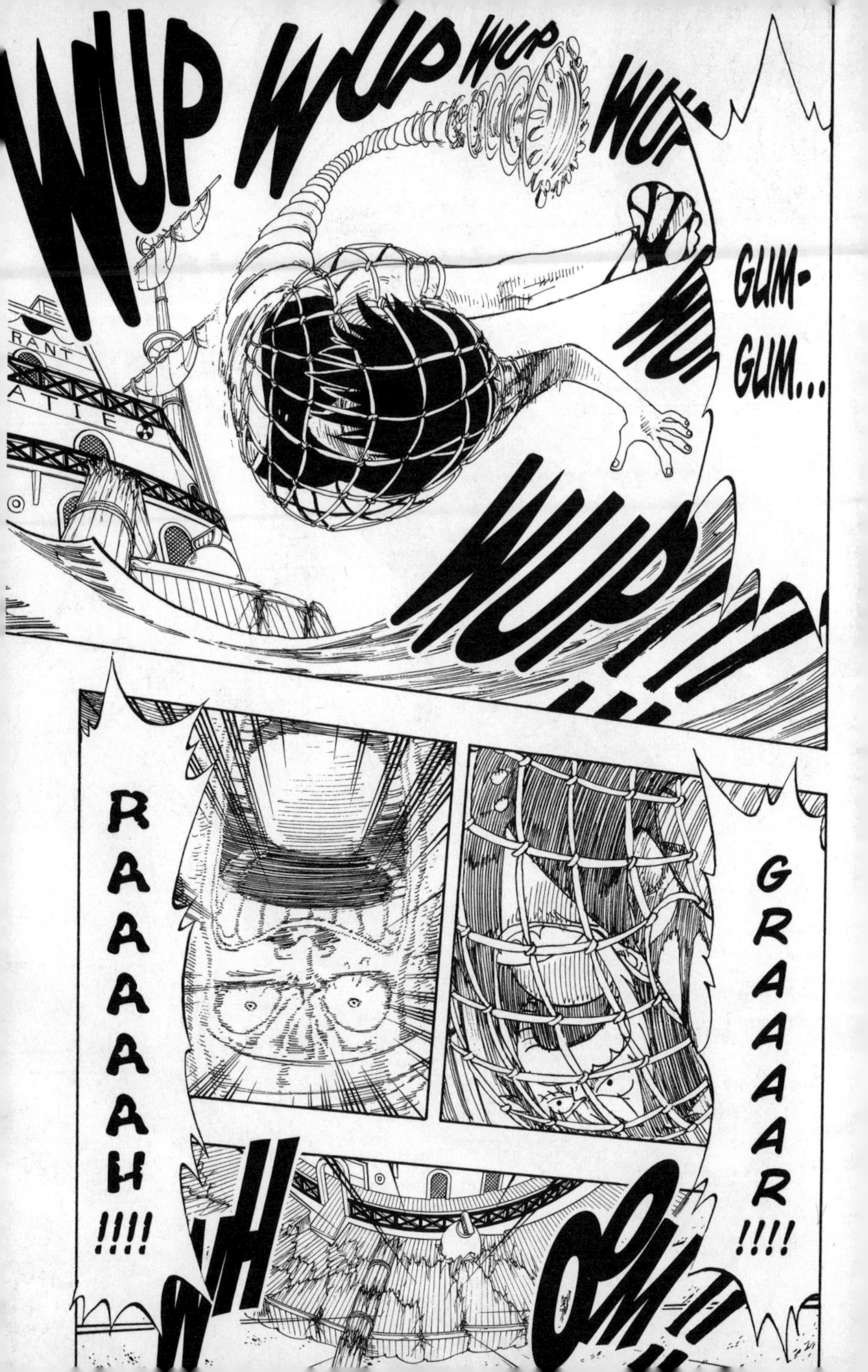
GUM-GUM...
WUP WUP WUP
WUP!!!
GRAAAAAR!!!!
RAAAAAAH!!!!
WHOOM!!

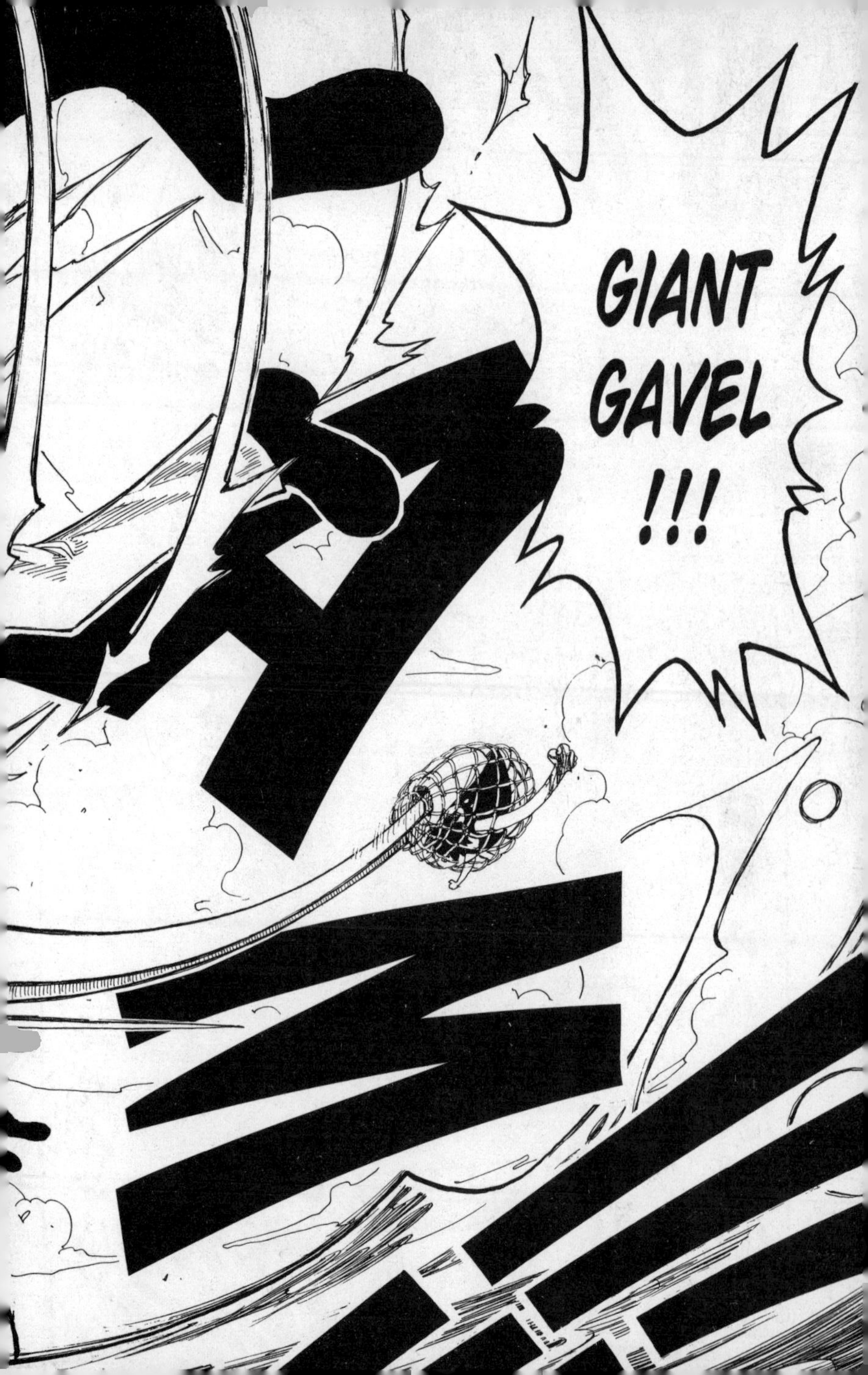
GIANT GAVEL !!!

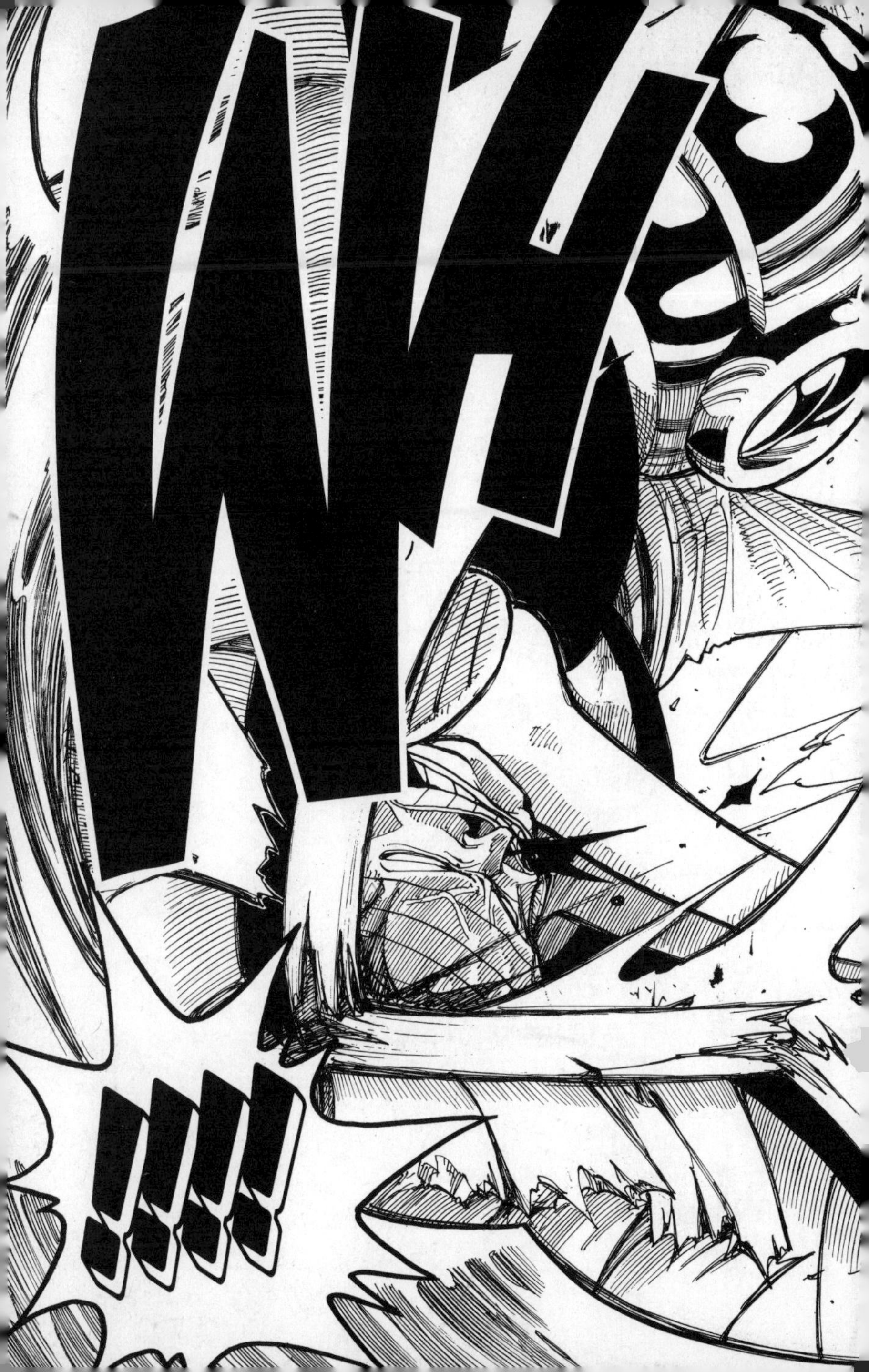
!!!!

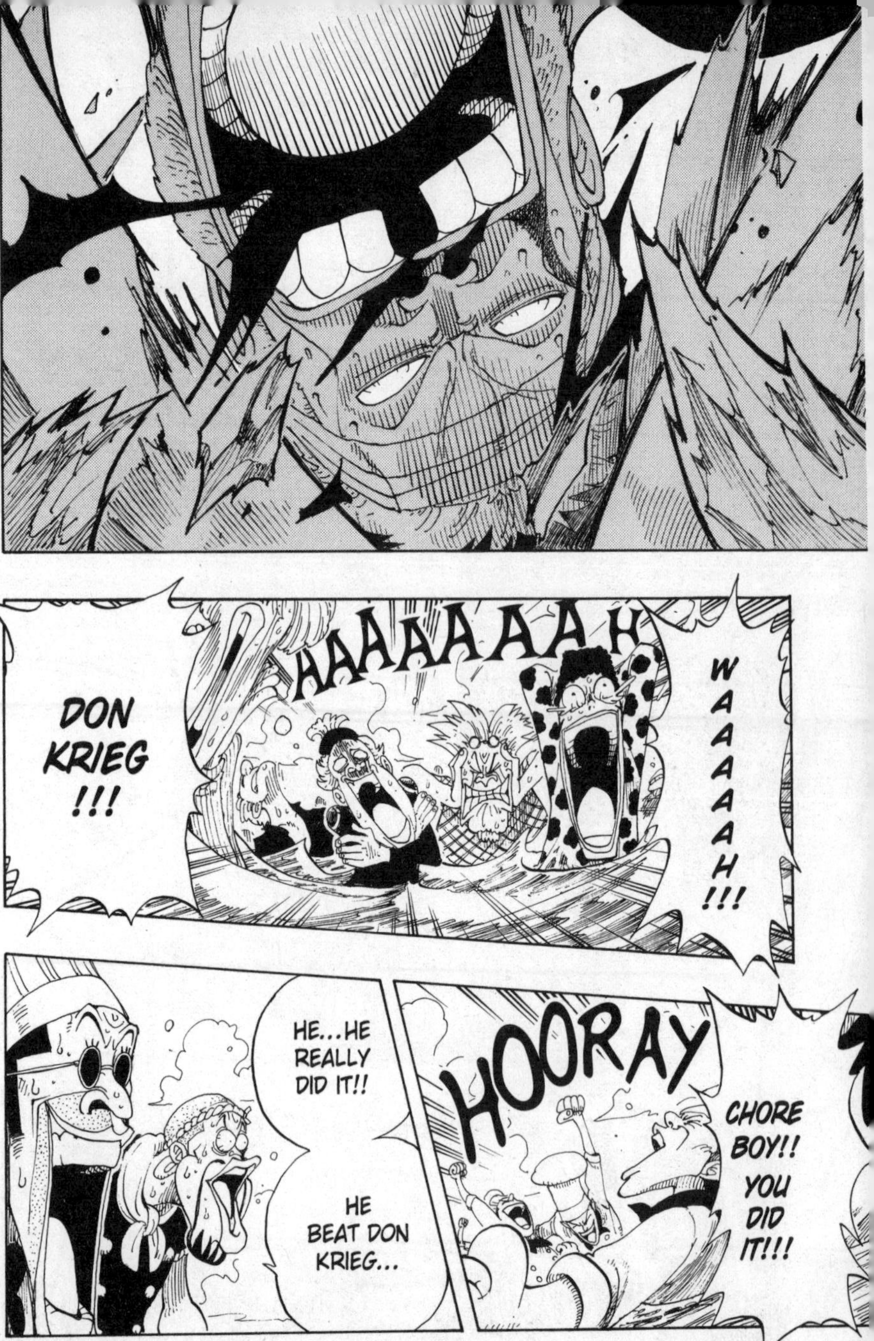
WAAAAAAH!!!
AAAAAAAH
DON KRIEG!!!
HOORAY
CHORE BOY!!
YOU DID IT!!!
HE...HE REALLY DID IT!!
HE BEAT DON KRIEG...

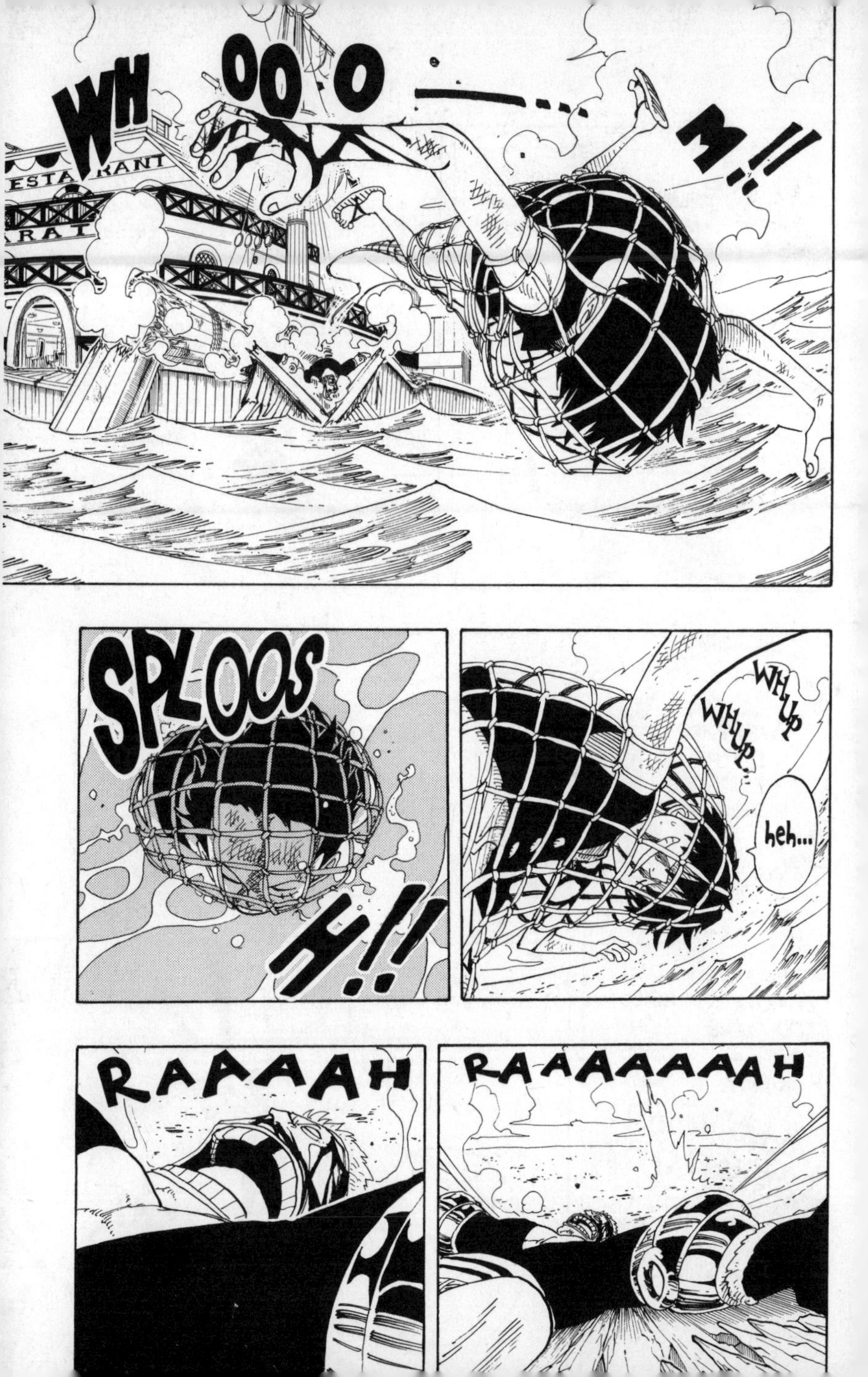
WHOO-O——...M!!
RESTARANT
BARAT
WHUP
WHUP...
heh...
SPLOOSH!!
RAAAAAAAH
RAAAAH

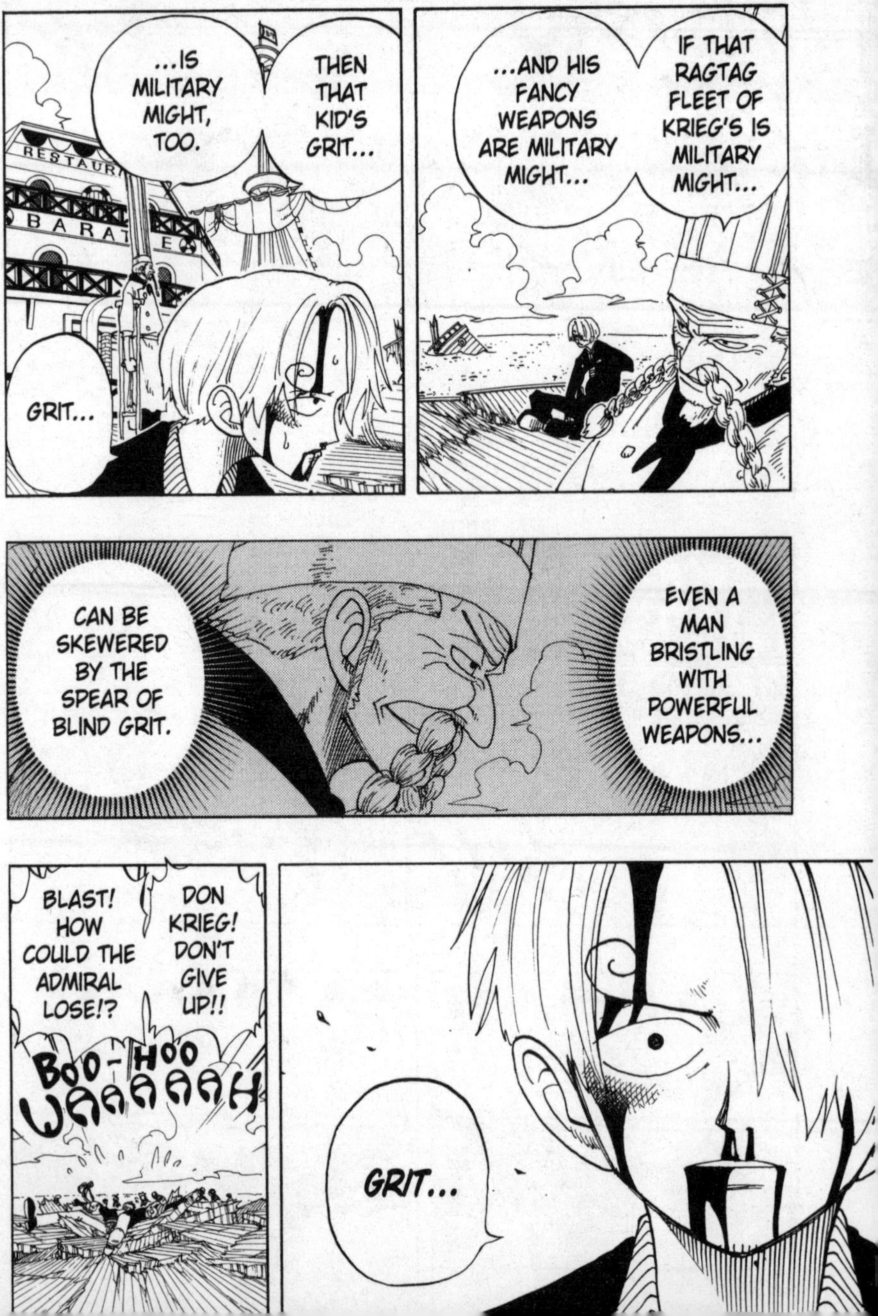
IF THAT RAGTAG FLEET OF KRIEG'S IS MILITARY MIGHT...
...AND HIS FANCY WEAPONS ARE MILITARY MIGHT...
THEN THAT KID'S GRIT...
...IS MILITARY MIGHT, TOO.
GRIT...
EVEN A MAN BRISTLING WITH POWERFUL WEAPONS...
CAN BE SKEWERED BY THE SPEAR OF BLIND GRIT.
GRIT...
DON KRIEG! DON'T GIVE UP!!
BLAST! HOW COULD THE ADMIRAL LOSE!?
BOO-HOO
WAAAAAAH

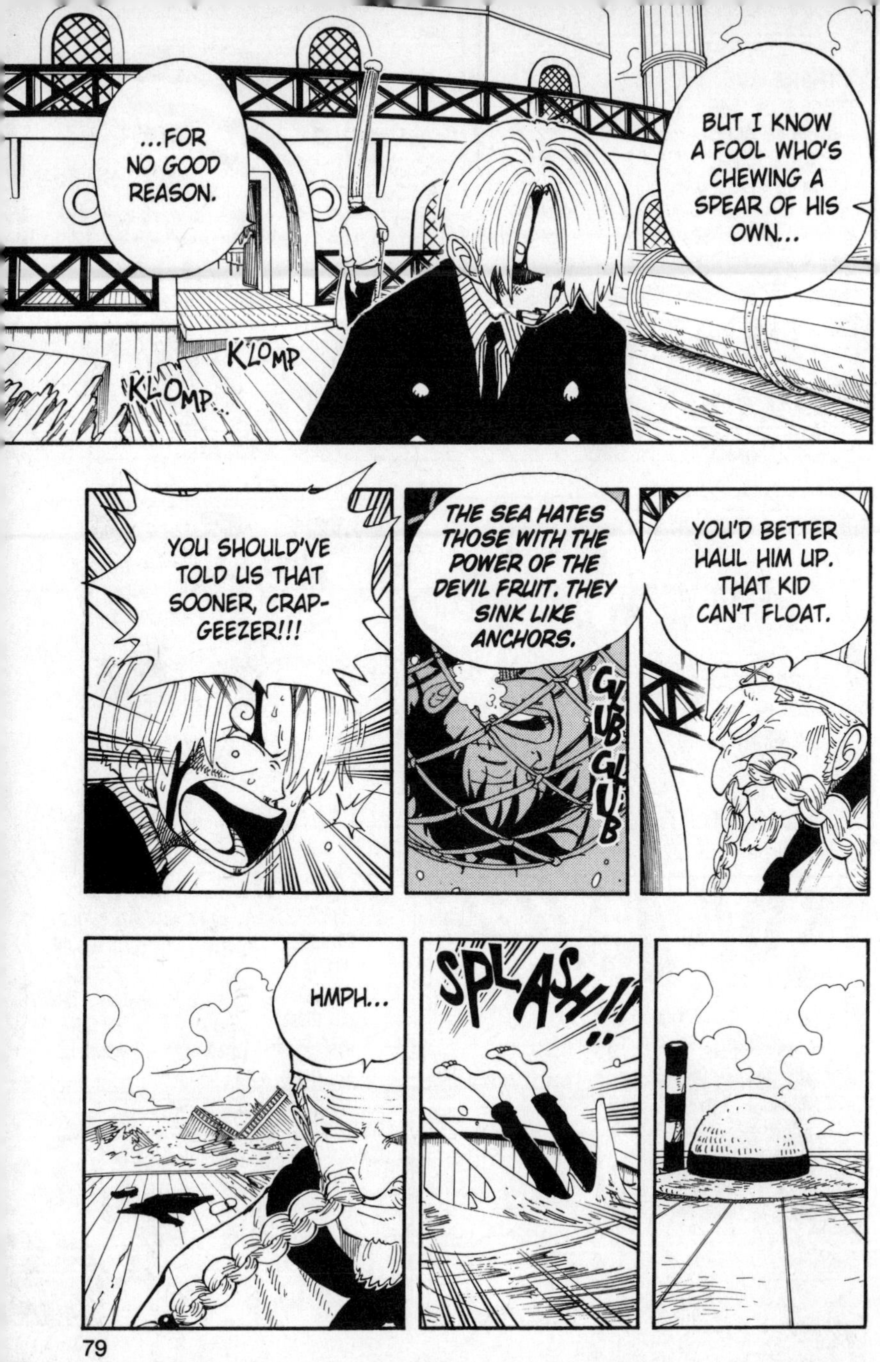
BUT I KNOW A FOOL WHO'S CHEWING A SPEAR OF HIS OWN...
...FOR NO GOOD REASON.
KLOMP
KLOMP...
YOU'D BETTER HAUL HIM UP. THAT KID CAN'T FLOAT.
THE SEA HATES THOSE WITH THE POWER OF THE DEVIL FRUIT. THEY SINK LIKE ANCHORS.
GLUB GLUB GLUB
YOU SHOULD'VE TOLD US THAT SOONER, CRAP-GEEZER!!!
SPLASH!!
HMPH...

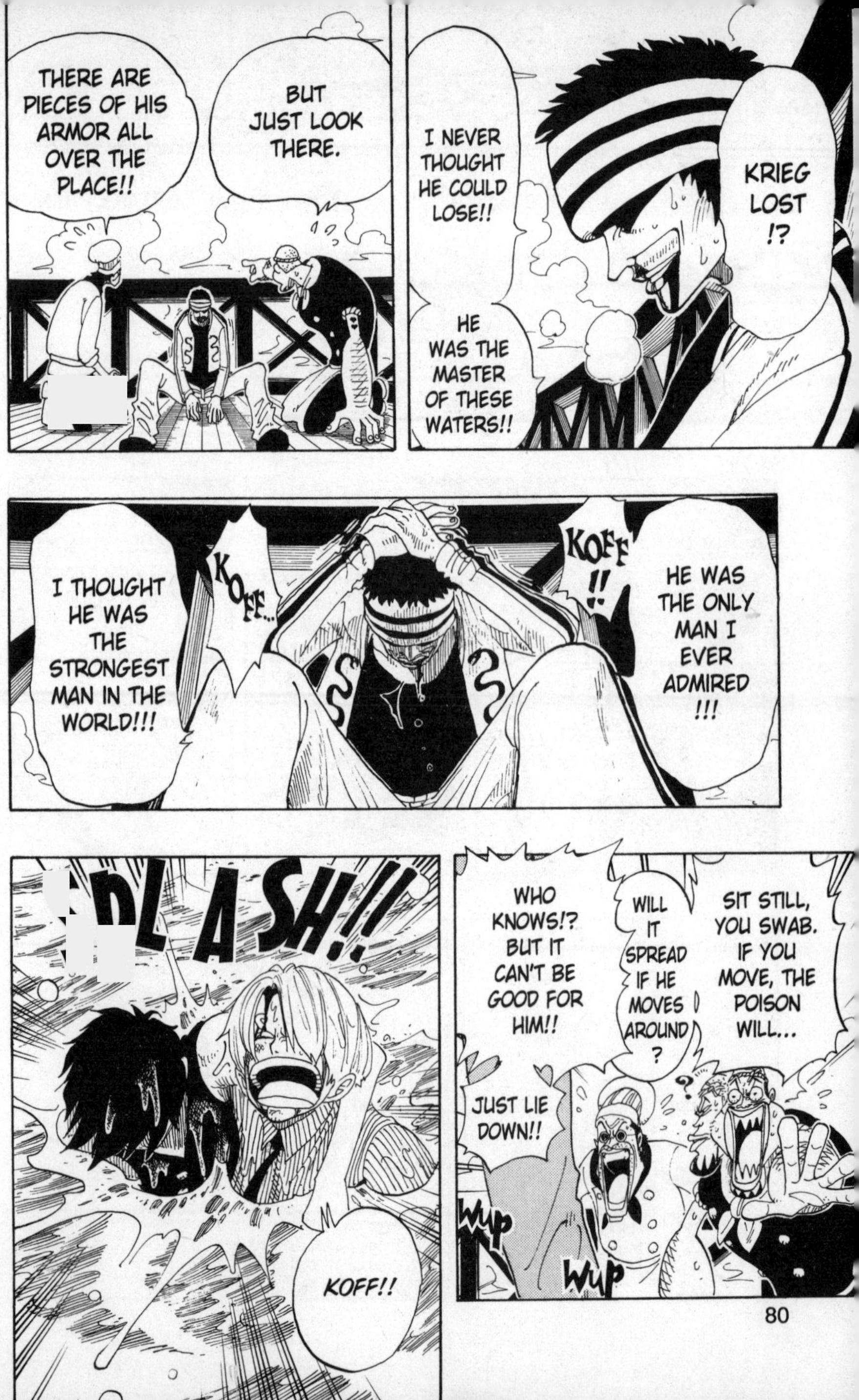
KRIEG LOST !?
I NEVER THOUGHT HE COULD LOSE!!
HE WAS THE MASTER OF THESE WATERS!!
BUT JUST LOOK THERE.
THERE ARE PIECES OF HIS ARMOR ALL OVER THE PLACE!!
KOFF !!
HE WAS THE ONLY MAN I EVER ADMIRED !!!
KOFF...
I THOUGHT HE WAS THE STRONGEST MAN IN THE WORLD!!!
SIT STILL, YOU SWAB. IF YOU MOVE, THE POISON WILL...
WILL IT SPREAD IF HE MOVES AROUND ?
WHO KNOWS!? BUT IT CAN'T BE GOOD FOR HIM!!
JUST LIE DOWN!!
WUP
WUP
PLASH!!
KOFF!!

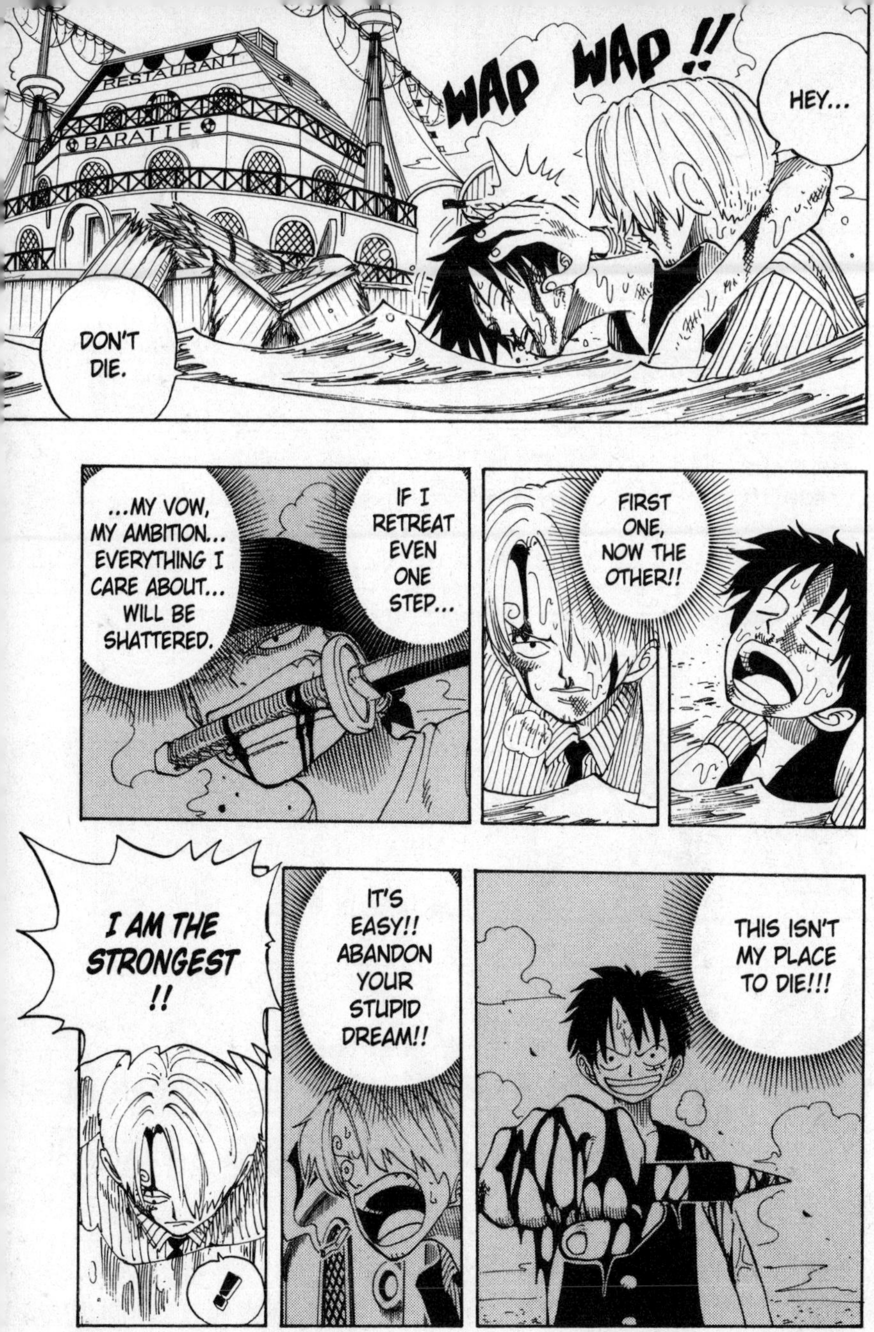
HEY...
WAP WAP!!
DON'T DIE.
FIRST ONE, NOW THE OTHER!!
IF I RETREAT EVEN ONE STEP...
...MY VOW, MY AMBITION... EVERYTHING I CARE ABOUT... WILL BE SHATTERED.
THIS ISN'T MY PLACE TO DIE!!!
IT'S EASY!! ABANDON YOUR STUPID DREAM!!
I AM THE STRONGEST!!
!

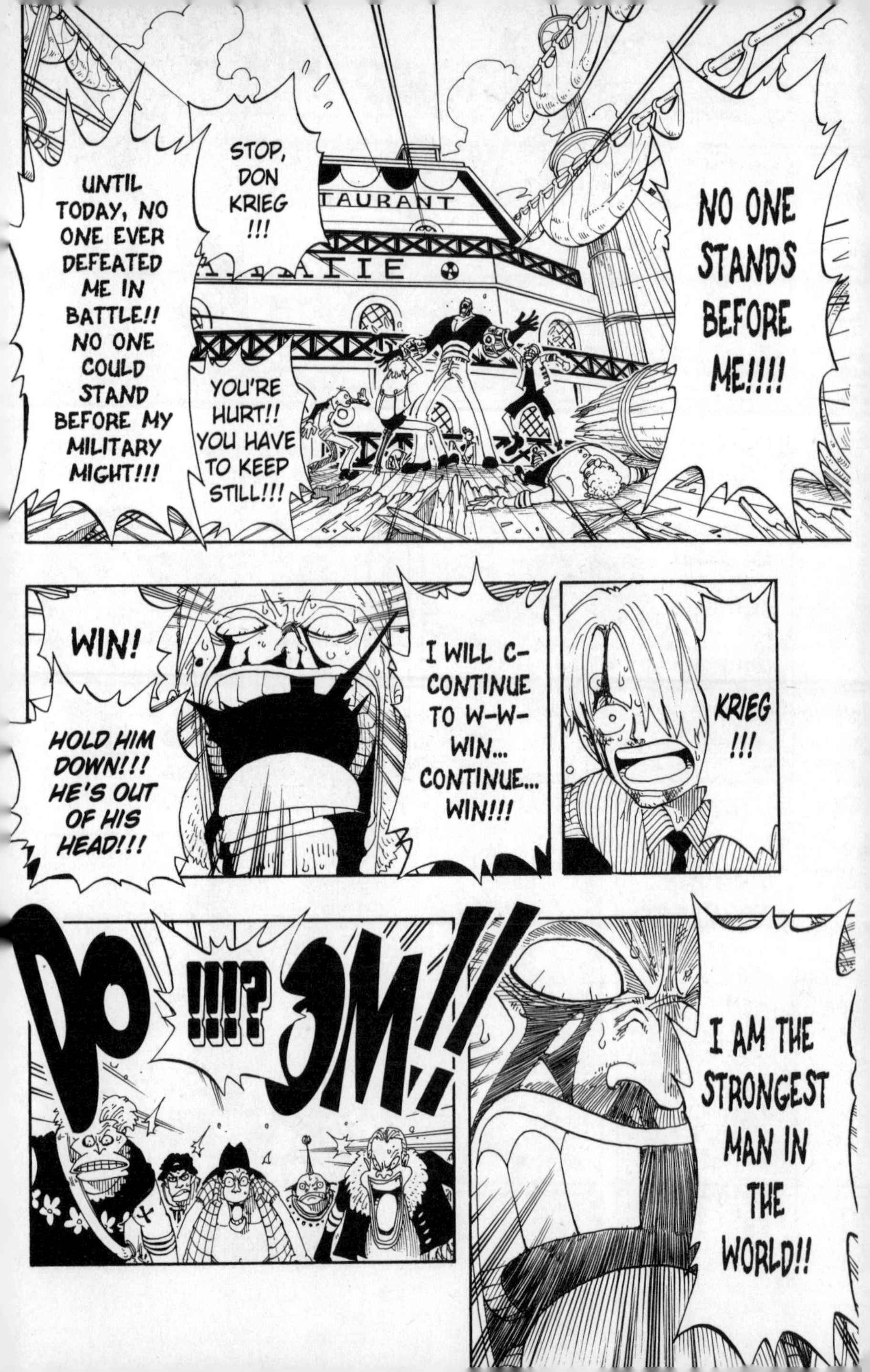

NO ONE STANDS BEFORE ME!!!!
STOP, DON KRIEG!!!
UNTIL TODAY, NO ONE EVER DEFEATED ME IN BATTLE!! NO ONE COULD STAND BEFORE MY MILITARY MIGHT!!!
YOU'RE HURT!! YOU HAVE TO KEEP STILL!!!
KRIEG!!!
I WILL C-CONTINUE TO W-W-WIN... CONTINUE... WIN!!!
WIN!
HOLD HIM DOWN!!! HE'S OUT OF HIS HEAD!!!
I AM THE STRONGEST MAN IN THE WORLD!!
DOOM!!
!!!?

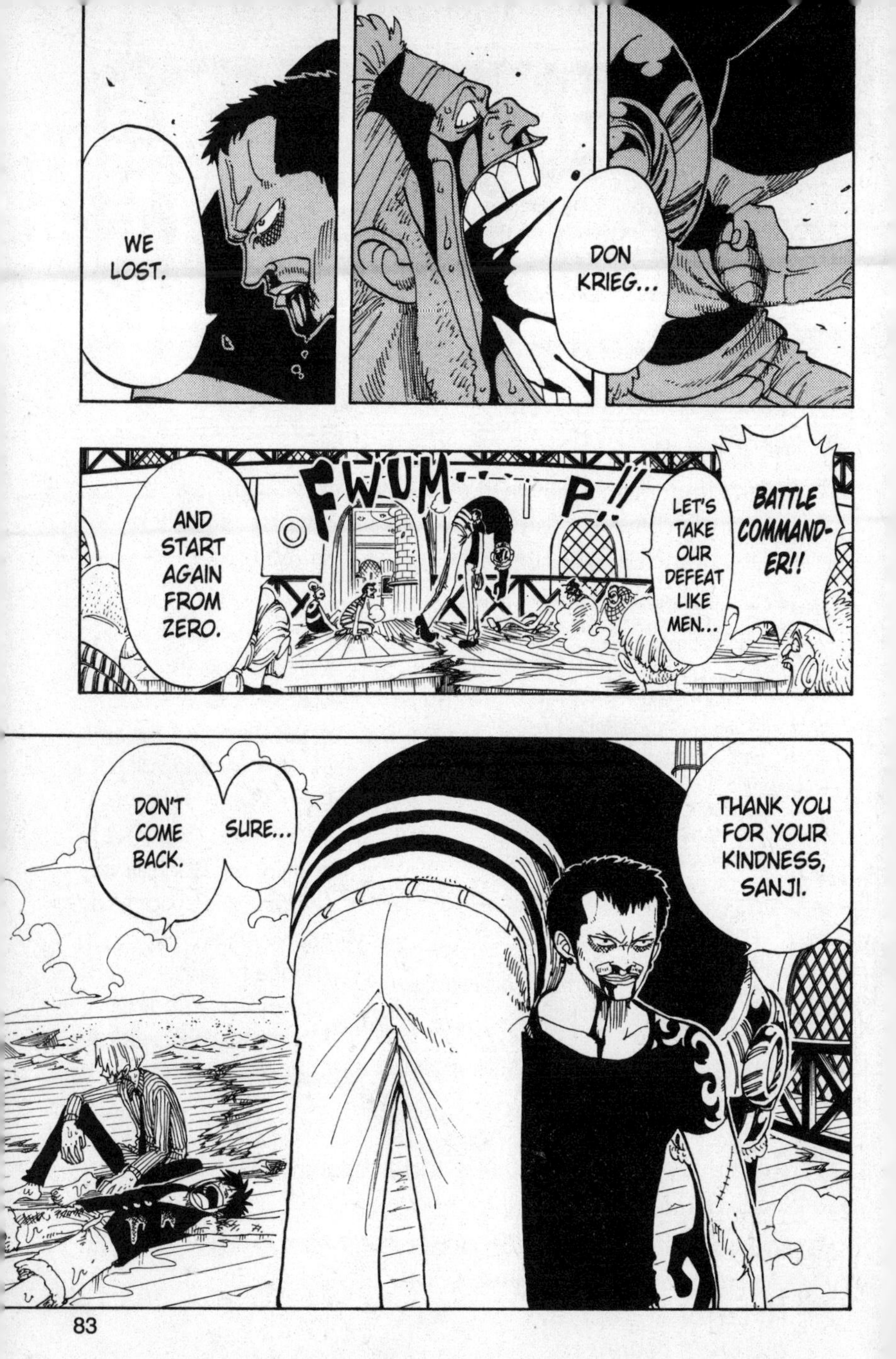
DON KRIEG...
WE LOST.
BATTLE COMMANDER!!
LET'S TAKE OUR DEFEAT LIKE MEN...
FWUMP!!
AND START AGAIN FROM ZERO.
THANK YOU FOR YOUR KINDNESS, SANJI.
SURE...
DON'T COME BACK.

Q: Does Sanji like to say crap?

A: He loves to.

Q: I don't understand the naval rank system very well. Is a captain the highest position? Is Koby at Navy Headquarters or at a branch office? How high up is Lt. Fullbody?

A:

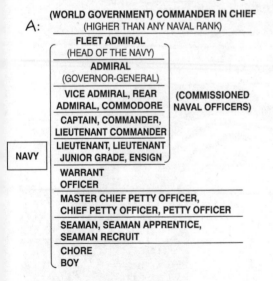

NAVY		
(WORLD GOVERNMENT) COMMANDER IN CHIEF (HIGHER THAN ANY NAVAL RANK)		
FLEET ADMIRAL (HEAD OF THE NAVY)		
ADMIRAL (GOVERNOR-GENERAL)		
VICE ADMIRAL, REAR ADMIRAL, COMMODORE	**(COMMISSIONED NAVAL OFFICERS)**	
CAPTAIN, COMMANDER, LIEUTENANT COMMANDER		
LIEUTENANT, LIEUTENANT JUNIOR GRADE, ENSIGN		
WARRANT OFFICER		
MASTER CHIEF PETTY OFFICER, CHIEF PETTY OFFICER, PETTY OFFICER		
SEAMAN, SEAMAN APPRENTICE, SEAMAN RECRUIT		
CHORE BOY		

The ranks work something like this, But this only holds true for the navy in the world of One Piece. KoBy is at Branch 153. The Branches scattered around the world are commanded By officers with a rank higher than captain. MayBe someday KoBy will Be an officer.

Q: In volume 5, page 159 panel 3, there's a fat guy. Did he steal some of that girl's food?

A: Very perceptive!! Wow!! That's Mr. Motzel, the Gourmand. Yes, he filched some of her food. Afterward, they Got into a fight. The Girl is Mr. Motzel's daughter.

Chapter 67: THE SOUP

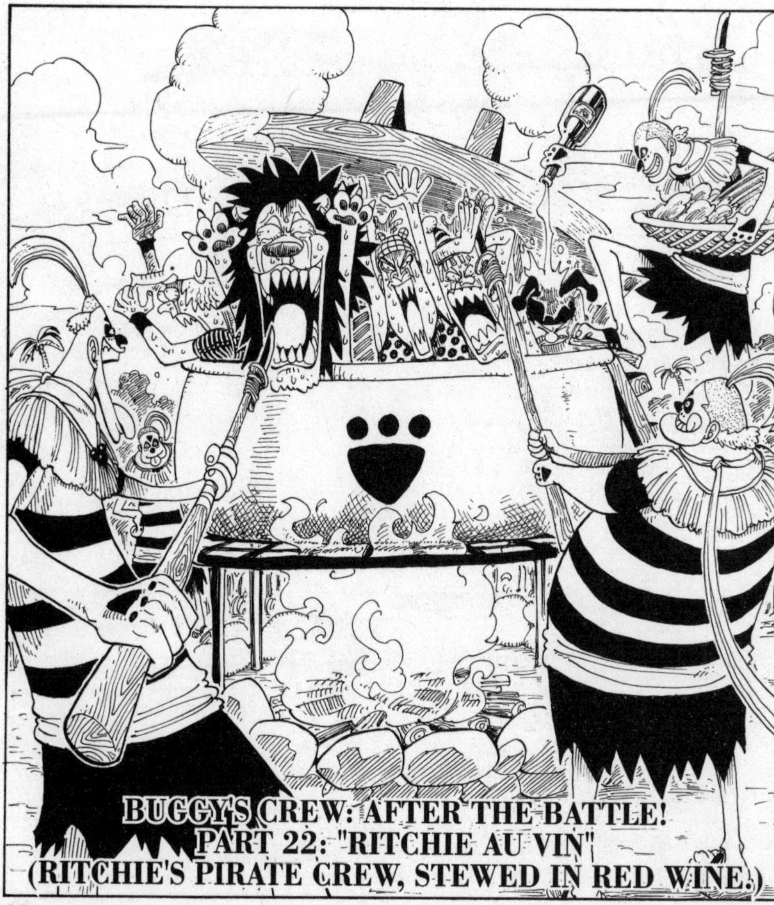
BUGGY'S CREW: AFTER THE BATTLE!
PART 22: "RITCHIE AU VIN"
(RITCHIE'S PIRATE CREW, STEWED IN RED WINE.)

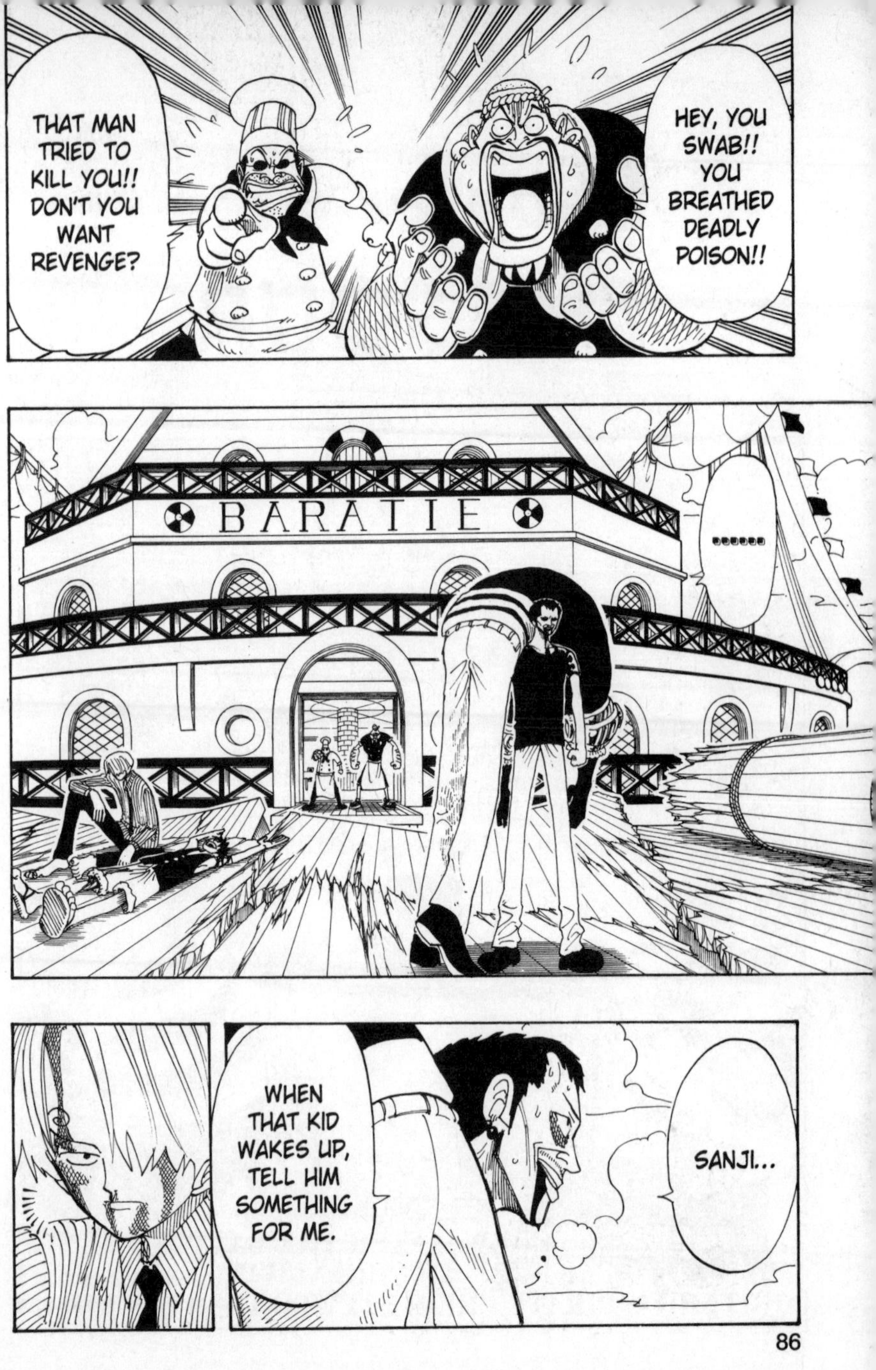
HEY, YOU SWAB!! YOU BREATHED DEADLY POISON!!
THAT MAN TRIED TO KILL YOU!! DON'T YOU WANT REVENGE?
......
BARATIE
SANJI...
WHEN THAT KID WAKES UP, TELL HIM SOMETHING FOR ME.

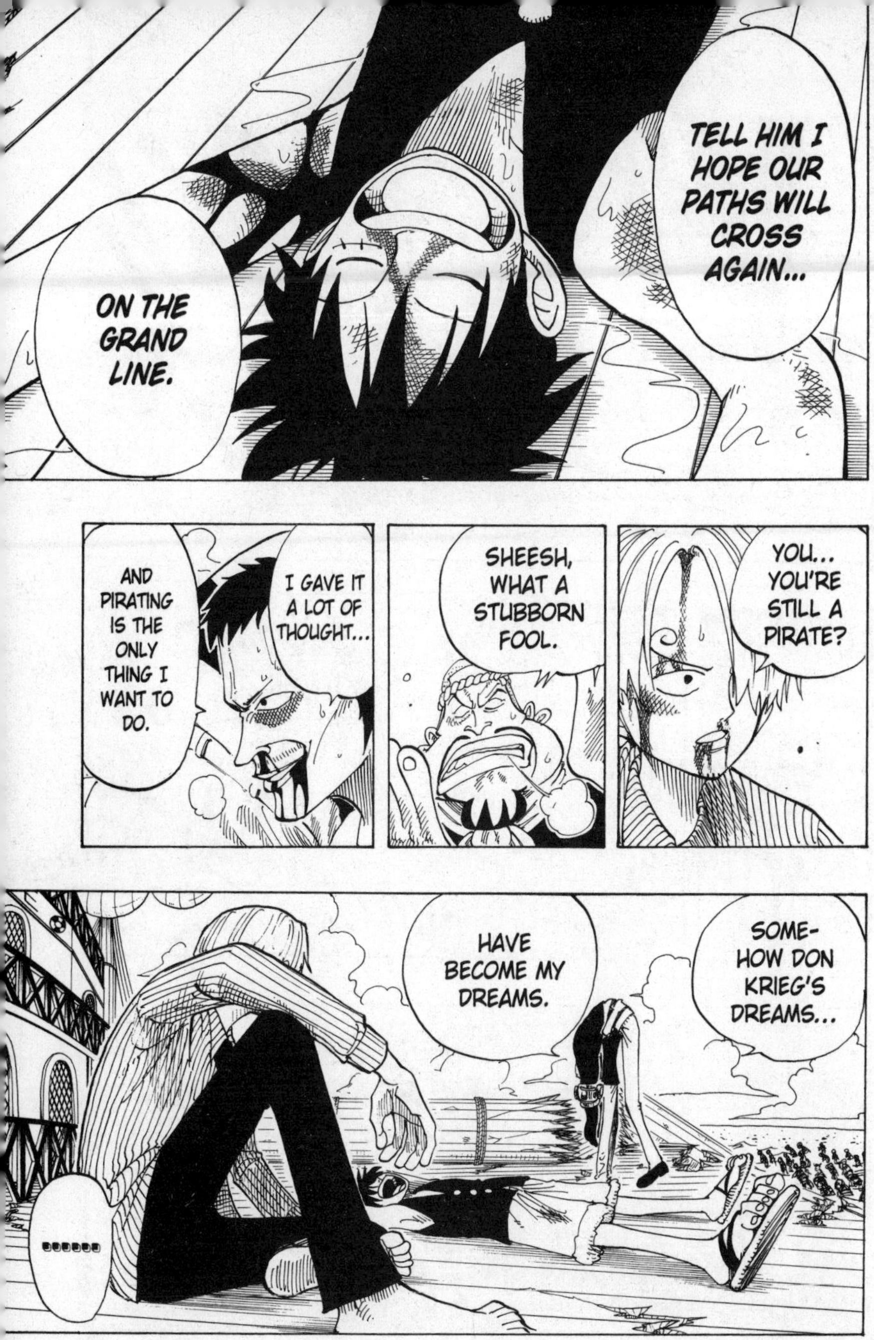
TELL HIM I HOPE OUR PATHS WILL CROSS AGAIN...
ON THE GRAND LINE.
YOU... YOU'RE STILL A PIRATE?
SHEESH, WHAT A STUBBORN FOOL.
I GAVE IT A LOT OF THOUGHT...
AND PIRATING IS THE ONLY THING I WANT TO DO.
SOME-HOW DON KRIEG'S DREAMS...
HAVE BECOME MY DREAMS.
......

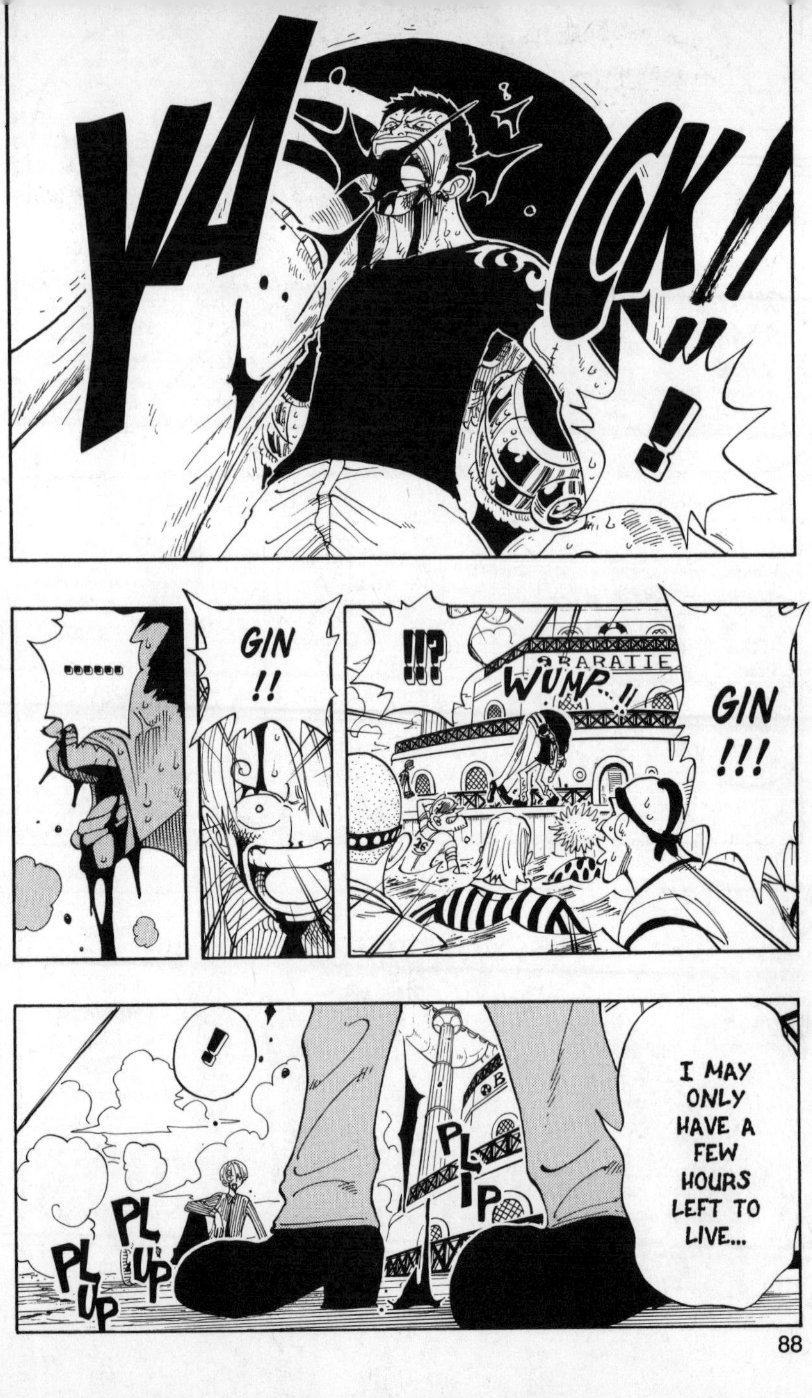
YA-CK!!
!
GIN !!!
!!?
BARATIE
WUMP..!!
GIN !!
......
I MAY ONLY HAVE A FEW HOURS LEFT TO LIVE...
PLIP
!
PLUP
PLUP

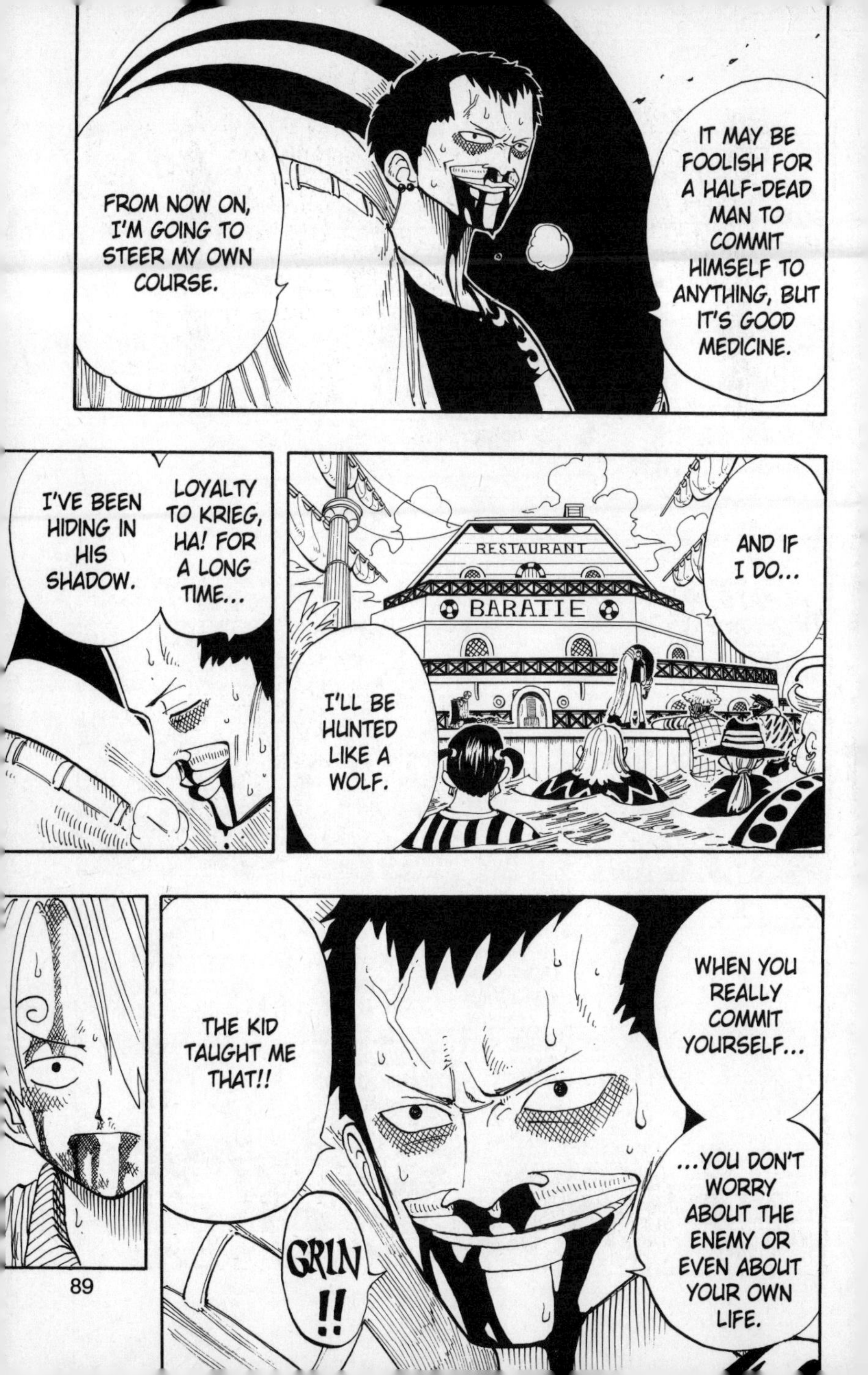
IT MAY BE FOOLISH FOR A HALF-DEAD MAN TO COMMIT HIMSELF TO ANYTHING, BUT IT'S GOOD MEDICINE.
FROM NOW ON, I'M GOING TO STEER MY OWN COURSE.
RESTAURANT
BARATIE
AND IF I DO...
I'LL BE HUNTED LIKE A WOLF.
LOYALTY TO KRIEG, HA! FOR A LONG TIME...
I'VE BEEN HIDING IN HIS SHADOW.
WHEN YOU REALLY COMMIT YOURSELF...
...YOU DON'T WORRY ABOUT THE ENEMY OR EVEN ABOUT YOUR OWN LIFE.
THE KID TAUGHT ME THAT!!
GRIN !!

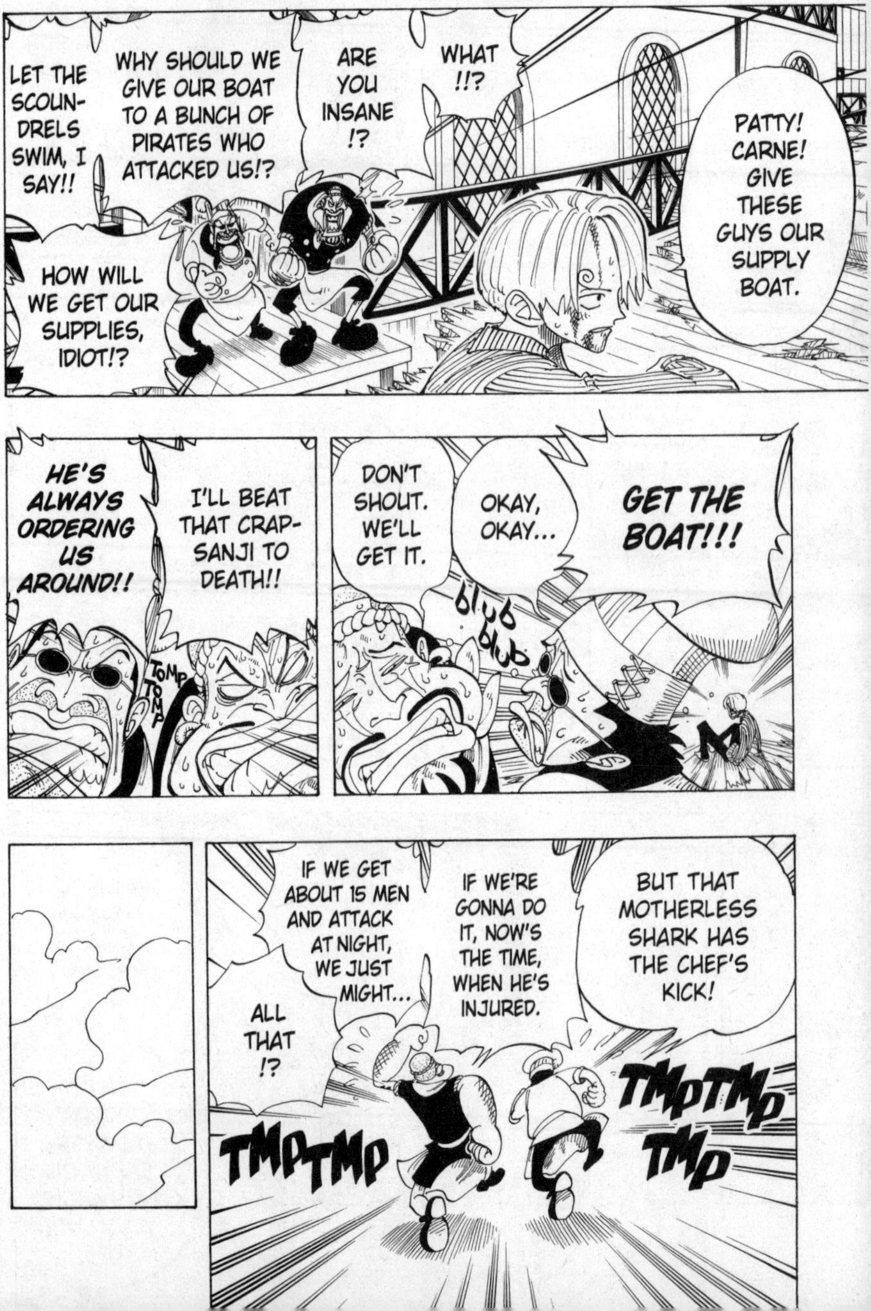
PATTY! CARNE! GIVE THESE GUYS OUR SUPPLY BOAT.
WHAT !!?
ARE YOU INSANE !?
WHY SHOULD WE GIVE OUR BOAT TO A BUNCH OF PIRATES WHO ATTACKED US!?
LET THE SCOUN-DRELS SWIM, I SAY!!
HOW WILL WE GET OUR SUPPLIES, IDIOT!?
GET THE BOAT!!!
OKAY, OKAY...
DON'T SHOUT. WE'LL GET IT.
blub blub
I'LL BEAT THAT CRAP-SANJI TO DEATH!!
TOMP TOMP TOMP
HE'S ALWAYS ORDERING US AROUND!!
BUT THAT MOTHERLESS SHARK HAS THE CHEF'S KICK!
IF WE'RE GONNA DO IT, NOW'S THE TIME, WHEN HE'S INJURED.
IF WE GET ABOUT 15 MEN AND ATTACK AT NIGHT, WE JUST MIGHT...
ALL THAT !?
TMPTMP TMP
TMPTMP

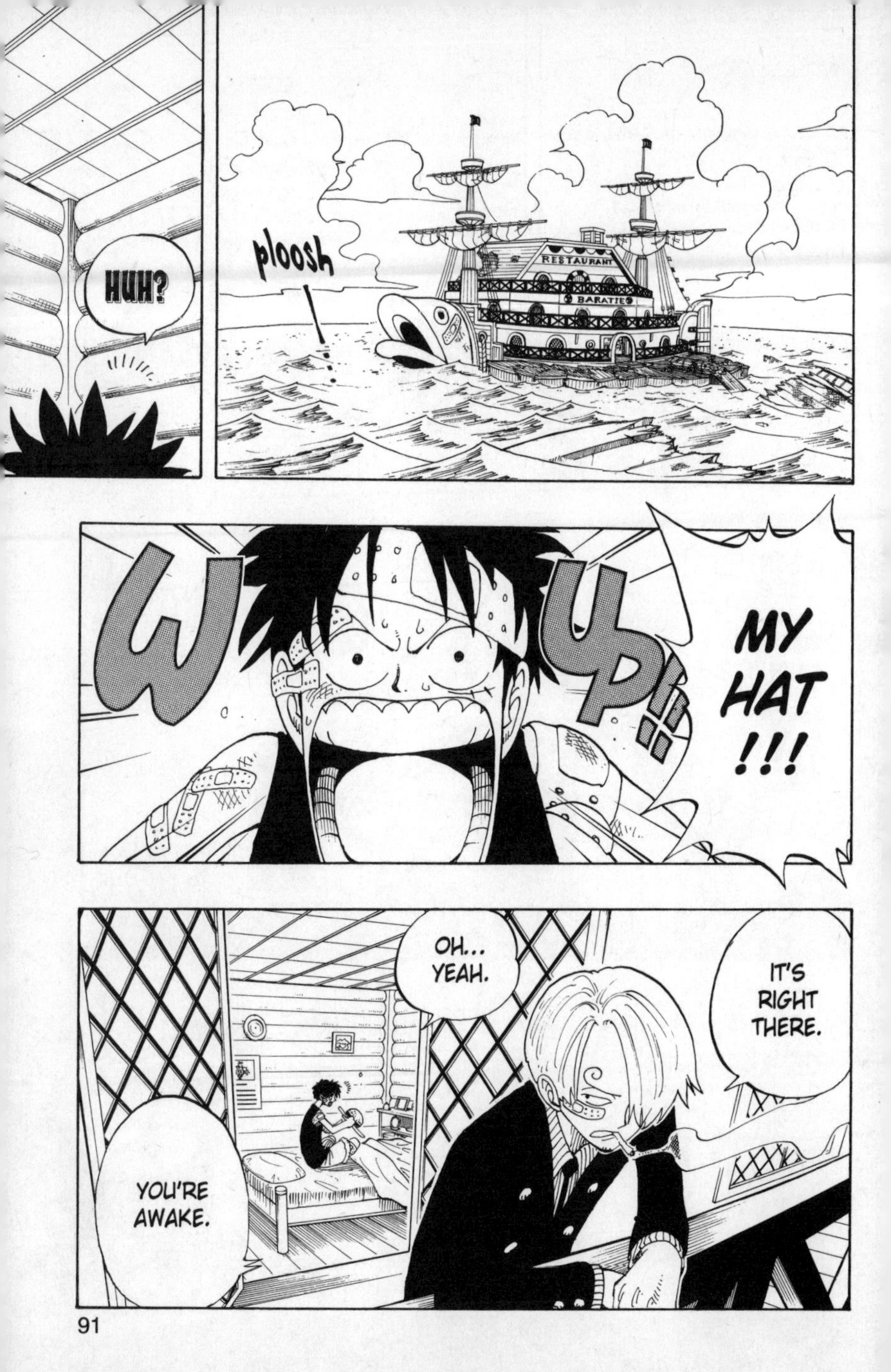
ploosh
HUH?
MY HAT!!!
WUP!!
IT'S RIGHT THERE.
OH... YEAH.
YOU'RE AWAKE.

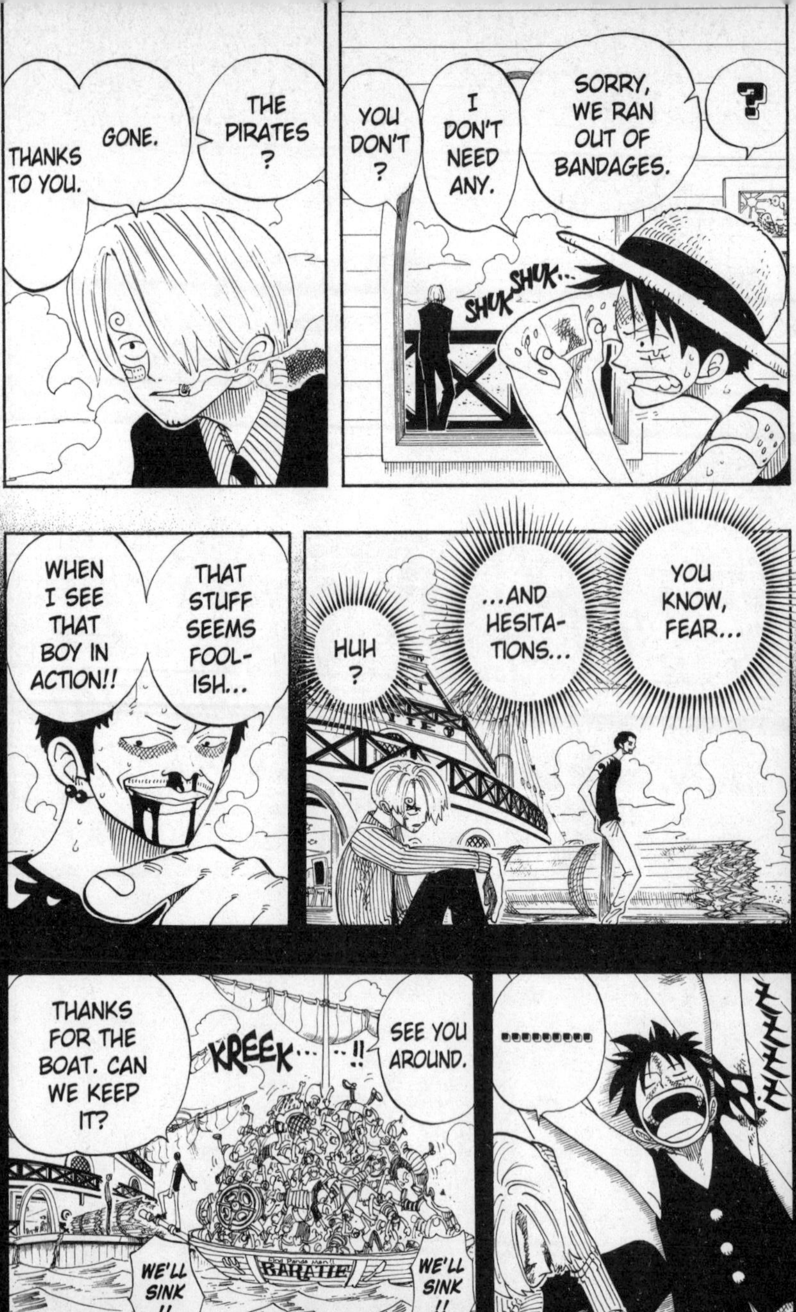
?
SORRY, WE RAN OUT OF BANDAGES.
I DON'T NEED ANY.
YOU DON'T ?
SHUK-SHUK...
THE PIRATES ?
GONE.
THANKS TO YOU.
YOU KNOW, FEAR...
...AND HESITATIONS...
HUH ?
THAT STUFF SEEMS FOOLISH...
WHEN I SEE THAT BOY IN ACTION!!
....
SEE YOU AROUND.
KREEK... ..!!
THANKS FOR THE BOAT. CAN WE KEEP IT?
WE'LL SINK !!
BARATIE
WE'LL SINK !!

READ THIS WAY

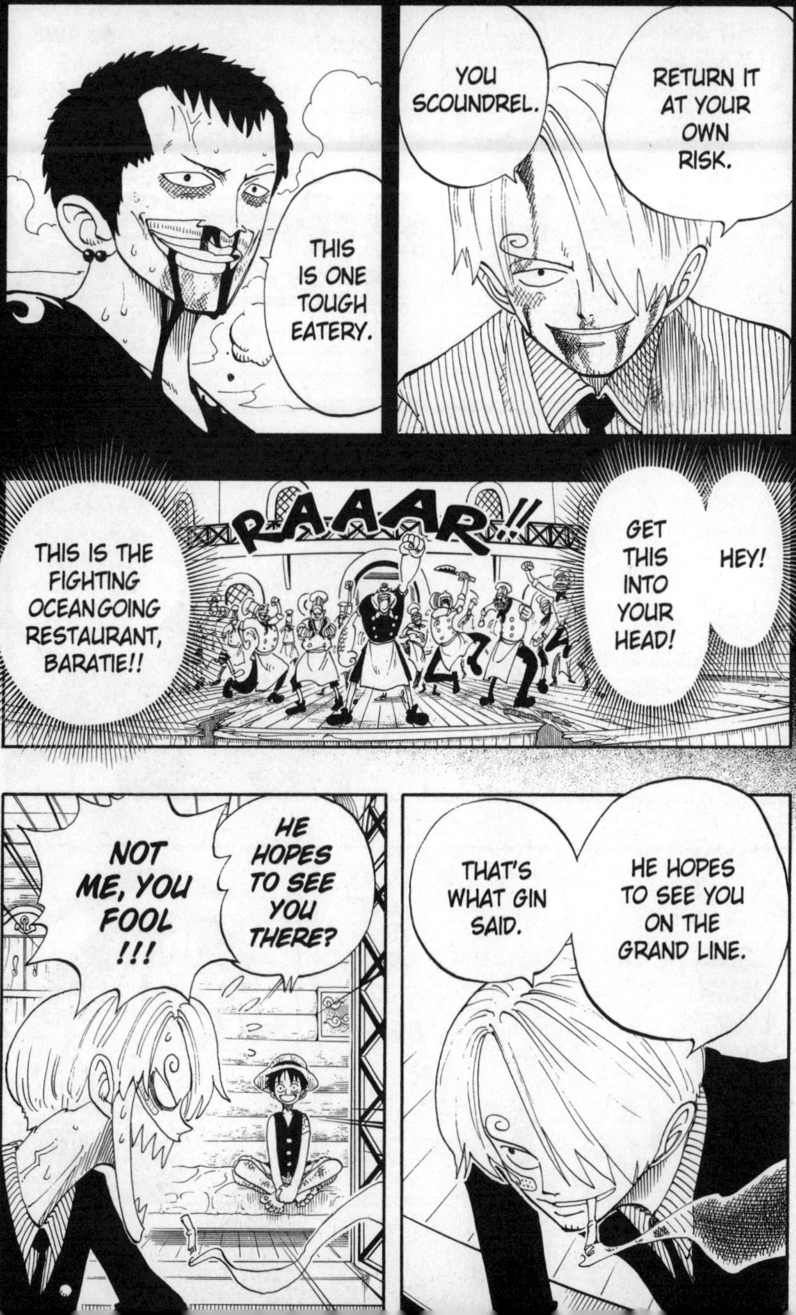
RETURN IT AT YOUR OWN RISK.
YOU SCOUNDREL.
THIS IS ONE TOUGH EATERY.
HEY!
GET THIS INTO YOUR HEAD!
RAAAR!!
THIS IS THE FIGHTING OCEANGOING RESTAURANT, BARATIE!!
HE HOPES TO SEE YOU ON THE GRAND LINE.
THAT'S WHAT GIN SAID.
HE HOPES TO SEE YOU THERE?
NOT ME, YOU FOOL!!!

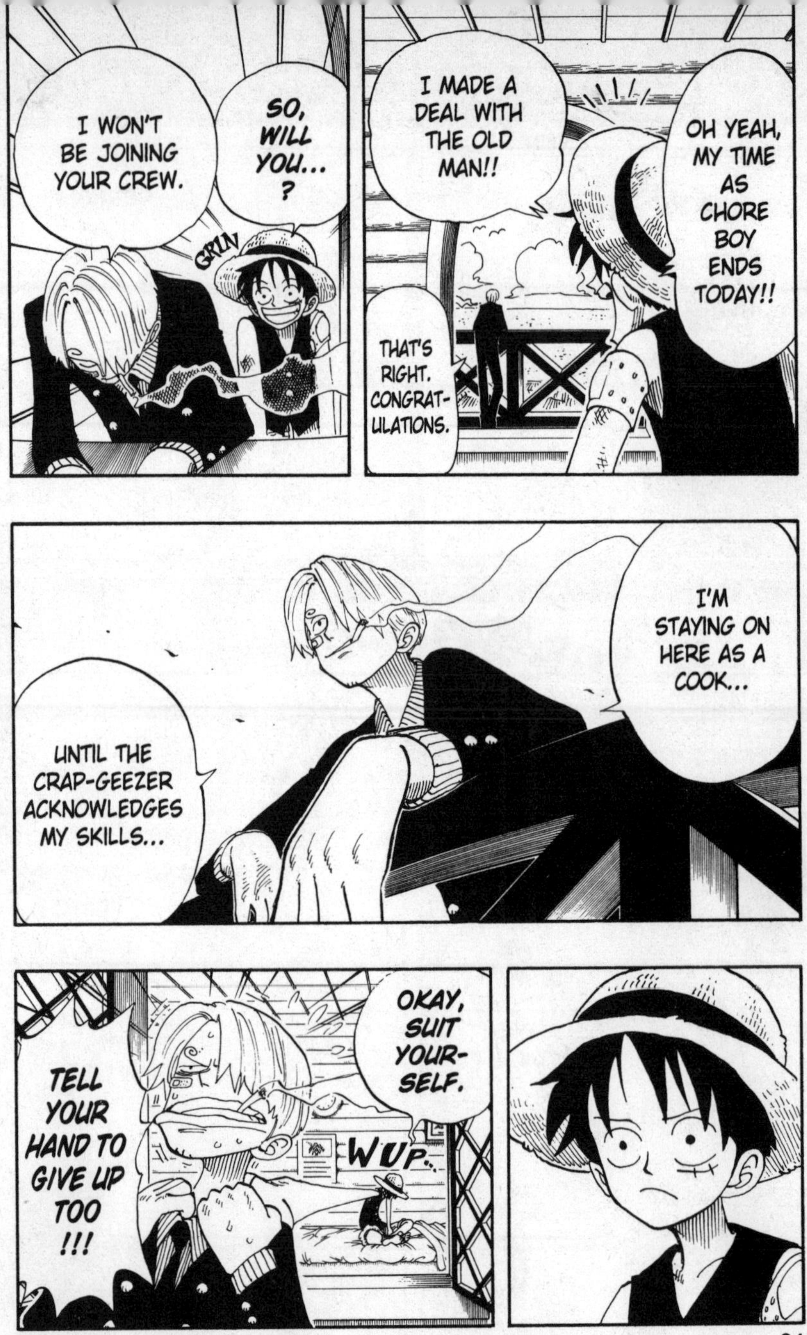

OH YEAH, MY TIME AS CHORE BOY ENDS TODAY!!
I MADE A DEAL WITH THE OLD MAN!!
THAT'S RIGHT. CONGRATULATIONS.
SO, WILL YOU... ?
I WON'T BE JOINING YOUR CREW.
GRIN
I'M STAYING ON HERE AS A COOK...
UNTIL THE CRAP-GEEZER ACKNOWLEDGES MY SKILLS...
OKAY, SUIT YOURSELF.
WUP..
TELL YOUR HAND TO GIVE UP TOO !!!

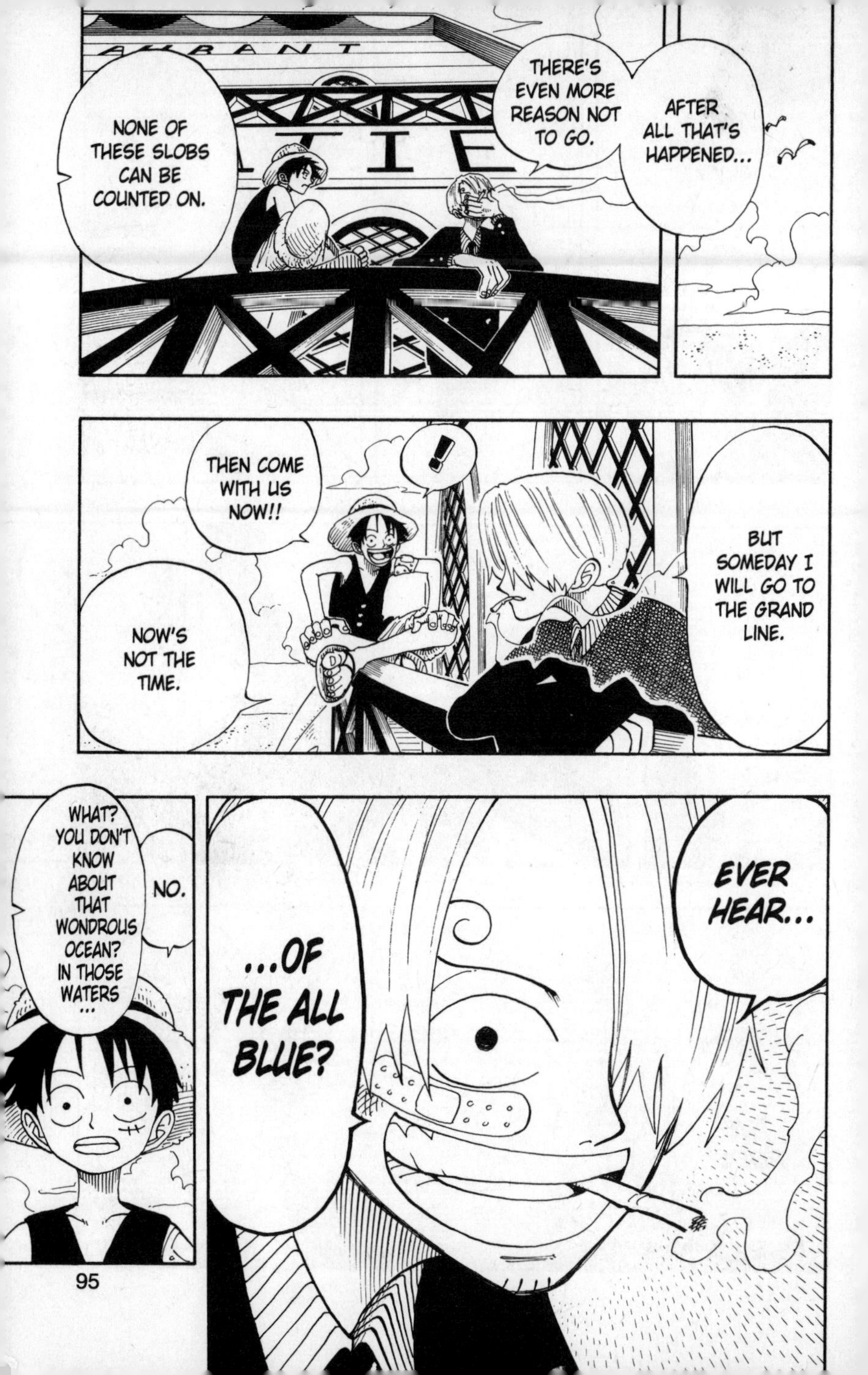
AFTER ALL THAT'S HAPPENED...
THERE'S EVEN MORE REASON NOT TO GO.
NONE OF THESE SLOBS CAN BE COUNTED ON.
BUT SOMEDAY I WILL GO TO THE GRAND LINE.
!
THEN COME WITH US NOW!!
NOW'S NOT THE TIME.
EVER HEAR...
...OF THE ALL BLUE?
NO.
WHAT? YOU DON'T KNOW ABOUT THAT WONDROUS OCEAN? IN THOSE WATERS...

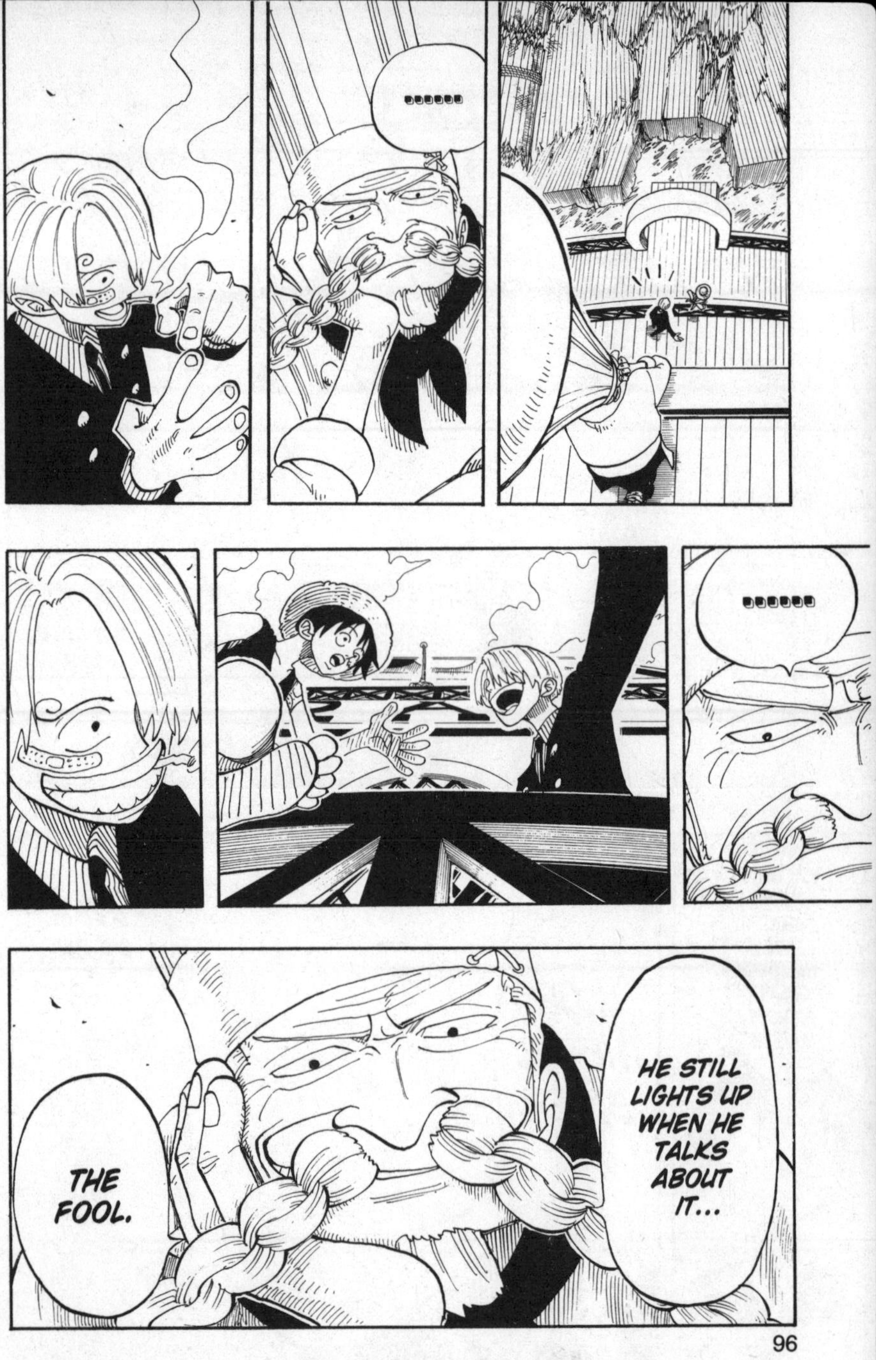
......
......
HE STILL LIGHTS UP WHEN HE TALKS ABOUT IT...
THE FOOL.

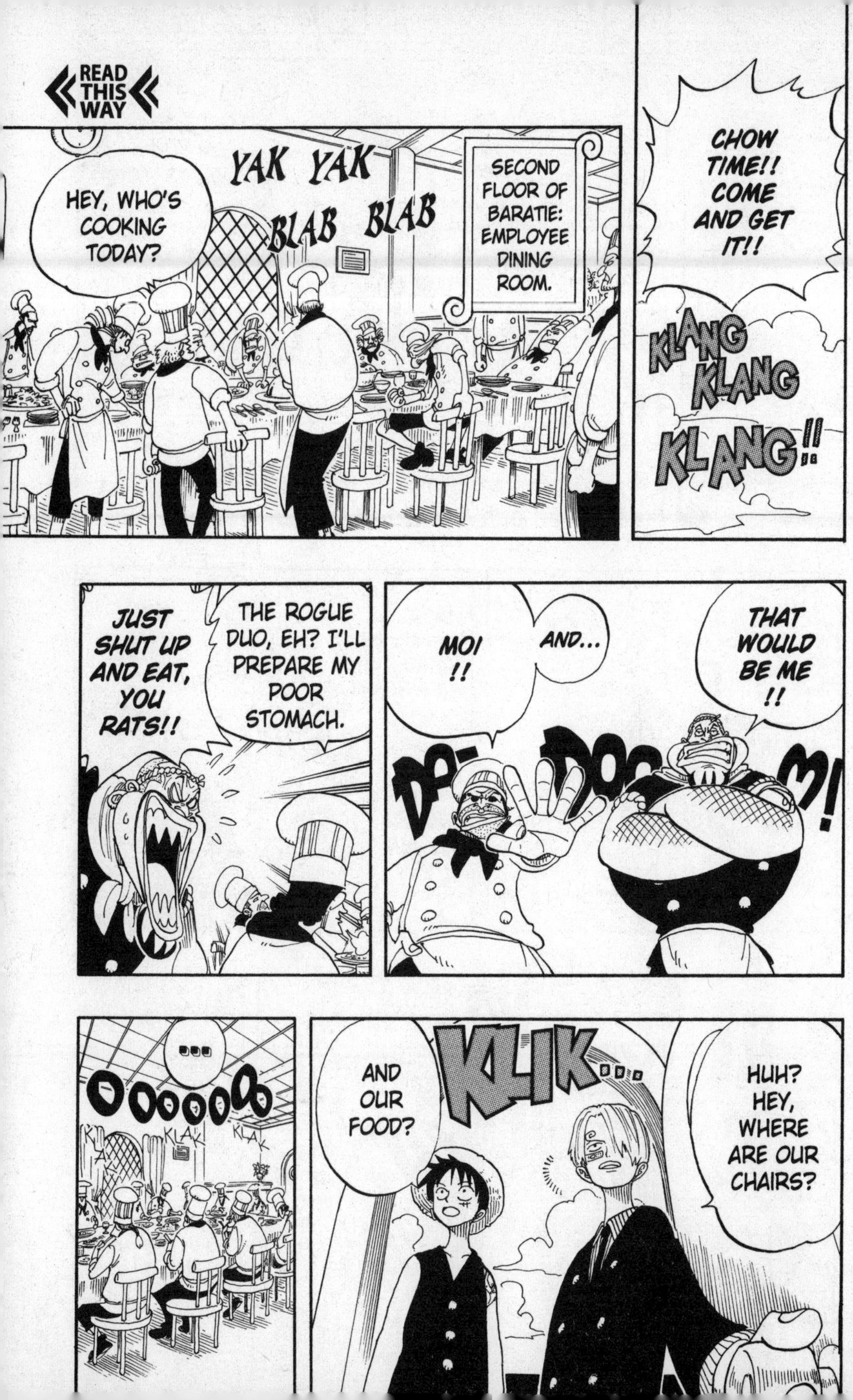
READ THIS WAY
CHOW TIME!! COME AND GET IT!!
KLANG KLANG KLANG!!
SECOND FLOOR OF BARATIE: EMPLOYEE DINING ROOM.
YAK YAK BLAB BLAB
HEY, WHO'S COOKING TODAY?
THAT WOULD BE ME !!
AND...
MOI !!
DO- DOO M!
THE ROGUE DUO, EH? I'LL PREPARE MY POOR STOMACH.
JUST SHUT UP AND EAT, YOU RATS!!
HUH? HEY, WHERE ARE OUR CHAIRS?
KLIK...
AND OUR FOOD?
...
KLAK KLAK

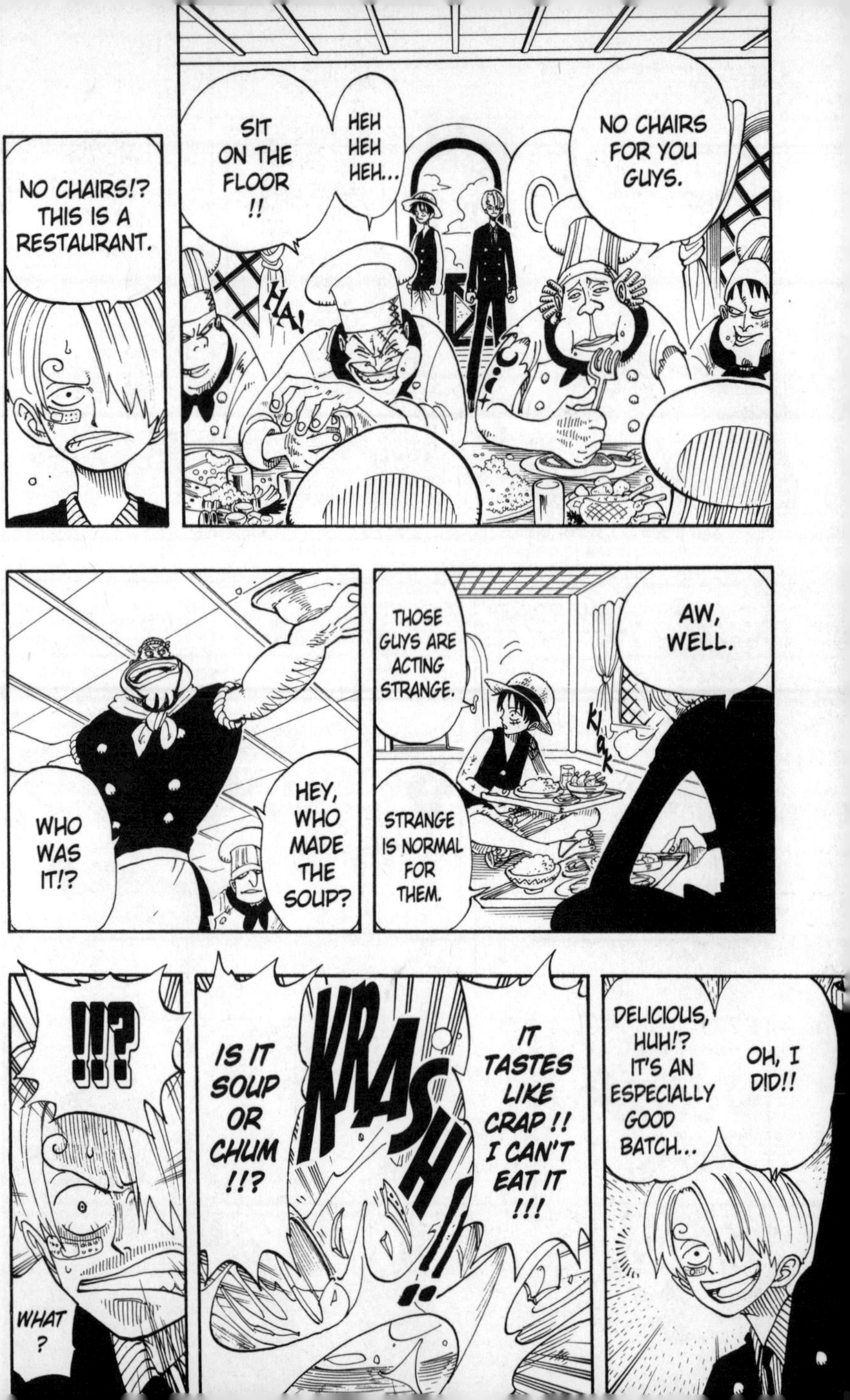
NO CHAIRS FOR YOU GUYS.
HEH HEH HEH...
SIT ON THE FLOOR !!
HA!
NO CHAIRS!? THIS IS A RESTAURANT.
AW, WELL.
THOSE GUYS ARE ACTING STRANGE.
KLAK
STRANGE IS NORMAL FOR THEM.
HEY, WHO MADE THE SOUP?
WHO WAS IT!?
OH, I DID!!
DELICIOUS, HUH!? IT'S AN ESPECIALLY GOOD BATCH...
IT TASTES LIKE CRAP !! I CAN'T EAT IT !!!
KRASH!!
IS IT SOUP OR CHUM !!?
!!?
WHAT ?

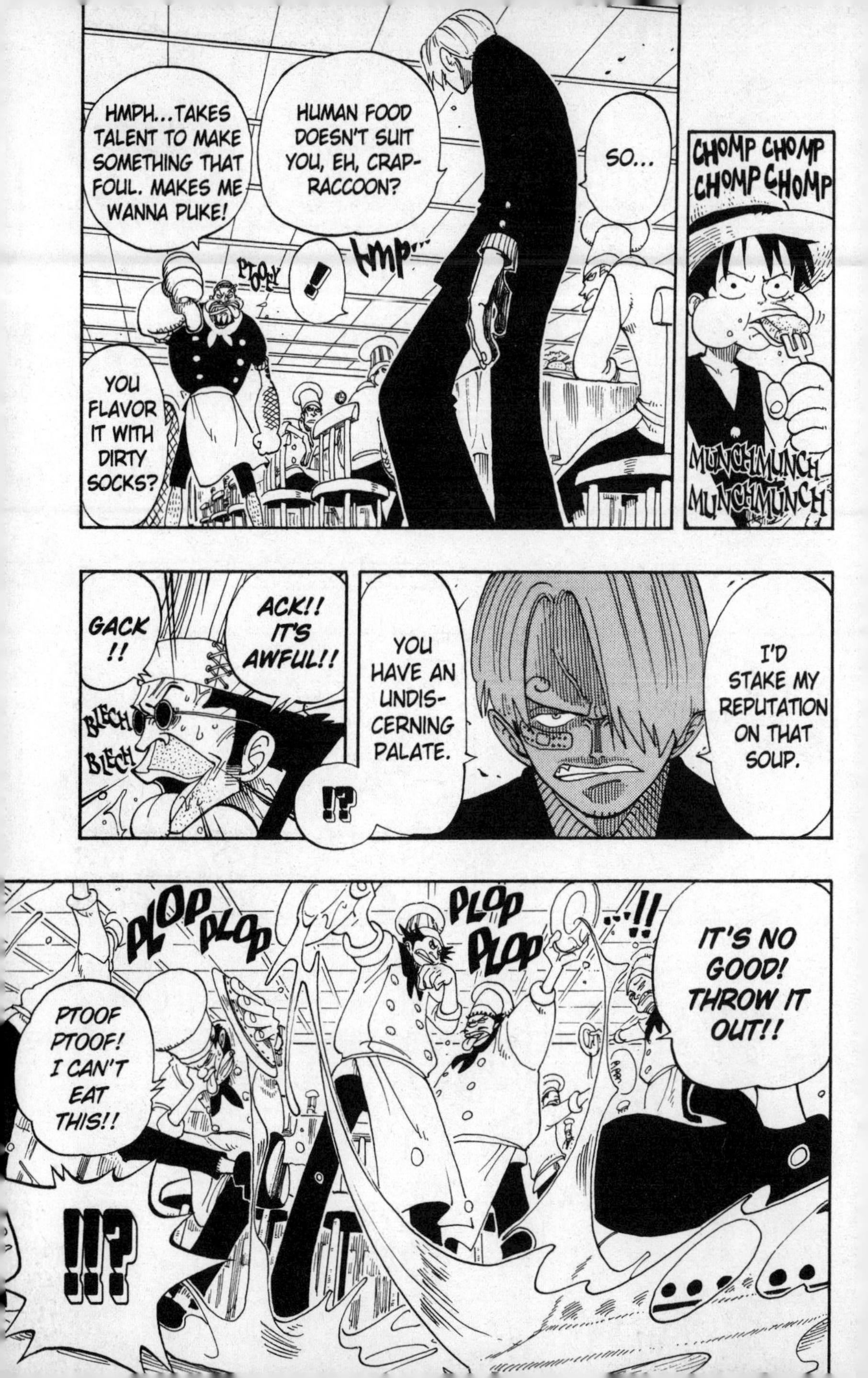
CHOMP CHOMP CHOMP CHOMP
MUNCHMUNCH MUNCHMUNCH
SO...
HUMAN FOOD DOESN'T SUIT YOU, EH, CRAP-RACCOON?
HMP...
!
HMPH...TAKES TALENT TO MAKE SOMETHING THAT FOUL. MAKES ME WANNA PUKE!
PTOOEY
YOU FLAVOR IT WITH DIRTY SOCKS?
I'D STAKE MY REPUTATION ON THAT SOUP.
YOU HAVE AN UNDISCERNING PALATE.
!?
ACK!! IT'S AWFUL!!
GACK !!
BLECH BLECH
IT'S NO GOOD! THROW IT OUT!!
...!!
PLOP PLOP
PLOP PLOP
PTOOF PTOOF! I CAN'T EAT THIS!!
!!?
......

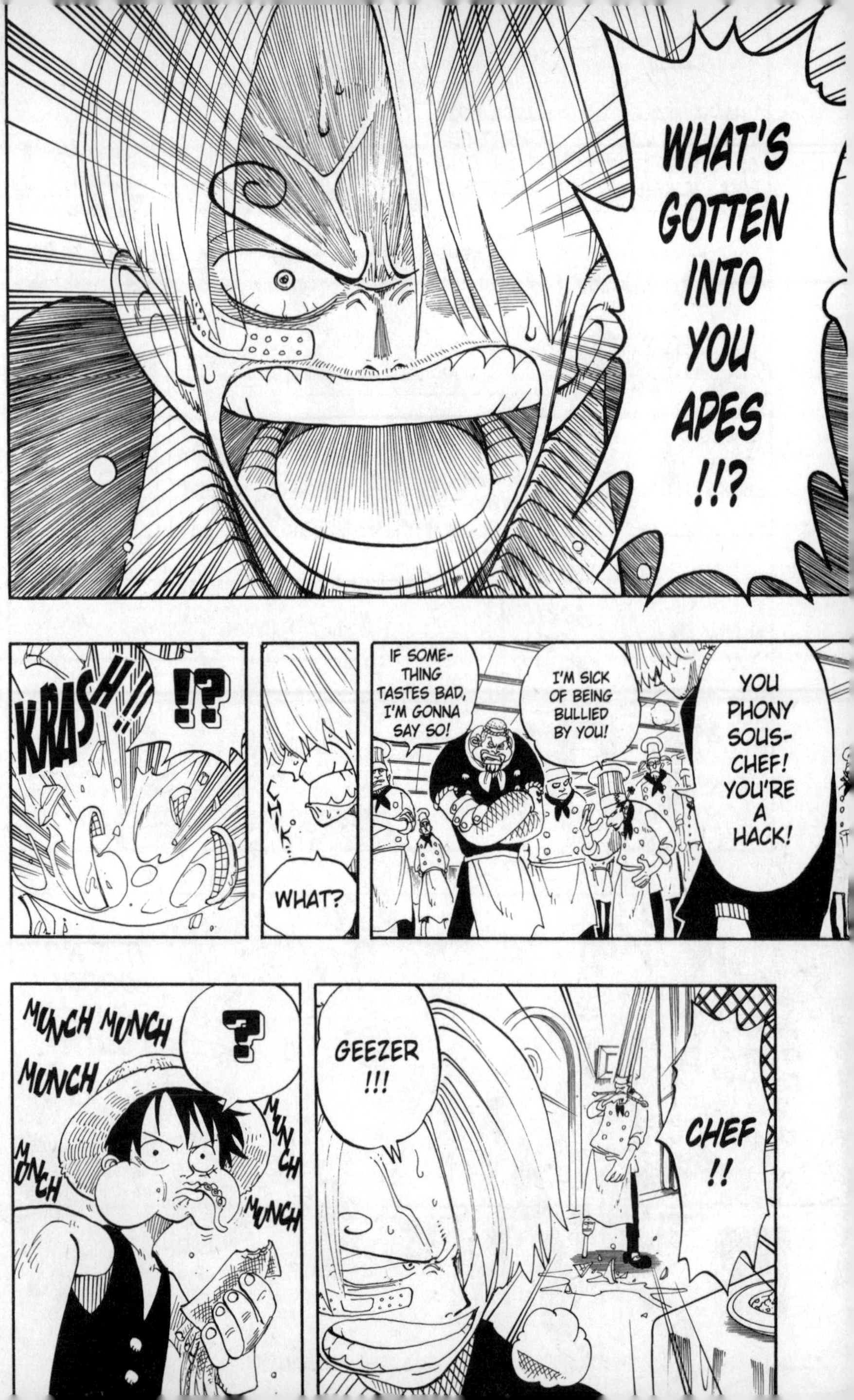
WHAT'S GOTTEN INTO YOU APES !!?
YOU PHONY SOUS-CHEF! YOU'RE A HACK!
I'M SICK OF BEING BULLIED BY YOU!
IF SOME-THING TASTES BAD, I'M GONNA SAY SO!
CHIK...
WHAT?
!?
KRASH!!
CHEF !!
GEEZER !!!
MUNCH
MUNCH
?
MUNCH MUNCH
MUNCH
MUNCH

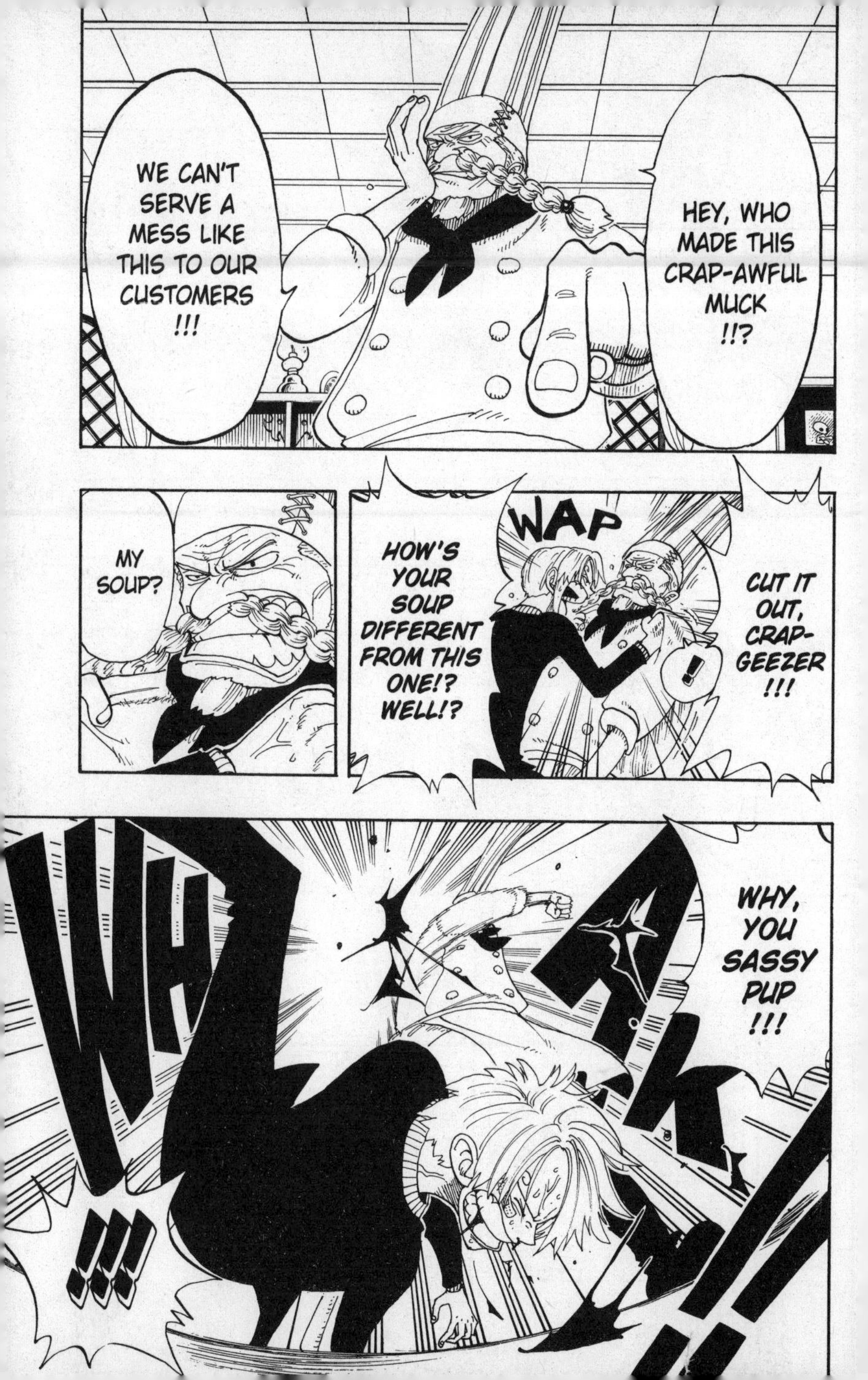
HEY, WHO MADE THIS CRAP-AWFUL MUCK !!?
WE CAN'T SERVE A MESS LIKE THIS TO OUR CUSTOMERS !!!
CUT IT OUT, CRAP-GEEZER !!!
WAP
HOW'S YOUR SOUP DIFFERENT FROM THIS ONE!? WELL!?
MY SOUP?
WHY, YOU SASSY PUP !!!
WHAK!!!

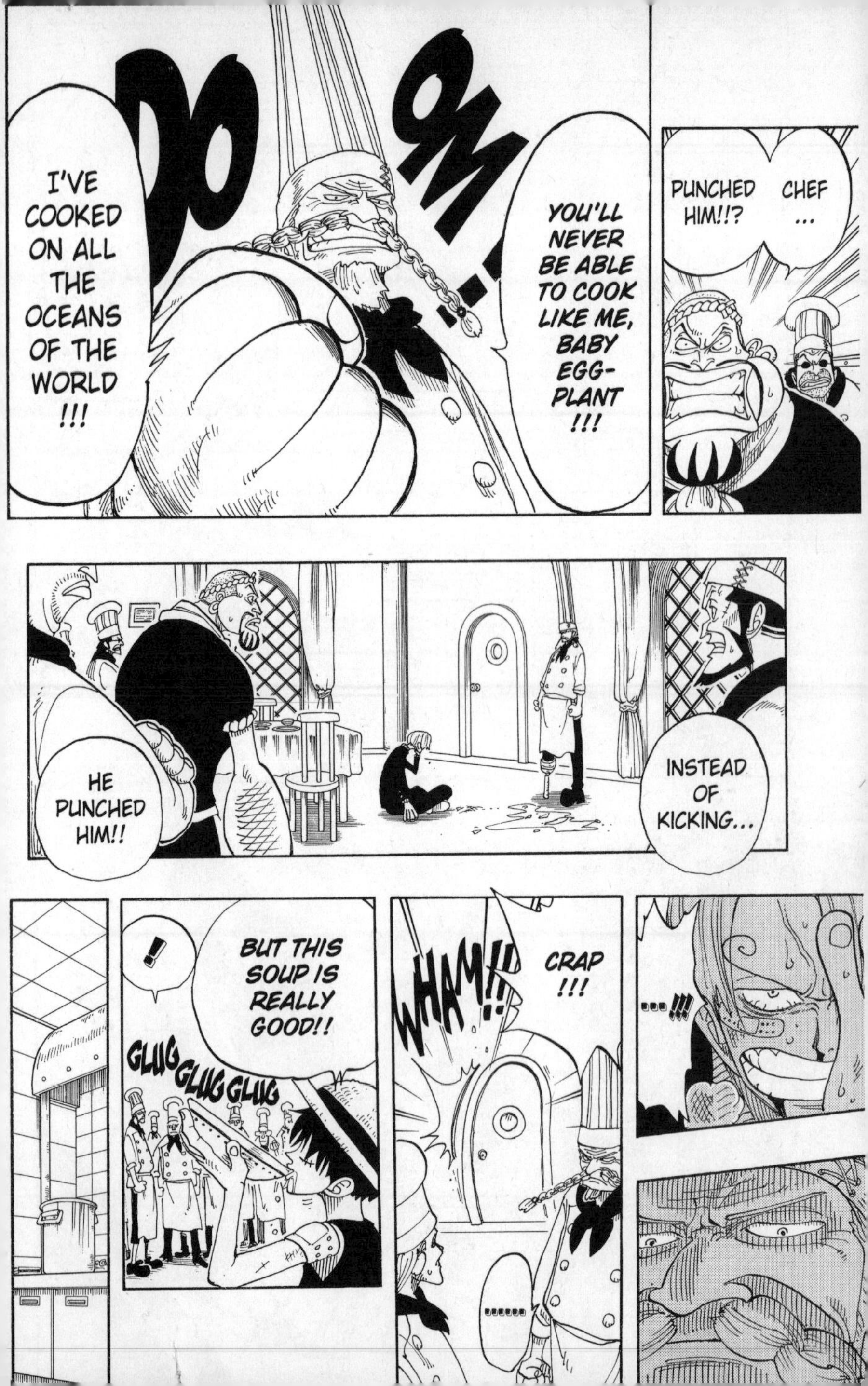
CHEF ...
PUNCHED HIM!!?
YOU'LL NEVER BE ABLE TO COOK LIKE ME, BABY EGG-PLANT!!!
DOOM...!
I'VE COOKED ON ALL THE OCEANS OF THE WORLD!!!
INSTEAD OF KICKING...
HE PUNCHED HIM!!
...!!!
CRAP!!!
WHAM!!
......
!
BUT THIS SOUP IS REALLY GOOD!!
GLUG GLUG GLUG

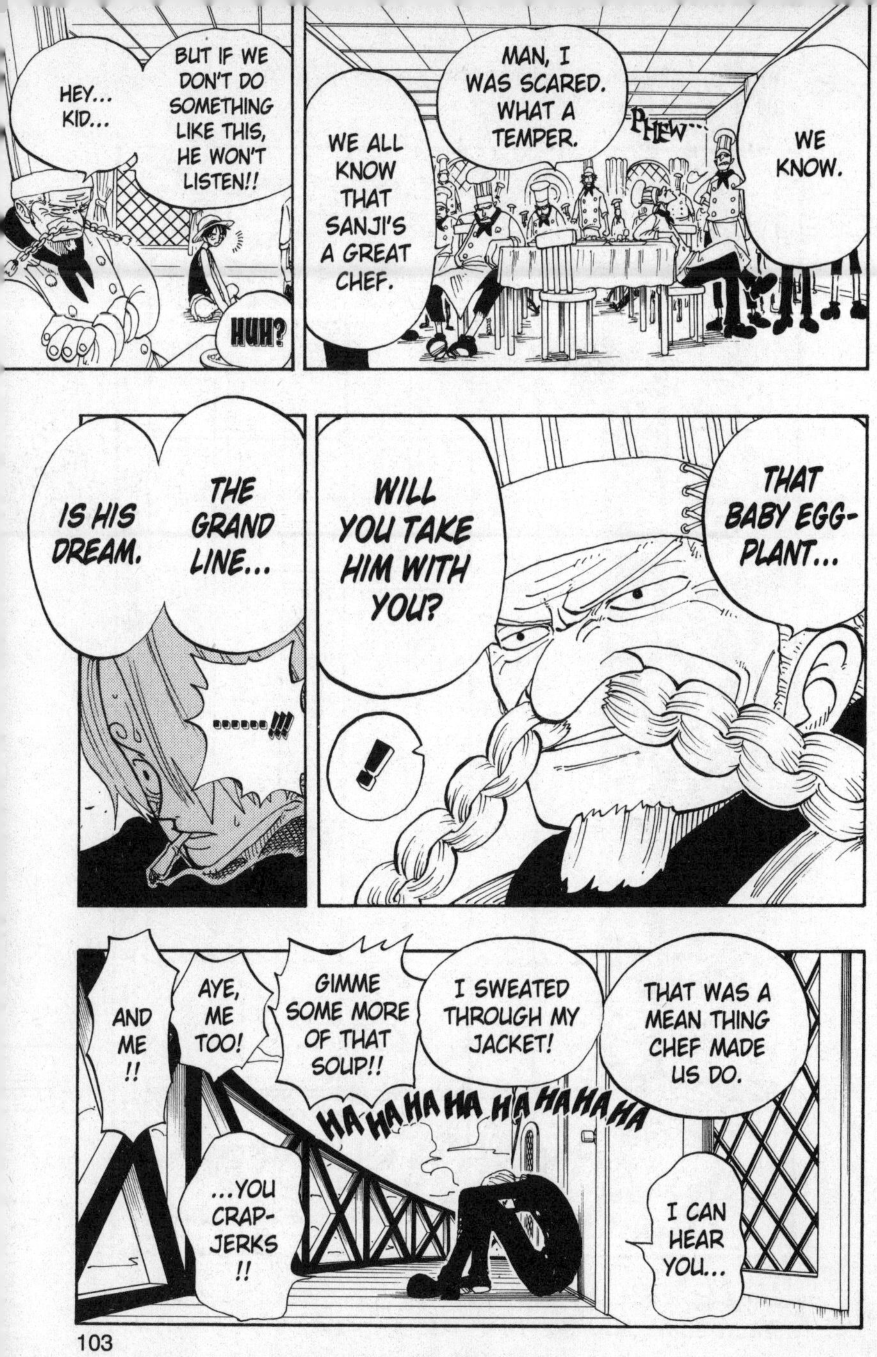
WE KNOW.
PHEW...
MAN, I WAS SCARED. WHAT A TEMPER.
WE ALL KNOW THAT SANJI'S A GREAT CHEF.
BUT IF WE DON'T DO SOMETHING LIKE THIS, HE WON'T LISTEN!!
HEY... KID...
HUH?
THAT BABY EGG-PLANT...
WILL YOU TAKE HIM WITH YOU?
!
THE GRAND LINE...
IS HIS DREAM.
......!!!
THAT WAS A MEAN THING CHEF MADE US DO.
I SWEATED THROUGH MY JACKET!
GIMME SOME MORE OF THAT SOUP!!
AYE, ME TOO!
AND ME !!
HAHAHAHA HAHAHAHAHA
I CAN HEAR YOU...
...YOU CRAP-JERKS !!

Q: Sensei, there's something I really want to have--
a *One Piece* Class Schedule!!

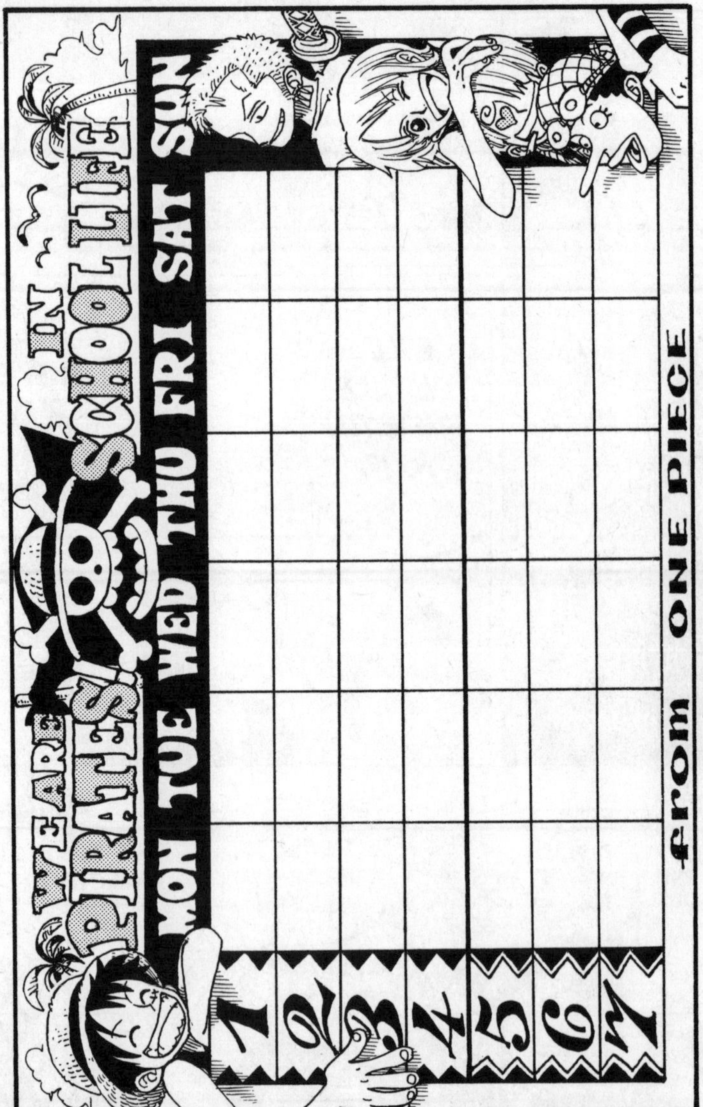
WE ARE PIRATES! IN SCHOOL LIFE
MON TUE WED THU FRI SAT SUN
1
2
3
4
5
6
7
from ONE PIECE

A: Class Schedule...ahhh...that brings back memories! How about something like this!? Use a copier to enlarge it or shrink it, and use it however you like!! Are there schools with seven periods? I drew it that way, just in case.

Chapter 68:
THE FOURTH PERSON

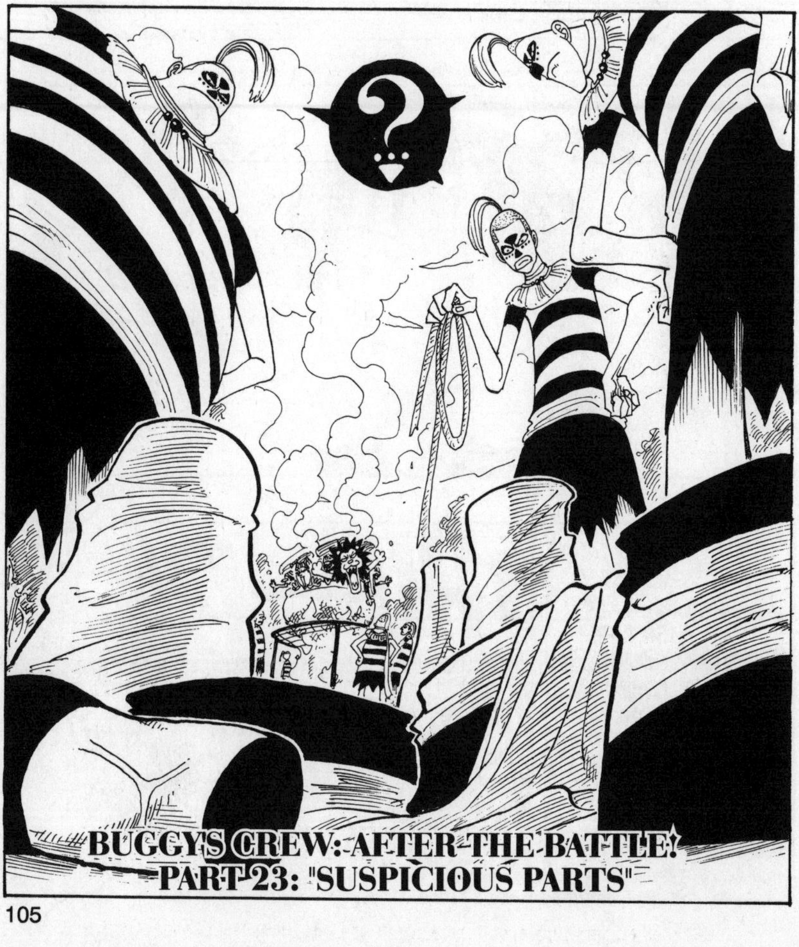
BUGGY'S CREW: AFTER THE BATTLE!
PART 23: "SUSPICIOUS PARTS"

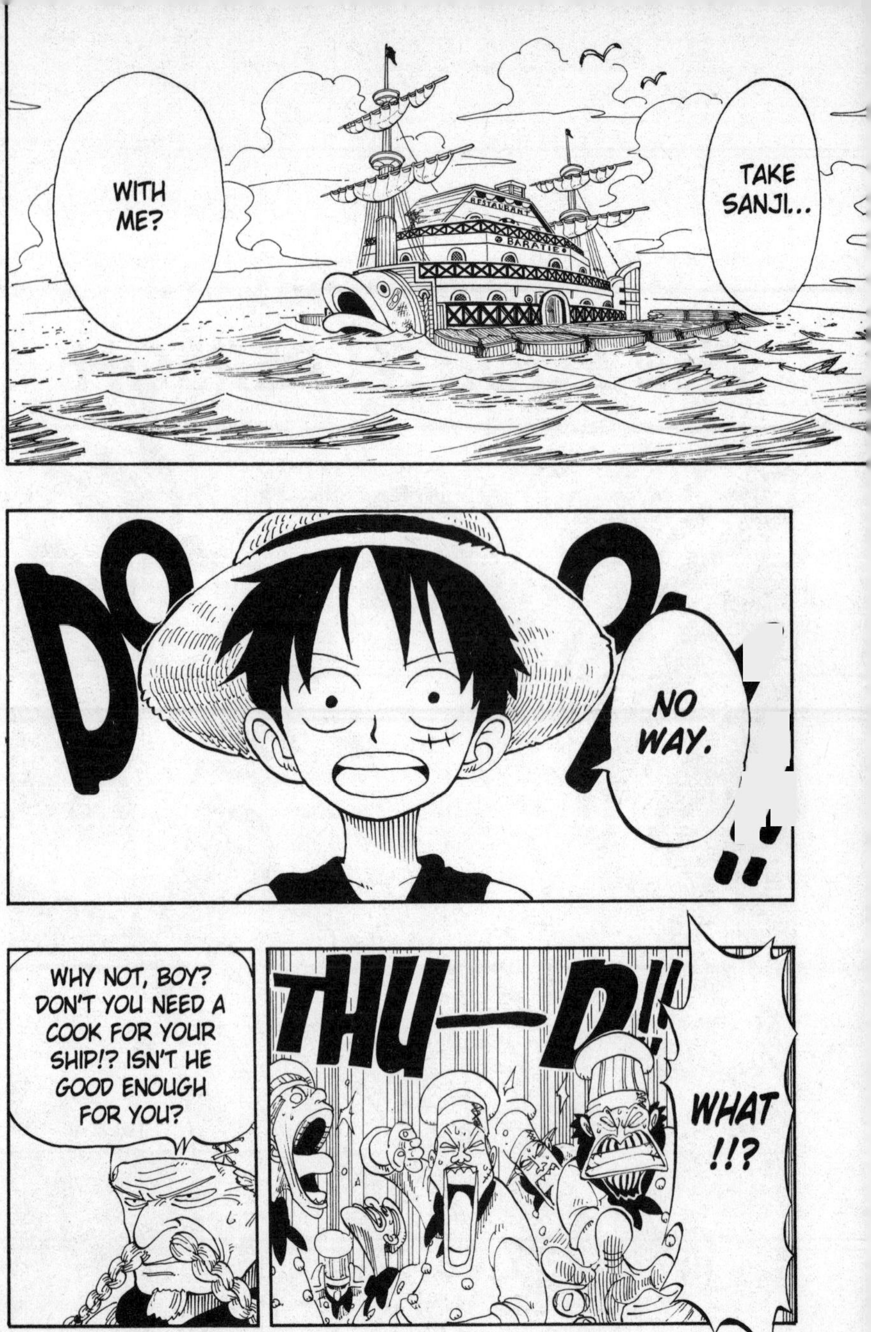
TAKE SANJI...
WITH ME?
NO WAY.
THU—D!!
WHAT !!?
WHY NOT, BOY? DON'T YOU NEED A COOK FOR YOUR SHIP!? ISN'T HE GOOD ENOUGH FOR YOU?

READ THIS WAY

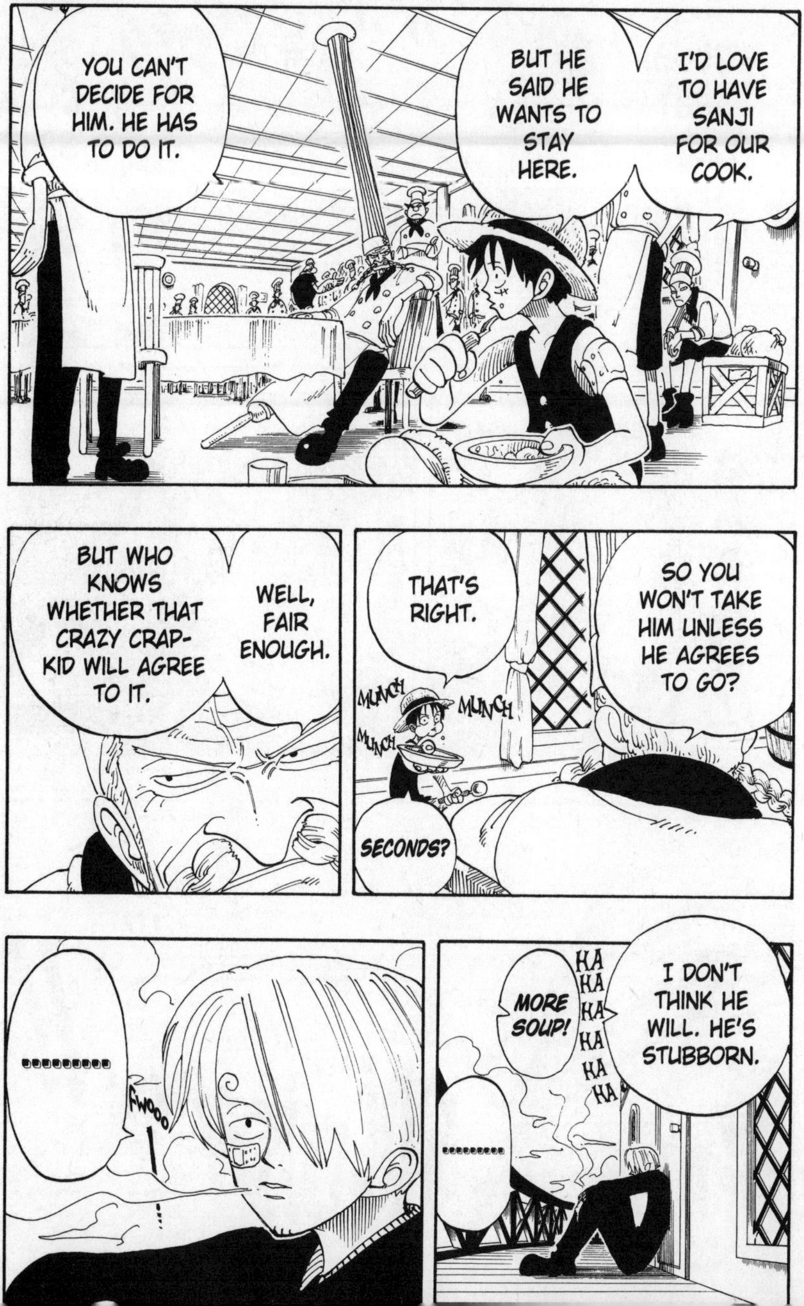
I'D LOVE TO HAVE SANJI FOR OUR COOK.
BUT HE SAID HE WANTS TO STAY HERE.
YOU CAN'T DECIDE FOR HIM. HE HAS TO DO IT.
SO YOU WON'T TAKE HIM UNLESS HE AGREES TO GO?
THAT'S RIGHT.
MUNCH
MUNCH
MUNCH
SECONDS?
WELL, FAIR ENOUGH.
BUT WHO KNOWS WHETHER THAT CRAZY CRAP-KID WILL AGREE TO IT.
I DON'T THINK HE WILL. HE'S STUBBORN.
HA HA HA HA HA HA HA
MORE SOUP!
....
....
FWOOO

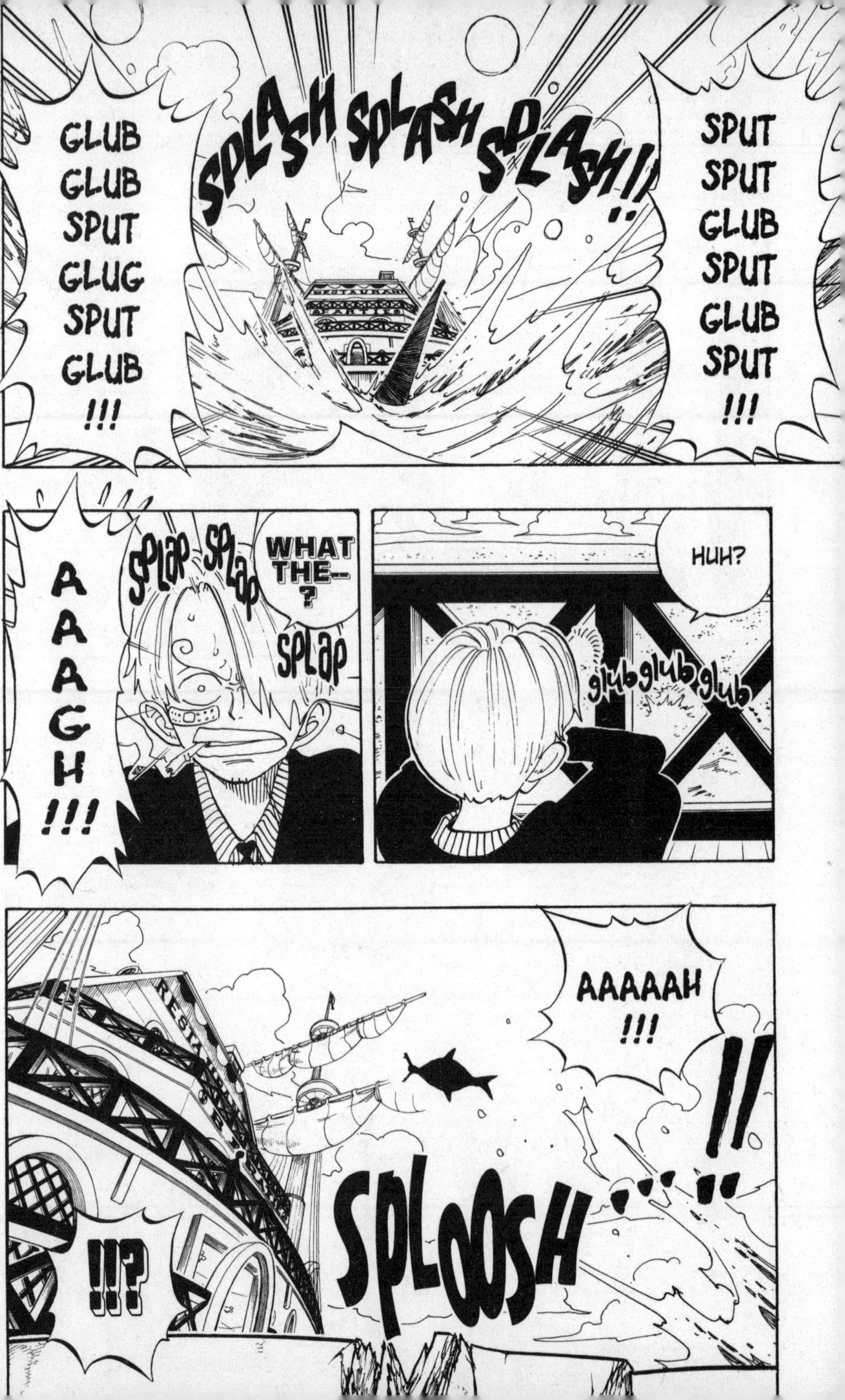
SPUT SPUT GLUB SPUT GLUB SPUT!!!
SPLASH SPLASH SPLASH!!
GLUB GLUB SPUT GLUG SPUT GLUB!!!
HUH?
glub glub glub
WHAT THE--?
SPLAP
SPLAP
SPLAP
AAAGH!!!
AAAAAH!!!
!!
SPLOOSH
!!?

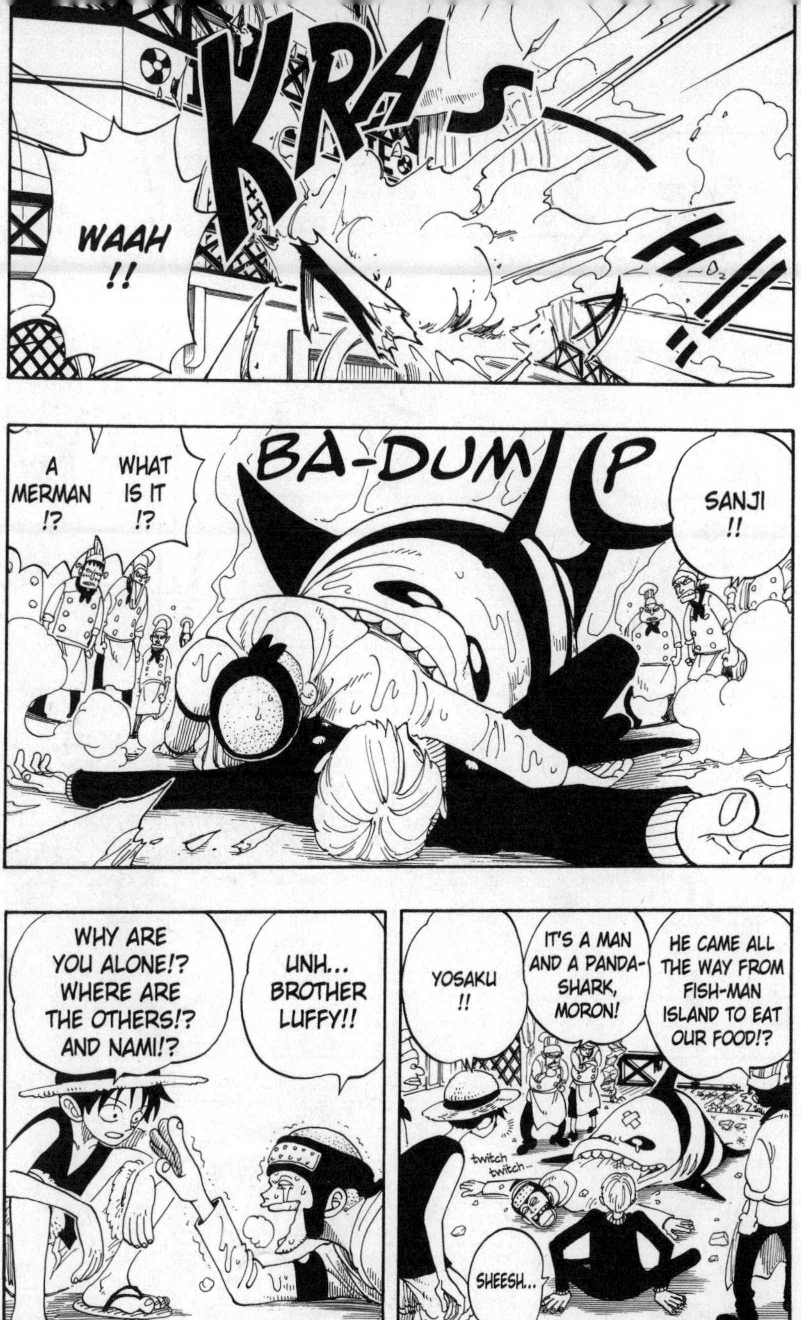

KRA-SH!!
WAAH!!
SANJI!!
BA-DUMP
WHAT IS IT!?
A MERMAN!?
HE CAME ALL THE WAY FROM FISH-MAN ISLAND TO EAT OUR FOOD!?
IT'S A MAN AND A PANDA-SHARK, MORON!
YOSAKU!!
twitch twitch...
SHEESH...
UNH... BROTHER LUFFY!!
WHY ARE YOU ALONE!? WHERE ARE THE OTHERS!? AND NAMI!?

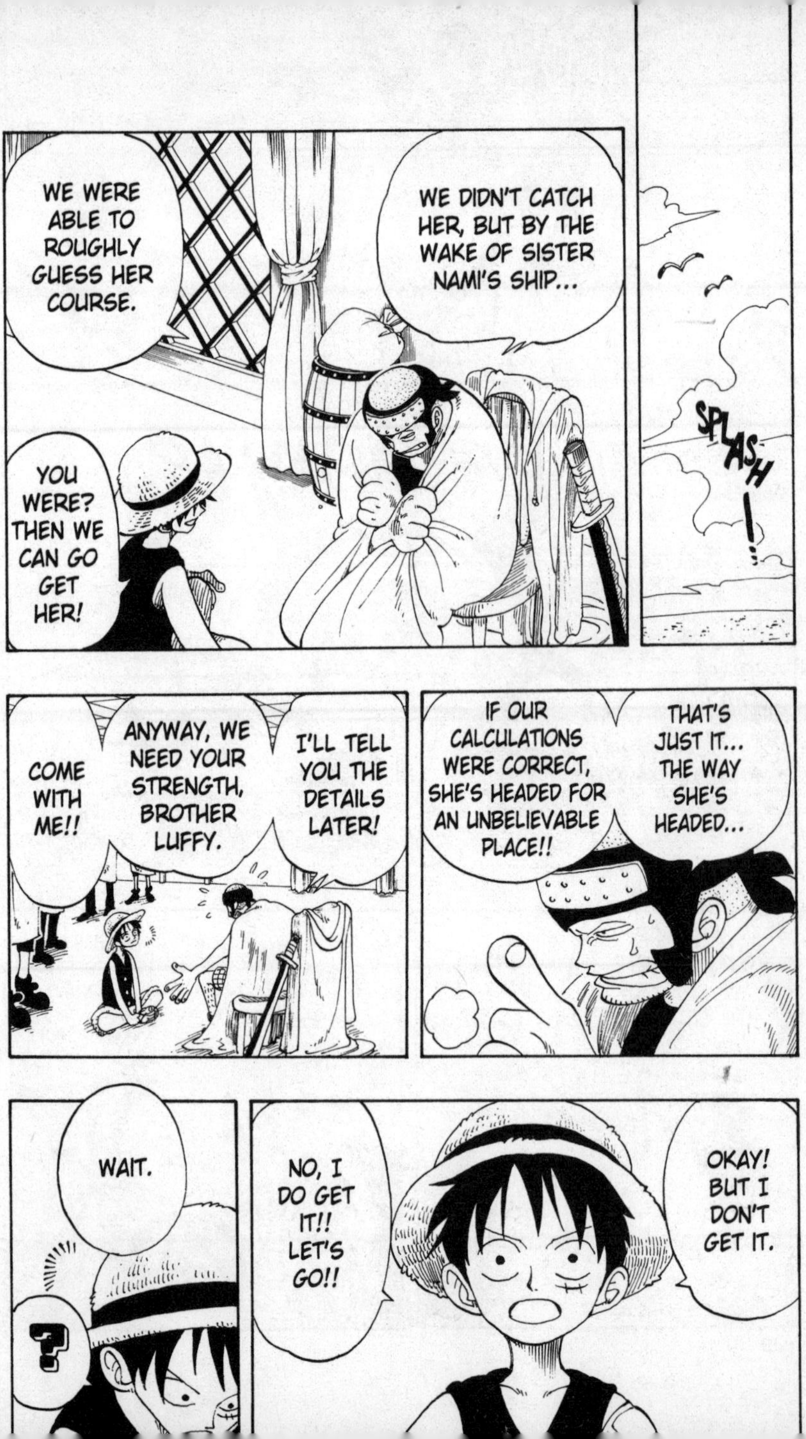
SPLASH!!
WE DIDN'T CATCH HER, BUT BY THE WAKE OF SISTER NAMI'S SHIP...
WE WERE ABLE TO ROUGHLY GUESS HER COURSE.
YOU WERE? THEN WE CAN GO GET HER!
THAT'S JUST IT... THE WAY SHE'S HEADED...
IF OUR CALCULATIONS WERE CORRECT, SHE'S HEADED FOR AN UNBELIEVABLE PLACE!!
I'LL TELL YOU THE DETAILS LATER!
ANYWAY, WE NEED YOUR STRENGTH, BROTHER LUFFY.
COME WITH ME!!
OKAY! BUT I DON'T GET IT.
NO, I DO GET IT!! LET'S GO!!
WAIT.
?

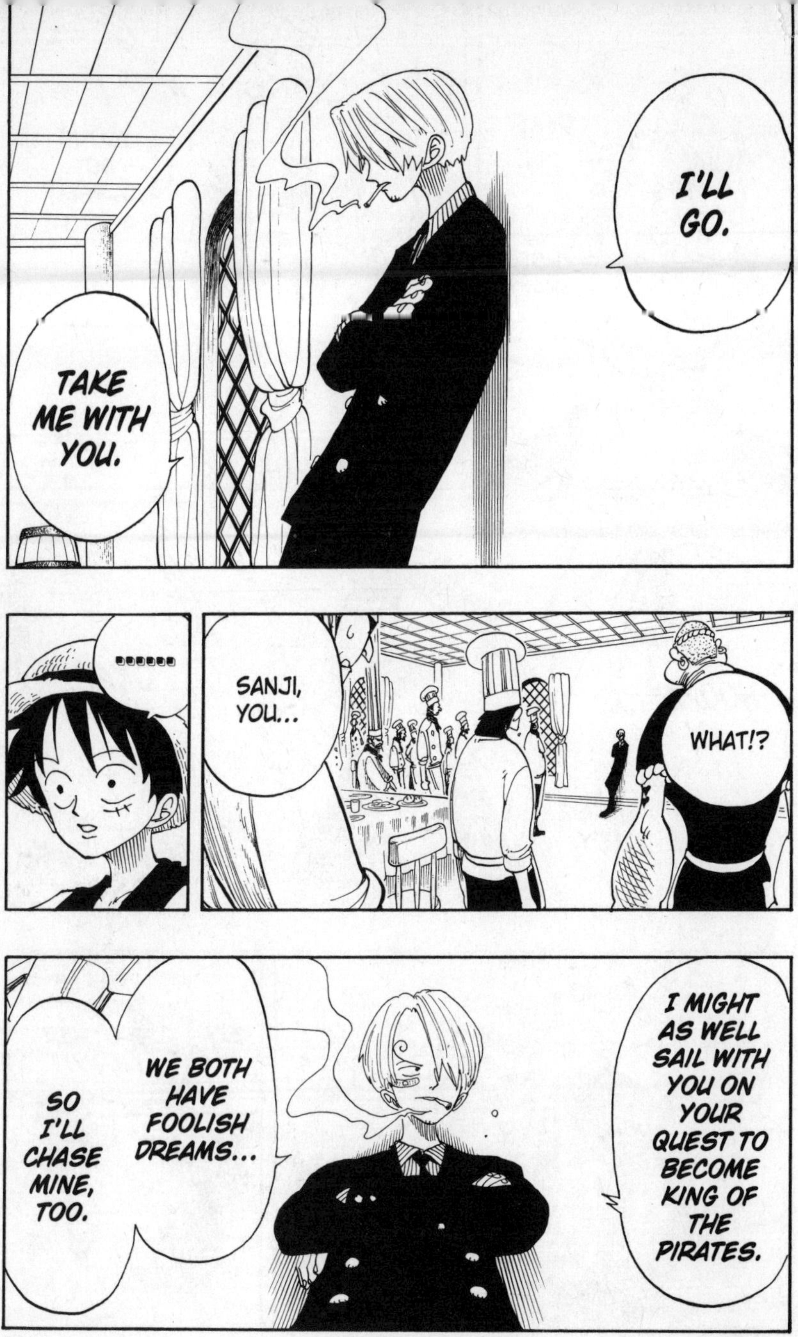
I'LL GO.
TAKE ME WITH YOU.
WHAT!?
SANJI, YOU...
......
I MIGHT AS WELL SAIL WITH YOU ON YOUR QUEST TO BECOME KING OF THE PIRATES.
WE BOTH HAVE FOOLISH DREAMS...
SO I'LL CHASE MINE, TOO.

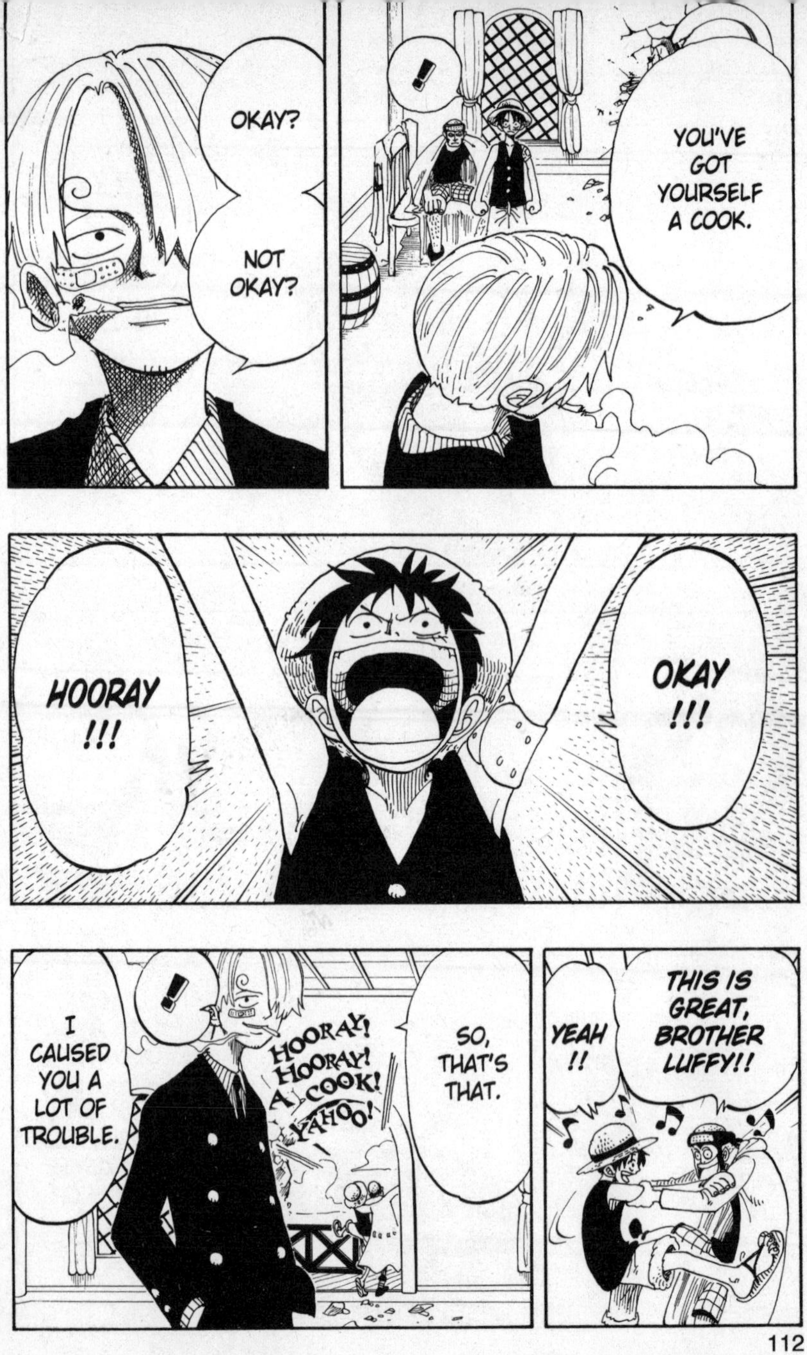
YOU'VE GOT YOURSELF A COOK.
!
OKAY?
NOT OKAY?
OKAY !!!
HOORAY !!!
THIS IS GREAT, BROTHER LUFFY!!
YEAH !!
SO, THAT'S THAT.
HOORAY! HOORAY! A COOK! YAHOO!
!
I CAUSED YOU A LOT OF TROUBLE.

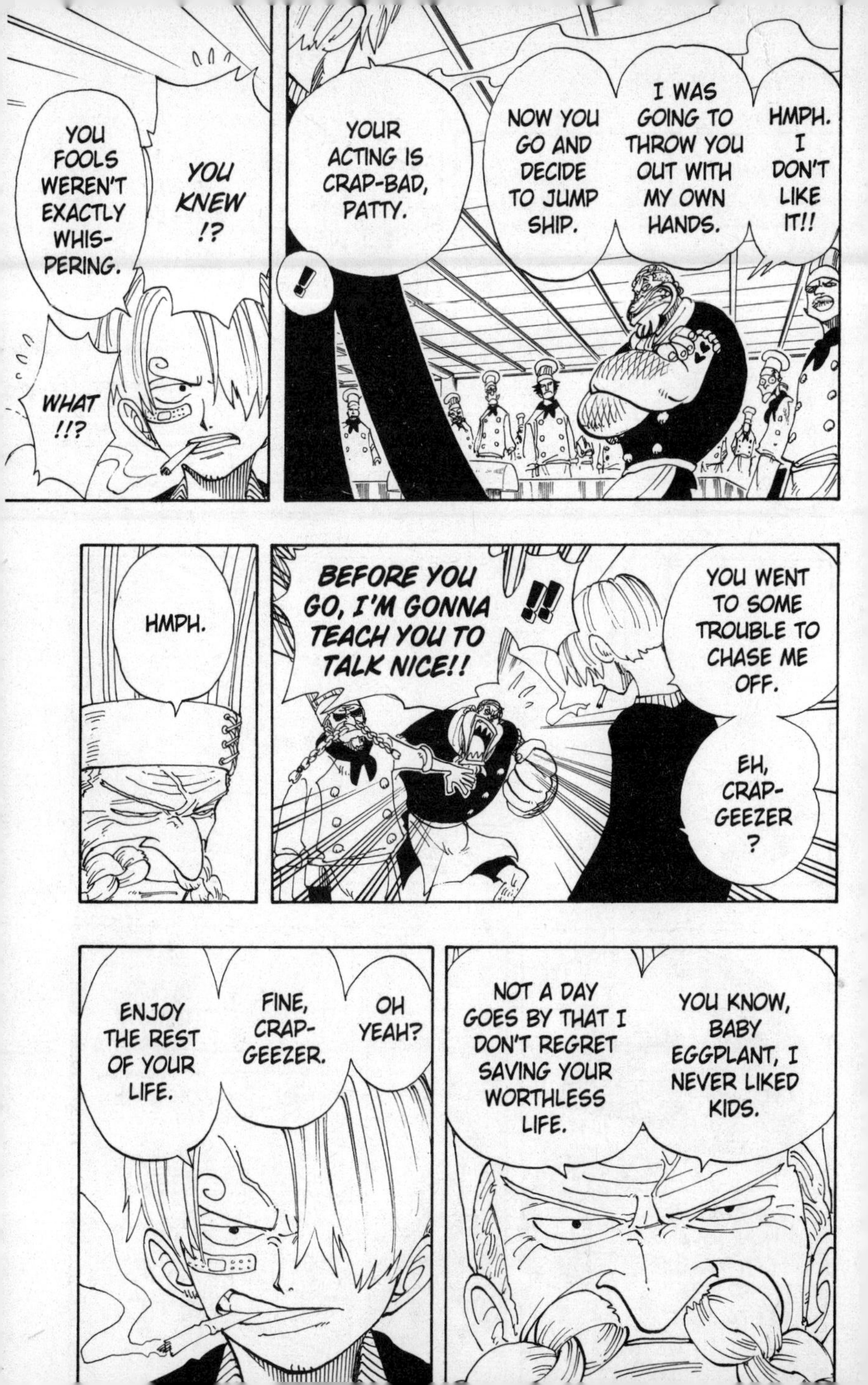
HMPH. I DON'T LIKE IT!!
I WAS GOING TO THROW YOU OUT WITH MY OWN HANDS.
NOW YOU GO AND DECIDE TO JUMP SHIP.
YOUR ACTING IS CRAP-BAD, PATTY.
!
YOU KNEW!?
YOU FOOLS WEREN'T EXACTLY WHISPERING.
WHAT!!?
YOU WENT TO SOME TROUBLE TO CHASE ME OFF.
EH, CRAP-GEEZER?
!!
BEFORE YOU GO, I'M GONNA TEACH YOU TO TALK NICE!!
HMPH.
YOU KNOW, BABY EGGPLANT, I NEVER LIKED KIDS.
NOT A DAY GOES BY THAT I DON'T REGRET SAVING YOUR WORTHLESS LIFE.
OH YEAH?
FINE, CRAP-GEEZER.
ENJOY THE REST OF YOUR LIFE.

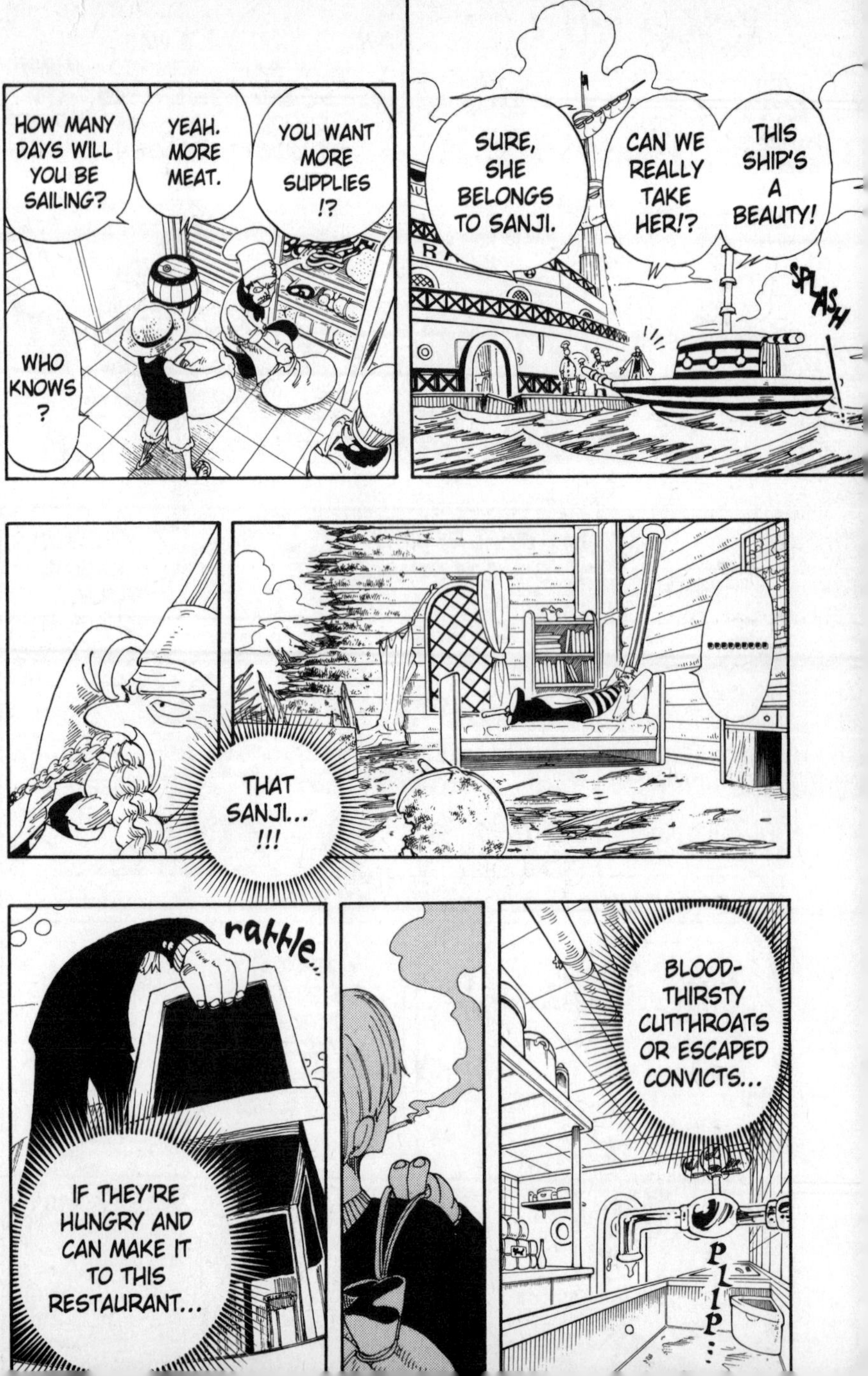
THIS SHIP'S A BEAUTY!
CAN WE REALLY TAKE HER!?
SURE, SHE BELONGS TO SANJI.
SPLASH
YOU WANT MORE SUPPLIES !?
YEAH. MORE MEAT.
HOW MANY DAYS WILL YOU BE SAILING?
WHO KNOWS ?
....
THAT SANJI... !!!
BLOOD-THIRSTY CUTTHROATS OR ESCAPED CONVICTS...
PLIP...
rattle...
IF THEY'RE HUNGRY AND CAN MAKE IT TO THIS RESTAURANT...

READ THIS WAY

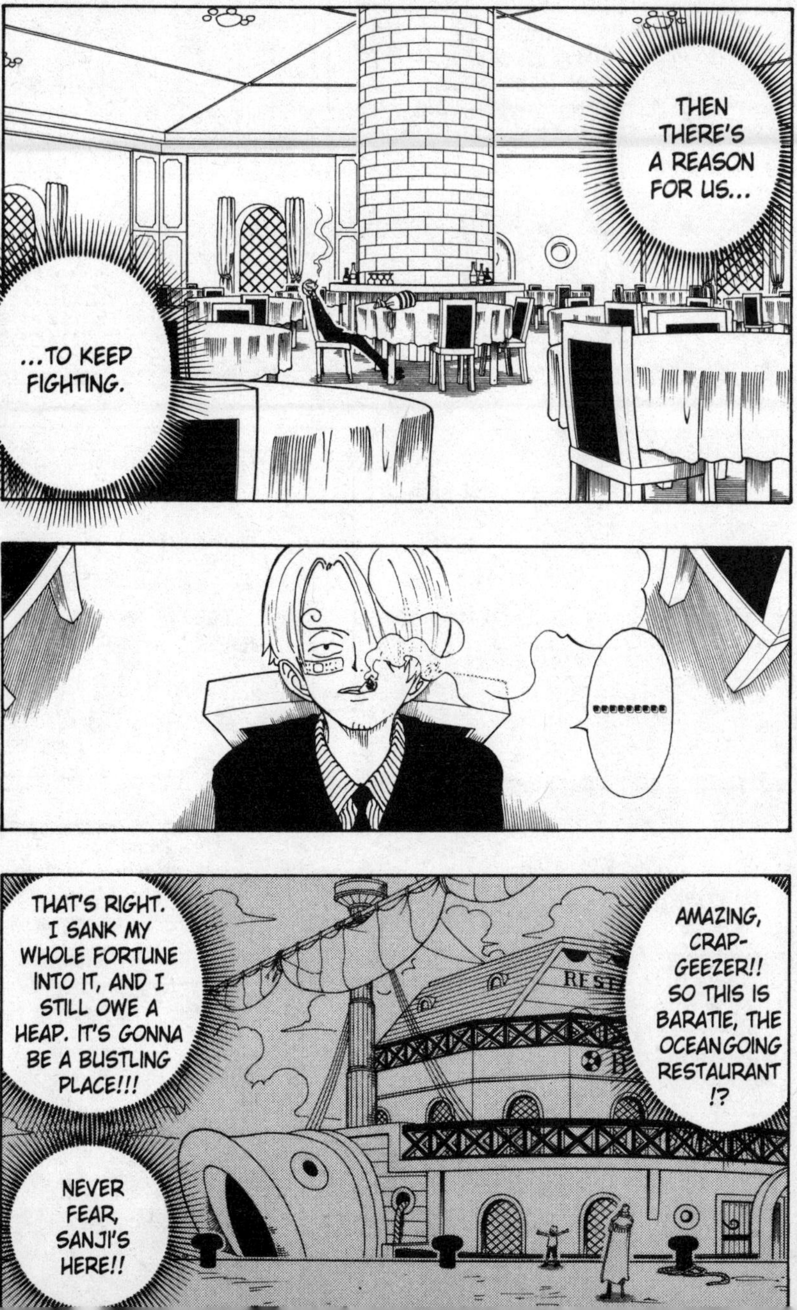
THEN THERE'S A REASON FOR US...
...TO KEEP FIGHTING.
....
AMAZING, CRAP-GEEZER!! SO THIS IS BARATIE, THE OCEANGOING RESTAURANT!?
THAT'S RIGHT. I SANK MY WHOLE FORTUNE INTO IT, AND I STILL OWE A HEAP. IT'S GONNA BE A BUSTLING PLACE!!!
NEVER FEAR, SANJI'S HERE!!

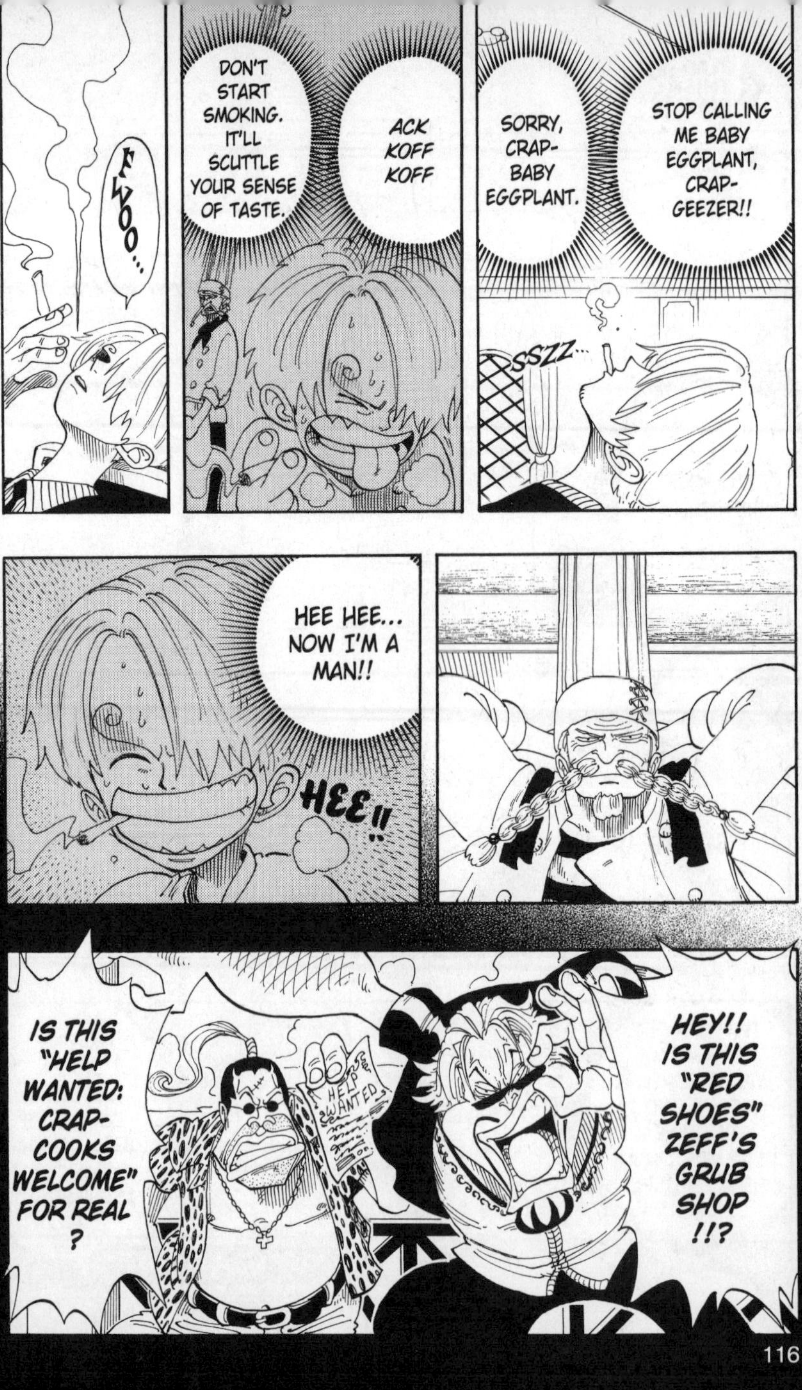
STOP CALLING ME BABY EGGPLANT, CRAP-GEEZER!!
SORRY, CRAP-BABY EGGPLANT.
SSZZ...
ACK KOFF KOFF
DON'T START SMOKING. IT'LL SCUTTLE YOUR SENSE OF TASTE.
FWOO...
HEE HEE... NOW I'M A MAN!!
HEE!!
HEY!! IS THIS "RED SHOES" ZEFF'S GRUB SHOP !!?
IS THIS "HELP WANTED: CRAP-COOKS WELCOME" FOR REAL ?
HELP WANTED

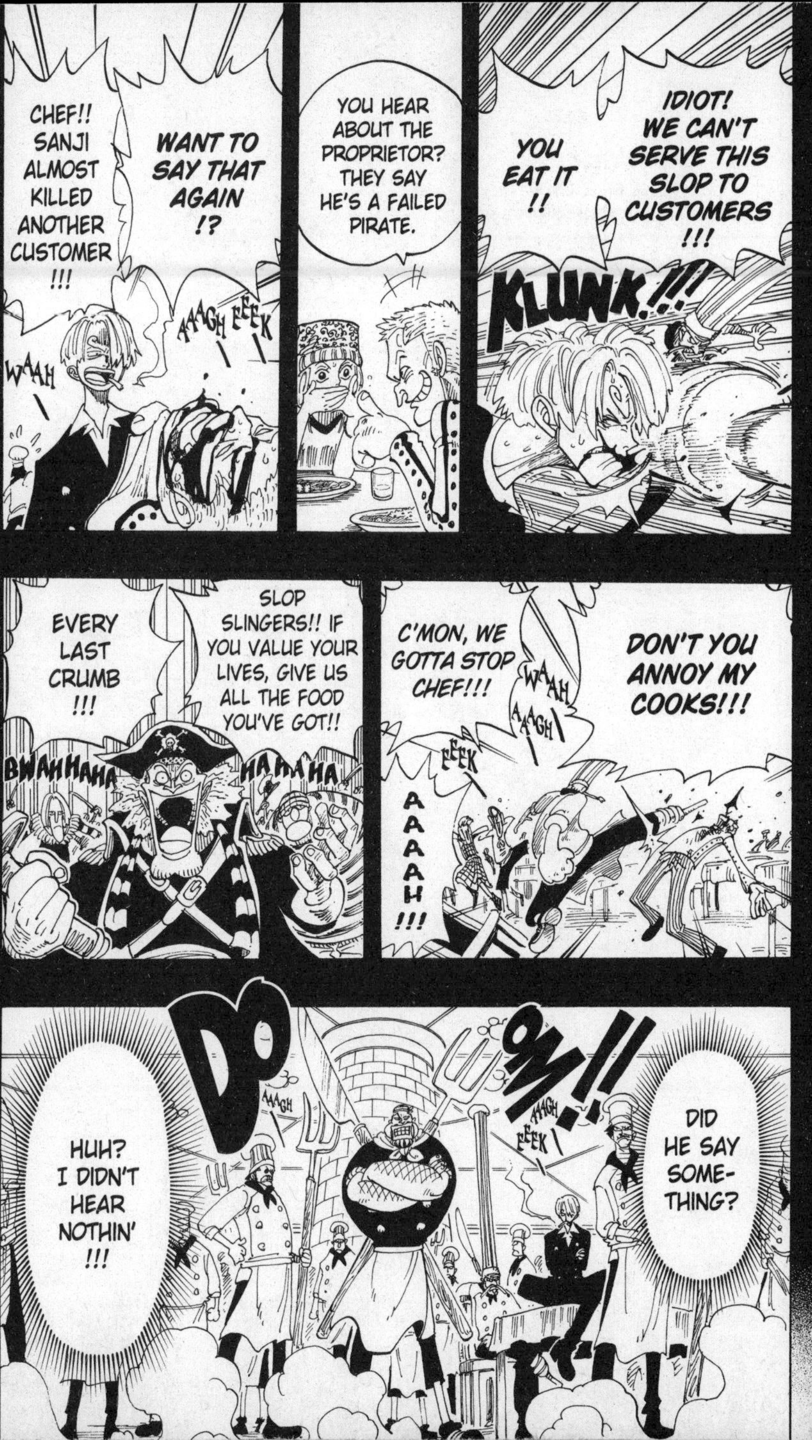
IDIOT! WE CAN'T SERVE THIS SLOP TO CUSTOMERS!!!
YOU EAT IT!!
KLUNK!!!
YOU HEAR ABOUT THE PROPRIETOR? THEY SAY HE'S A FAILED PIRATE.
WANT TO SAY THAT AGAIN!?
CHEF!! SANJI ALMOST KILLED ANOTHER CUSTOMER!!!
AAAGH
EEEK
WAAH
DON'T YOU ANNOY MY COOKS!!!
C'MON, WE GOTTA STOP CHEF!!!
WAAH
AAAGH
EEEK
AAAAAH!!!
SLOP SLINGERS!! IF YOU VALUE YOUR LIVES, GIVE US ALL THE FOOD YOU'VE GOT!!
EVERY LAST CRUMB!!!
HAHAHA
BWAHHAHA
DOOM!!
DID HE SAY SOMETHING?
AAAGH
EEEK
AAAGH
HUH? I DIDN'T HEAR NOTHIN'!!!

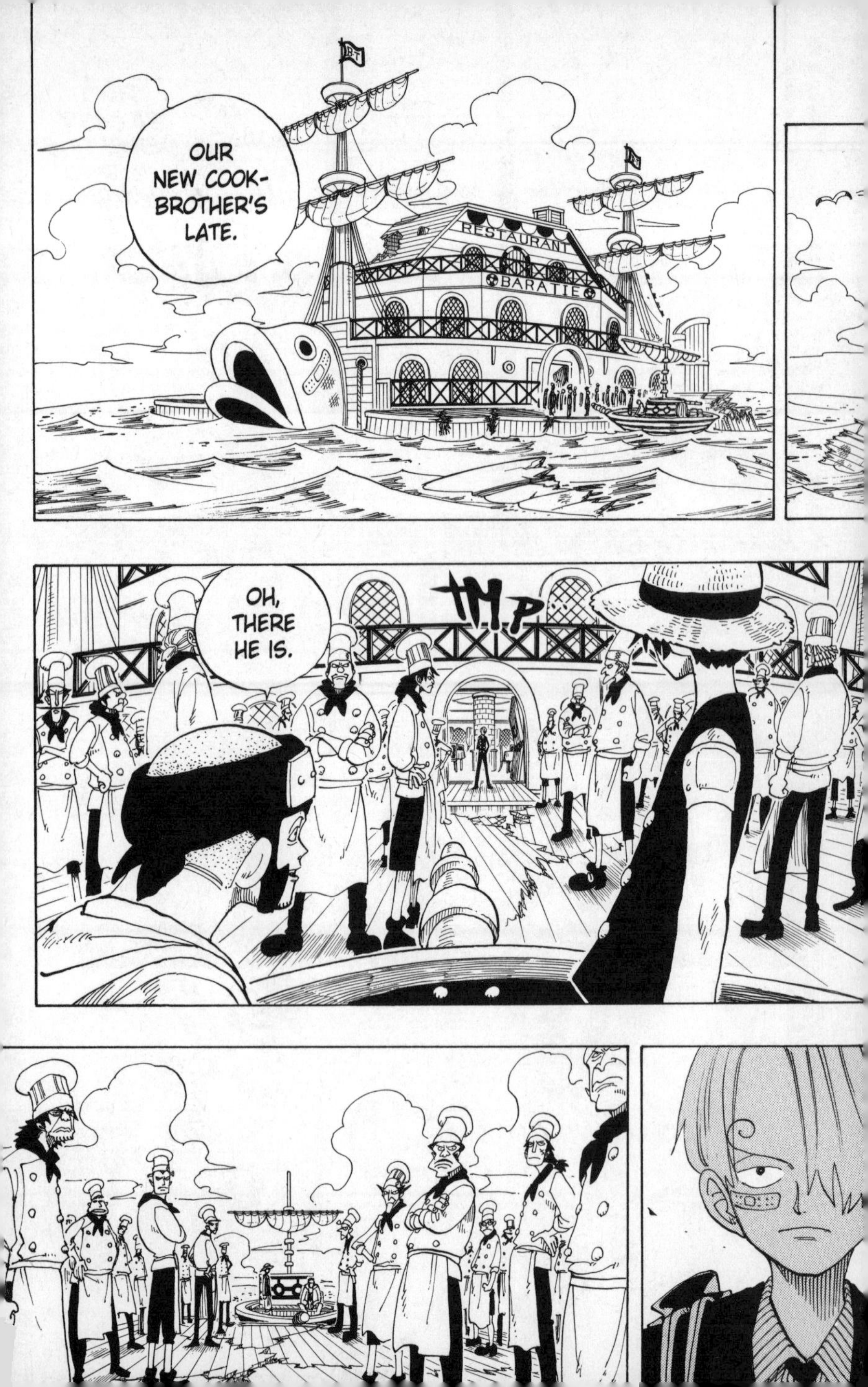
OUR NEW COOK-BROTHER'S LATE.
TMP
OH, THERE HE IS.

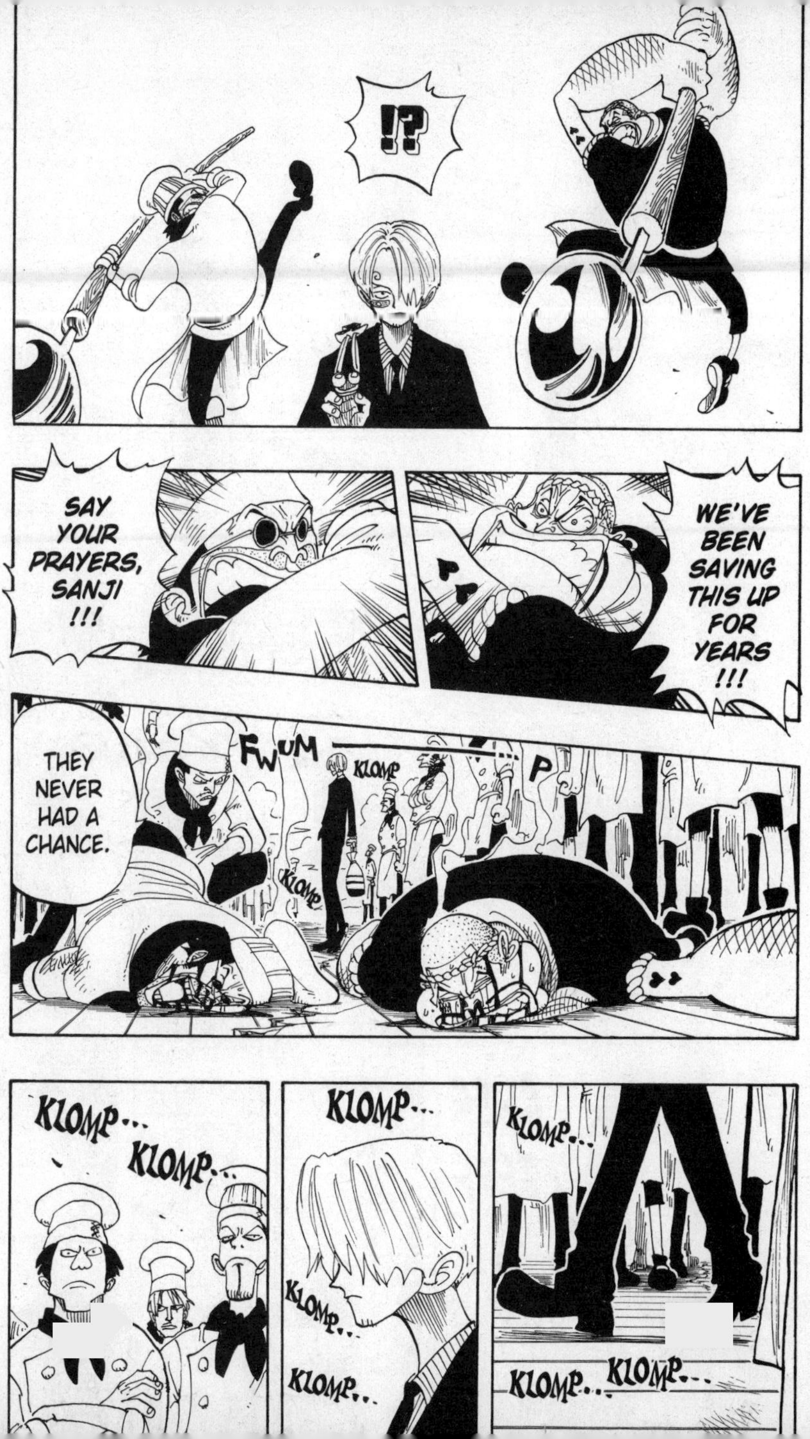
!?
WE'VE BEEN SAVING THIS UP FOR YEARS!!!
SAY YOUR PRAYERS, SANJI!!!
FWUM P
KLOMP
KLOMP
THEY NEVER HAD A CHANCE.
KLOMP...
KLOMP...
KLOMP...
KLOMP...
KLOMP...
KLOMP...
KLOMP...
KLOMP...

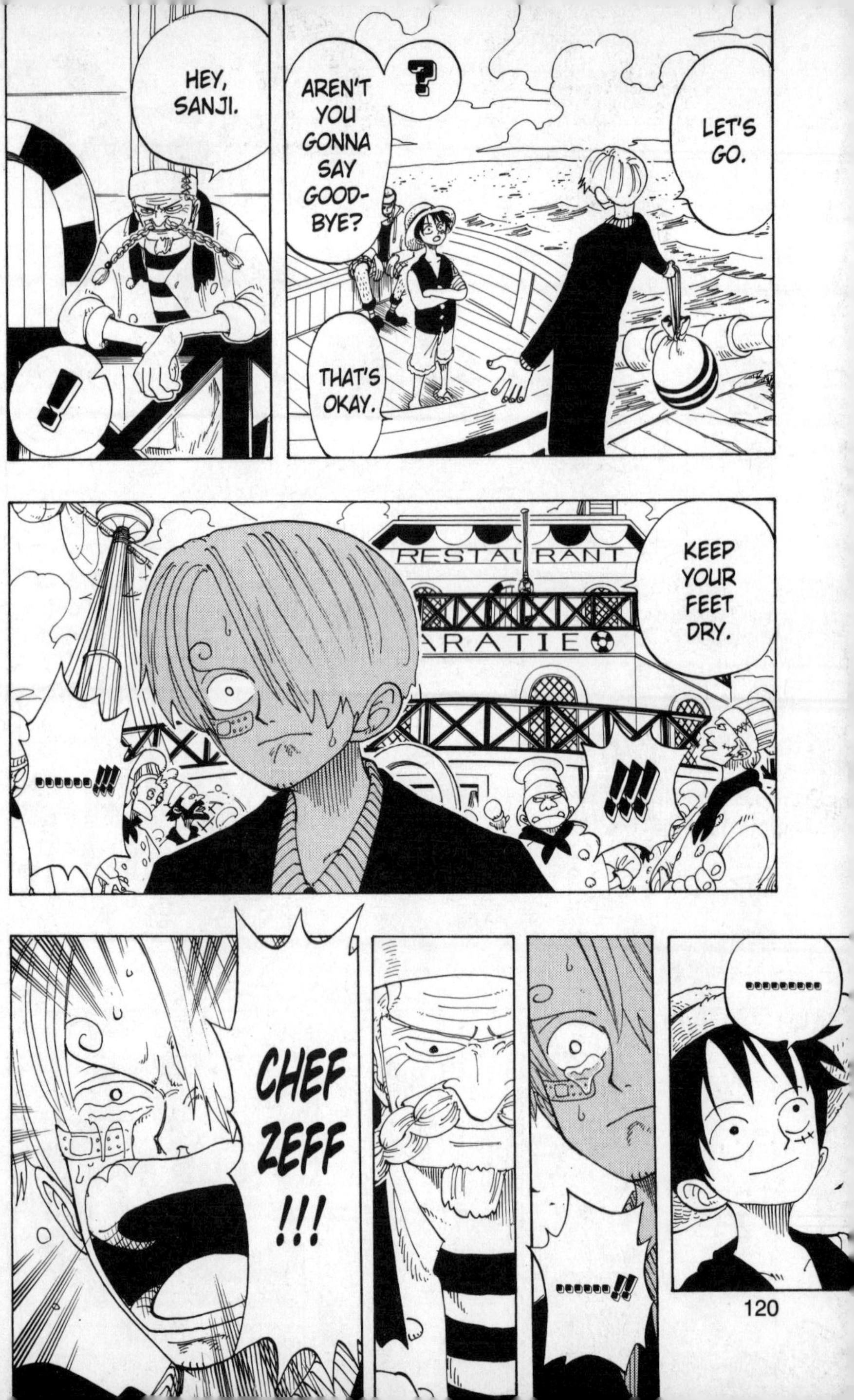
LET'S GO.
?
AREN'T YOU GONNA SAY GOOD-BYE?
THAT'S OKAY.
HEY, SANJI.
!
KEEP YOUR FEET DRY.
!!!!
......!!!
....
......!!
CHEF ZEFF!!!

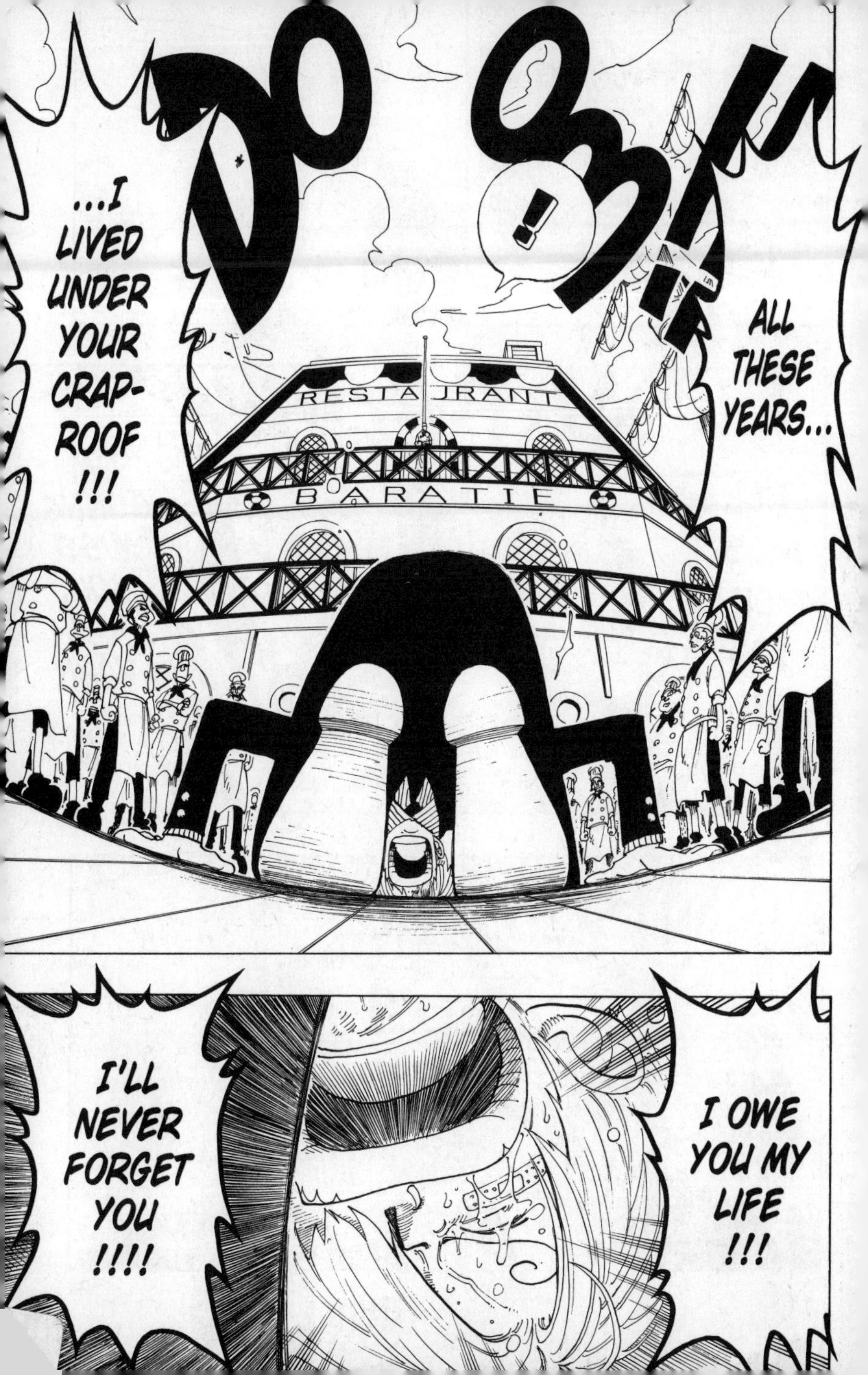
ALL THESE YEARS...
...I LIVED UNDER YOUR CRAP-ROOF!!!
RESTAURANT
BARATIE
I OWE YOU MY LIFE!!!
I'LL NEVER FORGET YOU!!!!

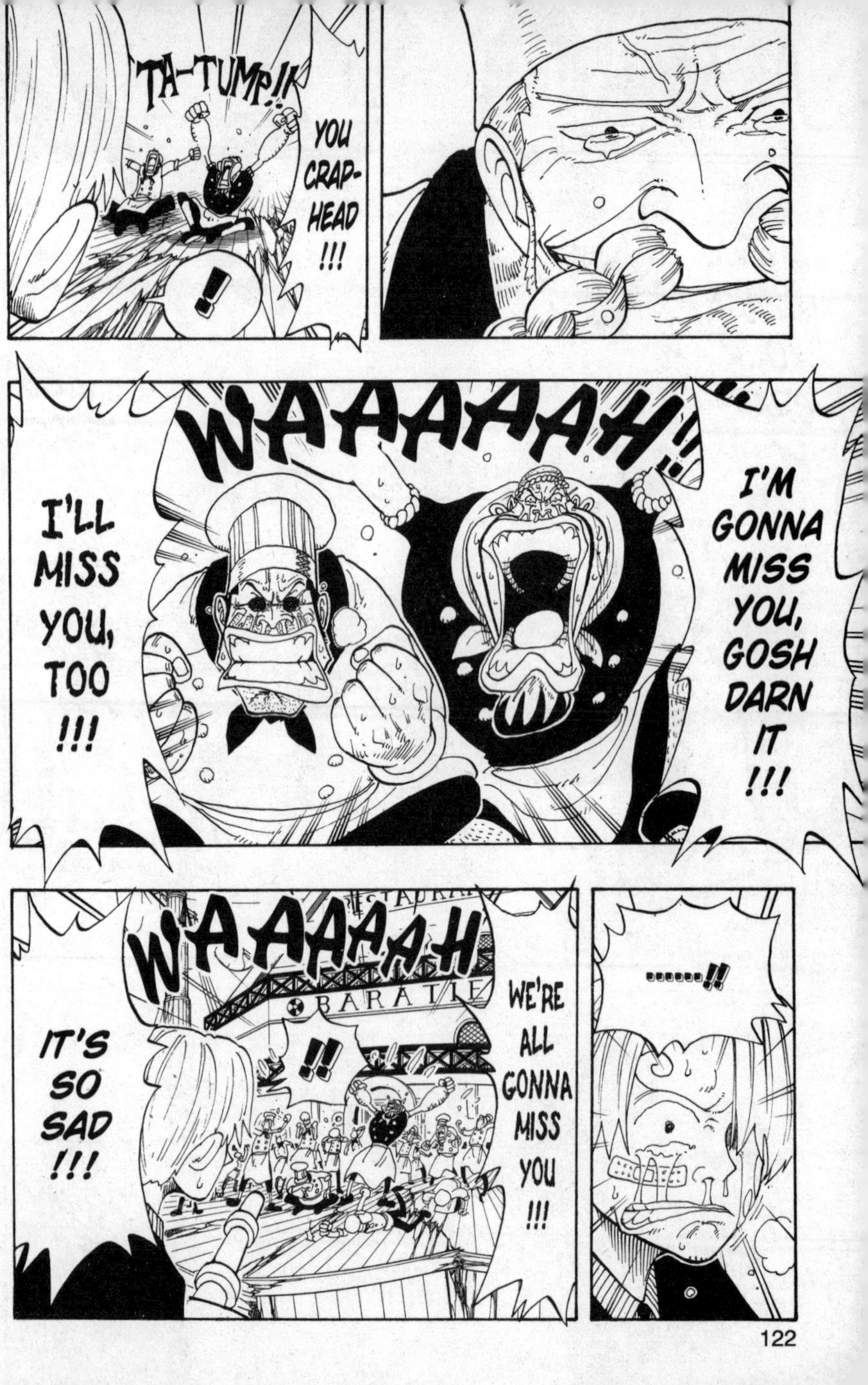
TA-TUMP!!
YOU CRAP-HEAD!!!
!
WAAAAAH!!
I'M GONNA MISS YOU, GOSH DARN IT!!!
I'LL MISS YOU, TOO!!!
......!!
WAAAAAH
BARATIE
WE'RE ALL GONNA MISS YOU!!!
!!
IT'S SO SAD!!!

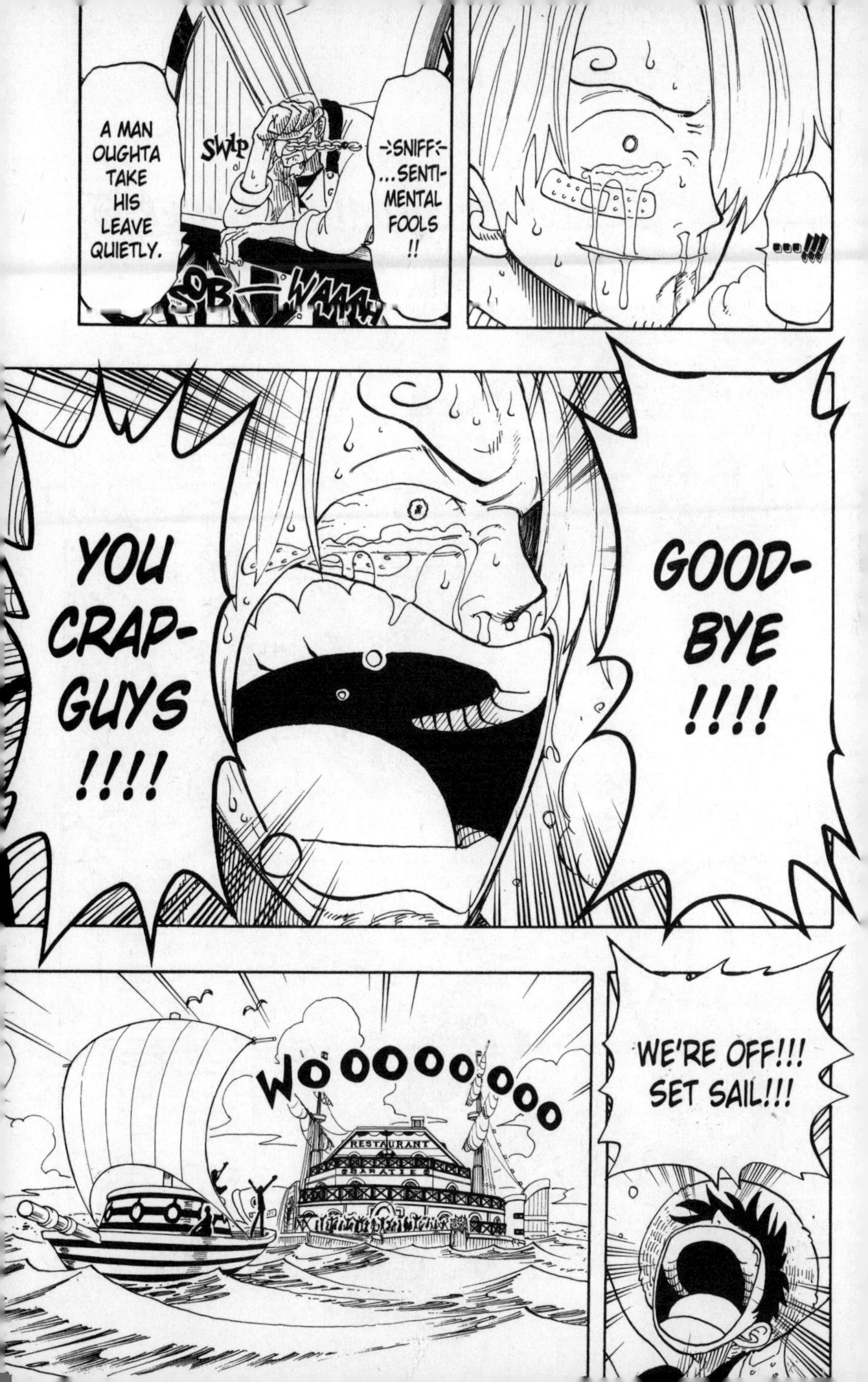
...!!!
SNIFF ...SENTIMENTAL FOOLS!!
SWLP
A MAN OUGHTA TAKE HIS LEAVE QUIETLY.
SOB WAAAH
YOU CRAP-GUYS!!!!
GOOD-BYE!!!!
WE'RE OFF!!! SET SAIL!!!
WOOOOOOOO
RESTAURANT
BARATIE

◎COLORING CORNER◎

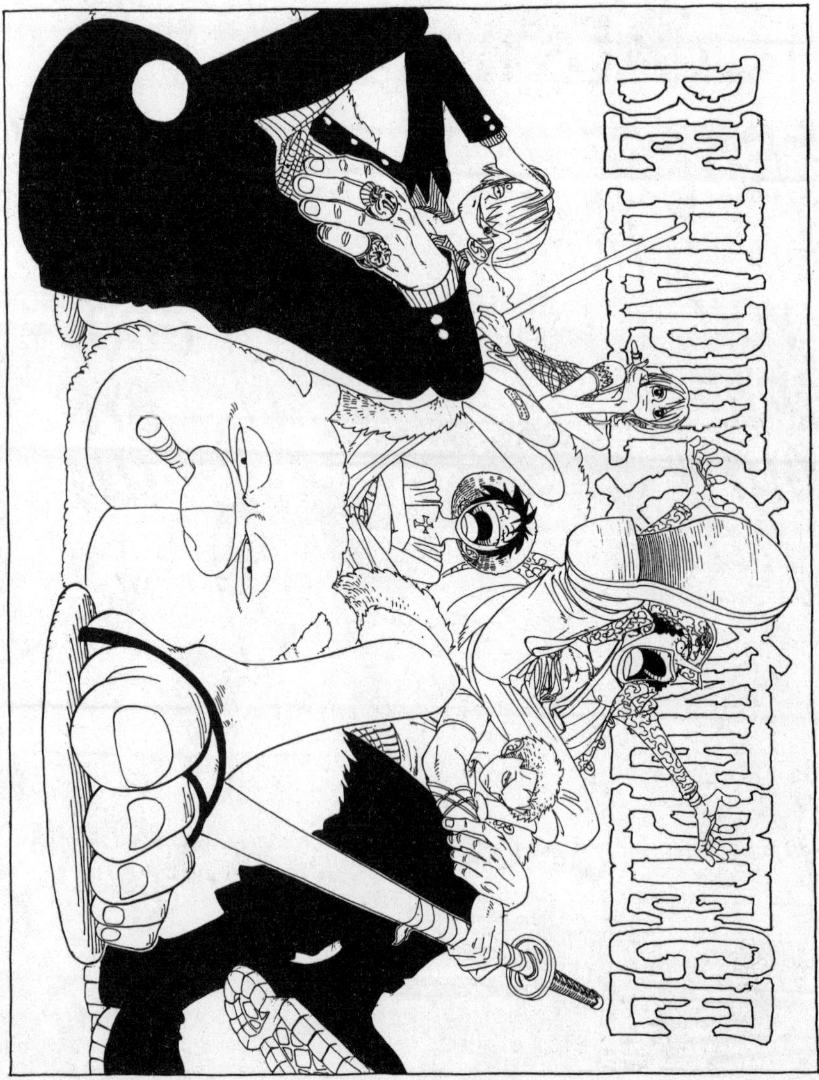

Chapter 69:
ARLONG PARK

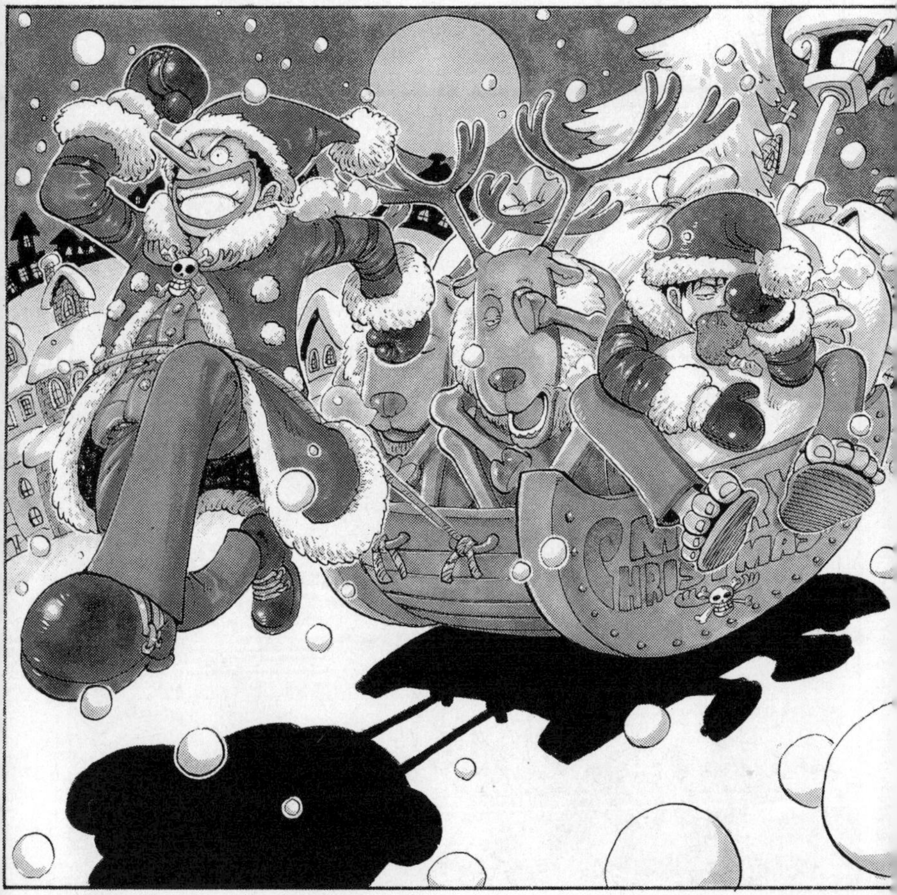

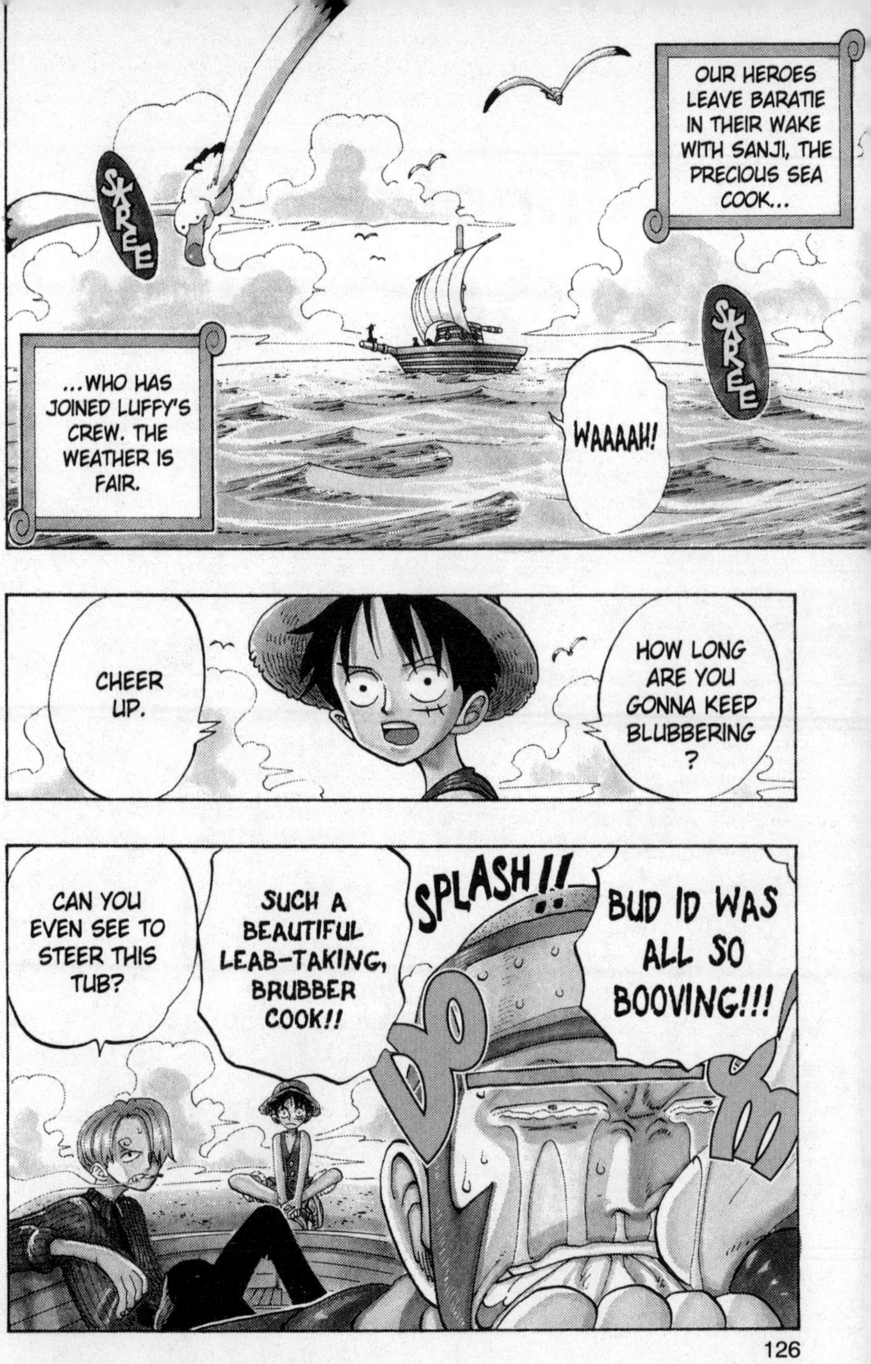
OUR HEROES LEAVE BARATIE IN THEIR WAKE WITH SANJI, THE PRECIOUS SEA COOK...
SKREE
SKREE
WAAAAH!
...WHO HAS JOINED LUFFY'S CREW. THE WEATHER IS FAIR.
HOW LONG ARE YOU GONNA KEEP BLUBBERING ?
CHEER UP.
BUD ID WAS ALL SO BOOVING!!!
SPLASH!!
SUCH A BEAUTIFUL LEAB-TAKING, BRUBBER COOK!!
CAN YOU EVEN SEE TO STEER THIS TUB?

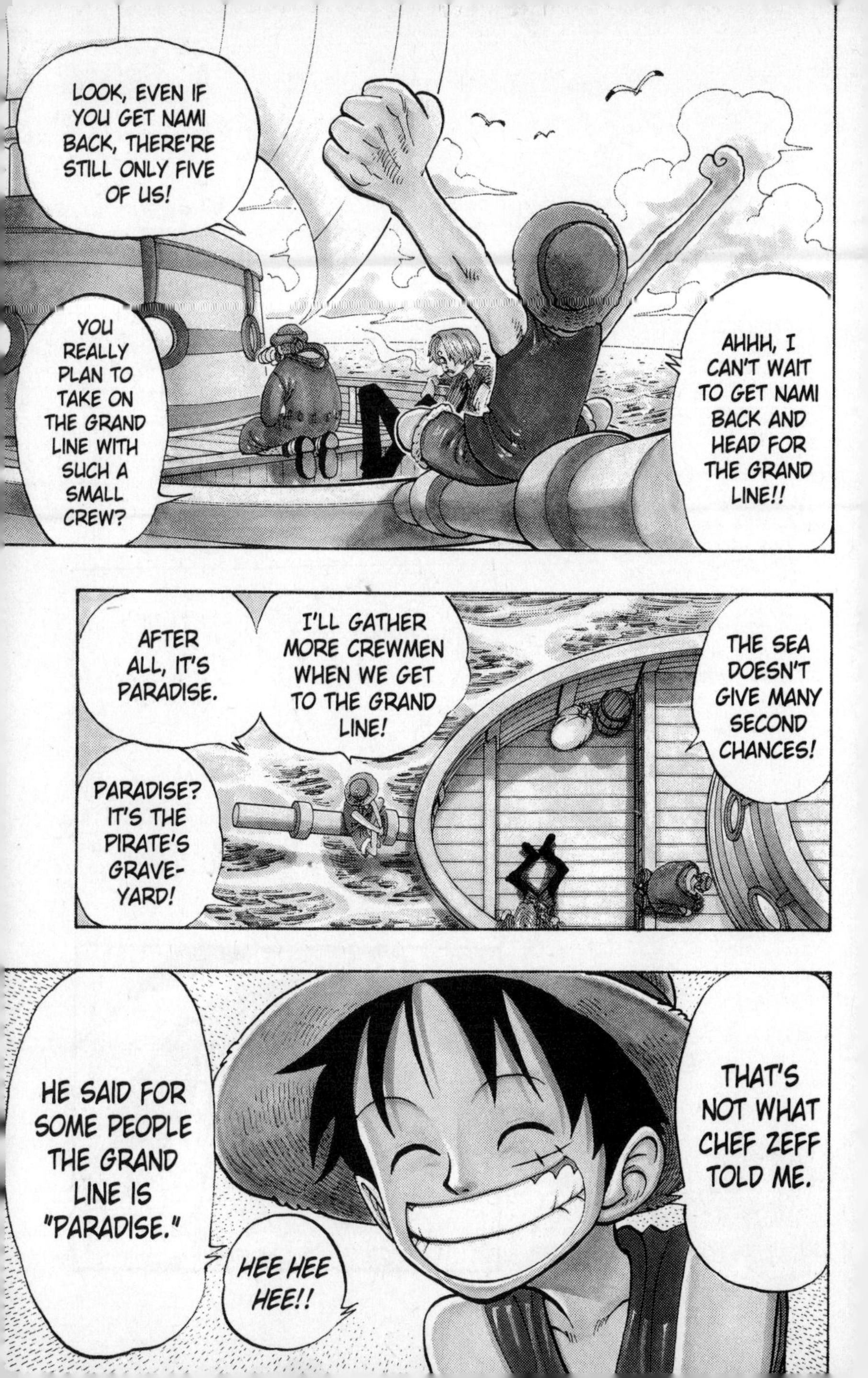
AHHH, I CAN'T WAIT TO GET NAMI BACK AND HEAD FOR THE GRAND LINE!!
YOU REALLY PLAN TO TAKE ON THE GRAND LINE WITH SUCH A SMALL CREW?
LOOK, EVEN IF YOU GET NAMI BACK, THERE'RE STILL ONLY FIVE OF US!
THE SEA DOESN'T GIVE MANY SECOND CHANCES!
I'LL GATHER MORE CREWMEN WHEN WE GET TO THE GRAND LINE!
AFTER ALL, IT'S PARADISE.
PARADISE? IT'S THE PIRATE'S GRAVE-YARD!
THAT'S NOT WHAT CHEF ZEFF TOLD ME.
HE SAID FOR SOME PEOPLE THE GRAND LINE IS "PARADISE."
HEE HEE HEE!!

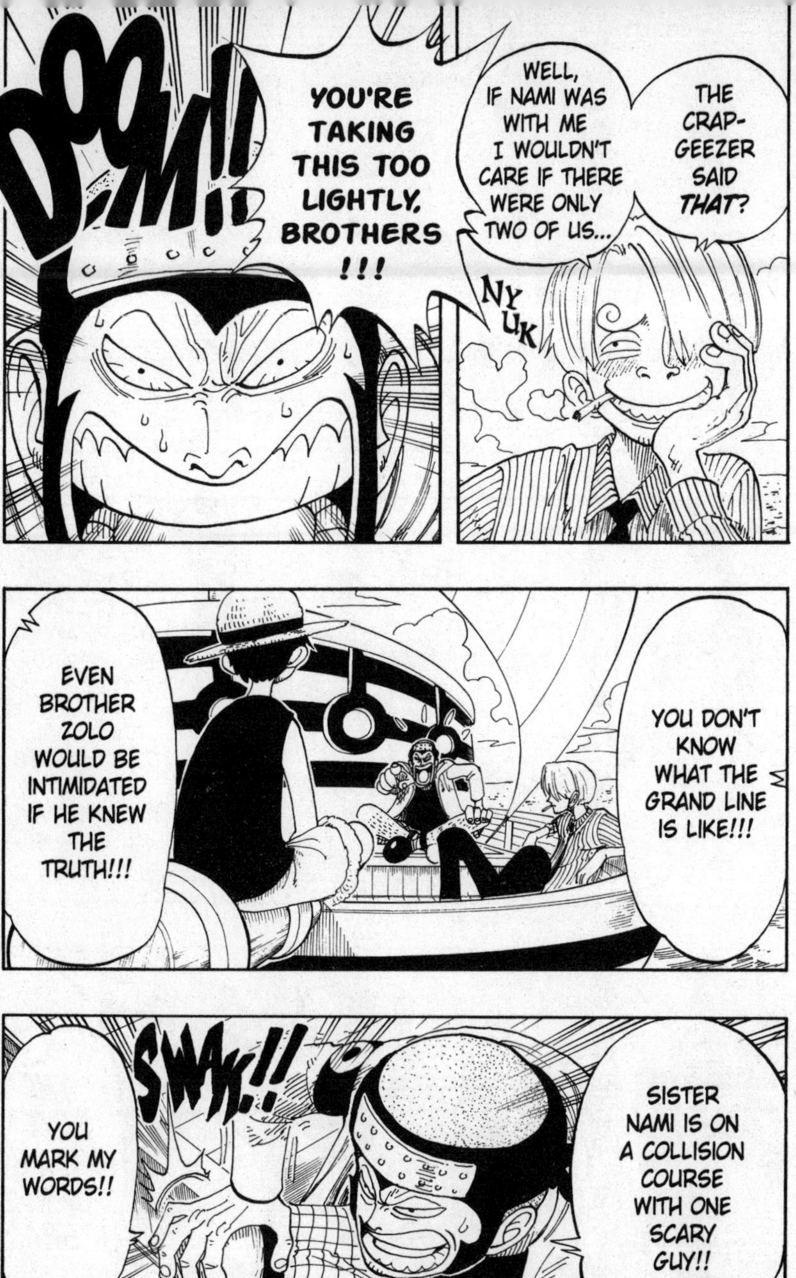
THE CRAP-GEEZER SAID *THAT*?
WELL, IF NAMI WAS WITH ME I WOULDN'T CARE IF THERE WERE ONLY TWO OF US...
NYUK
YOU'RE TAKING THIS TOO LIGHTLY, BROTHERS!!!
DOOM!!
YOU DON'T KNOW WHAT THE GRAND LINE IS LIKE!!!
EVEN BROTHER ZOLO WOULD BE INTIMIDATED IF HE KNEW THE TRUTH!!!
SISTER NAMI IS ON A COLLISION COURSE WITH ONE SCARY GUY!!
SWAK!!
YOU MARK MY WORDS!!

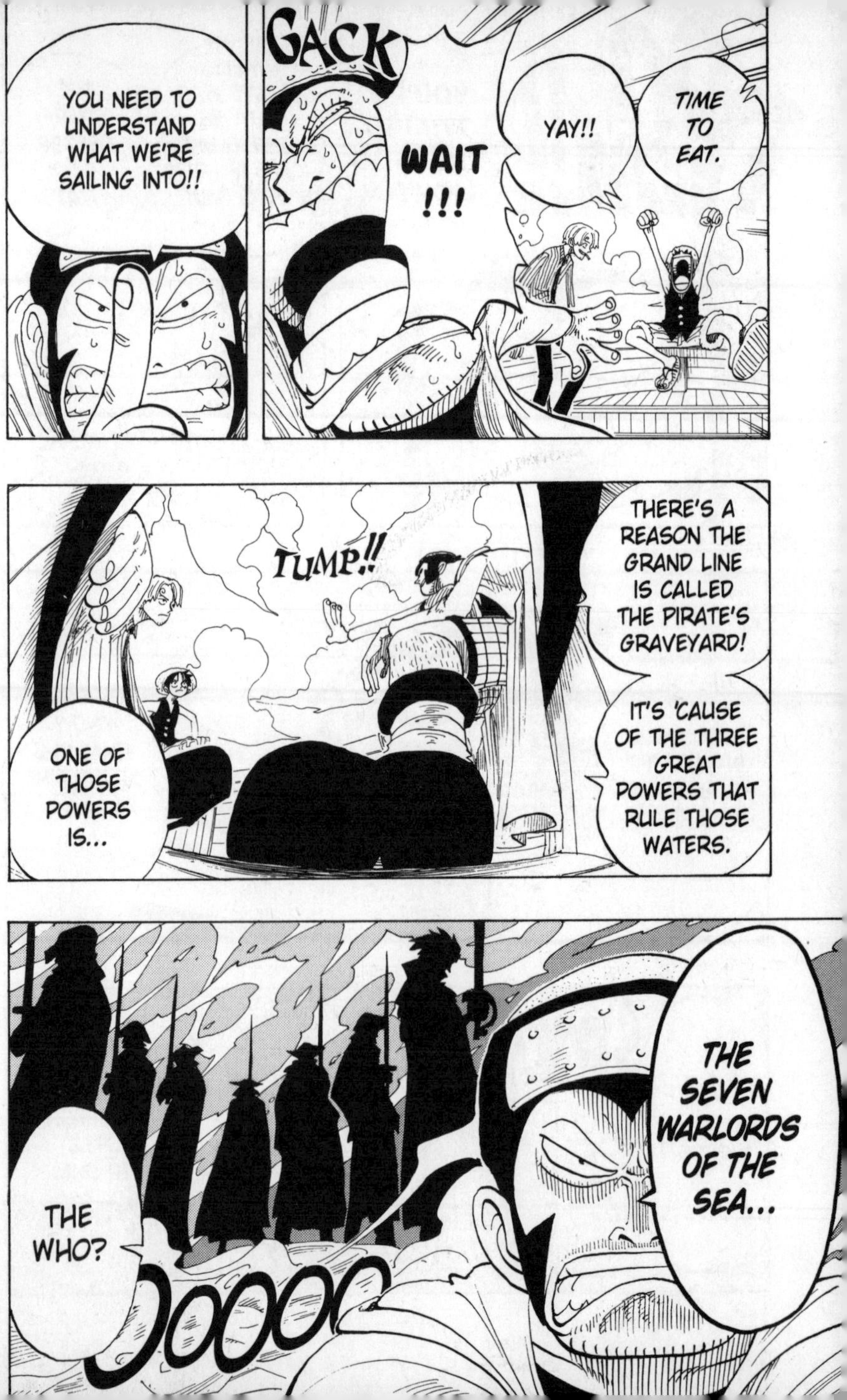

TIME TO EAT.
YAY!!
GACK
WAIT !!!
YOU NEED TO UNDERSTAND WHAT WE'RE SAILING INTO!!
THERE'S A REASON THE GRAND LINE IS CALLED THE PIRATE'S GRAVEYARD!
IT'S 'CAUSE OF THE THREE GREAT POWERS THAT RULE THOSE WATERS.
TUMP!!
ONE OF THOSE POWERS IS...
THE SEVEN WARLORDS OF THE SEA...
THE WHO?

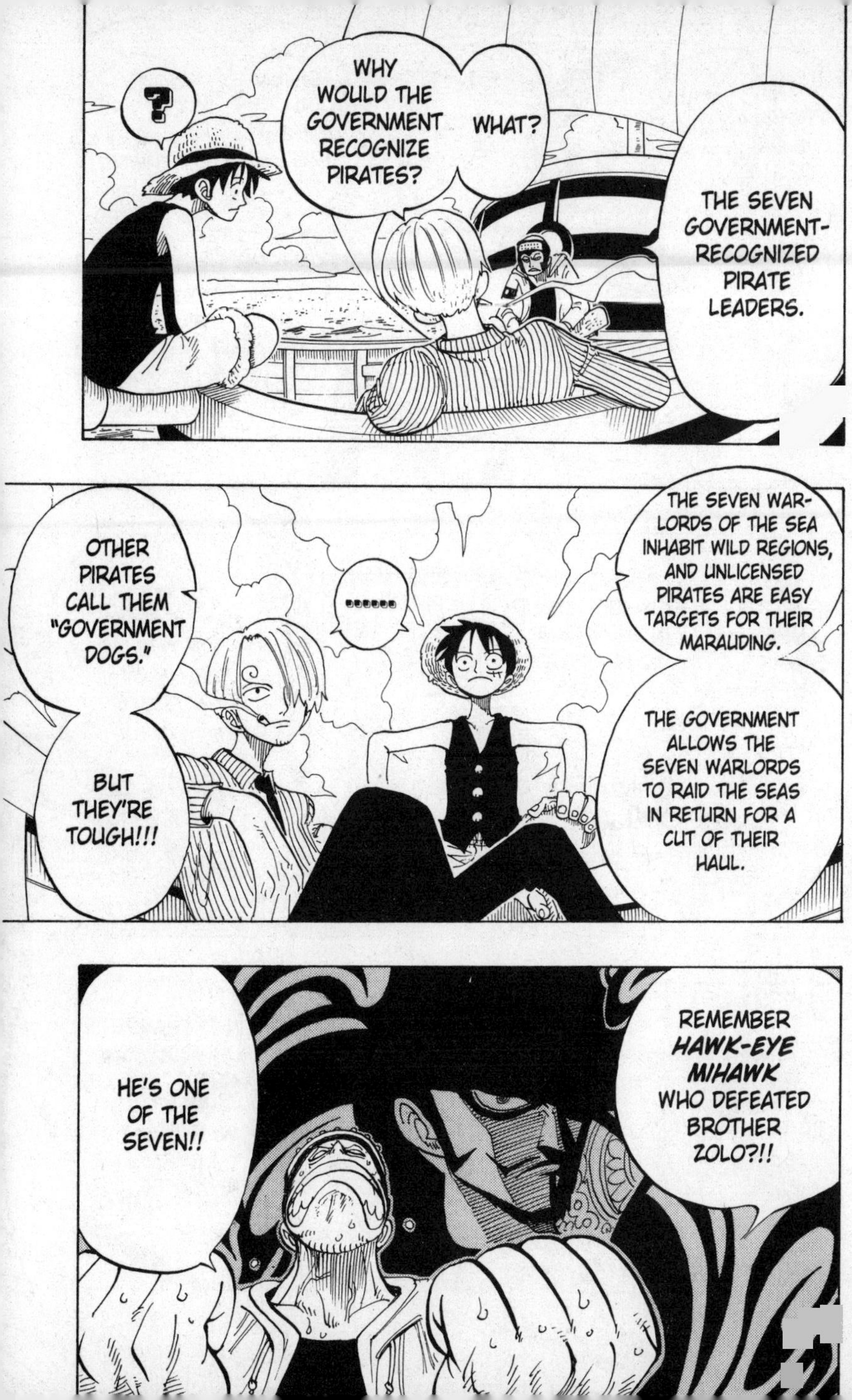
THE SEVEN GOVERNMENT-RECOGNIZED PIRATE LEADERS.
WHAT?
WHY WOULD THE GOVERNMENT RECOGNIZE PIRATES?
?
THE SEVEN WARLORDS OF THE SEA INHABIT WILD REGIONS, AND UNLICENSED PIRATES ARE EASY TARGETS FOR THEIR MARAUDING.
THE GOVERNMENT ALLOWS THE SEVEN WARLORDS TO RAID THE SEAS IN RETURN FOR A CUT OF THEIR HAUL.
......
OTHER PIRATES CALL THEM "GOVERNMENT DOGS."
BUT THEY'RE TOUGH!!!
REMEMBER *HAWK-EYE MIHAWK* WHO DEFEATED BROTHER ZOLO?!!
HE'S ONE OF THE SEVEN!!

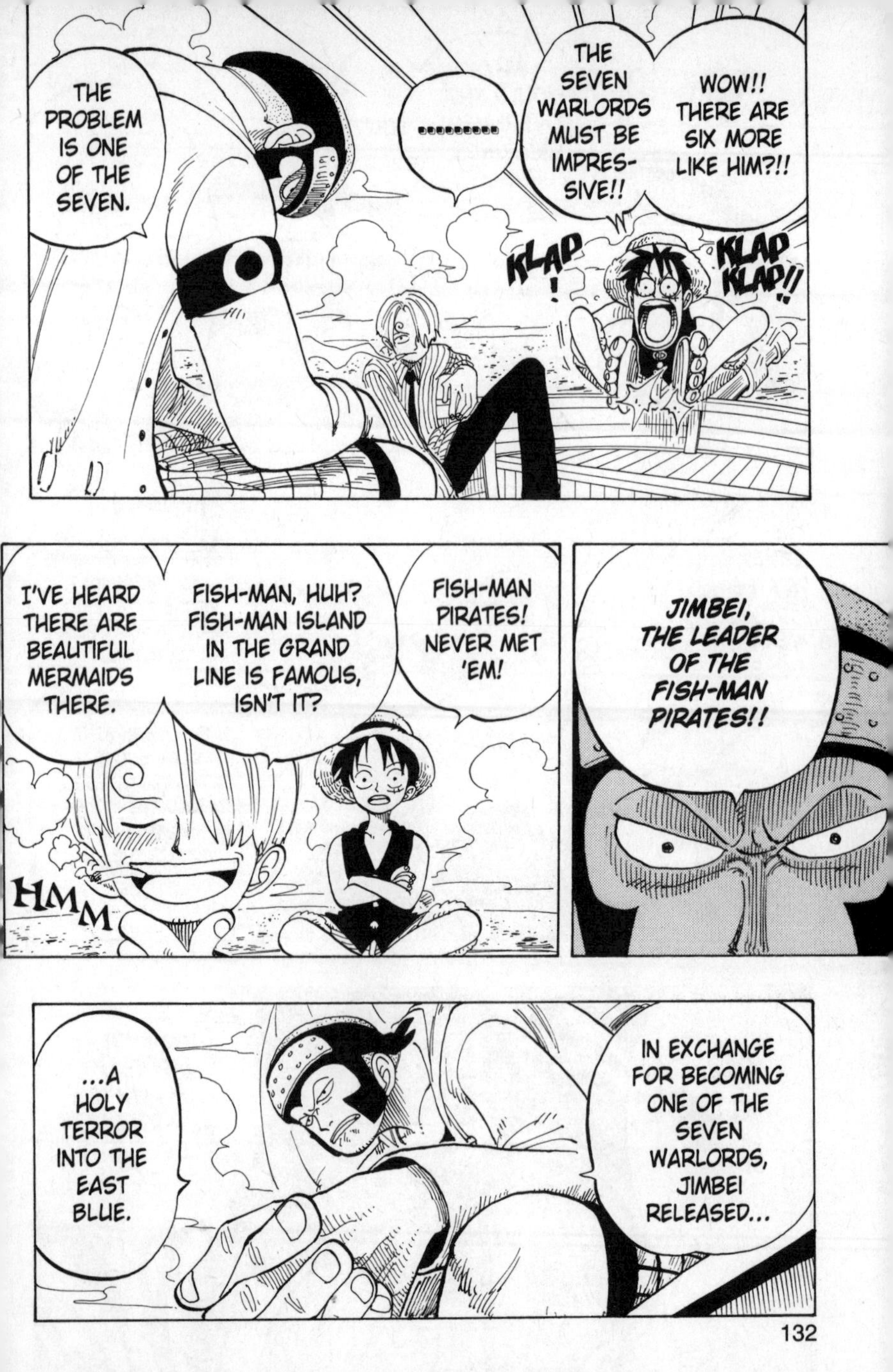

WOW!! THERE ARE SIX MORE LIKE HIM?!!
THE SEVEN WARLORDS MUST BE IMPRES-SIVE!!
KLAP KLAP!!
KLAP!
....
THE PROBLEM IS ONE OF THE SEVEN.
JIMBEI, THE LEADER OF THE FISH-MAN PIRATES!!
FISH-MAN PIRATES! NEVER MET 'EM!
FISH-MAN, HUH? FISH-MAN ISLAND IN THE GRAND LINE IS FAMOUS, ISN'T IT?
I'VE HEARD THERE ARE BEAUTIFUL MERMAIDS THERE.
HMM
IN EXCHANGE FOR BECOMING ONE OF THE SEVEN WARLORDS, JIMBEI RELEASED...
...A HOLY TERROR INTO THE EAST BLUE.

READ THIS WAY

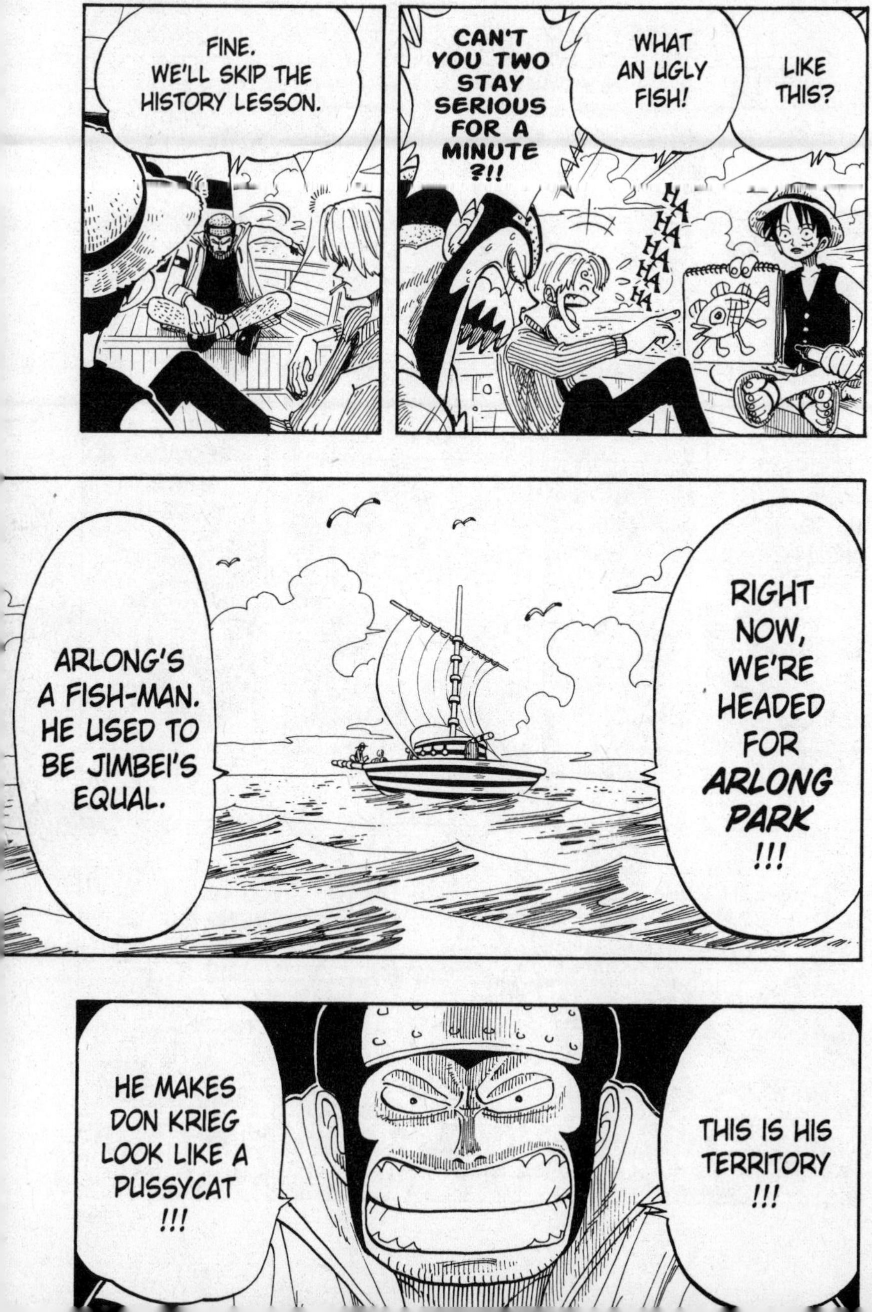
LIKE THIS?
WHAT AN UGLY FISH!
HA HA HA HA HA
CAN'T YOU TWO STAY SERIOUS FOR A MINUTE?!!
FINE. WE'LL SKIP THE HISTORY LESSON.
RIGHT NOW, WE'RE HEADED FOR ARLONG PARK!!!
ARLONG'S A FISH-MAN. HE USED TO BE JIMBEI'S EQUAL.
THIS IS HIS TERRITORY!!!
HE MAKES DON KRIEG LOOK LIKE A PUSSYCAT!!!

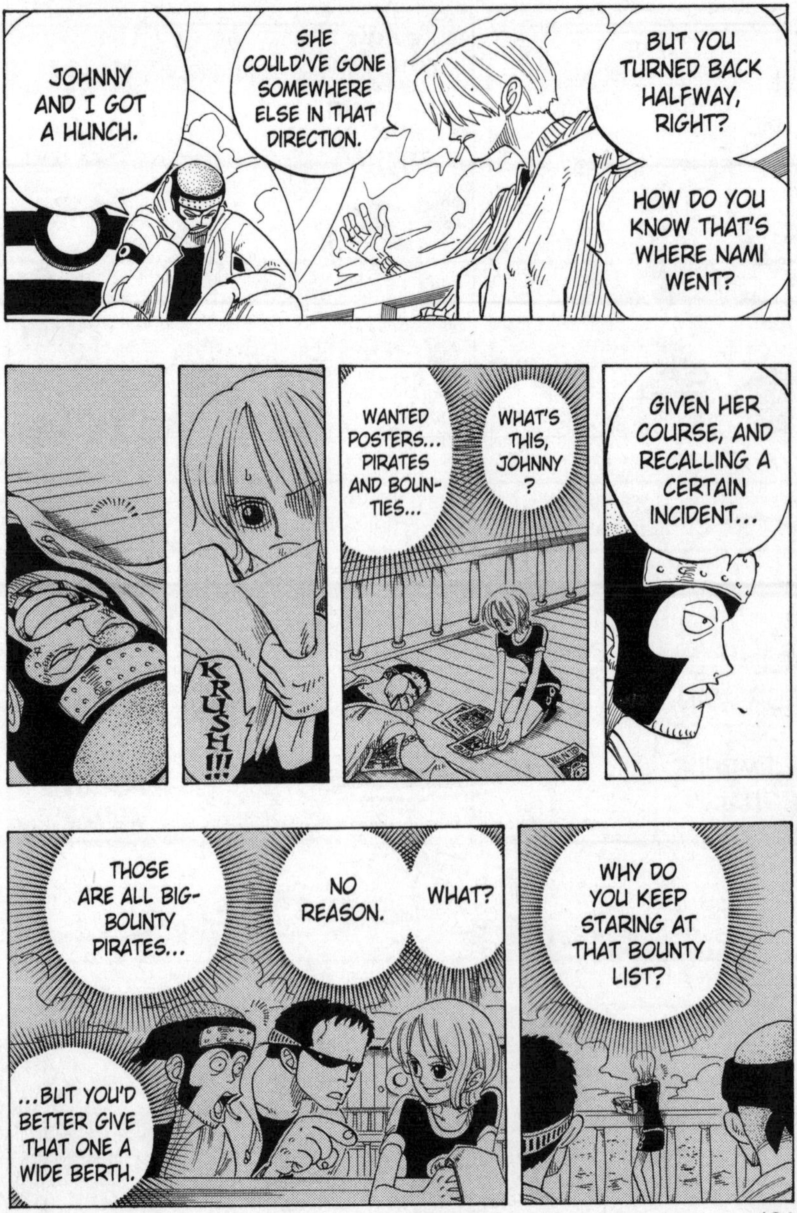
BUT YOU TURNED BACK HALFWAY, RIGHT?
HOW DO YOU KNOW THAT'S WHERE NAMI WENT?
SHE COULD'VE GONE SOMEWHERE ELSE IN THAT DIRECTION.
JOHNNY AND I GOT A HUNCH.
GIVEN HER COURSE, AND RECALLING A CERTAIN INCIDENT...
WHAT'S THIS, JOHNNY?
WANTED POSTERS... PIRATES AND BOUN-TIES...
KRUSH!!!
WHY DO YOU KEEP STARING AT THAT BOUNTY LIST?
WHAT?
NO REASON.
THOSE ARE ALL BIG-BOUNTY PIRATES...
...BUT YOU'D BETTER GIVE THAT ONE A WIDE BERTH.

READ THIS WAY

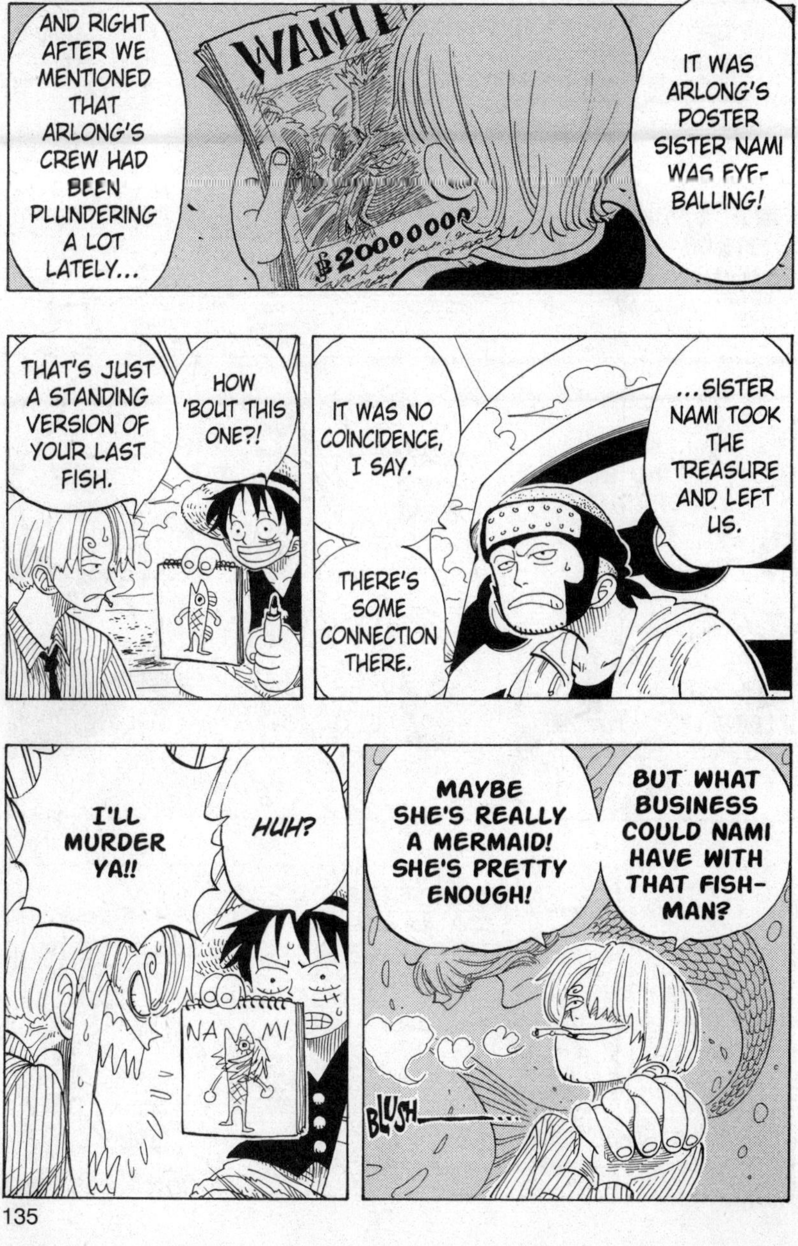

IT WAS ARLONG'S POSTER SISTER NAMI WAS EYE-BALLING!
WANTE
AND RIGHT AFTER WE MENTIONED THAT ARLONG'S CREW HAD BEEN PLUNDERING A LOT LATELY...
...SISTER NAMI TOOK THE TREASURE AND LEFT US.
IT WAS NO COINCIDENCE, I SAY.
THERE'S SOME CONNECTION THERE.
HOW 'BOUT THIS ONE?!
THAT'S JUST A STANDING VERSION OF YOUR LAST FISH.
BUT WHAT BUSINESS COULD NAMI HAVE WITH THAT FISH-MAN?
MAYBE SHE'S REALLY A MERMAID! SHE'S PRETTY ENOUGH!
BLUSH
HUH?
I'LL MURDER YA!!
NA MI

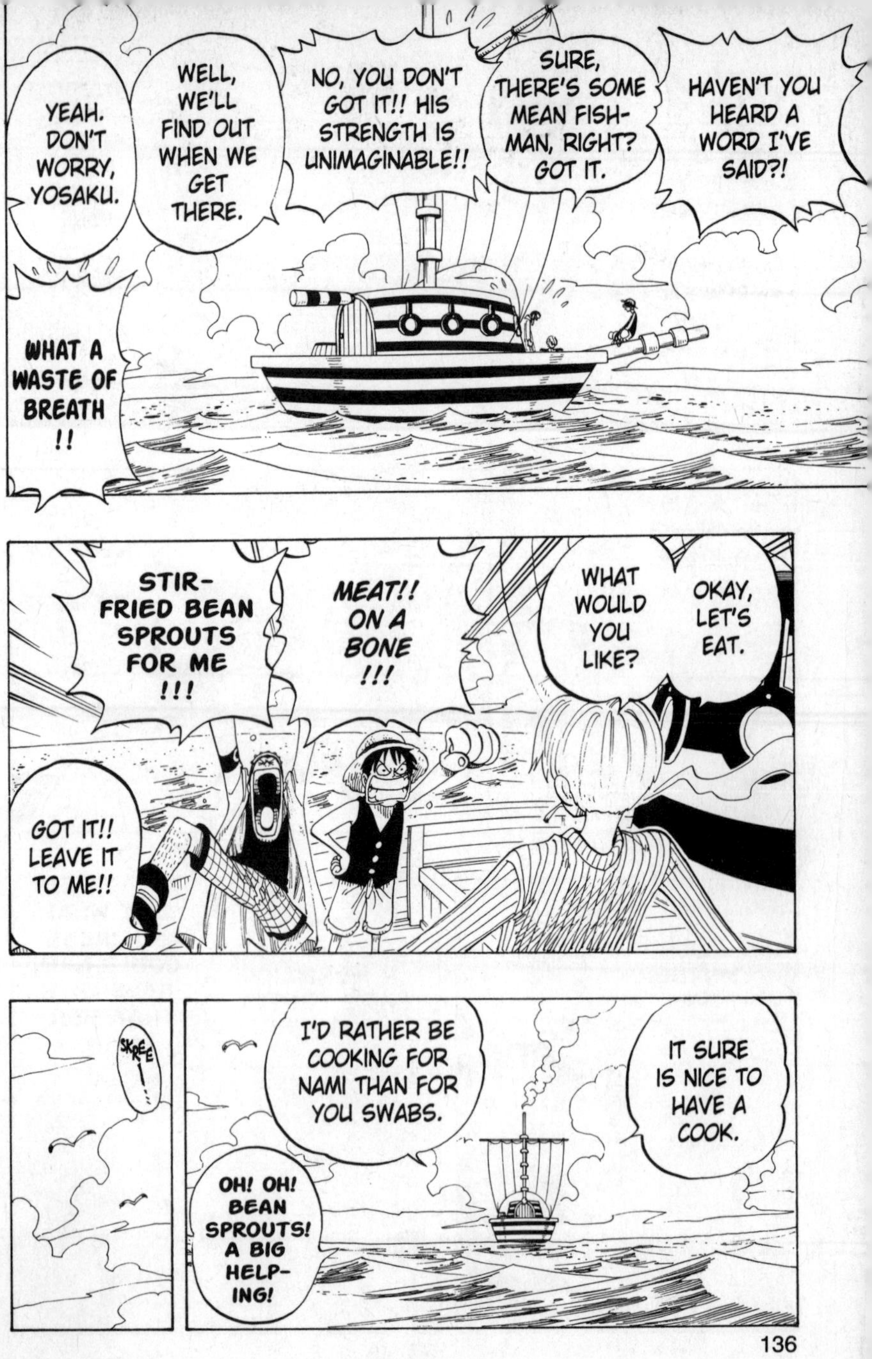
HAVEN'T YOU HEARD A WORD I'VE SAID?!
SURE, THERE'S SOME MEAN FISH-MAN, RIGHT? GOT IT.
NO, YOU DON'T GOT IT!! HIS STRENGTH IS UNIMAGINABLE!!
WELL, WE'LL FIND OUT WHEN WE GET THERE.
YEAH. DON'T WORRY, YOSAKU.
WHAT A WASTE OF BREATH!!
OKAY, LET'S EAT.
WHAT WOULD YOU LIKE?
MEAT!! ON A BONE!!!
STIR-FRIED BEAN SPROUTS FOR ME!!!
GOT IT!! LEAVE IT TO ME!!
IT SURE IS NICE TO HAVE A COOK.
I'D RATHER BE COOKING FOR NAMI THAN FOR YOU SWABS.
OH! OH! BEAN SPROUTS! A BIG HELPING!
SKREEE

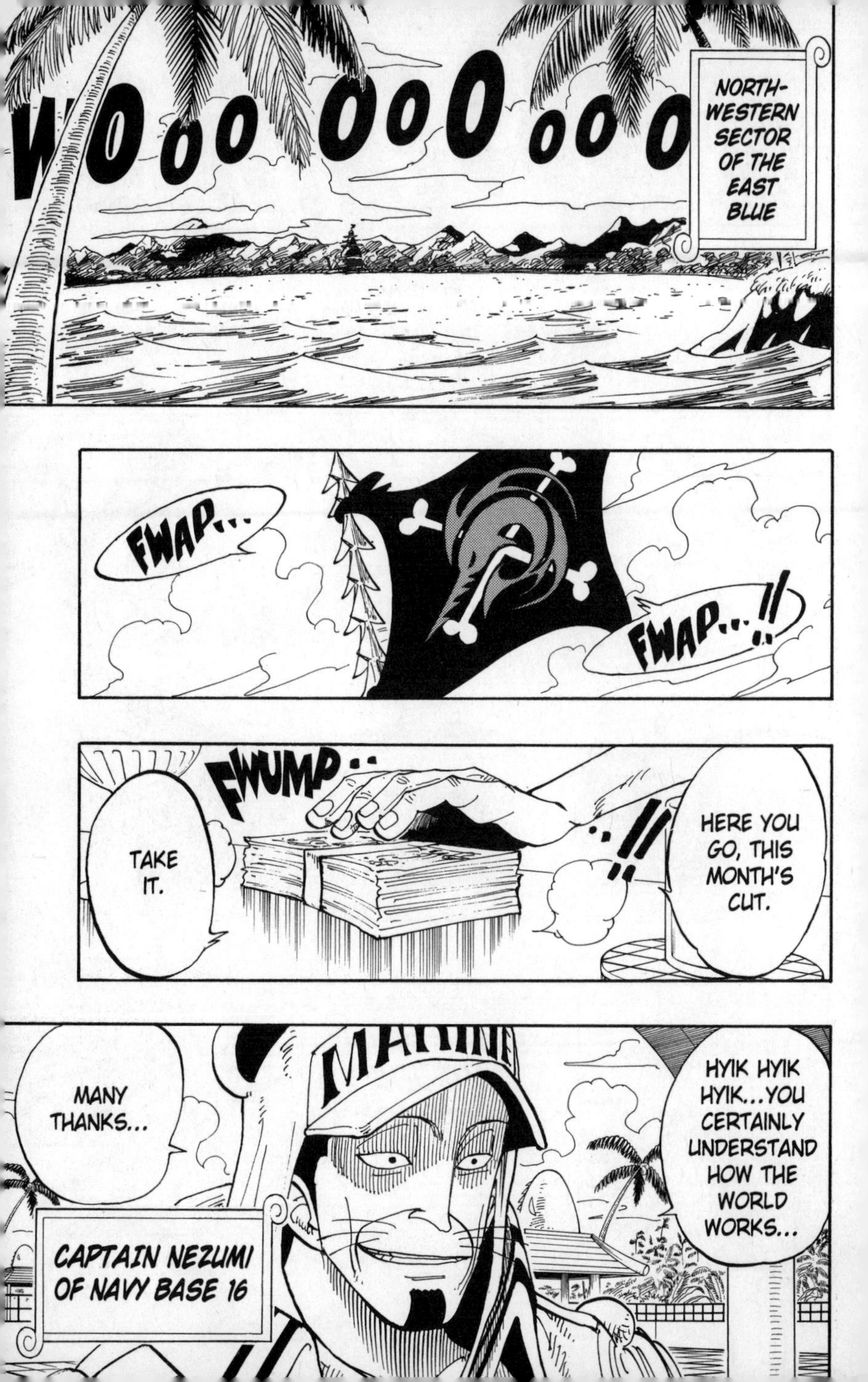
NORTH-WESTERN SECTOR OF THE EAST BLUE
WOOOOOOOOO
FWAP...!!
FWAP...
HERE YOU GO, THIS MONTH'S CUT.
..!!
FWUMP..
TAKE IT.
HYIK HYIK HYIK...YOU CERTAINLY UNDERSTAND HOW THE WORLD WORKS...
MANY THANKS...
CAPTAIN NEZUMI OF NAVY BASE 16

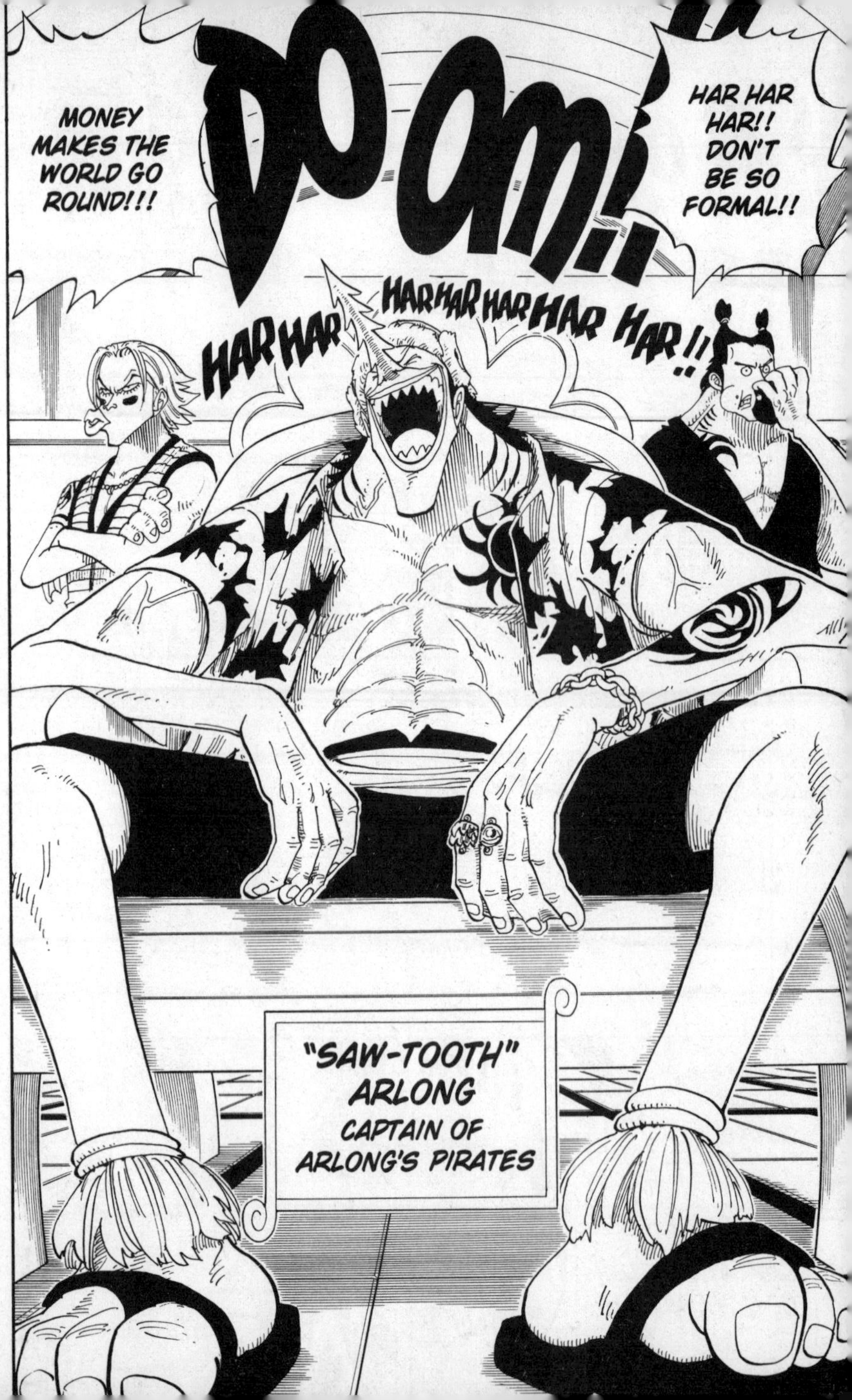
HAR HAR HAR!! DON'T BE SO FORMAL!!
DOOM!!
MONEY MAKES THE WORLD GO ROUND!!!
HAR HAR HAR HAR HAR HAR HAR!!
"SAW-TOOTH" ARLONG
CAPTAIN OF ARLONG'S PIRATES

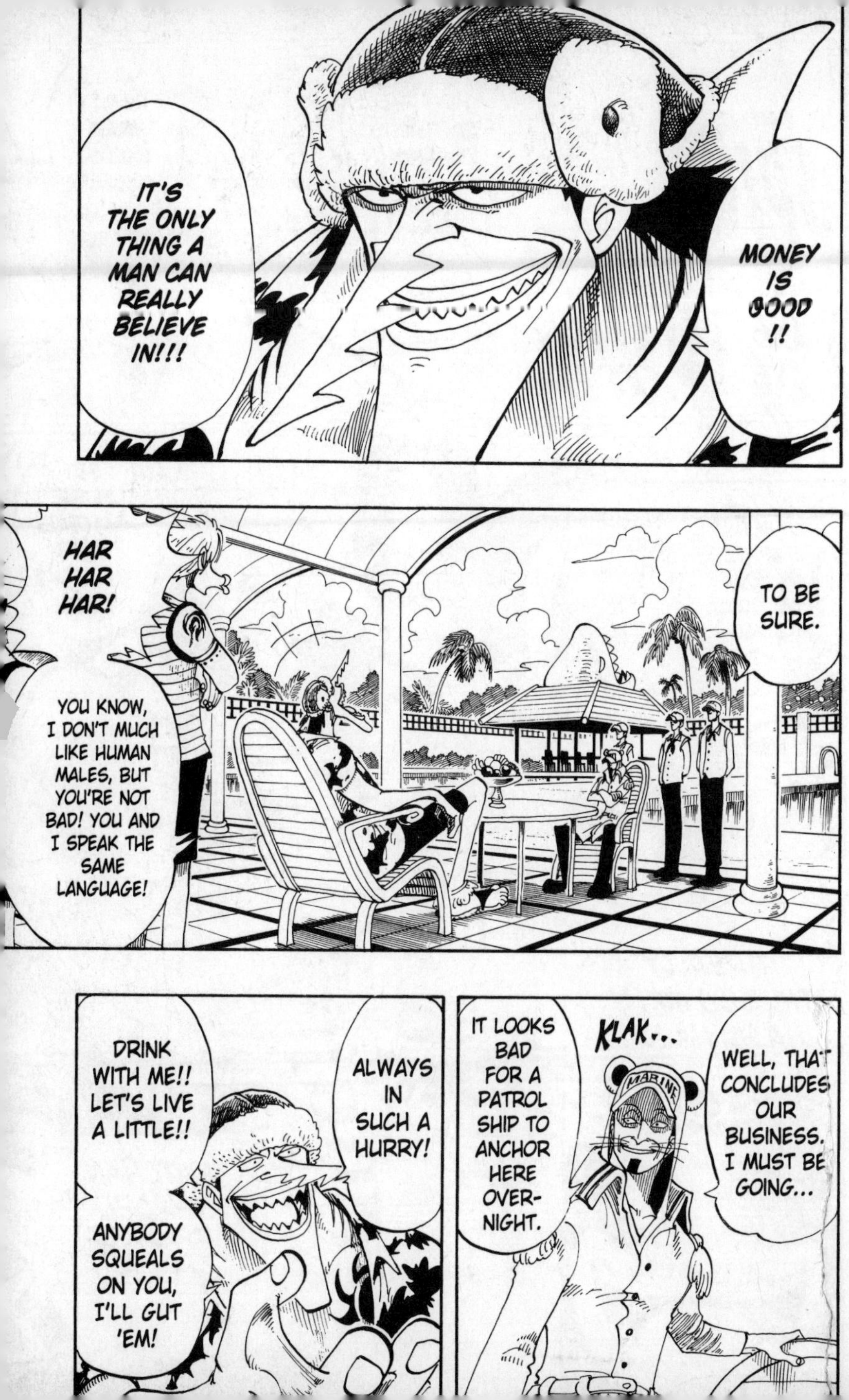
MONEY IS GOOD!!
IT'S THE ONLY THING A MAN CAN REALLY BELIEVE IN!!!
TO BE SURE.
HAR HAR HAR!
YOU KNOW, I DON'T MUCH LIKE HUMAN MALES, BUT YOU'RE NOT BAD! YOU AND I SPEAK THE SAME LANGUAGE!
WELL, THAT CONCLUDES OUR BUSINESS. I MUST BE GOING...
KLAK...
MARINE
IT LOOKS BAD FOR A PATROL SHIP TO ANCHOR HERE OVER-NIGHT.
ALWAYS IN SUCH A HURRY!
DRINK WITH ME!! LET'S LIVE A LITTLE!!
ANYBODY SQUEALS ON YOU, I'LL GUT 'EM!

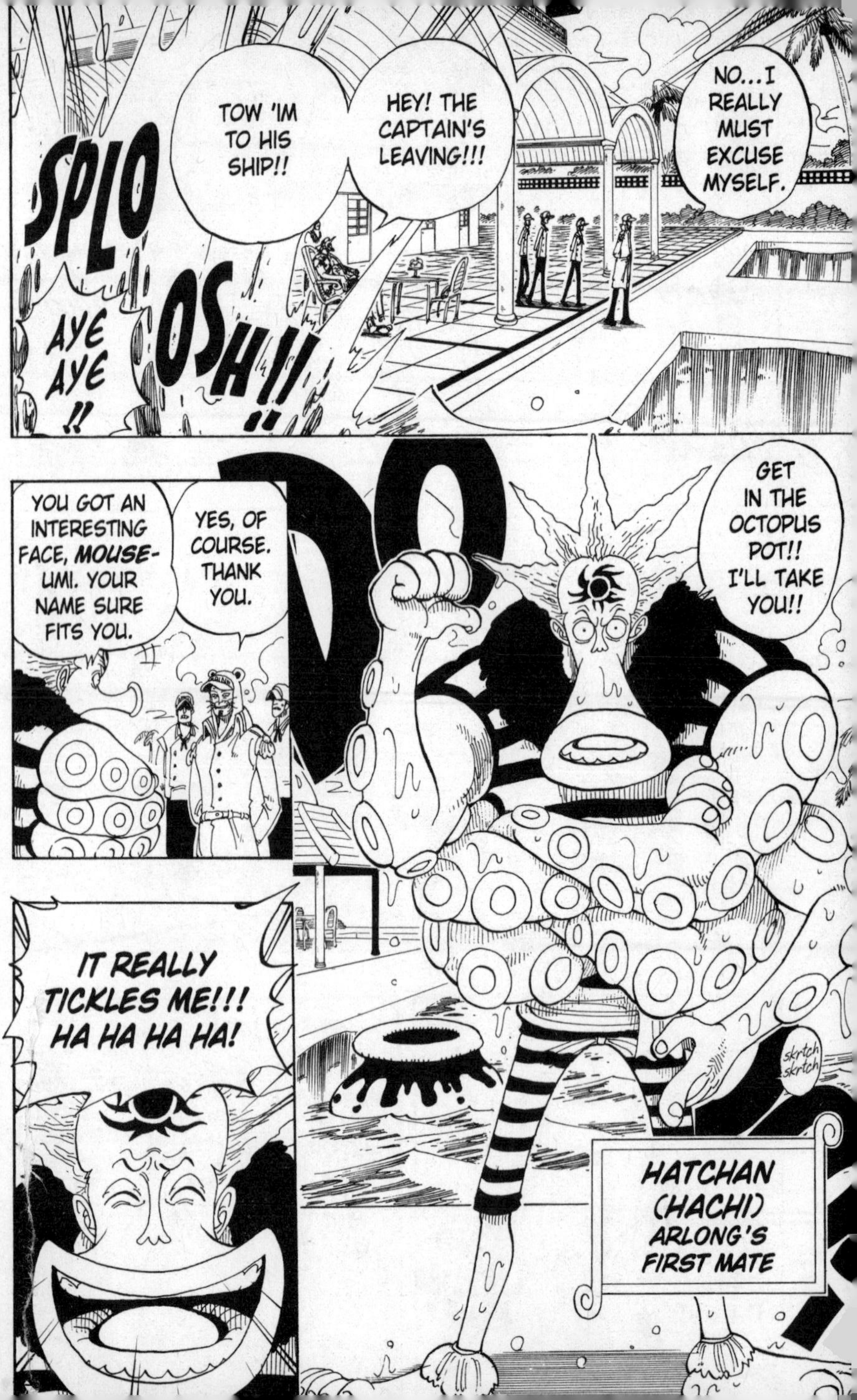
NO...I REALLY MUST EXCUSE MYSELF.
HEY! THE CAPTAIN'S LEAVING!!!
TOW 'IM TO HIS SHIP!!
SPLOOSH!!
AYE AYE!!
DO
GET IN THE OCTOPUS POT!! I'LL TAKE YOU!!
skrtch skrtch
HATCHAN (HACHI) ARLONG'S FIRST MATE
YES, OF COURSE. THANK YOU.
YOU GOT AN INTERESTING FACE, *MOUSE-UMI*. YOUR NAME SURE FITS YOU.
IT REALLY TICKLES ME!!! HA HA HA HA!

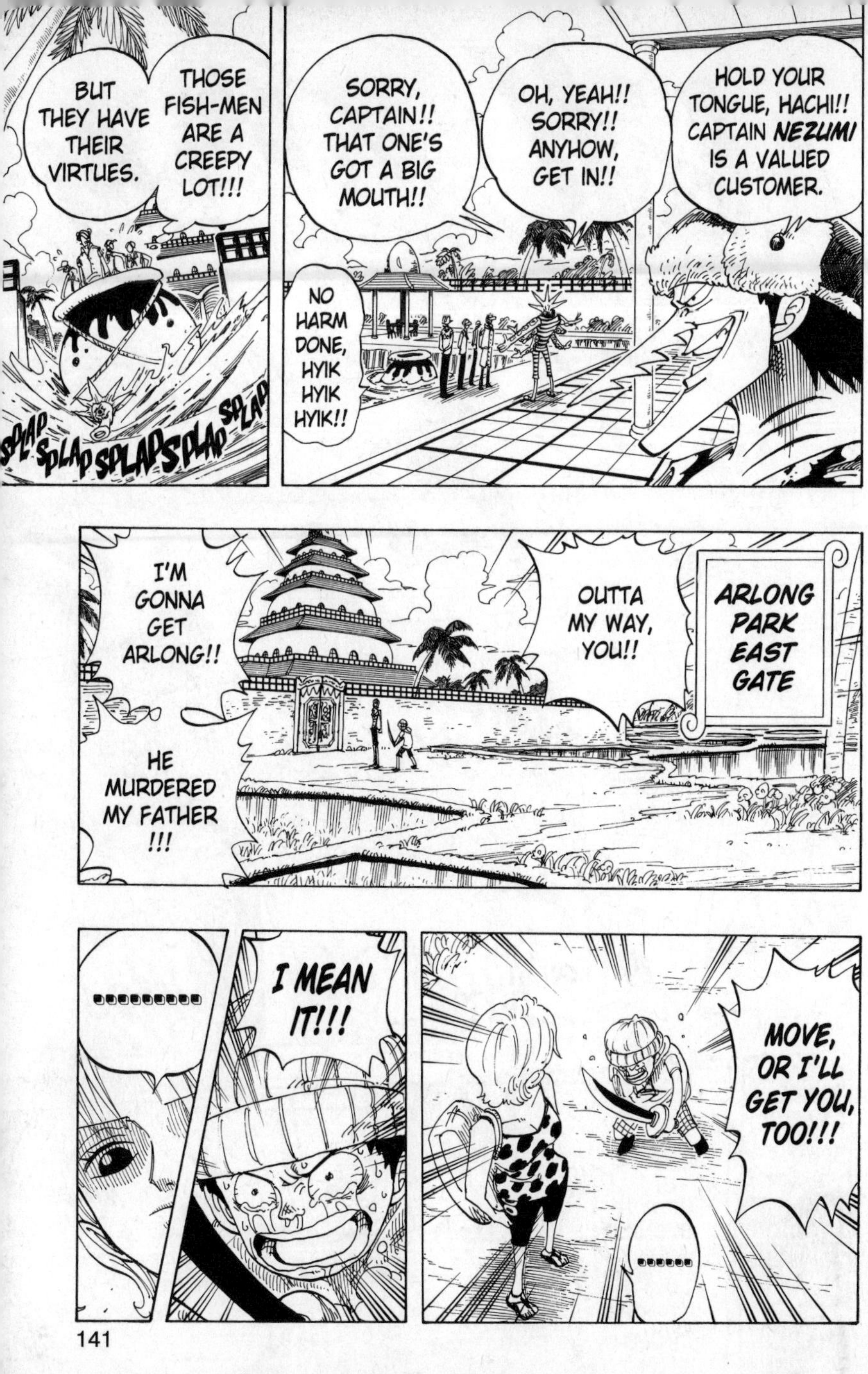
HOLD YOUR TONGUE, HACHI!! CAPTAIN NEZUMI IS A VALUED CUSTOMER.
OH, YEAH!! SORRY!! ANYHOW, GET IN!!
SORRY, CAPTAIN!! THAT ONE'S GOT A BIG MOUTH!!
NO HARM DONE, HYIK HYIK HYIK!!
THOSE FISH-MEN ARE A CREEPY LOT!!!
BUT THEY HAVE THEIR VIRTUES.
SPLAP SPLAP SPLAP SPLAP SPLAP
ARLONG PARK EAST GATE
OUTTA MY WAY, YOU!!
I'M GONNA GET ARLONG!!
HE MURDERED MY FATHER!!!
MOVE, OR I'LL GET YOU, TOO!!!
......
I MEAN IT!!!
....

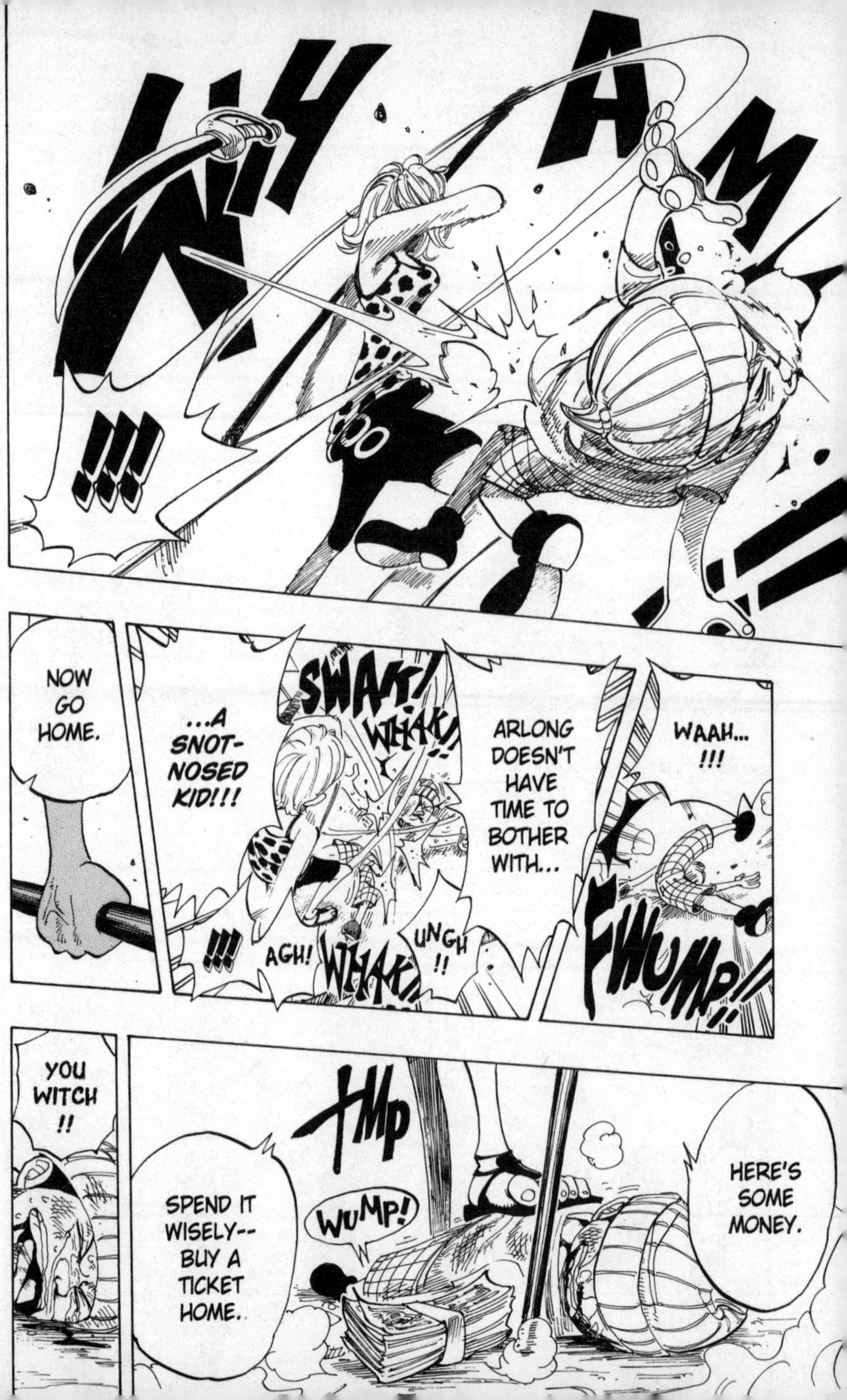
WHAM!!!
WAAH... !!!
FWUMP!!
ARLONG DOESN'T HAVE TIME TO BOTHER WITH...
...A SNOT-NOSED KID!!!
SWAK!
WHAK!
!!!
AGH!
WHAK!
UNGH !!
NOW GO HOME.
HERE'S SOME MONEY.
HMP
WUMP!
SPEND IT WISELY-- BUY A TICKET HOME..
YOU WITCH !!

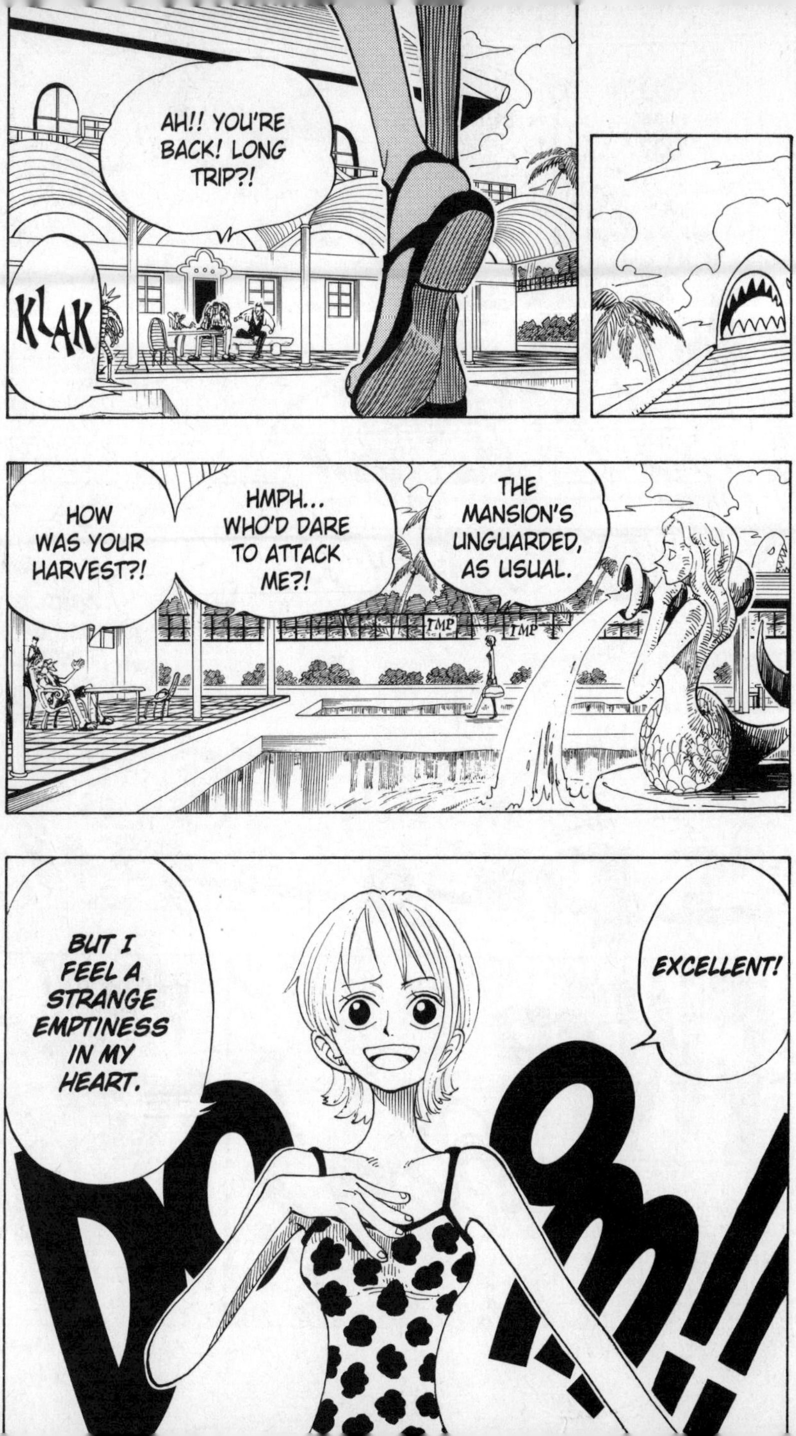
AH!! YOU'RE BACK! LONG TRIP?!
KLAK
THE MANSION'S UNGUARDED, AS USUAL.
HMPH... WHO'D DARE TO ATTACK ME?!
HOW WAS YOUR HARVEST?!
EXCELLENT!
BUT I FEEL A STRANGE EMPTINESS IN MY HEART.
DOOM!!

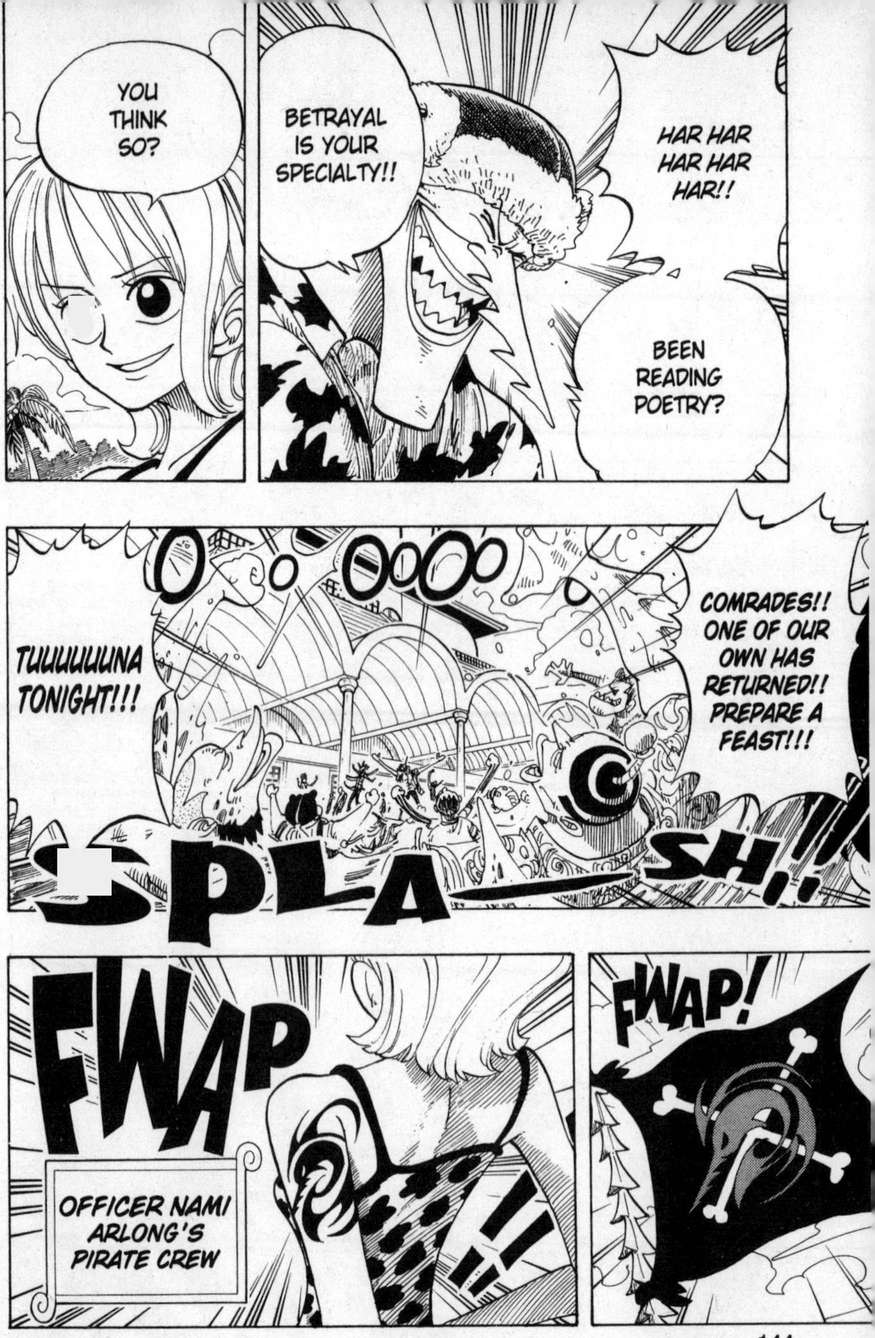
HAR HAR HAR HAR HAR!!
BEEN READING POETRY?
BETRAYAL IS YOUR SPECIALTY!!
YOU THINK SO?
COMRADES!! ONE OF OUR OWN HAS RETURNED!! PREPARE A FEAST!!!
OOOOOOO
TUUUUUUNA TONIGHT!!!
SPLA—SH!!
FWAP!
FWAP
OFFICER NAMI ARLONG'S PIRATE CREW

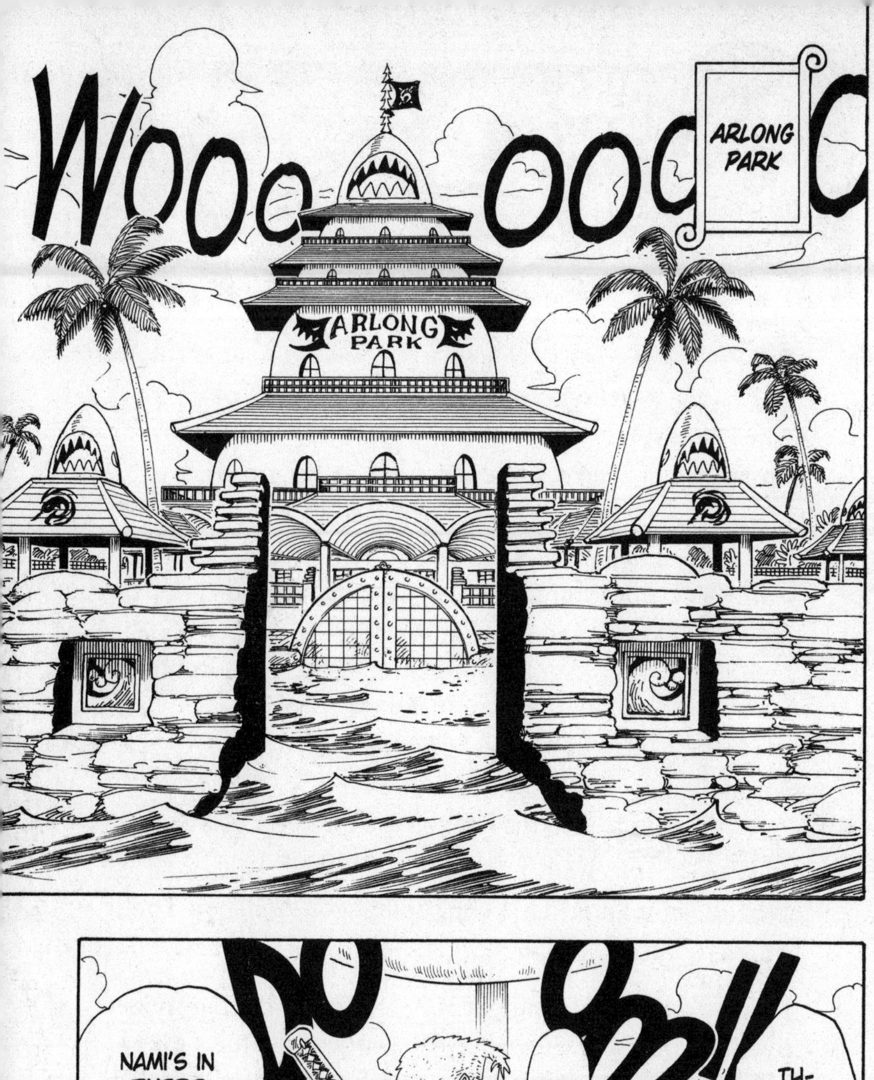
ARLONG PARK
WOOO OOOO
ARLONG PARK

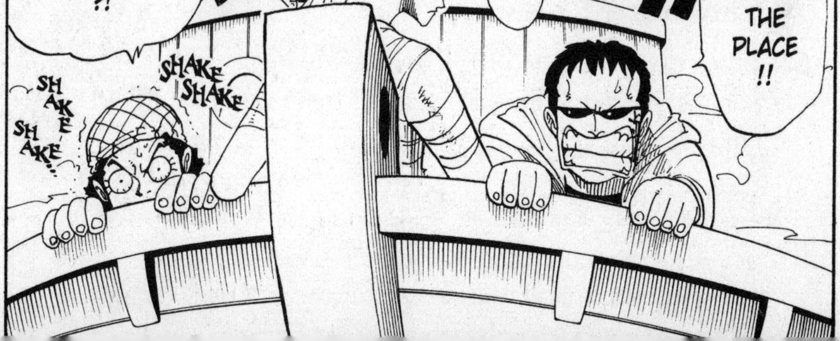
DO OM!!
TH-THAT'S THE PLACE !!
......
NAMI'S IN THERE ?!
SHAKE SHAKE
SHAKE SHAKE

Q: To become a **girl** who is as cool and strong as Zolo, what should I do?

A: Hmm...a girl? Let's see... First of all, do squats!! And eat sardines to strengthen your mental powers!!

Q: Oda Sensei, hello, or rather, *ni hao*!! I used my whole brain to compose Luffy's song. Please read it, dance, and cry!

First verse: Gum$^{\times 3}$ Gum Ya-a-ay
Am I a Gum-Gum Person, or a Rubber Man?
Gum$^{\times 3}$ Gum Yahoo
Lalalalaa Lalaa Lalalalaa Oooh

Second verse: Gum$^{\times 3}$ Gum Stretch
I'm the King of the Pirates, I'm amazing!!
(Gum$^{\times 3}$ Gum) $^{\times 2}$ Amooon

What do you think? Do I win? Shall I go? Well, here I go!!

A: Yay!! Yes, go!! Go far!!

Q: Is Luffy natural or synthetic rubber? This is an inquiry from the Meteorological Agency (with cooperation from the Ministry of Education).

A: Natural ~~dumb~~ rubber.

Q: When my friends and I talk about *One Piece*, I like Shanks, Friend S. likes Zolo, and Friend I. likes Luffy, but R. likes Buggy and Django. Should he see a doctor?

A: One would have to be seriously ill to like those two. Please tell him to rest quietly at home and drink plenty of liquids. And tell him that if he perseveres, good things will come to him...

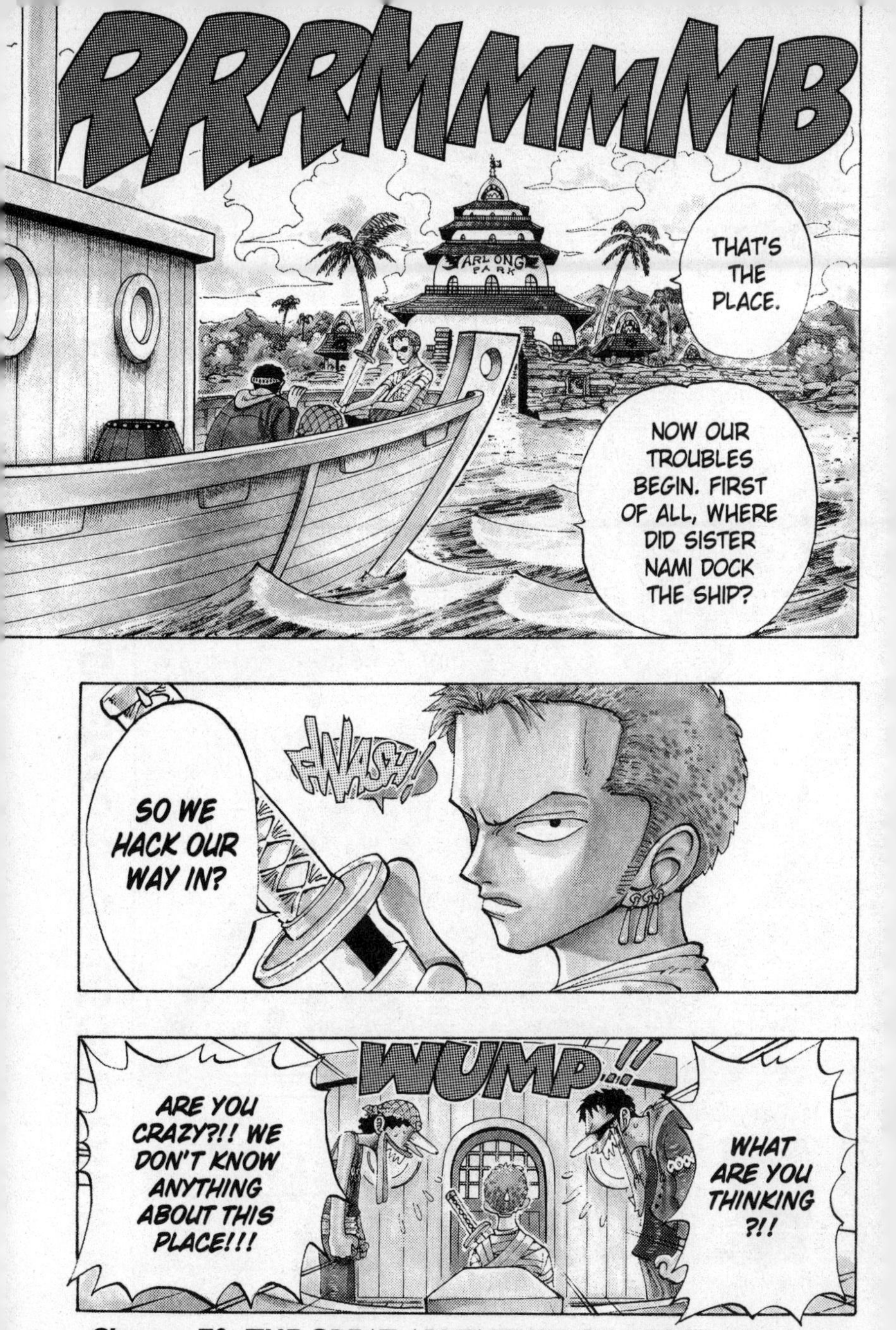
RRRMMMMMB
ARLONG PARK
THAT'S THE PLACE.
NOW OUR TROUBLES BEGIN. FIRST OF ALL, WHERE DID SISTER NAMI DOCK THE SHIP?
FWASH!
SO WE HACK OUR WAY IN?
WUMP!!
WHAT ARE YOU THINKING?!!
ARE YOU CRAZY?!! WE DON'T KNOW ANYTHING ABOUT THIS PLACE!!!

Chapter 70: THE GREAT ADVENTURE OF USOPP THE MAN

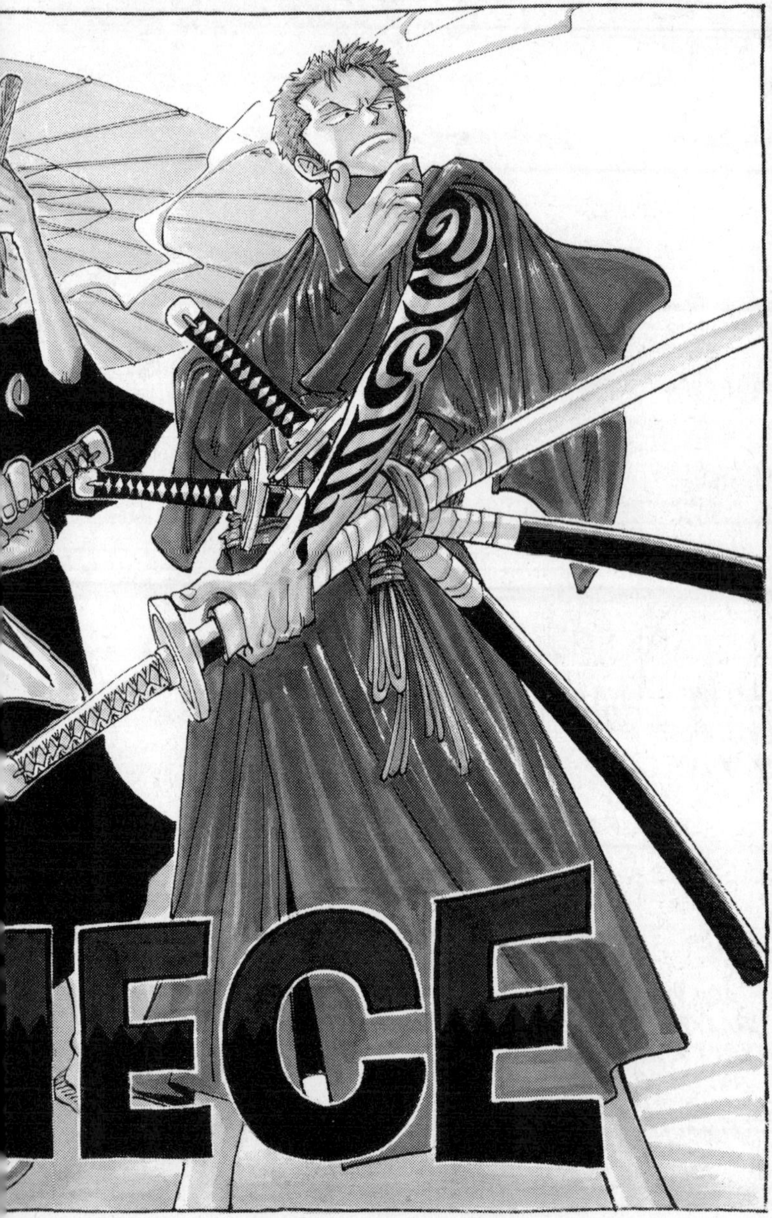
IECE

Chapter 70: THE GREAT ADVENTURE OF USOPP THE MAN

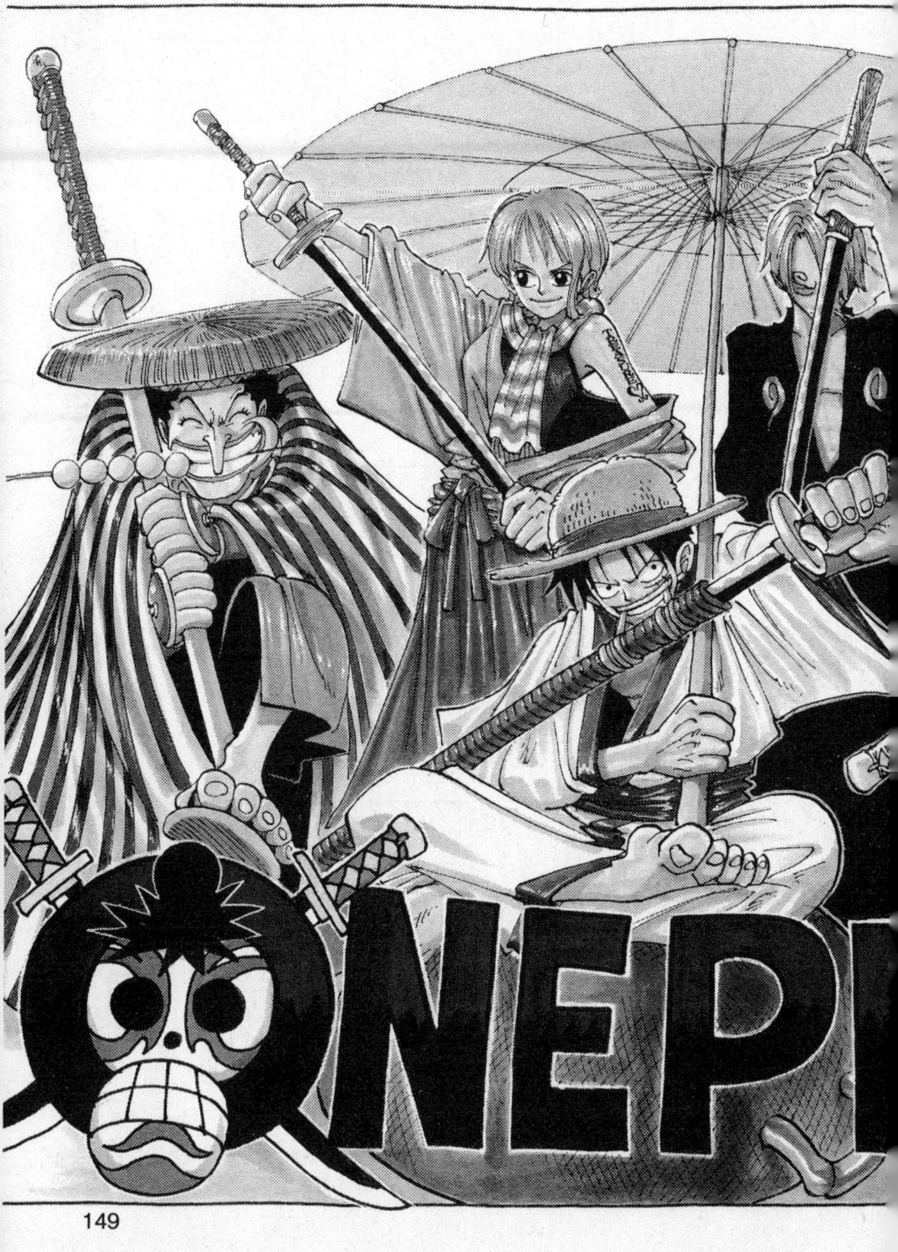

READ THIS WAY

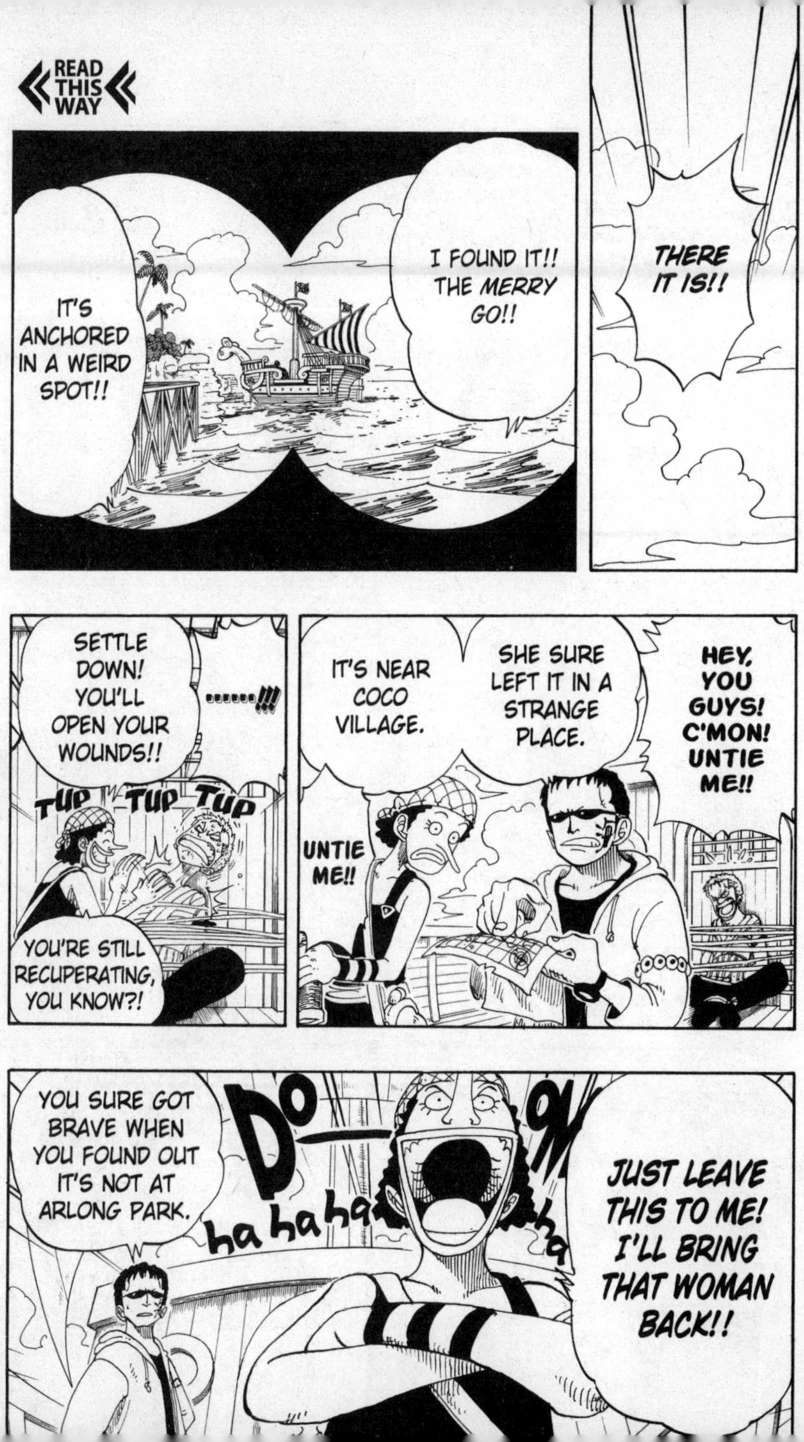
THERE IT IS!!
I FOUND IT!! THE MERRY GO!!
IT'S ANCHORED IN A WEIRD SPOT!!
HEY, YOU GUYS! C'MON! UNTIE ME!!
SHE SURE LEFT IT IN A STRANGE PLACE.
IT'S NEAR COCO VILLAGE.
UNTIE ME!!
SETTLE DOWN! YOU'LL OPEN YOUR WOUNDS!!
......!!!
TUP TUP TUP
YOU'RE STILL RECUPERATING, YOU KNOW?!
JUST LEAVE THIS TO ME! I'LL BRING THAT WOMAN BACK!!
DO—ON
ha ha ha ha
YOU SURE GOT BRAVE WHEN YOU FOUND OUT IT'S NOT AT ARLONG PARK.

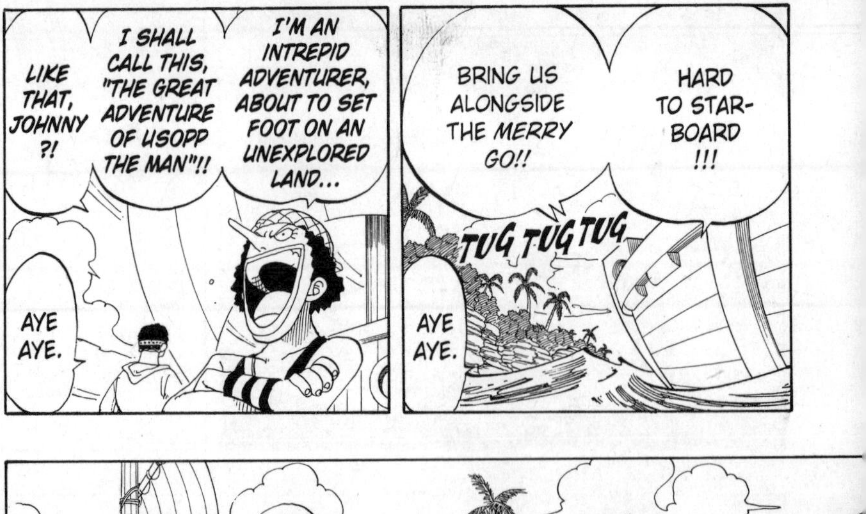
HARD TO STAR-BOARD !!!
BRING US ALONGSIDE THE MERRY GO!!
TUG TUG TUG
AYE AYE.
I'M AN INTREPID ADVENTURER, ABOUT TO SET FOOT ON AN UNEXPLORED LAND...
I SHALL CALL THIS, "THE GREAT ADVENTURE OF USOPP THE MAN"!!
LIKE THAT, JOHNNY ?!
AYE AYE.
?
SHWOOO...

UNLIKE THE INFAMOUS SWASTIKA OF NAZI GERMANY, THE BUDDHIST *MANJI* IS DEPICTED AS A SQUARE (RATHER THAN DIAMOND SHAPE), AND CAN POINT EITHER CLOCKWISE OR COUNTER-CLOCKWISE. AN ANCIENT SYMBOL, THE *MANJI* CAN BE SEEN ON THE CHEST, PALMS AND FEET OF BUDDHA, REPRESENTING GOOD LUCK. YOU'LL ALSO SEE IT ON THE BELLY OF THE FISHY BAD-BOY BELOW.

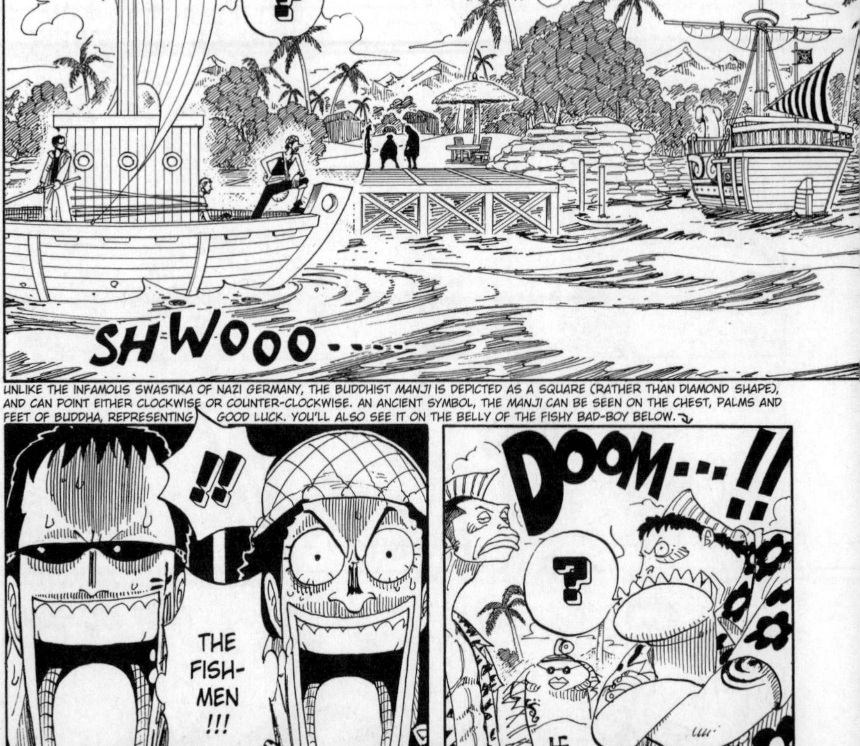
DOOM...!!
?
!!
THE FISH-MEN !!!

READ THIS WAY

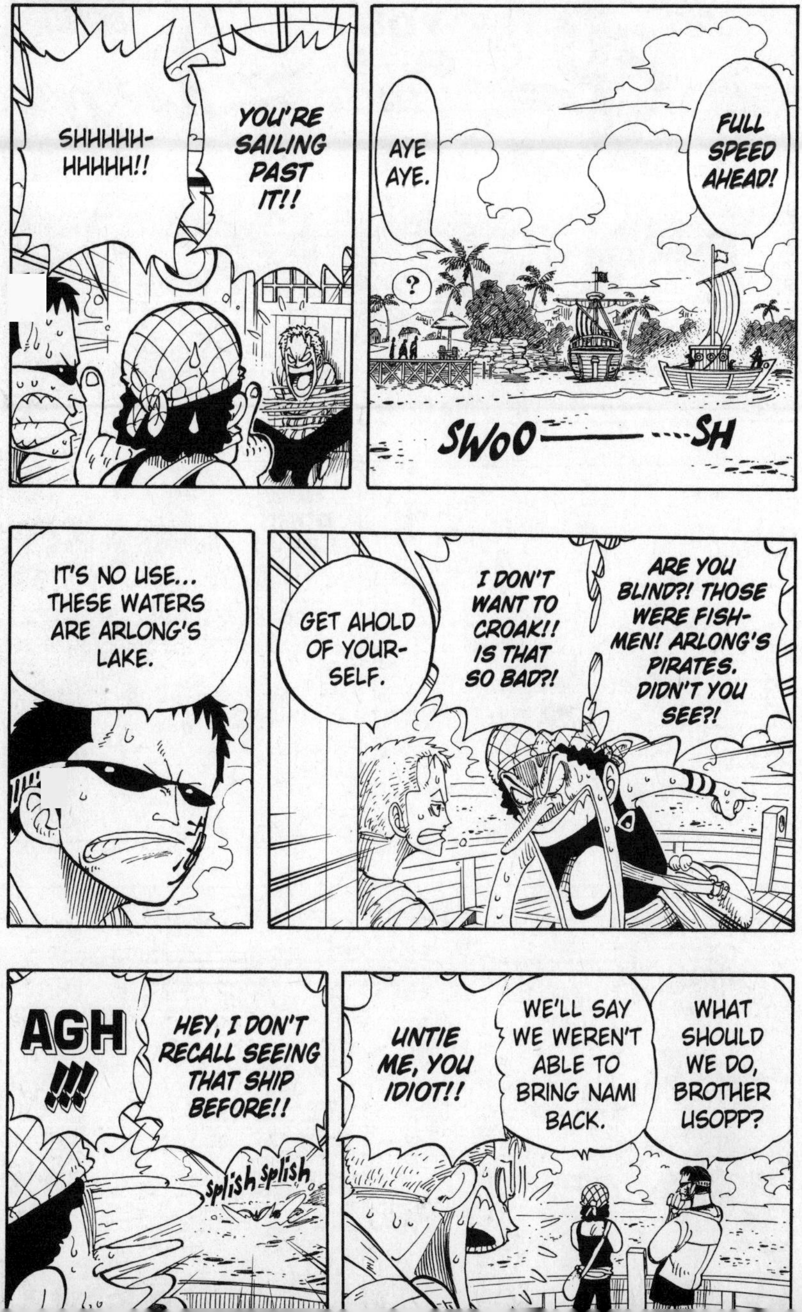
FULL SPEED AHEAD!
AYE AYE.
?
SWOO——SH
YOU'RE SAILING PAST IT!!
SHHHHHHHHHHH!!
ARE YOU BLIND?! THOSE WERE FISHMEN! ARLONG'S PIRATES. DIDN'T YOU SEE?!
I DON'T WANT TO CROAK!! IS THAT SO BAD?!
GET AHOLD OF YOURSELF.
IT'S NO USE... THESE WATERS ARE ARLONG'S LAKE.
WHAT SHOULD WE DO, BROTHER USOPP?
WE'LL SAY WE WEREN'T ABLE TO BRING NAMI BACK.
UNTIE ME, YOU IDIOT!!
HEY, I DON'T RECALL SEEING THAT SHIP BEFORE!!
AGH!!!
splish splish

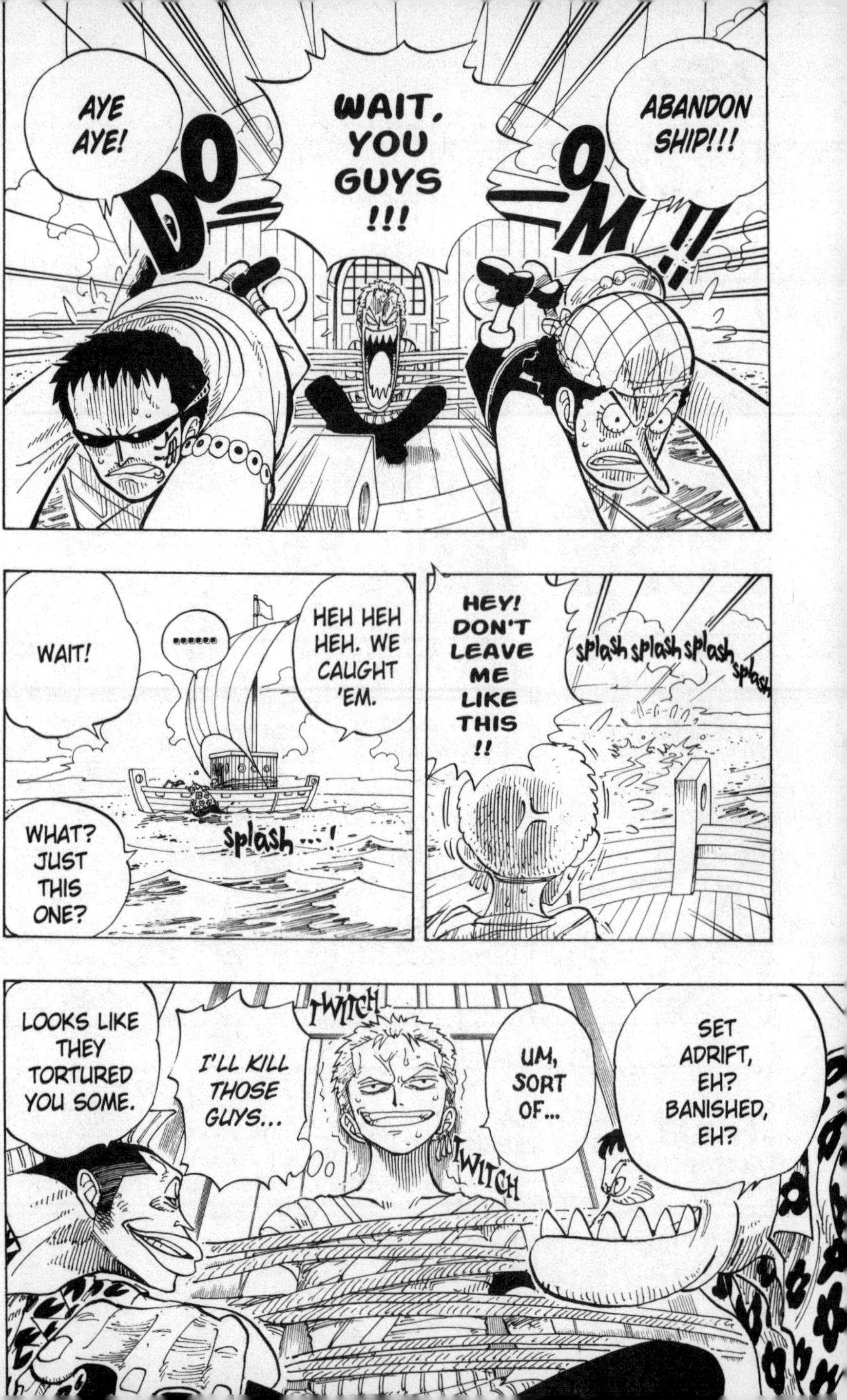
ABANDON SHIP!!!
AYE AYE!
DO—OM!!
WAIT. YOU GUYS!!!
HEY! DON'T LEAVE ME LIKE THIS!!
splash splash splash splash
HEH HEH HEH. WE CAUGHT 'EM.
......
WAIT!
WHAT? JUST THIS ONE?
splash...!
SET ADRIFT, EH? BANISHED, EH?
UM, SORT OF...
TWITCH
TWITCH
I'LL KILL THOSE GUYS...
LOOKS LIKE THEY TORTURED YOU SOME.

READ THIS WAY

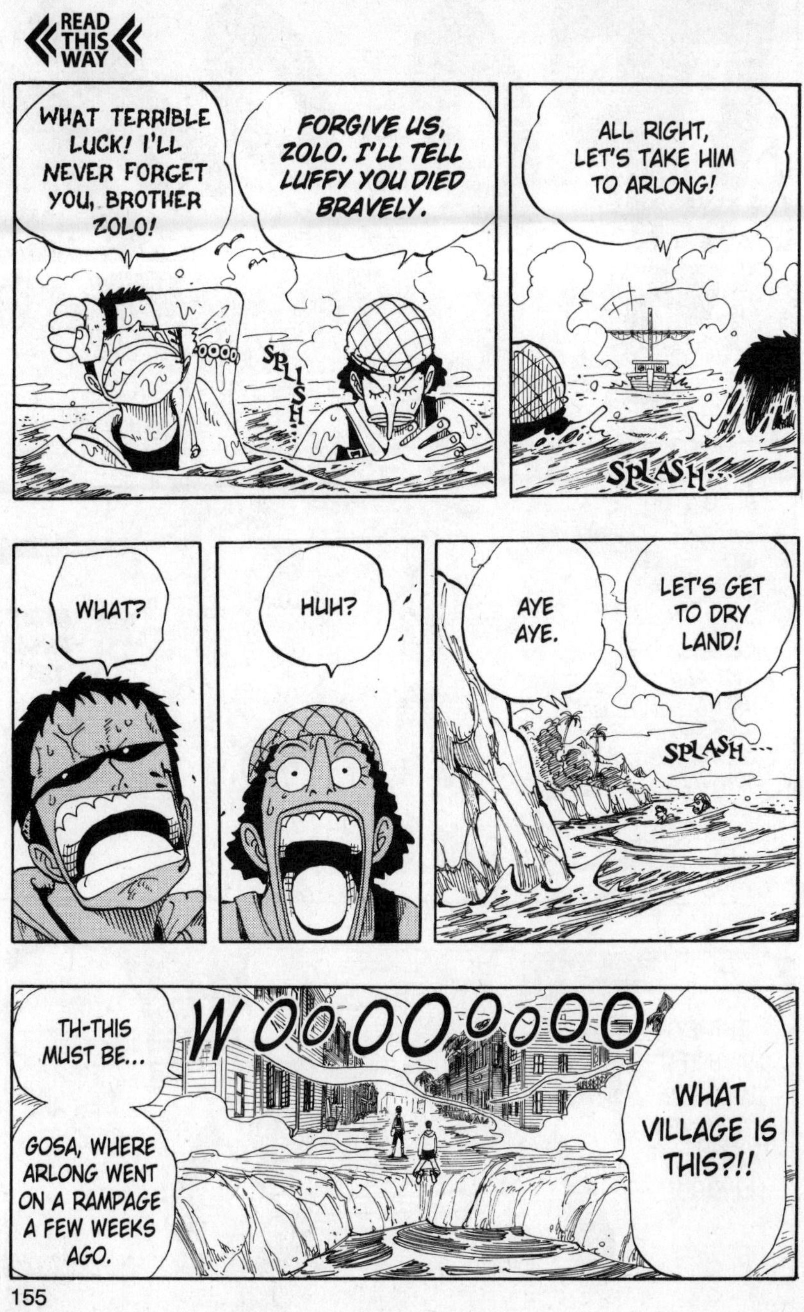
ALL RIGHT, LET'S TAKE HIM TO ARLONG!
SPLASH...
FORGIVE US, ZOLO. I'LL TELL LUFFY YOU DIED BRAVELY.
WHAT TERRIBLE LUCK! I'LL NEVER FORGET YOU, BROTHER ZOLO!
SPLISH!
LET'S GET TO DRY LAND!
AYE AYE.
SPLASH...
HUH?
WHAT?
WHAT VILLAGE IS THIS?!!
WOOOOOOOOO
TH-THIS MUST BE...
GOSA, WHERE ARLONG WENT ON A RAMPAGE A FEW WEEKS AGO.

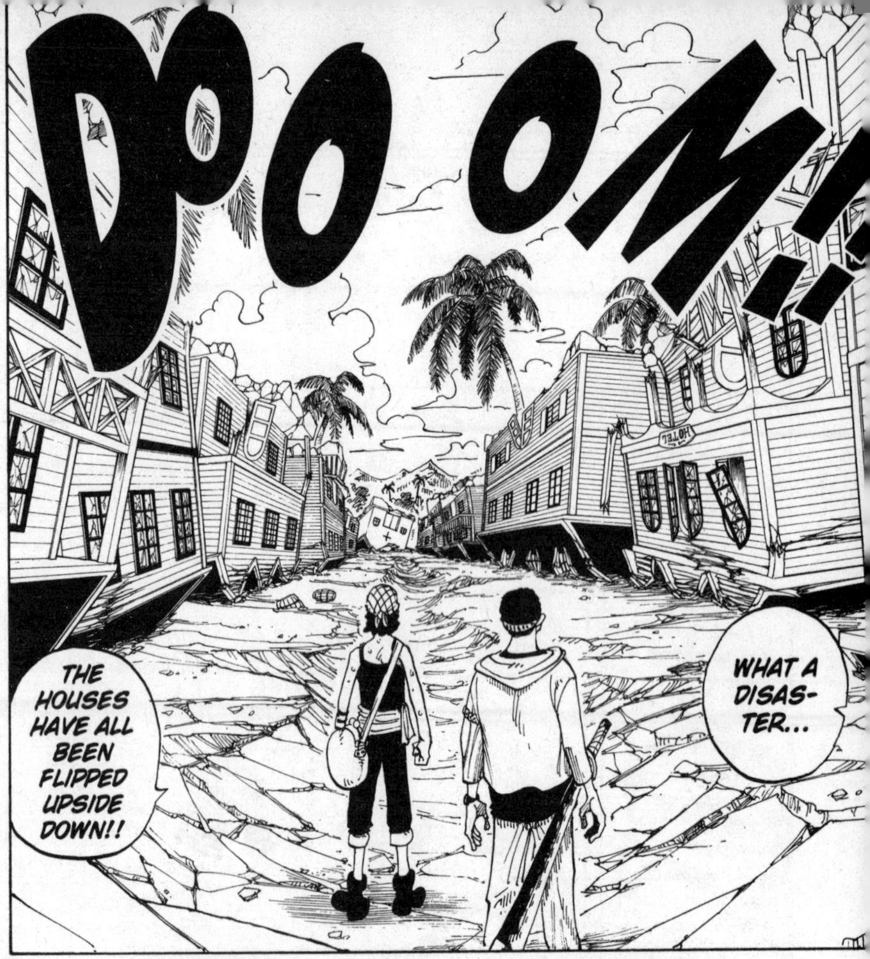
DOOM!!
WHAT A DISAS-TER...
THE HOUSES HAVE ALL BEEN FLIPPED UPSIDE DOWN!!

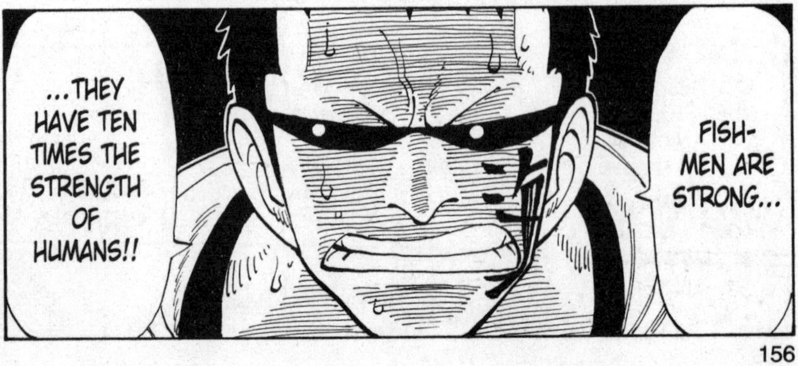
FISH-MEN ARE STRONG...
...THEY HAVE TEN TIMES THE STRENGTH OF HUMANS!!

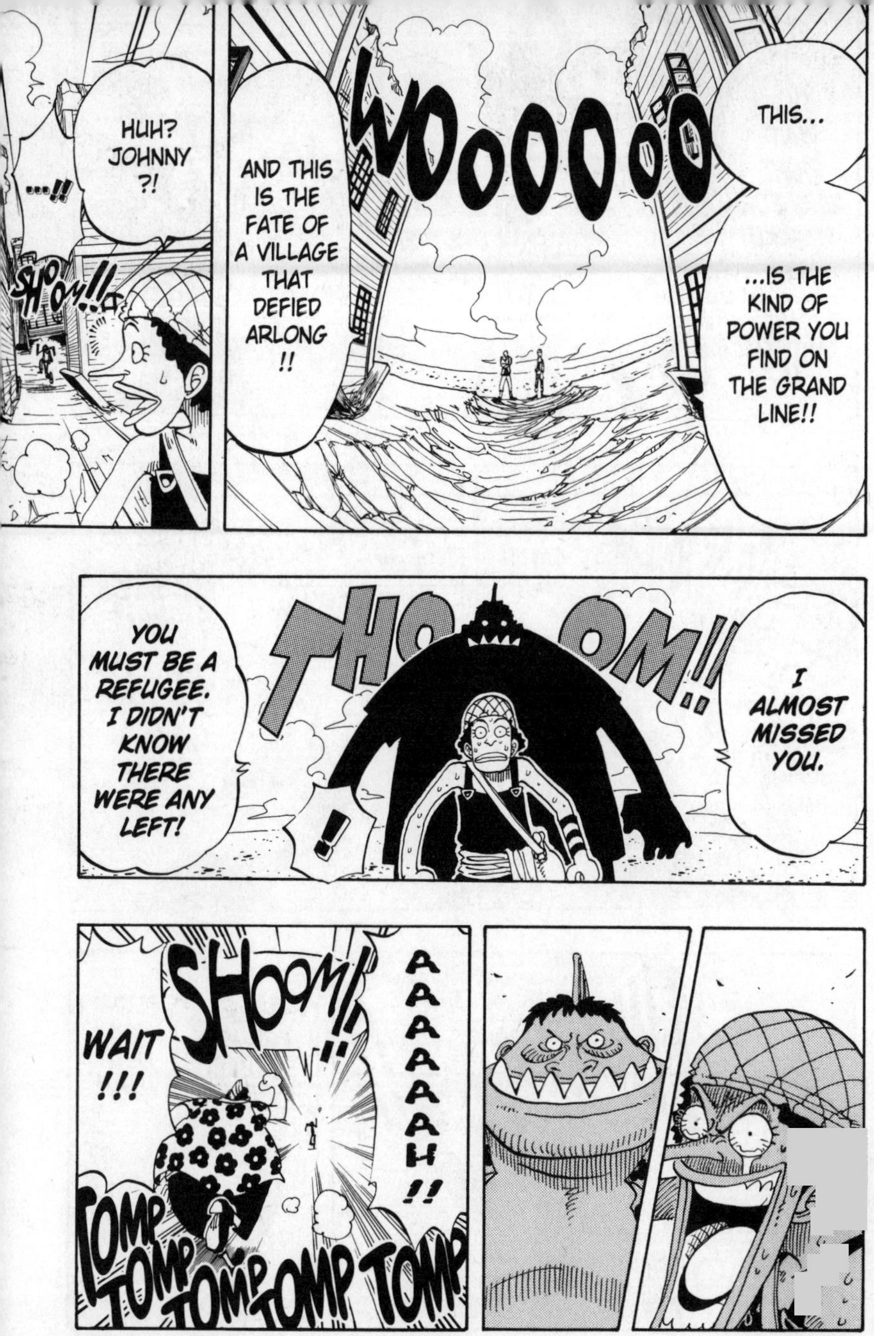
THIS...
...IS THE KIND OF POWER YOU FIND ON THE GRAND LINE!!
WOOOOOO
AND THIS IS THE FATE OF A VILLAGE THAT DEFIED ARLONG!!
HUH? JOHNNY?!
...!!
SHOOM!!
I ALMOST MISSED YOU.
THOOM!!
YOU MUST BE A REFUGEE. I DIDN'T KNOW THERE WERE ANY LEFT!
!
AAAAAAAH!!
SHOOM!!
WAIT!!!
TOMP TOMP TOMP TOMP TOMP

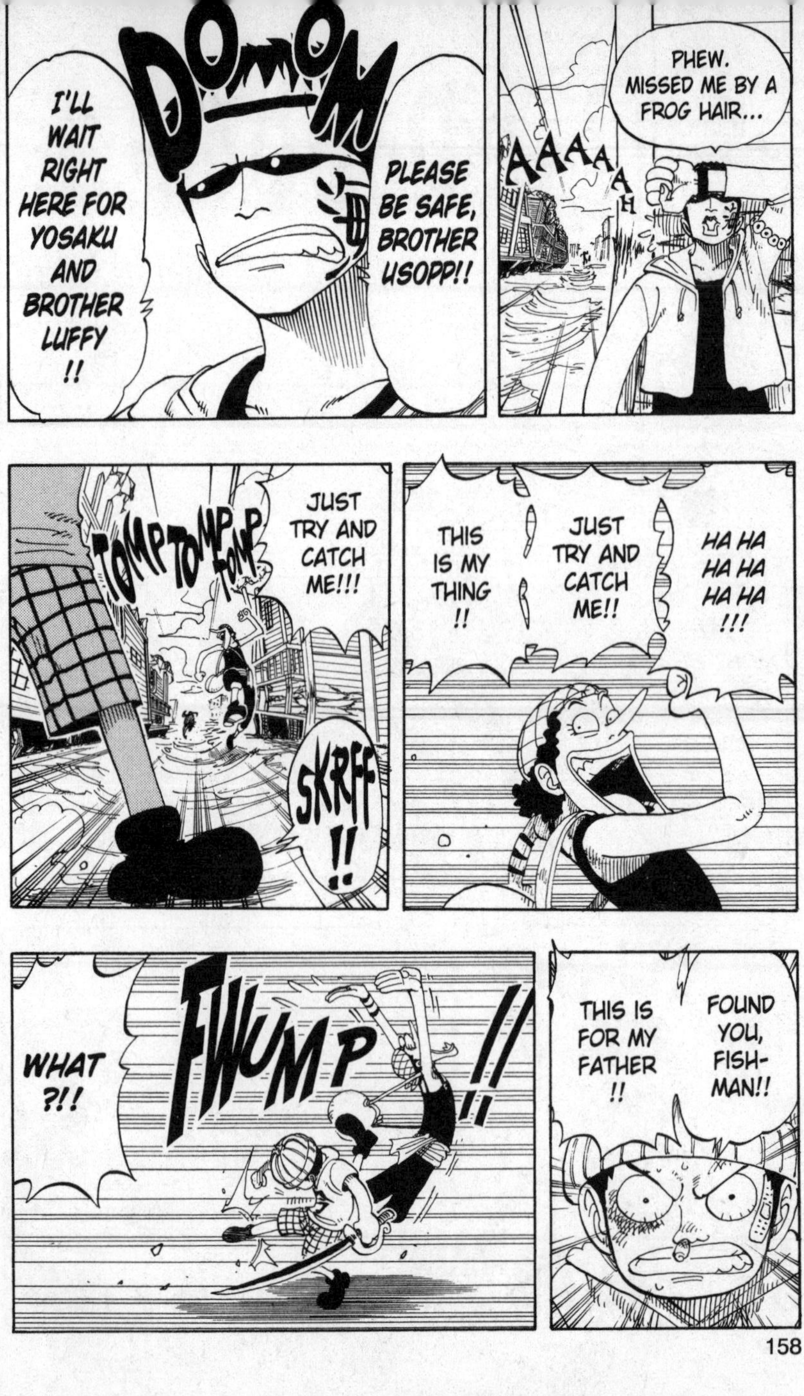
PHEW. MISSED ME BY A FROG HAIR...
AAAAAH
DOMON
PLEASE BE SAFE, BROTHER USOPP!!
I'LL WAIT RIGHT HERE FOR YOSAKU AND BROTHER LUFFY !!
HA HA HA HA HA HA !!!
JUST TRY AND CATCH ME!!
THIS IS MY THING !!
JUST TRY AND CATCH ME!!!
TOMPTOMPTOMP
SKRFF !!
FOUND YOU, FISH-MAN!!
THIS IS FOR MY FATHER !!
FWUMP!!
WHAT ?!!

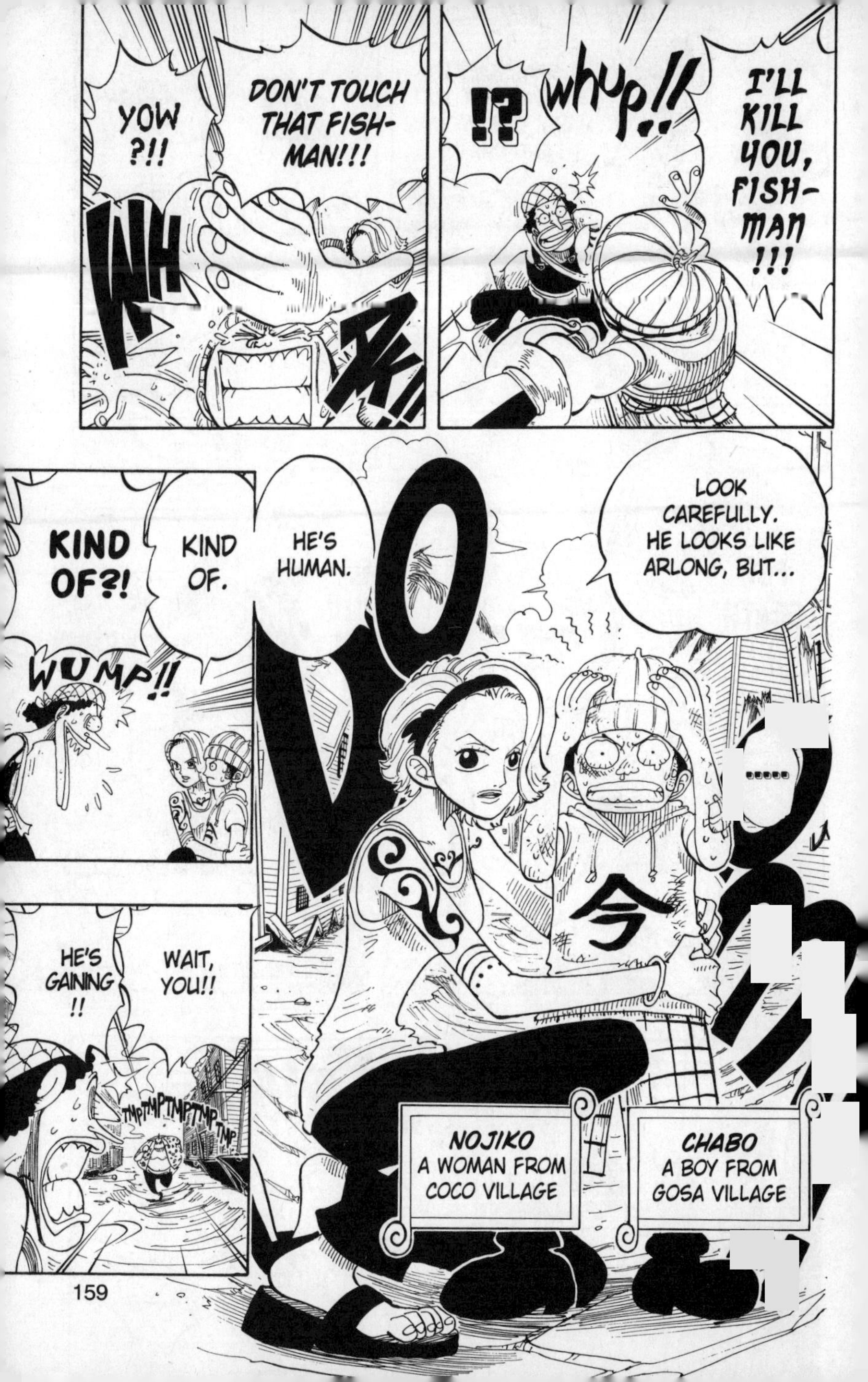

I'LL KILL YOU, FISH-MAN!!!
!?
WHUP!!
DON'T TOUCH THAT FISH-MAN!!!
YOW?!!
WHAK!!
LOOK CAREFULLY. HE LOOKS LIKE ARLONG, BUT...
HE'S HUMAN.
DO
......
CHABO
A BOY FROM GOSA VILLAGE
NOJIKO
A WOMAN FROM COCO VILLAGE
KIND OF.
KIND OF?!
WUMP!!
WAIT, YOU!!
HE'S GAINING!!
TMPTMPTMPTMPTMP

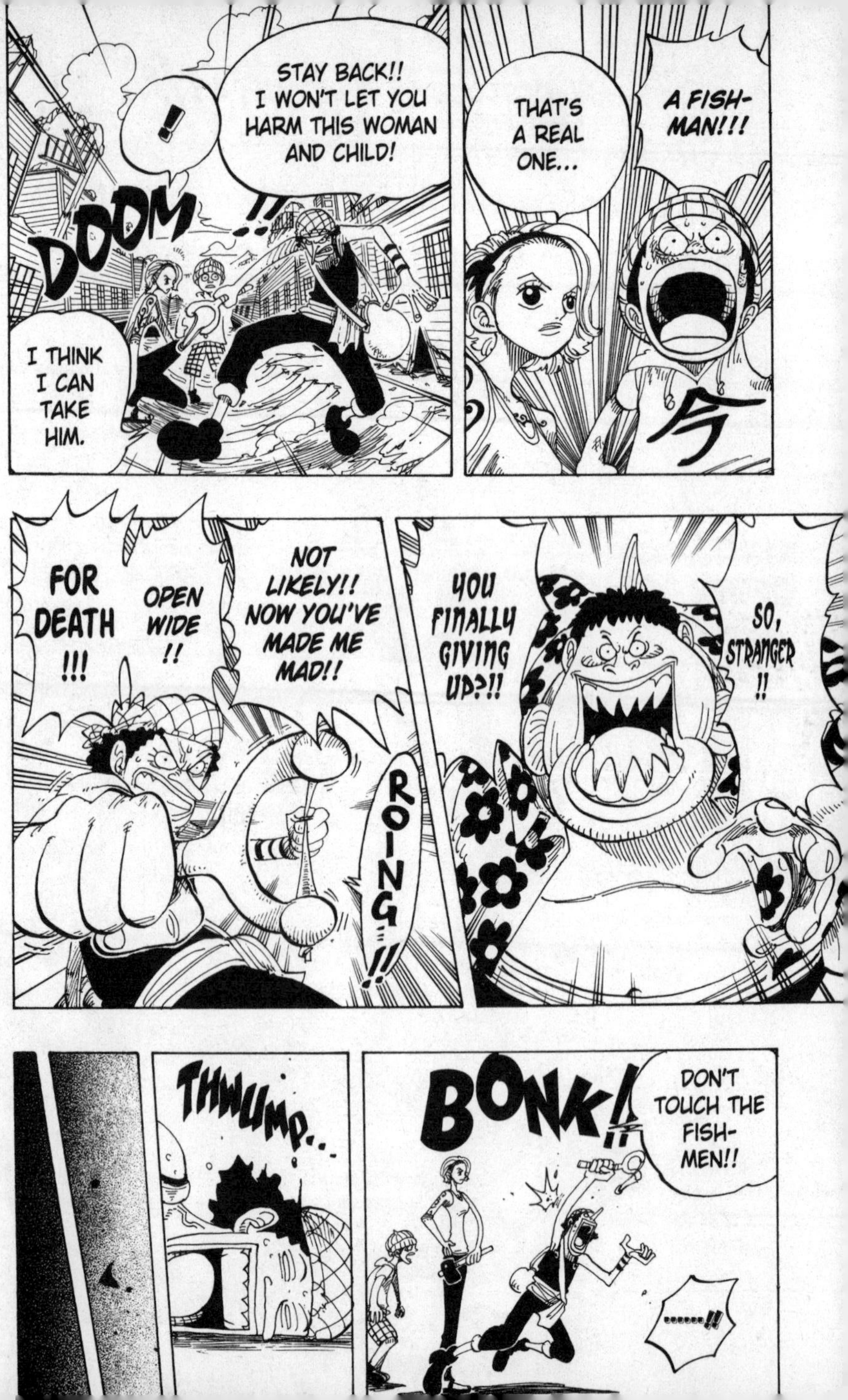
A FISH-MAN!!!
THAT'S A REAL ONE...
今
STAY BACK!! I WON'T LET YOU HARM THIS WOMAN AND CHILD!
!
DOOM
!!
I THINK I CAN TAKE HIM.
SO, STRANGER !!
YOU FINALLY GIVING UP?!!
NOT LIKELY!! NOW YOU'VE MADE ME MAD!!
OPEN WIDE !!
FOR DEATH !!!
ROING..!!
DON'T TOUCH THE FISH-MEN!!
BONK!!
......!!
THWUMP...

READ THIS WAY

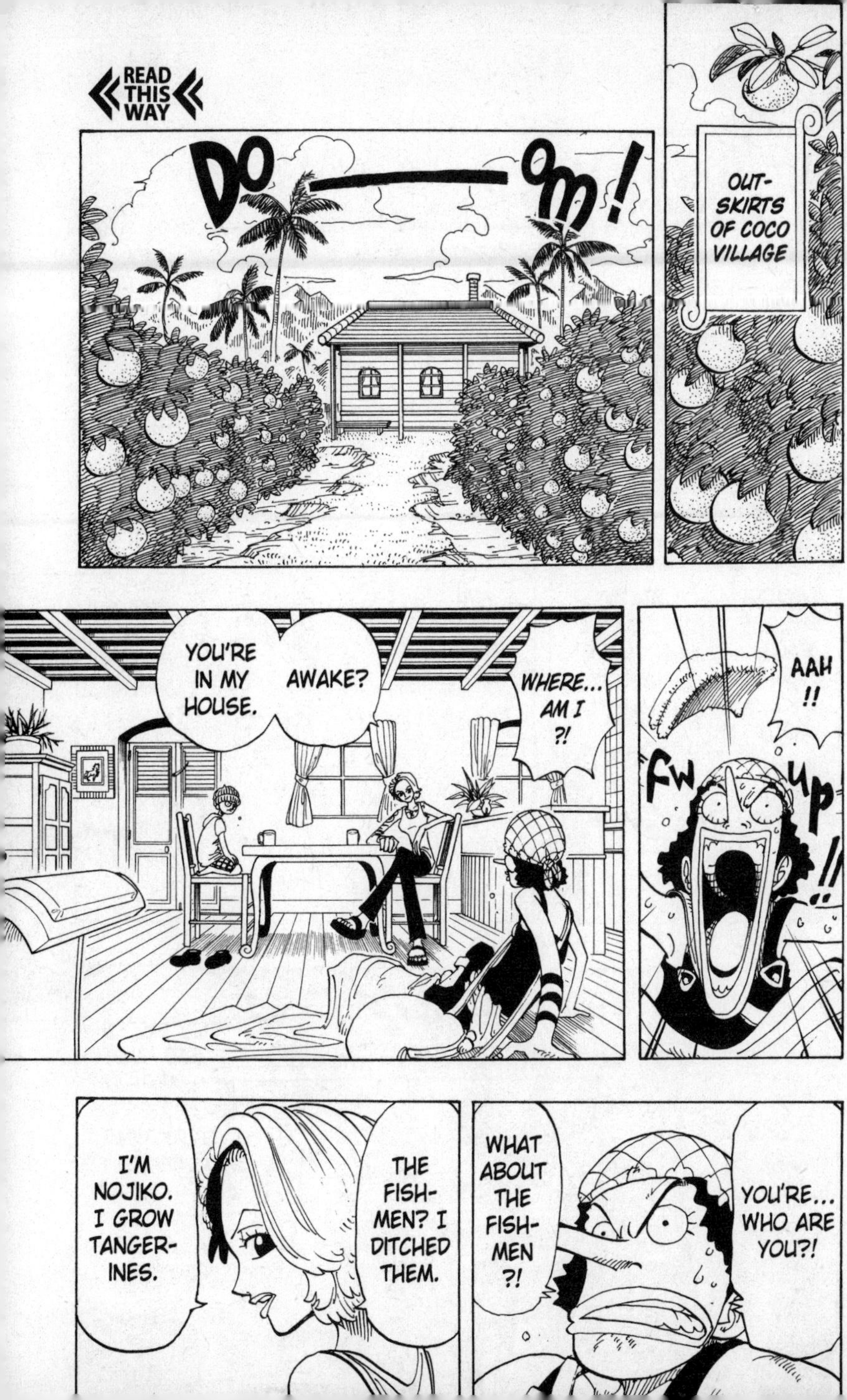
OUT-SKIRTS OF COCO VILLAGE
DO——OM!
AAH!!
FWUP!!
WHERE... AM I?!
AWAKE?
YOU'RE IN MY HOUSE.
YOU'RE... WHO ARE YOU?!
WHAT ABOUT THE FISH-MEN?!
THE FISH-MEN? I DITCHED THEM.
I'M NOJIKO. I GROW TANGER-INES.

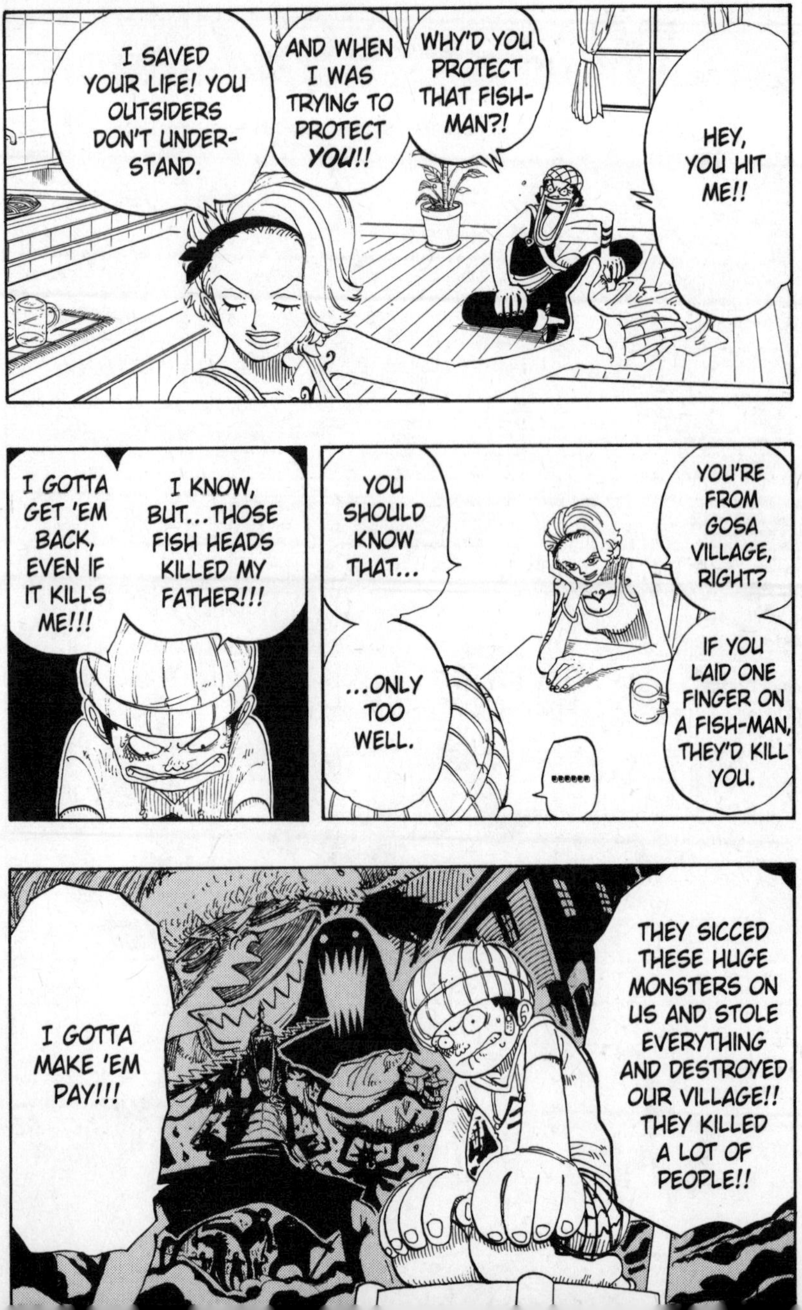
HEY, YOU HIT ME!!
WHY'D YOU PROTECT THAT FISH-MAN?!
AND WHEN I WAS TRYING TO PROTECT *YOU*!!
I SAVED YOUR LIFE! YOU OUTSIDERS DON'T UNDER-STAND.
YOU'RE FROM GOSA VILLAGE, RIGHT?
IF YOU LAID ONE FINGER ON A FISH-MAN, THEY'D KILL YOU.
......
YOU SHOULD KNOW THAT...
...ONLY TOO WELL.
I KNOW, BUT...THOSE FISH HEADS KILLED MY FATHER!!!
I GOTTA GET 'EM BACK, EVEN IF IT KILLS ME!!!
THEY SICCED THESE HUGE MONSTERS ON US AND STOLE EVERYTHING AND DESTROYED OUR VILLAGE!! THEY KILLED A LOT OF PEOPLE!!
I GOTTA MAKE 'EM PAY!!!

READ THIS WAY

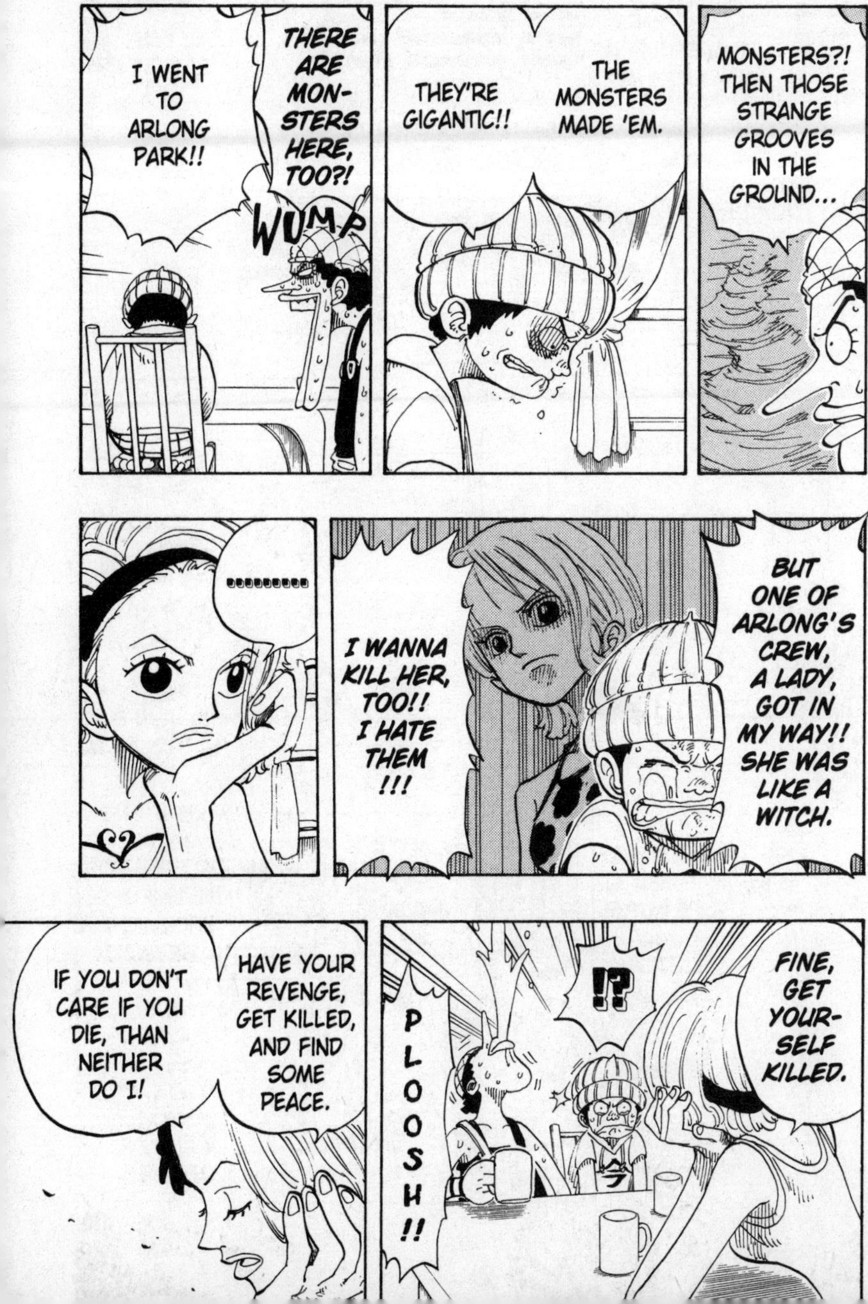
MONSTERS?! THEN THOSE STRANGE GROOVES IN THE GROUND...
THE MONSTERS MADE 'EM.
THEY'RE GIGANTIC!!
THERE ARE MON-STERS HERE, TOO?!
I WENT TO ARLONG PARK!!
WUMP
BUT ONE OF ARLONG'S CREW, A LADY, GOT IN MY WAY!! SHE WAS LIKE A WITCH.
I WANNA KILL HER, TOO!! I HATE THEM !!!
....
FINE, GET YOUR-SELF KILLED.
!?
PLOOSH!!
HAVE YOUR REVENGE, GET KILLED, AND FIND SOME PEACE.
IF YOU DON'T CARE IF YOU DIE, THAN NEITHER DO I!

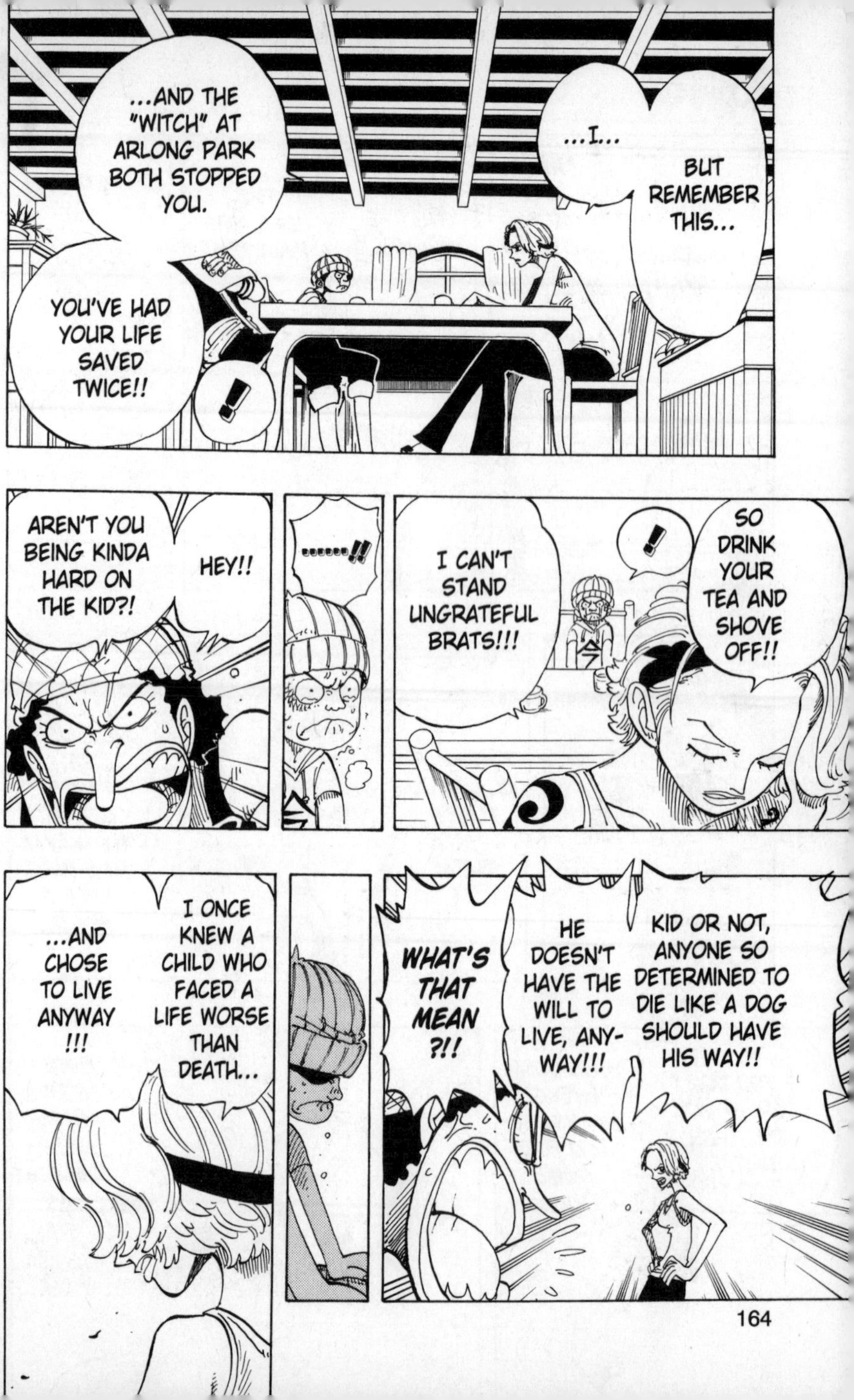
...I...
BUT REMEMBER THIS...
...AND THE "WITCH" AT ARLONG PARK BOTH STOPPED YOU.
YOU'VE HAD YOUR LIFE SAVED TWICE!!
!
SO DRINK YOUR TEA AND SHOVE OFF!!
!
I CAN'T STAND UNGRATEFUL BRATS!!!
......!!
HEY!!
AREN'T YOU BEING KINDA HARD ON THE KID?!
KID OR NOT, ANYONE SO DETERMINED TO DIE LIKE A DOG SHOULD HAVE HIS WAY!!
HE DOESN'T HAVE THE WILL TO LIVE, ANY-WAY!!!
WHAT'S THAT MEAN?!!
I ONCE KNEW A CHILD WHO FACED A LIFE WORSE THAN DEATH...
...AND CHOSE TO LIVE ANYWAY!!!

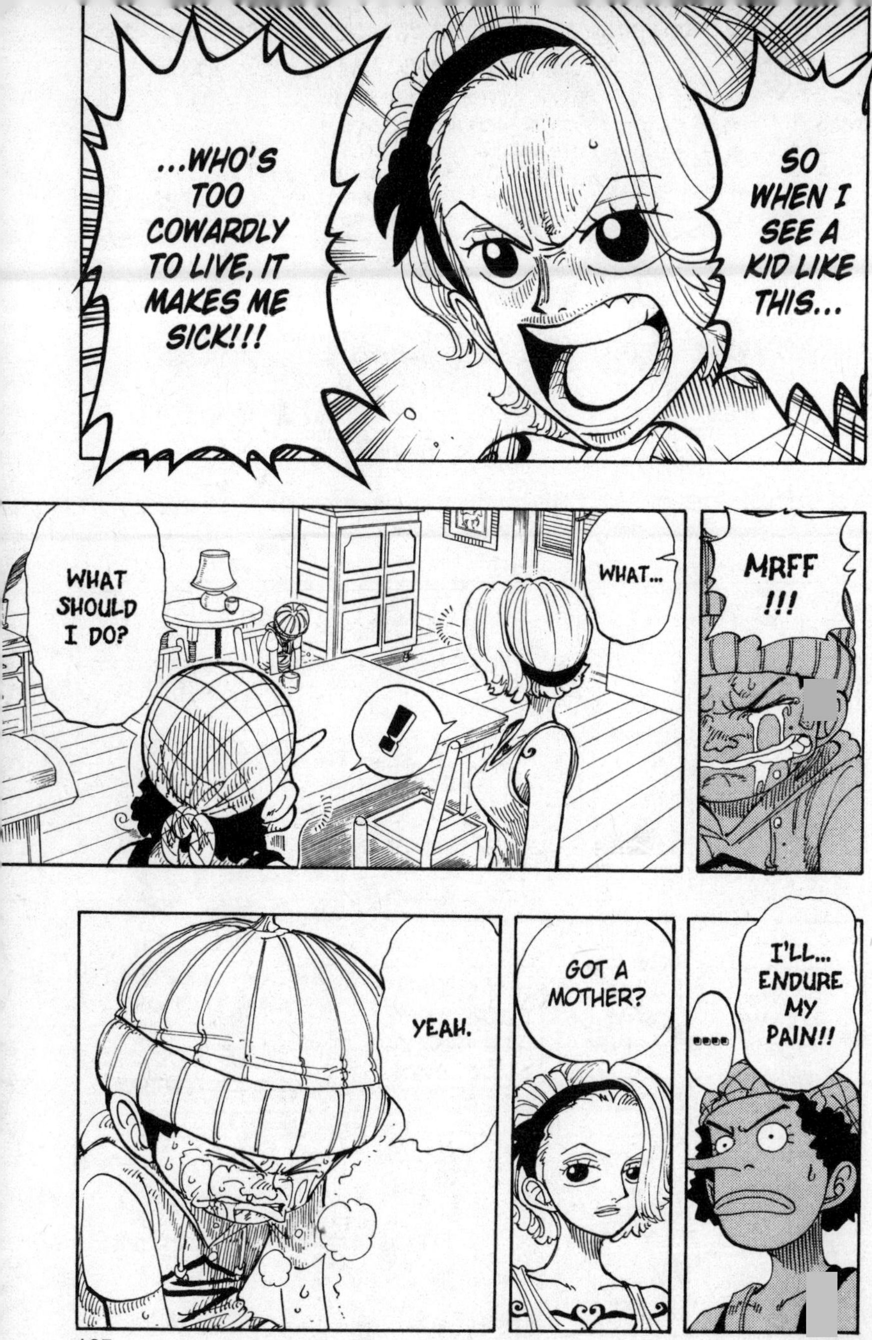
SO WHEN I SEE A KID LIKE THIS...
...WHO'S TOO COWARDLY TO LIVE, IT MAKES ME SICK!!!
MRFF !!!
WHAT...
WHAT SHOULD I DO?
!
I'LL... ENDURE MY PAIN!!
....
GOT A MOTHER?
YEAH.

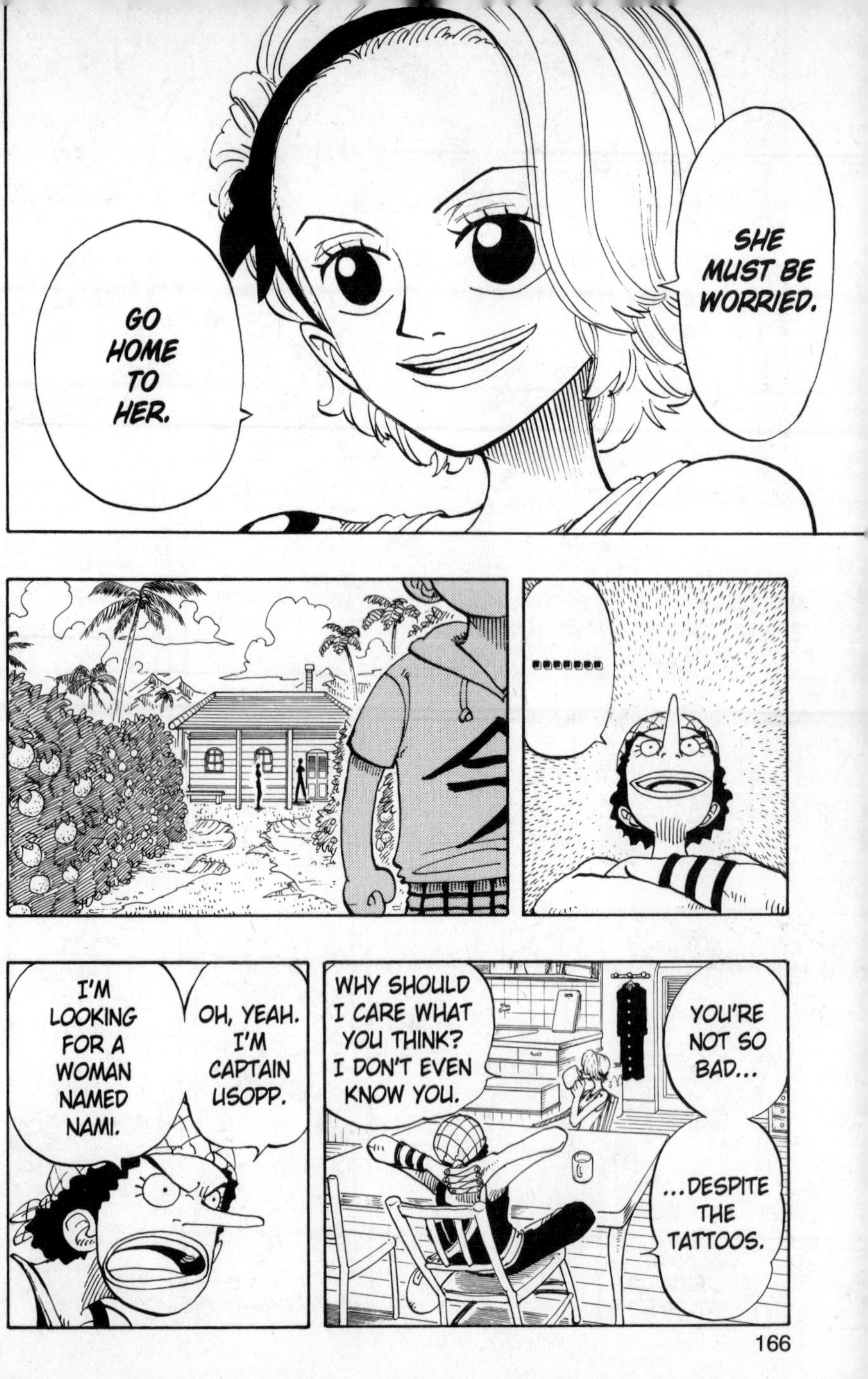
SHE MUST BE WORRIED.
GO HOME TO HER.
....
YOU'RE NOT SO BAD...
...DESPITE THE TATTOOS.
WHY SHOULD I CARE WHAT YOU THINK? I DON'T EVEN KNOW YOU.
OH, YEAH. I'M CAPTAIN USOPP.
I'M LOOKING FOR A WOMAN NAMED NAMI.

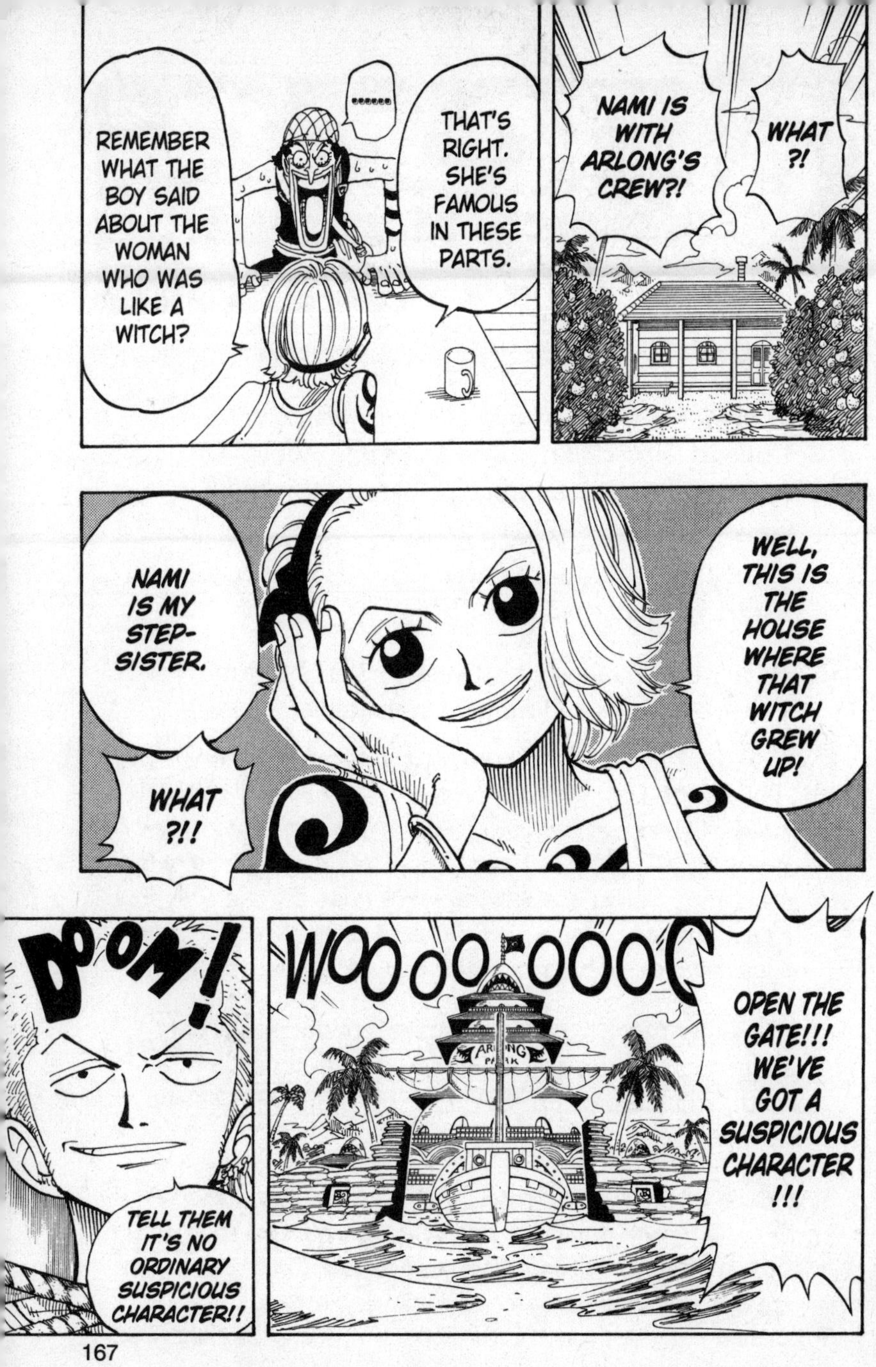
WHAT ?!
NAMI IS WITH ARLONG'S CREW?!
THAT'S RIGHT. SHE'S FAMOUS IN THESE PARTS.
......
REMEMBER WHAT THE BOY SAID ABOUT THE WOMAN WHO WAS LIKE A WITCH?
WELL, THIS IS THE HOUSE WHERE THAT WITCH GREW UP!
NAMI IS MY STEP-SISTER.
WHAT ?!!
WOOOOOOOOOO
OPEN THE GATE!!! WE'VE GOT A SUSPICIOUS CHARACTER !!!
DOOM!
TELL THEM IT'S NO ORDINARY SUSPICIOUS CHARACTER!!

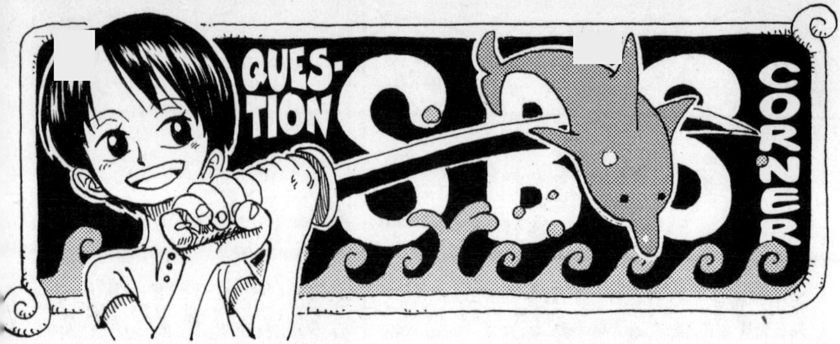
QUES-
TION
SBS
CORNER

Q: What does the D in Monkey D. Luffy stand for? Is it Donburi (a bowl of rice with topping)? Daibutsu (a statue of the Great Buddha)? What?! I gotta know!!

A: I get this question all the time.
But I can't answer it...yet. For now, don't worry about it. Just read it as "D."

Q: What's the relationship between pirates and rum? In books, pirates and rum are inseparable.

A: Not just pirates and rum, but all seafarers and rum. The short story is that rum was cheap, so the British navy in pirate times switched from brandy to rum for the sailors' grog rations, which led to hard-drinking mariners being associated with rum. By the way, the reason there was so much alcohol aboard the ships was that on long sea voyages, water would go bad.

Q: The other night, I met an inhabitant of the planet Gum-Gum. I asked him how long his arms stretched, and he said, "705 Poison Gum-Gums." How long is 705 Poison Gum-Gums?

A: You met a Gum-Gummian!! Amazing!! And lucky!! A "Poison Gum-Gum" is a unit equal to ten Gum-Gums. So that's 7,050 Gum-Gums!! We're talking cosmic distances!! But be warned--of all the races in the universe, the Gum-Gummians are the most likely to say ridiculous things.

Chapter 71:
LORDS OF ALL CREATION

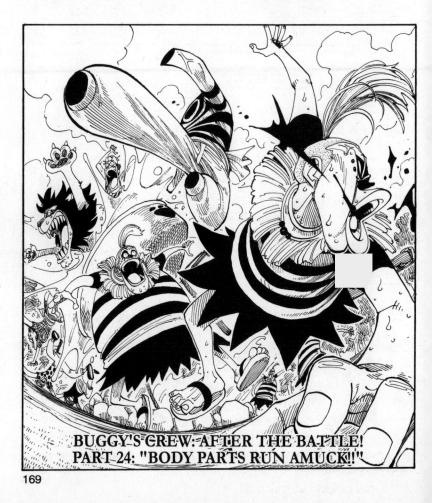

BUGGY'S CREW: AFTER THE BATTLE!
PART 24: "BODY PARTS RUN AMUCK!!"

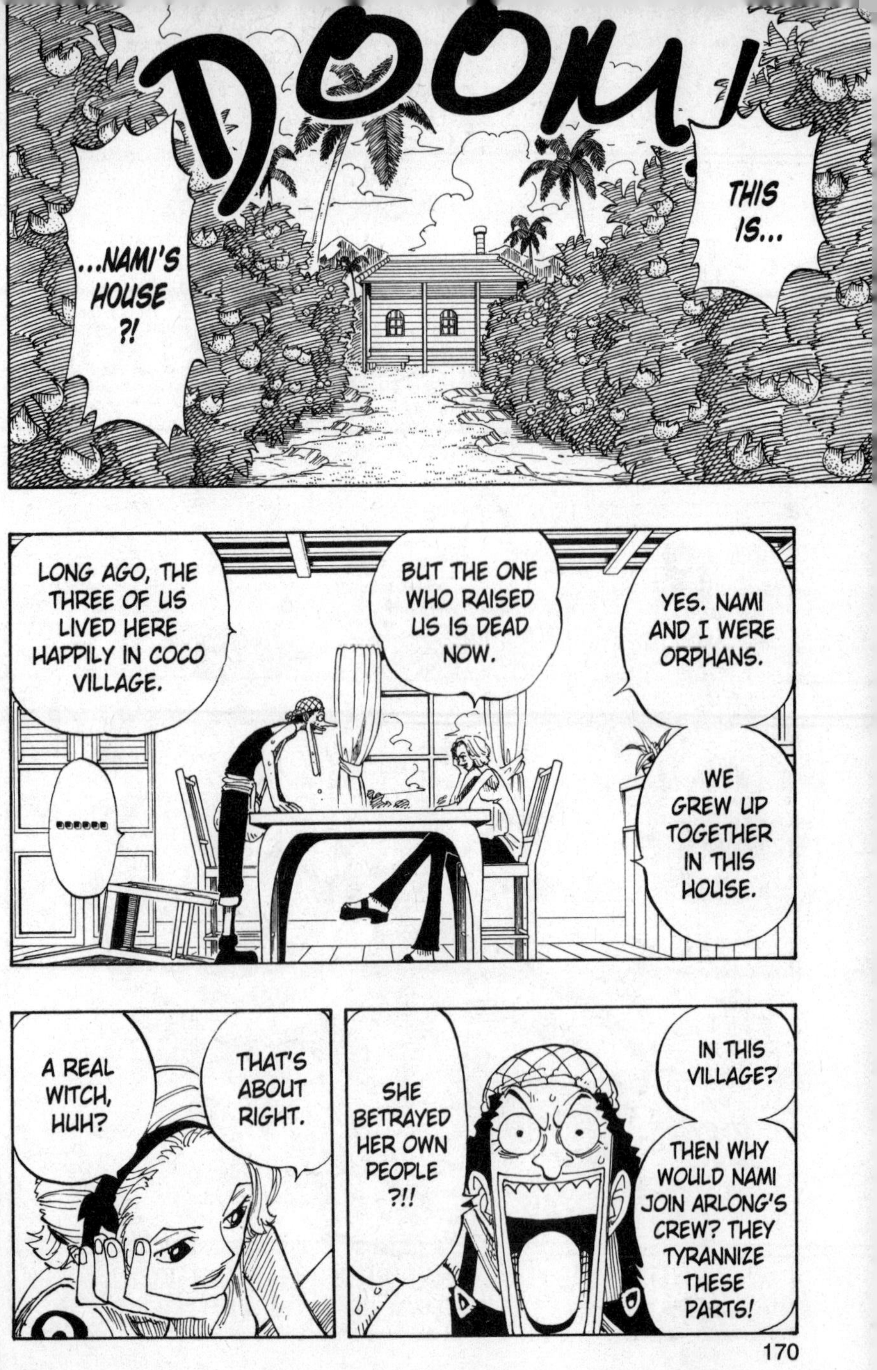
DOOM
THIS IS...
...NAMI'S HOUSE ?!
YES. NAMI AND I WERE ORPHANS.
WE GREW UP TOGETHER IN THIS HOUSE.
BUT THE ONE WHO RAISED US IS DEAD NOW.
LONG AGO, THE THREE OF US LIVED HERE HAPPILY IN COCO VILLAGE.
.....
IN THIS VILLAGE?
THEN WHY WOULD NAMI JOIN ARLONG'S CREW? THEY TYRANNIZE THESE PARTS!
SHE BETRAYED HER OWN PEOPLE ?!!
THAT'S ABOUT RIGHT.
A REAL WITCH, HUH?

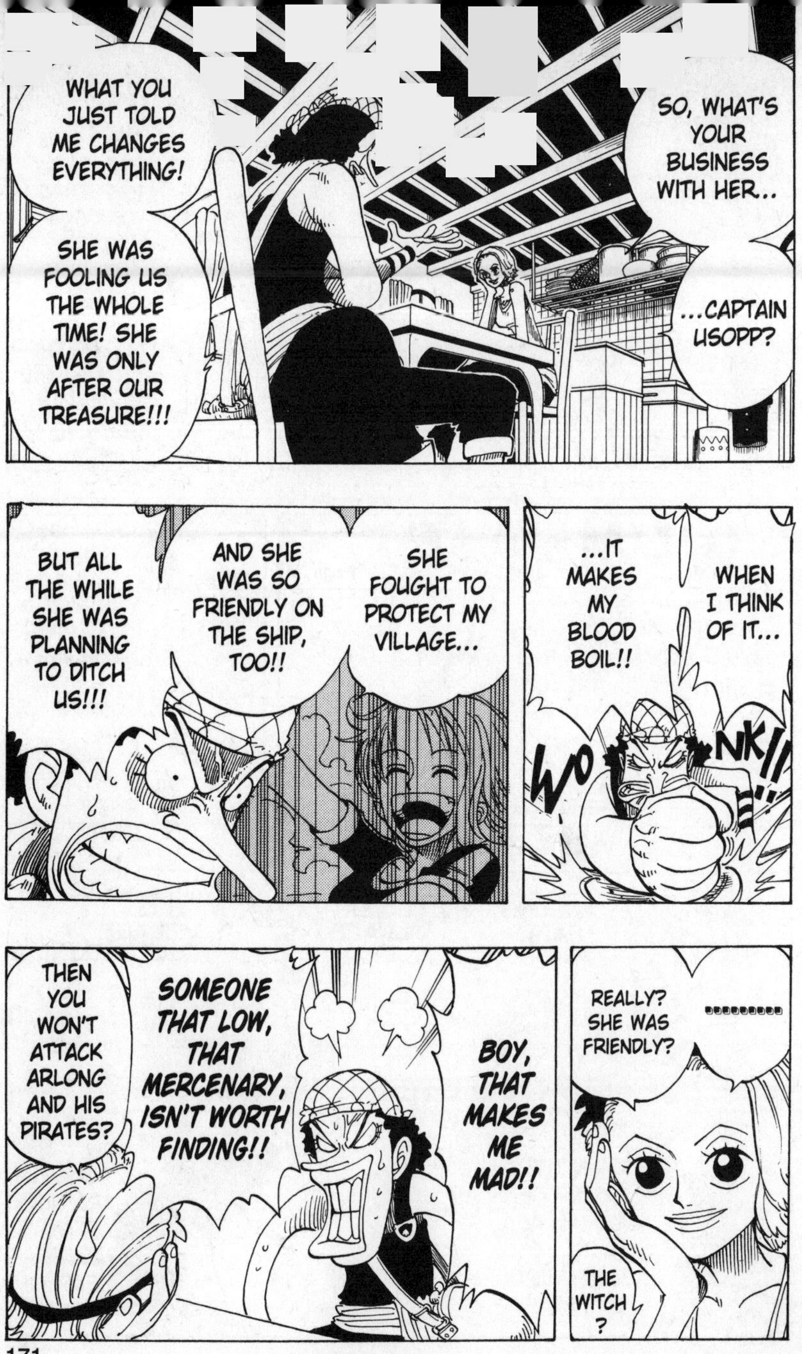
SO, WHAT'S YOUR BUSINESS WITH HER...
...CAPTAIN USOPP?
WHAT YOU JUST TOLD ME CHANGES EVERYTHING!
SHE WAS FOOLING US THE WHOLE TIME! SHE WAS ONLY AFTER OUR TREASURE!!!
WHEN I THINK OF IT...
...IT MAKES MY BLOOD BOIL!!
WO NK!!
SHE FOUGHT TO PROTECT MY VILLAGE...
AND SHE WAS SO FRIENDLY ON THE SHIP, TOO!!
BUT ALL THE WHILE SHE WAS PLANNING TO DITCH US!!!
....
REALLY? SHE WAS FRIENDLY?
THE WITCH ?
BOY, THAT MAKES ME MAD!!
SOMEONE THAT LOW, THAT MERCENARY, ISN'T WORTH FINDING!!
THEN YOU WON'T ATTACK ARLONG AND HIS PIRATES?

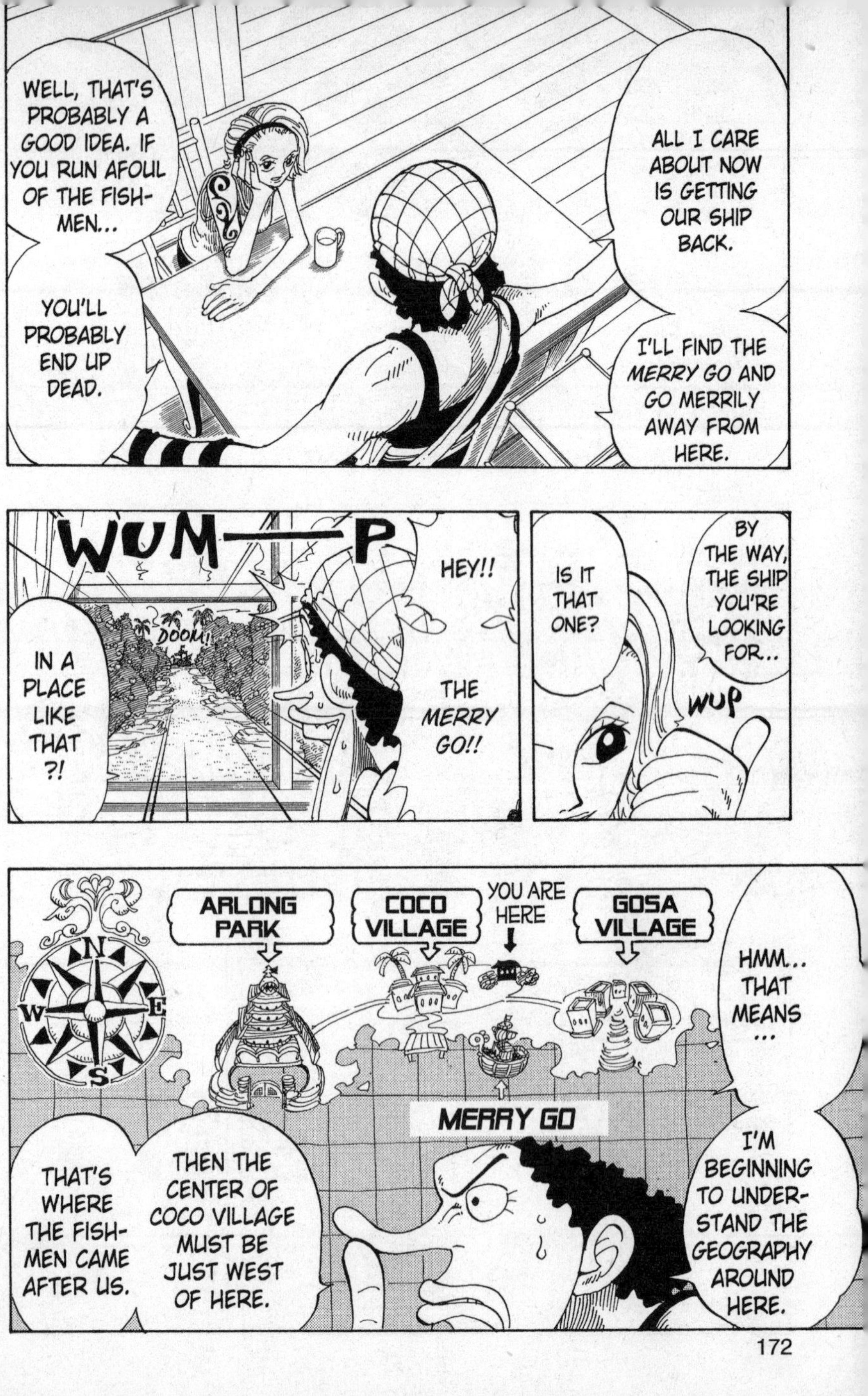
ALL I CARE ABOUT NOW IS GETTING OUR SHIP BACK.
I'LL FIND THE MERRY GO AND GO MERRILY AWAY FROM HERE.
WELL, THAT'S PROBABLY A GOOD IDEA. IF YOU RUN AFOUL OF THE FISH-MEN...
YOU'LL PROBABLY END UP DEAD.
BY THE WAY, THE SHIP YOU'RE LOOKING FOR...
IS IT THAT ONE?
WUP
HEY!!
THE MERRY GO!!
WUM—P
DOOM!
IN A PLACE LIKE THAT?!
HMM... THAT MEANS...
GOSA VILLAGE
YOU ARE HERE
COCO VILLAGE
ARLONG PARK
N
E
W
S
MERRY GO
I'M BEGINNING TO UNDER-STAND THE GEOGRAPHY AROUND HERE.
THEN THE CENTER OF COCO VILLAGE MUST BE JUST WEST OF HERE.
THAT'S WHERE THE FISH-MEN CAME AFTER US.

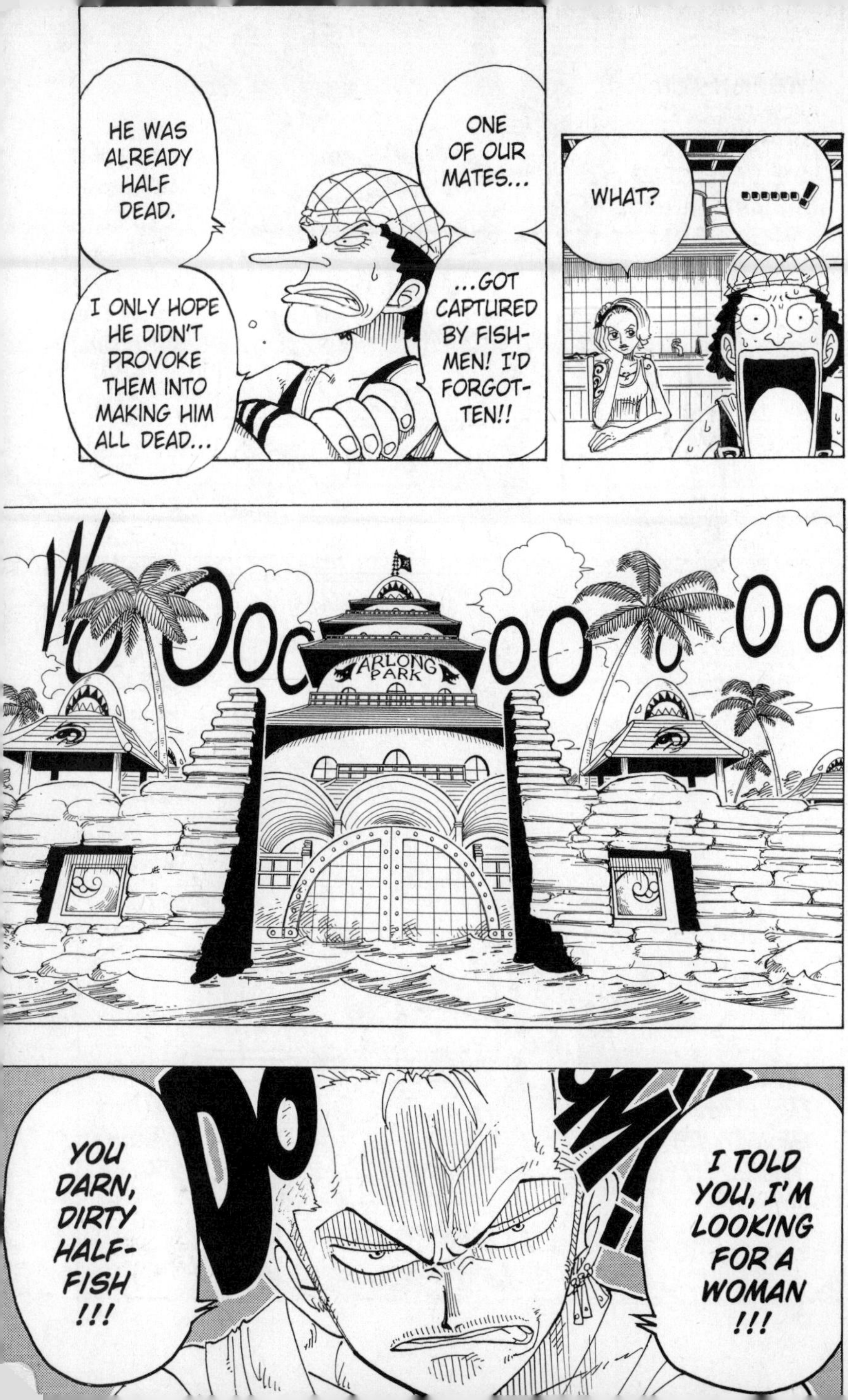
......!
WHAT?
ONE OF OUR MATES...
...GOT CAPTURED BY FISH-MEN! I'D FORGOT-TEN!!
HE WAS ALREADY HALF DEAD.
I ONLY HOPE HE DIDN'T PROVOKE THEM INTO MAKING HIM ALL DEAD...
WOOOOOOOO
ARLONG PARK
I TOLD YOU, I'M LOOKING FOR A WOMAN!!!
YOU DARN, DIRTY HALF-FISH!!!

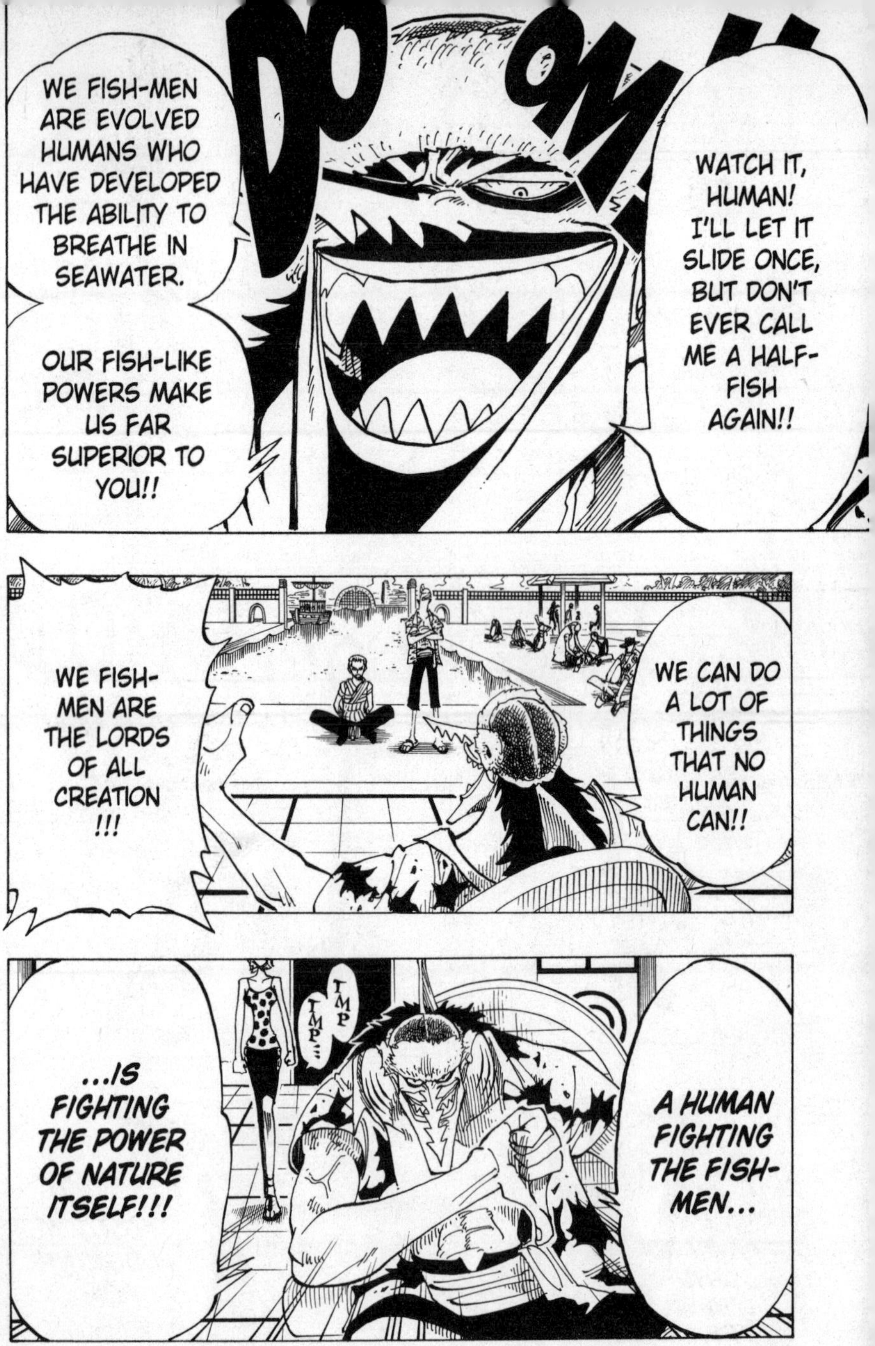
DOOM
WATCH IT, HUMAN! I'LL LET IT SLIDE ONCE, BUT DON'T EVER CALL ME A HALF-FISH AGAIN!!
WE FISH-MEN ARE EVOLVED HUMANS WHO HAVE DEVELOPED THE ABILITY TO BREATHE IN SEAWATER.
OUR FISH-LIKE POWERS MAKE US FAR SUPERIOR TO YOU!!
WE CAN DO A LOT OF THINGS THAT NO HUMAN CAN!!
WE FISH-MEN ARE THE LORDS OF ALL CREATION!!!
A HUMAN FIGHTING THE FISH-MEN...
TMP TMP...
...IS FIGHTING THE POWER OF NATURE ITSELF!!!

READ THIS WAY

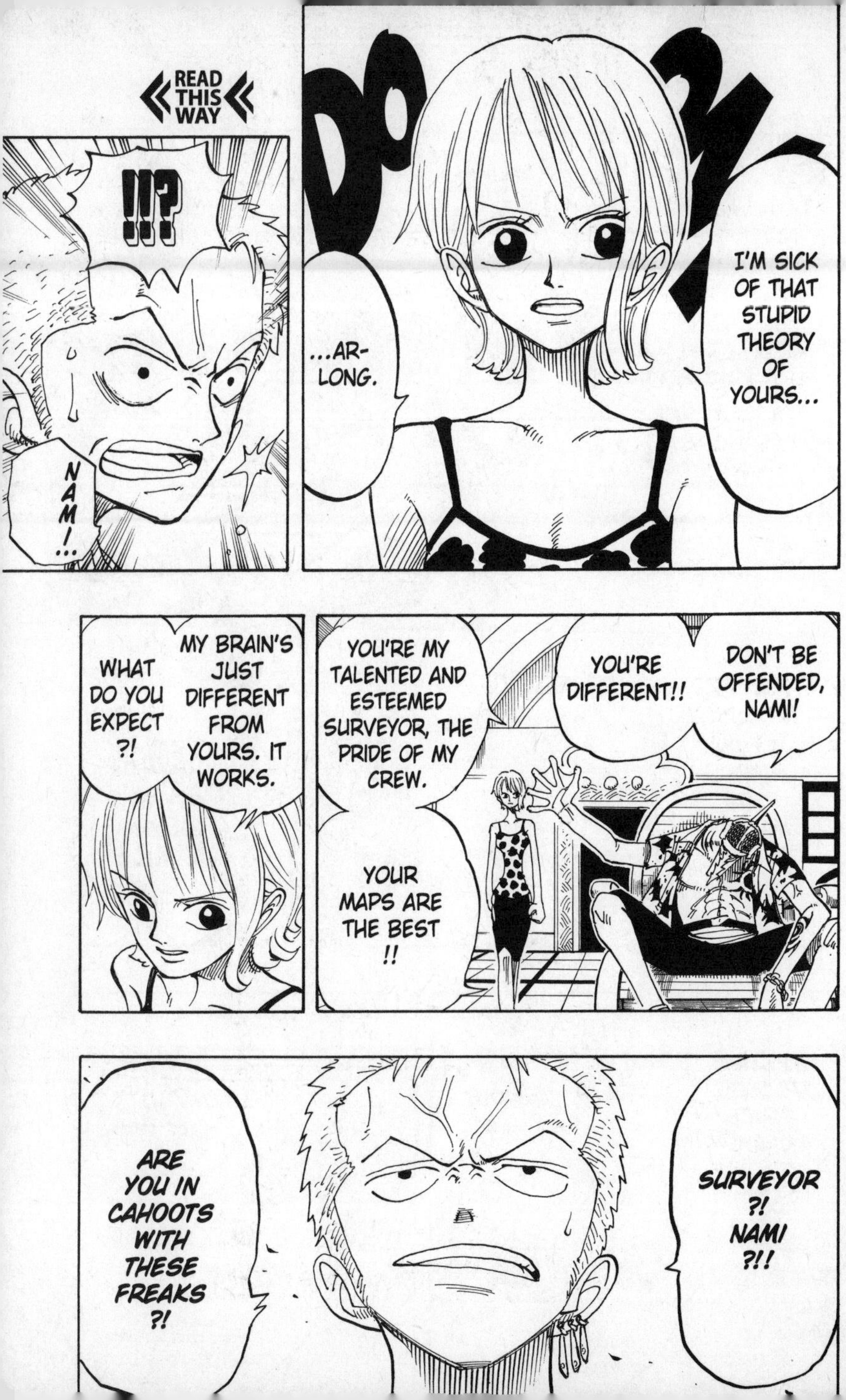
I'M SICK OF THAT STUPID THEORY OF YOURS...
...AR-LONG.
!!?
NAMI...
DON'T BE OFFENDED, NAMI!
YOU'RE DIFFERENT!!
YOU'RE MY TALENTED AND ESTEEMED SURVEYOR, THE PRIDE OF MY CREW.
YOUR MAPS ARE THE BEST!!
MY BRAIN'S JUST DIFFERENT FROM YOURS. IT WORKS.
WHAT DO YOU EXPECT?!
SURVEYOR?! NAMI?!!
ARE YOU IN CAHOOTS WITH THESE FREAKS?!

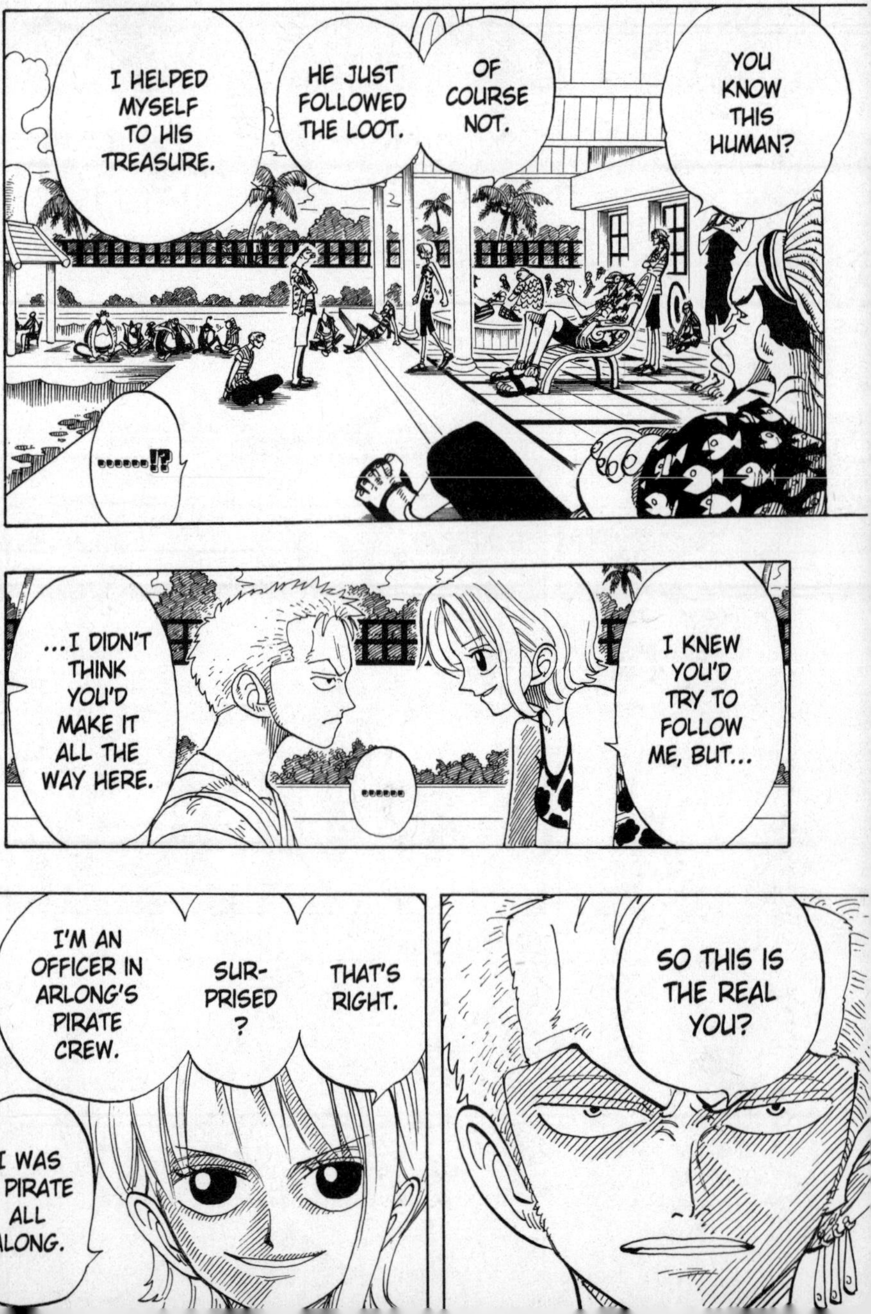
YOU KNOW THIS HUMAN?
OF COURSE NOT.
HE JUST FOLLOWED THE LOOT.
I HELPED MYSELF TO HIS TREASURE.
......!?
I KNEW YOU'D TRY TO FOLLOW ME, BUT...
......
...I DIDN'T THINK YOU'D MAKE IT ALL THE WAY HERE.
SO THIS IS THE REAL YOU?
THAT'S RIGHT.
SUR-PRISED?
I'M AN OFFICER IN ARLONG'S PIRATE CREW.
I WAS A PIRATE ALL ALONG.

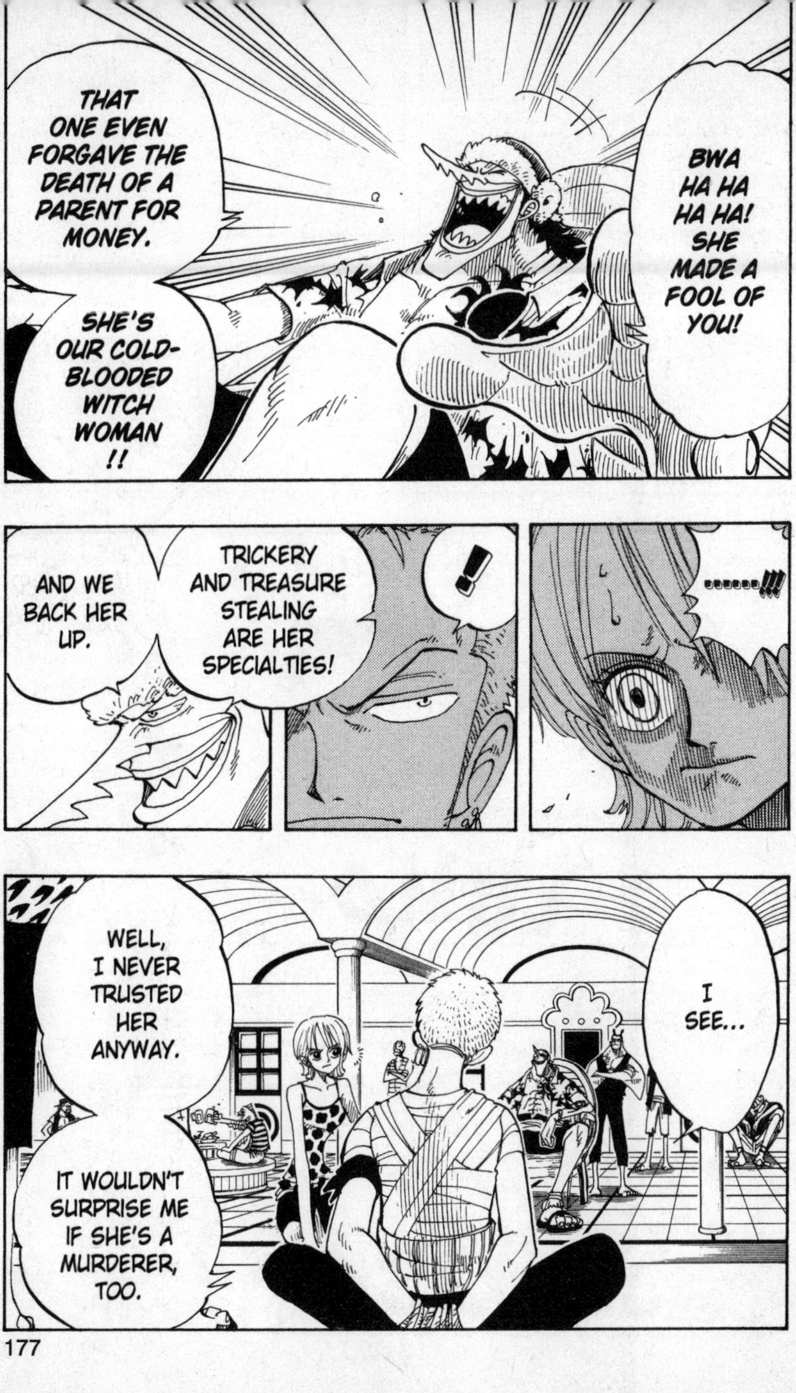
BWA HA HA HA HA! SHE MADE A FOOL OF YOU!
THAT ONE EVEN FORGAVE THE DEATH OF A PARENT FOR MONEY.
SHE'S OUR COLD-BLOODED WITCH WOMAN!!
......!!!
!
TRICKERY AND TREASURE STEALING ARE HER SPECIALTIES!
AND WE BACK HER UP.
I SEE...
WELL, I NEVER TRUSTED HER ANYWAY.
IT WOULDN'T SURPRISE ME IF SHE'S A MURDERER, TOO.

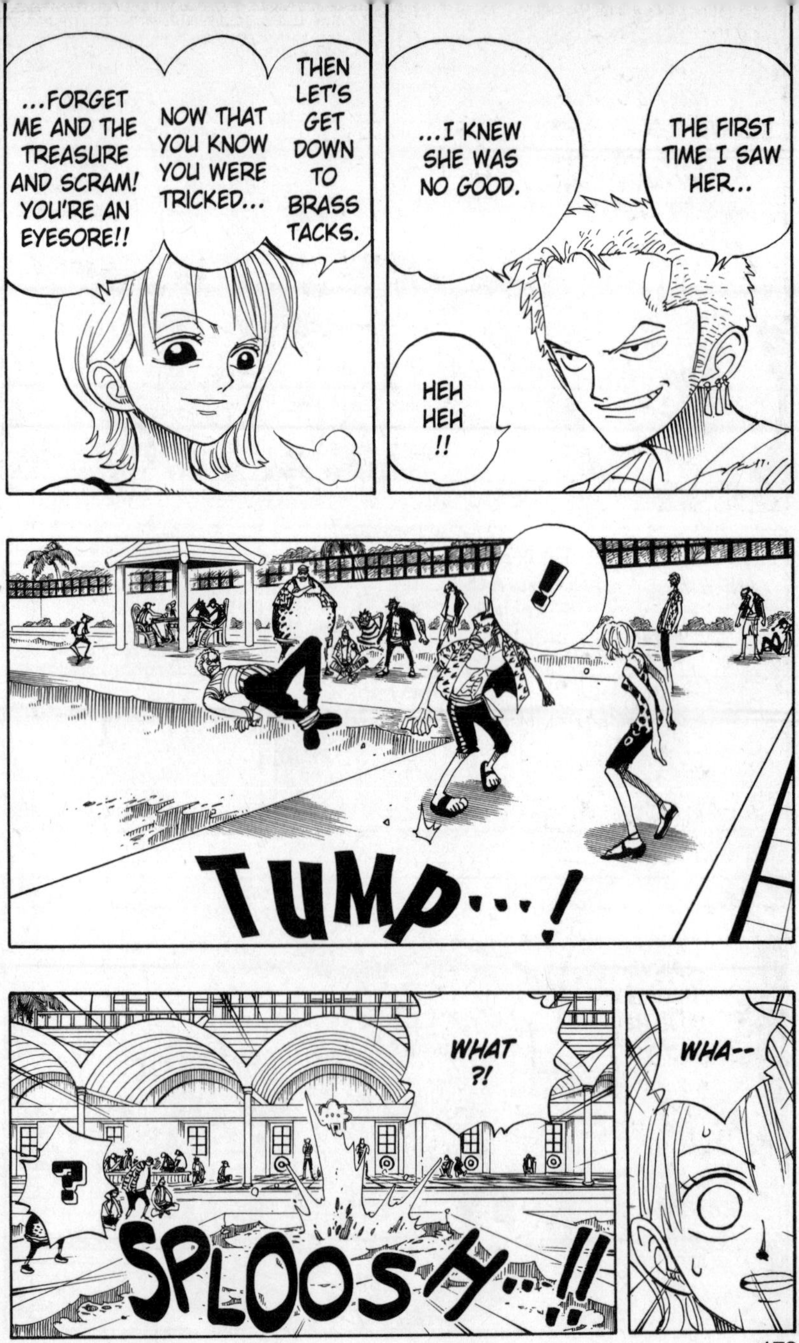
THE FIRST TIME I SAW HER...
...I KNEW SHE WAS NO GOOD.
HEH HEH !!
THEN LET'S GET DOWN TO BRASS TACKS.
NOW THAT YOU KNOW YOU WERE TRICKED...
...FORGET ME AND THE TREASURE AND SCRAM! YOU'RE AN EYESORE!!
!
TUMP...!
WHA--
WHAT ?!
?
SPLOOSH...!!

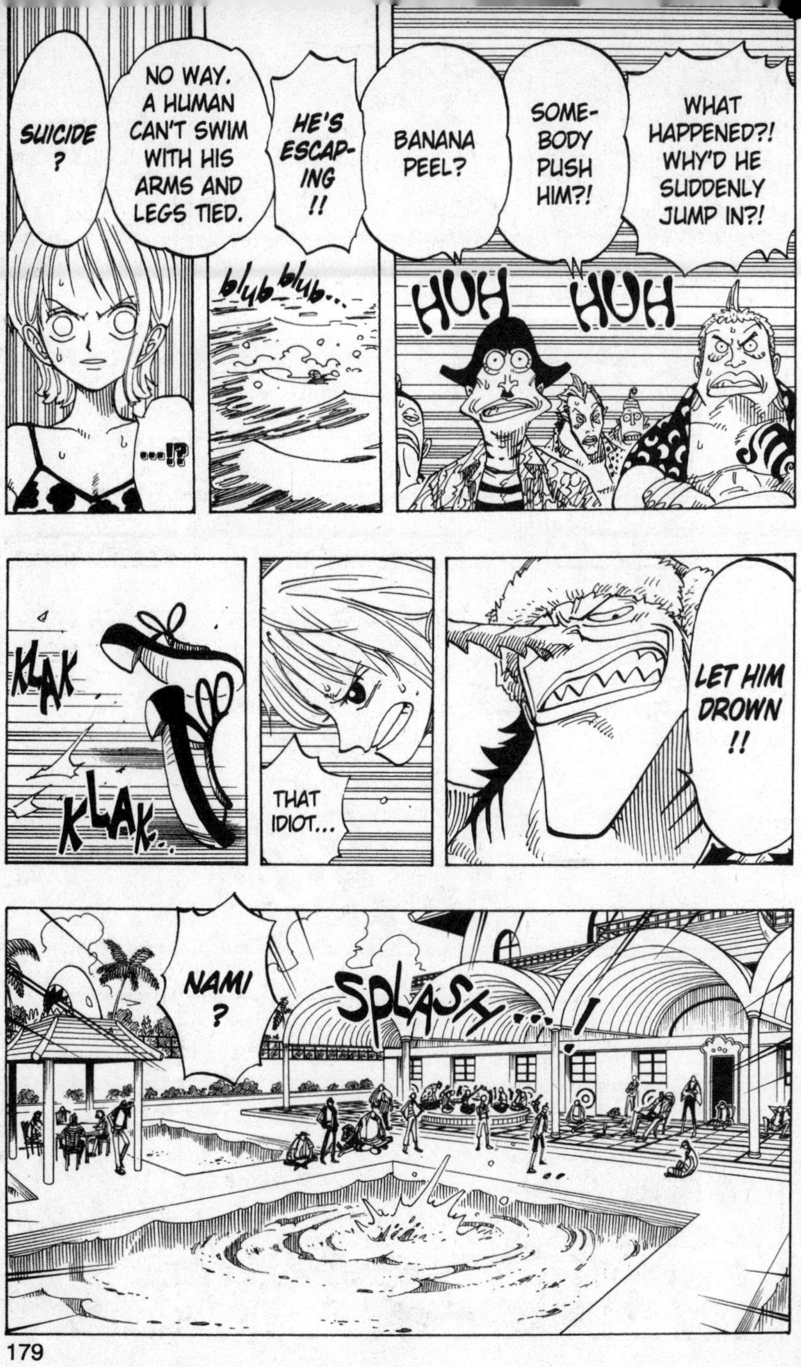
WHAT HAPPENED?! WHY'D HE SUDDENLY JUMP IN?!
SOME-BODY PUSH HIM?!
BANANA PEEL?
HUH HUH
HE'S ESCAP-ING!!
blub blub...
NO WAY. A HUMAN CAN'T SWIM WITH HIS ARMS AND LEGS TIED.
SUICIDE?
...!?
LET HIM DROWN!!
THAT IDIOT...
KLAK
KLAK..
SPLASH...!
NAMI?

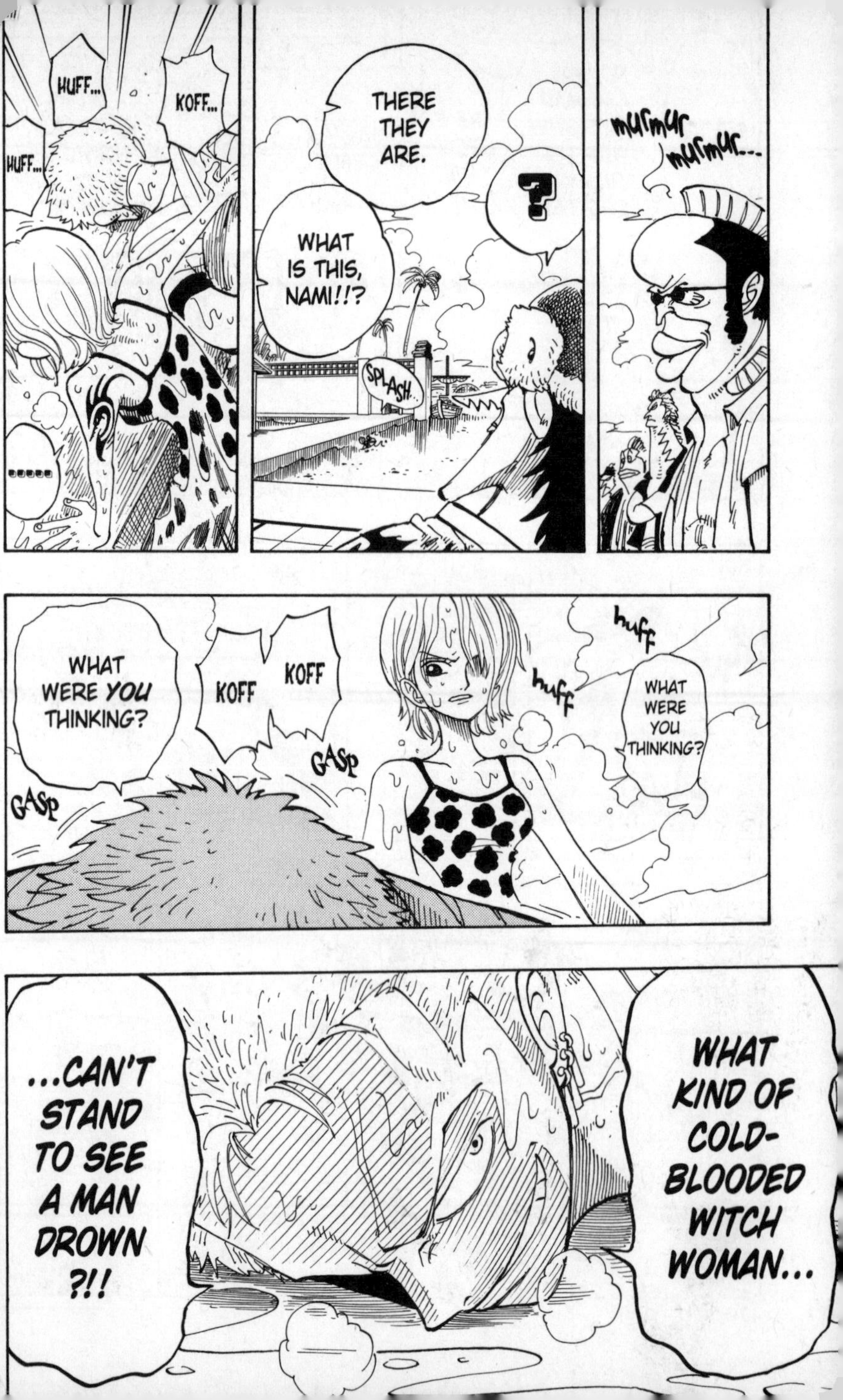
murmur
murmur...
THERE THEY ARE.
?
WHAT IS THIS, NAMI!!?
SPLASH
HUFF...
KOFF...
HUFF...
.....
huff
huff
WHAT WERE YOU THINKING?
GASP
KOFF
KOFF
WHAT WERE YOU THINKING?
GASP
WHAT KIND OF COLD-BLOODED WITCH WOMAN...
...CAN'T STAND TO SEE A MAN DROWN?!!

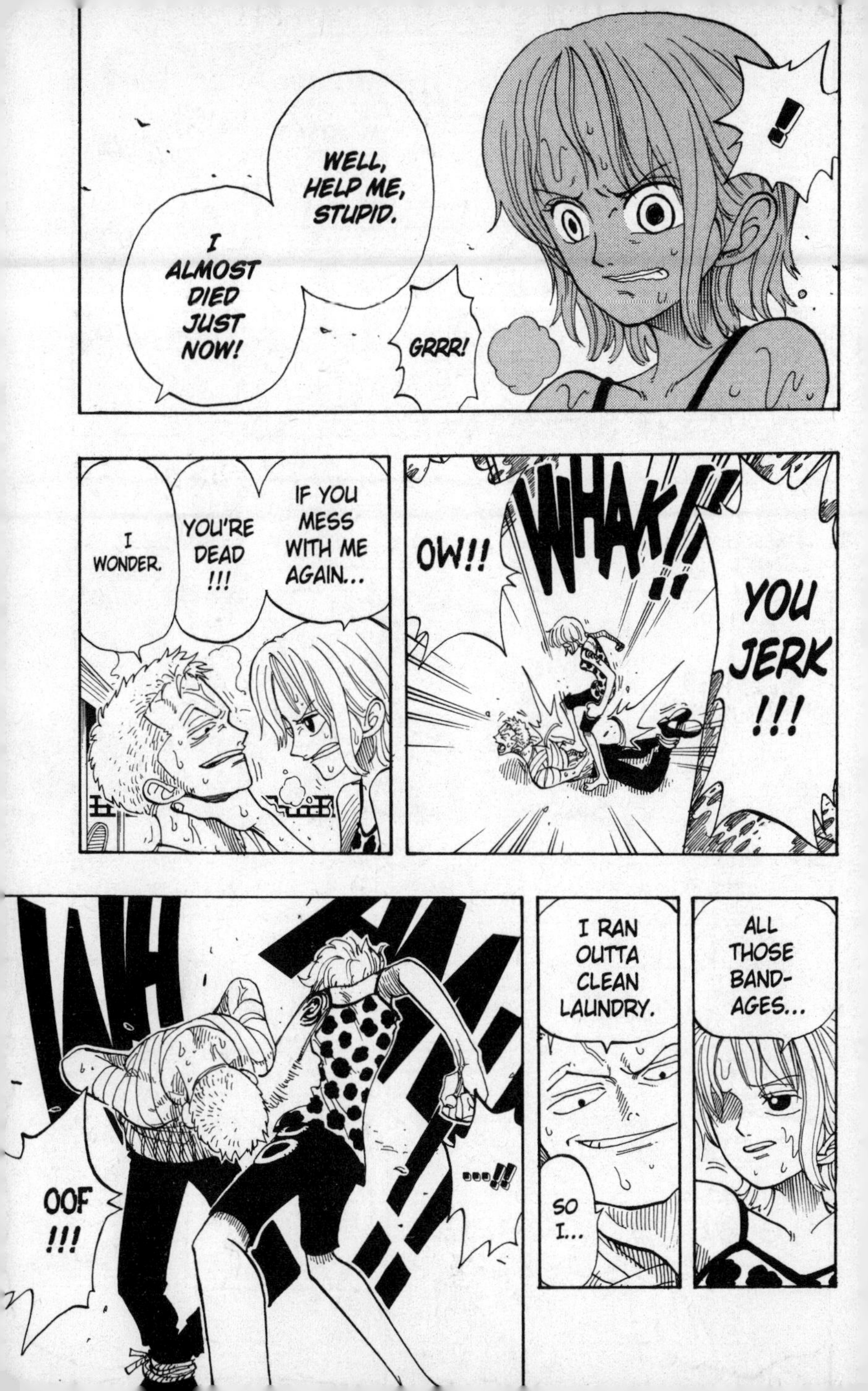
!
WELL, HELP ME, STUPID.
GRRR!
I ALMOST DIED JUST NOW!
WHAK!!
YOU JERK!!!
OW!!
IF YOU MESS WITH ME AGAIN...
YOU'RE DEAD!!!
I WONDER.
ALL THOSE BANDAGES...
I RAN OUTTA CLEAN LAUNDRY.
SO I...
...!!
OOF!!!

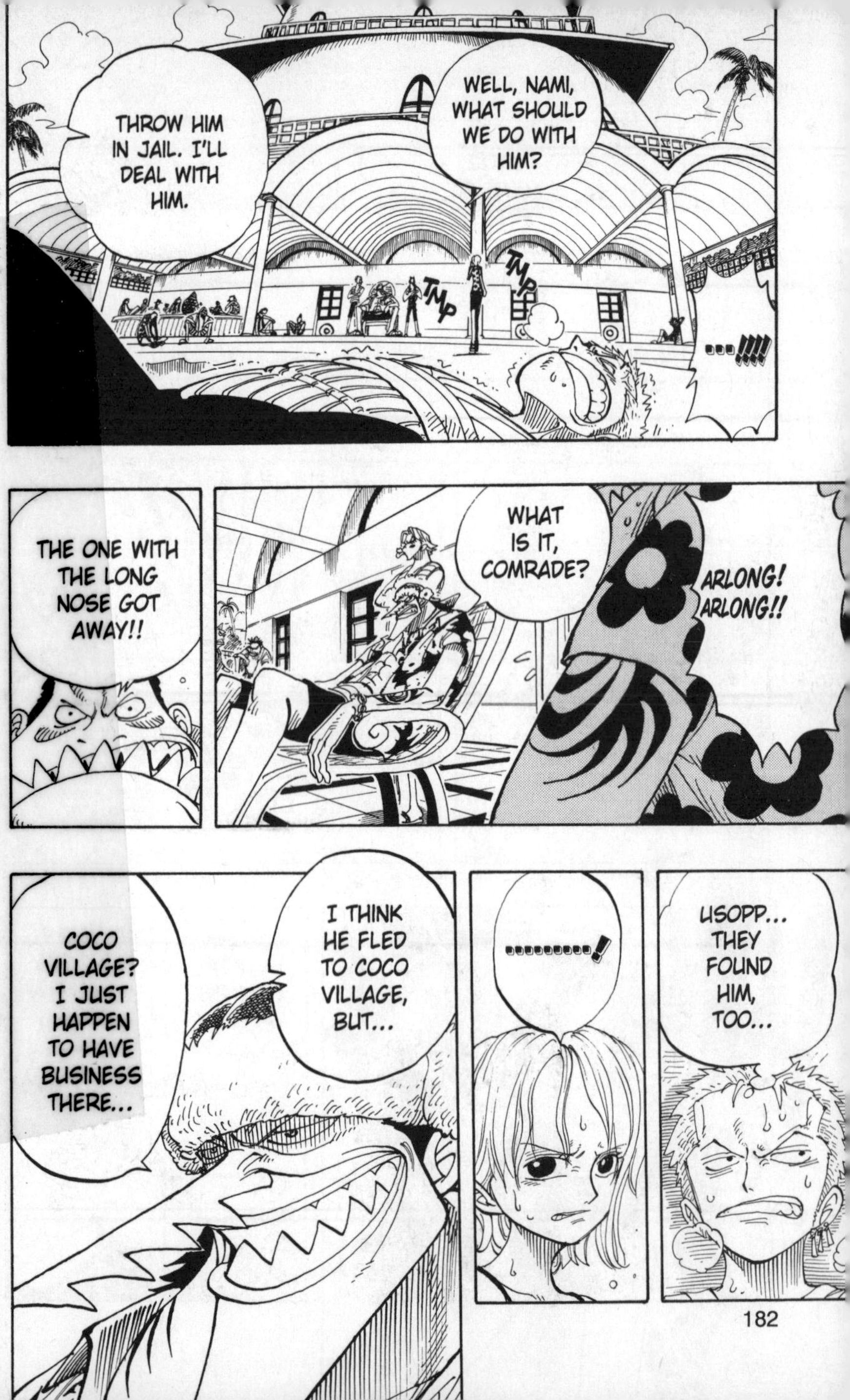
WELL, NAMI, WHAT SHOULD WE DO WITH HIM?
THROW HIM IN JAIL. I'LL DEAL WITH HIM.
TMP
TMP
...!!!!
ARLONG! ARLONG!!
WHAT IS IT, COMRADE?
THE ONE WITH THE LONG NOSE GOT AWAY!!
USOPP... THEY FOUND HIM, TOO...
.........!
I THINK HE FLED TO COCO VILLAGE, BUT...
COCO VILLAGE? I JUST HAPPEN TO HAVE BUSINESS THERE...

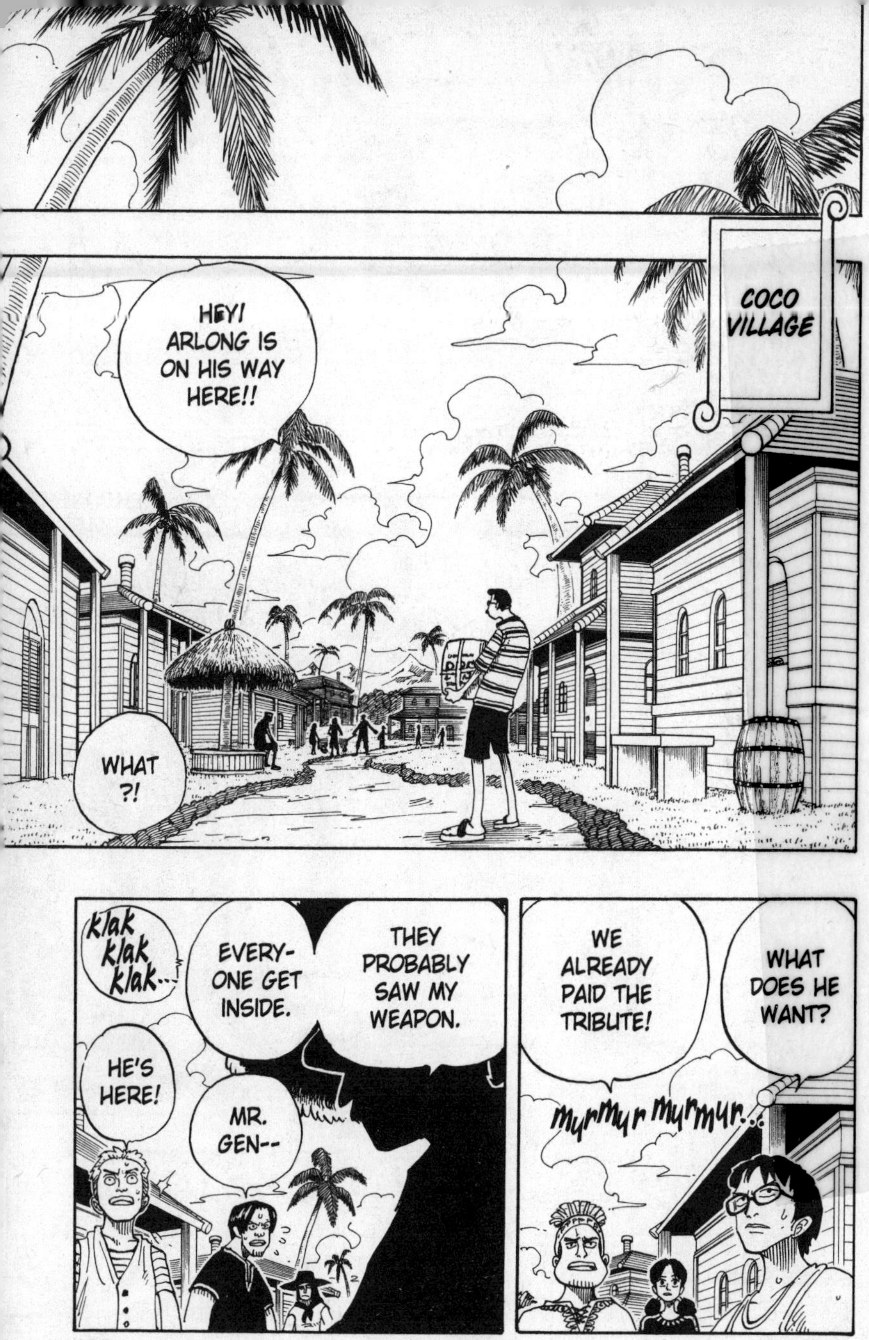
COCO VILLAGE
HEY! ARLONG IS ON HIS WAY HERE!!
WHAT ?!
WHAT DOES HE WANT?
WE ALREADY PAID THE TRIBUTE!
murmur murmur...
THEY PROBABLY SAW MY WEAPON.
EVERY-ONE GET INSIDE.
klak klak klak...
HE'S HERE!
MR. GEN--

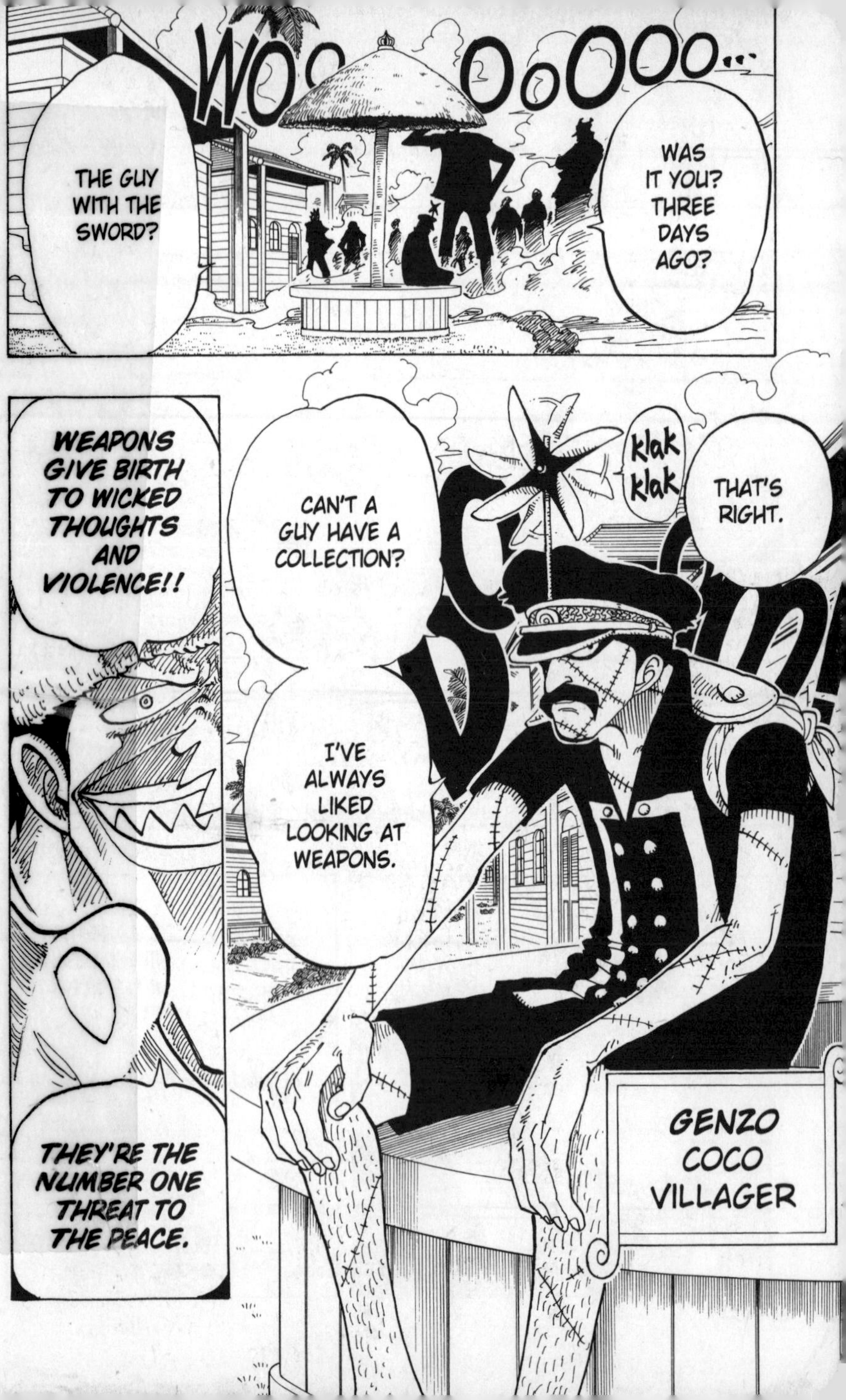
WOOoOOOo...
WAS IT YOU? THREE DAYS AGO?
THE GUY WITH THE SWORD?
klak klak
THAT'S RIGHT.
CAN'T A GUY HAVE A COLLECTION?
I'VE ALWAYS LIKED LOOKING AT WEAPONS.
GENZO COCO VILLAGER
WEAPONS GIVE BIRTH TO WICKED THOUGHTS AND VIOLENCE!!
THEY'RE THE NUMBER ONE THREAT TO THE PEACE.

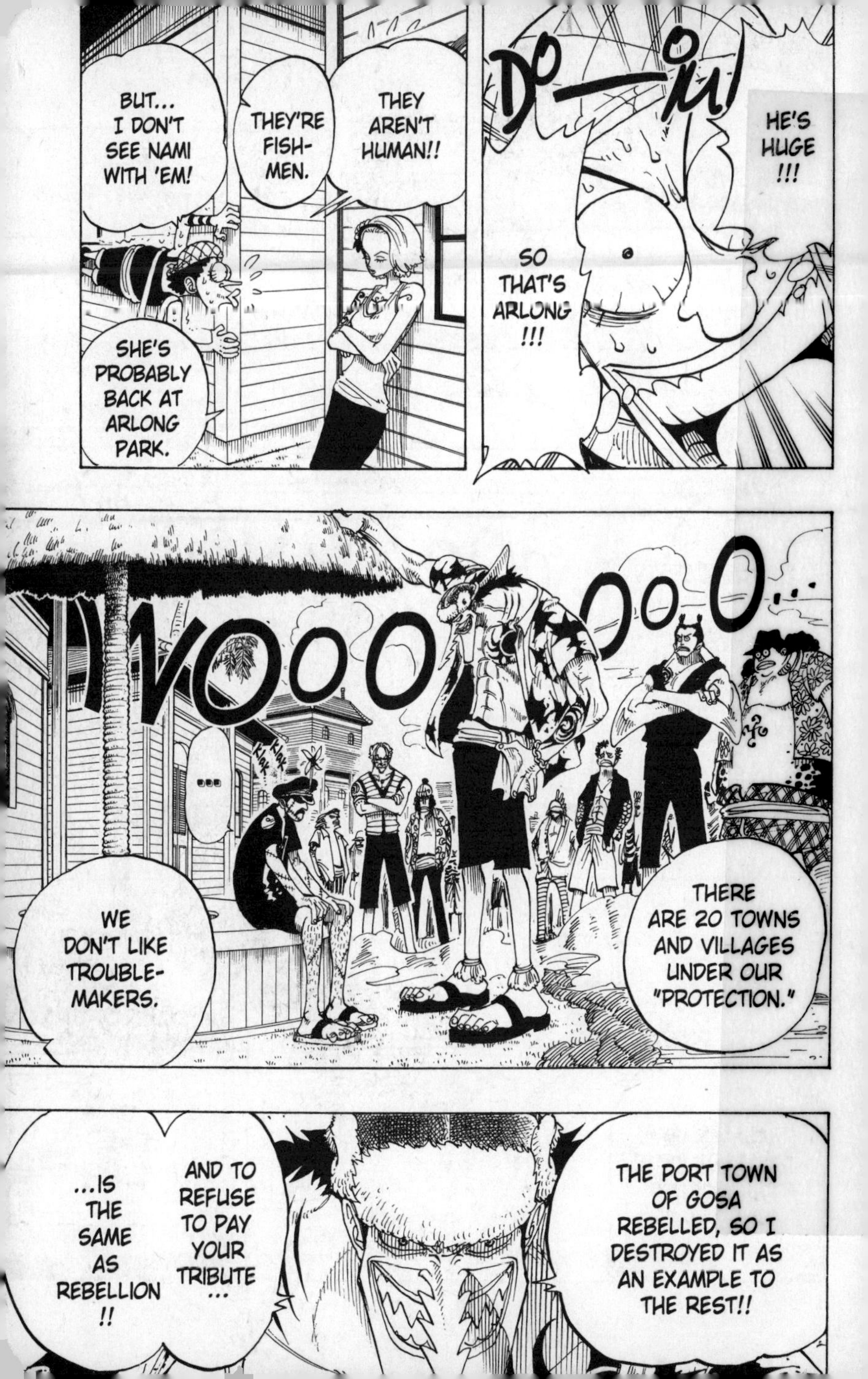
DO—OM
HE'S HUGE!!!
SO THAT'S ARLONG!!!
THEY AREN'T HUMAN!!
THEY'RE FISH-MEN.
BUT... I DON'T SEE NAMI WITH 'EM!
SHE'S PROBABLY BACK AT ARLONG PARK.
WOOOOOOOO...
THERE ARE 20 TOWNS AND VILLAGES UNDER OUR "PROTECTION."
...
KLAK KLAK
WE DON'T LIKE TROUBLE-MAKERS.
THE PORT TOWN OF GOSA REBELLED, SO I DESTROYED IT AS AN EXAMPLE TO THE REST!!
AND TO REFUSE TO PAY YOUR TRIBUTE...
...IS THE SAME AS REBELLION!!

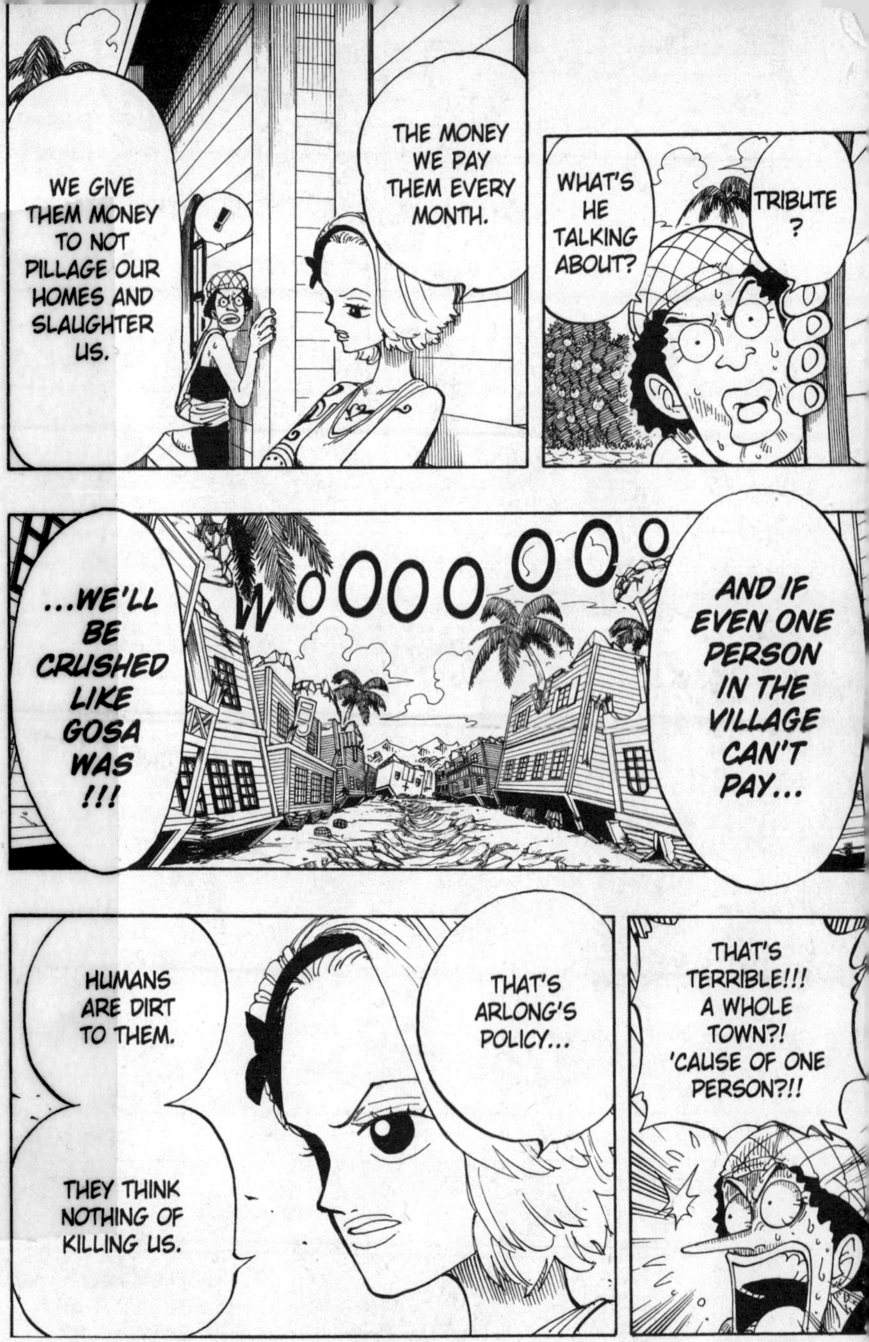
TRIBUTE ?
WHAT'S HE TALKING ABOUT?
THE MONEY WE PAY THEM EVERY MONTH.
!
WE GIVE THEM MONEY TO NOT PILLAGE OUR HOMES AND SLAUGHTER US.
AND IF EVEN ONE PERSON IN THE VILLAGE CAN'T PAY...
WOOOOOOOO
...WE'LL BE CRUSHED LIKE GOSA WAS !!!
THAT'S TERRIBLE!!! A WHOLE TOWN?! 'CAUSE OF ONE PERSON?!!
THAT'S ARLONG'S POLICY...
HUMANS ARE DIRT TO THEM.
THEY THINK NOTHING OF KILLING US.

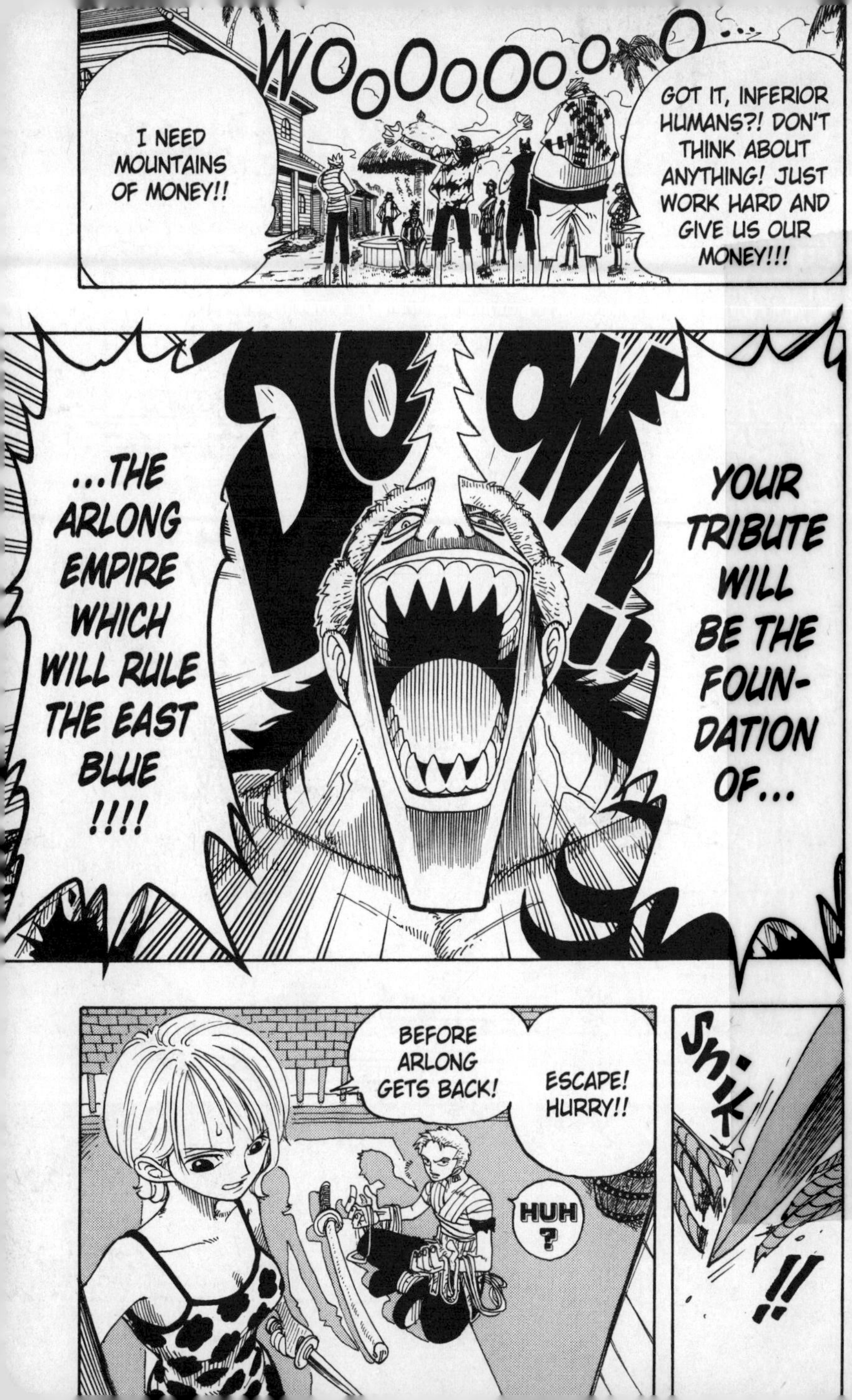
GOT IT, INFERIOR HUMANS?! DON'T THINK ABOUT ANYTHING! JUST WORK HARD AND GIVE US OUR MONEY!!!
WOOOOOOOO
I NEED MOUNTAINS OF MONEY!!
YOUR TRIBUTE WILL BE THE FOUN-DATION OF...
DOOM!!
...THE ARLONG EMPIRE WHICH WILL RULE THE EAST BLUE !!!!
SNIK
!!
ESCAPE! HURRY!!
BEFORE ARLONG GETS BACK!
HUH ?

COMING NEXT VOLUME:

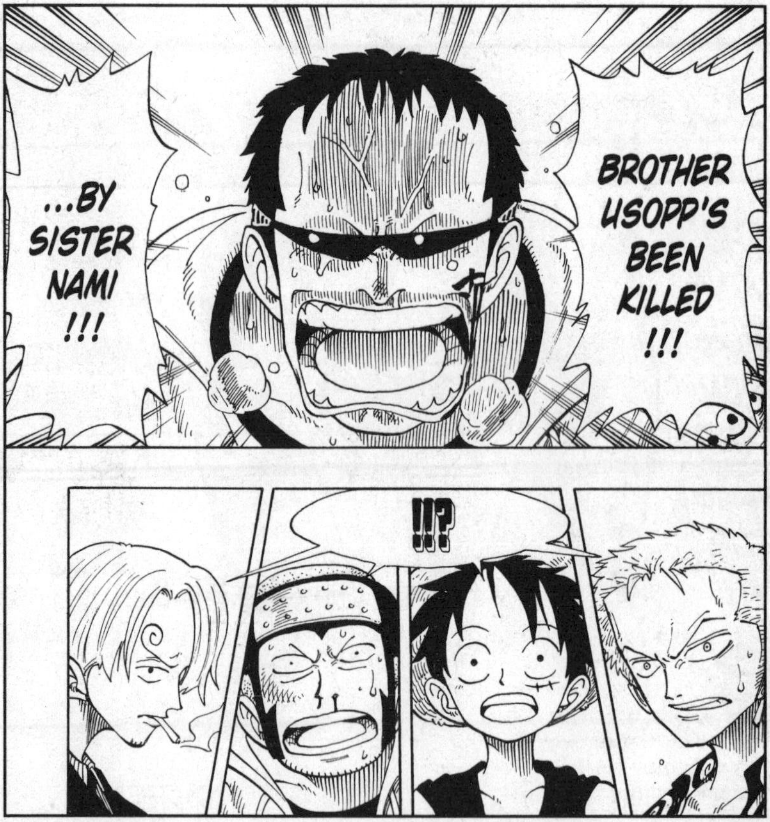
BROTHER USOPP'S BEEN KILLED!!!
...BY SISTER NAMI!!!
!!?

To save Coco Village eight years ago, Nami sealed an oath of loyalty to her old nemesis, Captain Arlong. But now that Luffy and his crew have joined the fray there's no telling how far she's willing to go to keep that wretched oath.

ON SALE NOW!

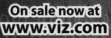

VIZ media
The World's Greatest Manga
Now available on your iPad

Full of FREE previews and tons of new manga for you to explore

From legendary manga like *Dragon Ball* to *Bakuman*, the newest series from the creators of *Death Note*, the best manga in the world is now available on the iPad through the official VIZ Manga app.

- ## Free App
- ## New content weekly
- ## Free chapter 1 previews

You're Reading in the Wrong Direction!!

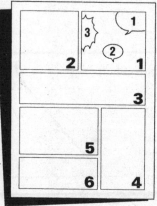

Whoops! Guess what? You're starting at the wrong end of the comic!

...It's true! In keeping with the original Japanese format, **One Piece** is meant to be read from right to left, starting in the upper-right corner.

Unlike English, which is read from left to right, Japanese is read from right to left, meaning that action, sound effects and word-balloon order are completely reversed... something which can make readers unfamiliar with Japanese feel pretty backwards themselves. For this reason, manga or Japanese comics published in the U.S. in English have sometimes been published "flopped"– that is, printed in exact reverse order, as though seen from the other side of a mirror.

By flopping pages, U.S. publishers can avoid confusing readers, but the compromise is not without its downside. For one thing, a character in a flopped manga series who once wore in the original Japanese version a T-shirt emblazoned with "M A Y" (as in "the merry month of") now wears one which reads "Y A M"! Additionally, many manga creators in Japan are themselves unhappy with the process, as some feel the mirror-imaging of their art skews their original intentions.

We are proud to bring you Eiichiro Oda's **One Piece** in the original unflopped format. For now, though, turn to the other side of the book and let the journey begin...!

—Editor